ALSO BY VIRGINIA T. HABEEB:

The American Home All-Purpose Cookbook
Learn to Cook Book

The
Ladies'
Home
Journal ART

of
HOMEMAKING

Everything you need to know
to run your home with ease and style

VIRGINIA T. HABEEB

With drawings by Loretta Trezzo

Simon and Schuster · New York

Manufactured in the United States of America

1   2   3   4   5   6   7   8   9   0

Library of Congress Cataloging Card Number 72-90393

ISBN 0-671-21487-X
ISBN 0-671-24210-5 Pbk.

® Title "Ladies' Home Journal" is registered at the U.S.
Patent Office and foreign countries by Downe Publishing Inc.

*To simplify much of the information found in this book, trade
names of products have been used. They are not intended as
endorsements. Neither is any criticism implied of products not
listed. Those listed may change from time to time.*

For permission to reprint in whole or in part material from previously
published works, the author wishes to thank the following:

American Druggist, for use of the chart "Counterdoses for the Home,"
copyright © 1972.

Dodd, Mead & Company, Inc., for material from *Management in the
Home* by Dr. Lillian M. Gilbreth, Dr. Orpha Mae Thomas, and Eleanor
Clymer, copyright © 1954, 1959 by Dr. Lillian M. Gilbreth, Dr. Orpha
Mae Thomas, and Eleanor Clymer.

The Macmillan Company, New York, for material from *Essentials of
Nutrition* by H. C. Sherman and C. S. Lanford, copyright © 1940, 1943,
1951, 1957 by The Macmillan Company.

William Morrow & Company, Inc., for material from *Male and Female*
by Margaret Mead, copyright © 1949 by Margaret Mead.

The New York State College of Human Ecology, a statutory college
of the State University, Cornell University, Ithaca, New York, for material
adapted from Home Economics Extension Leaflet No. 47, "When Is Food
Safe?" by Irene Downey and Marjorie Washbon, July 1969.

Exension Division, Virginia Polytechnic Institute and State University,
for material from Publication 359, "What's in Home Cleaning Products
and Why?" by Janice Woodward, Extension Specialist, Home Management.
Reprint, June 1972.

John Wiley & Sons, Inc., for material from *Work in the Home* by Rose
H. Steidl and Esther Crew Bratton, copyright © 1968 by John Wiley &
Sons, Inc.

To Mitch

Acknowledgments

The information in this book represents the experiences of hundreds of homemakers as well as many professionals, including home economists, educators, consumer service advisers, trade associations and their members, chemists, engineers, and the hundreds of people behind the scenes in industry and government who are constantly working to improve homemaking standards, products and services in a changing society.

The author wishes to express her thanks to the staffs of The Association of Interior Decor Specialists, Inc. (AIDS); M. Evans and Company, Inc.; The Culligan Water Institute; American National Standards Institute; The Electric Energy Association; Association of Home Appliance Manufacturers; Gas Appliance Manufacturers Association; American Gas Association; National Retail Merchants Association (NRMA); International Fabricare Institute; Soap and Detergent Association; National Canners Association; and their member companies and associate members for their advice and the use of materials.

In addition, this book also utilizes many special studies made and published by government agencies, such as the United States Department of Agriculture, and the work of research departments of colleges, universities and their extension services. Much is also the result of research compiled in the development of my own and other homemaking editorials and in the constant use of household products and services.

Although I cannot mention each by name, my special thanks go to: my editor Phyllis Grann whose special kind of enthusiasm

ACKNOWLEDGMENTS

and organization finally made short work of a long task, and Lois Myller, whose idea and patience made this book a reality, and to both of them for adding not only their literary talents but home-making talents as well. I also must thank my husband Mitchell Habeeb whose constant encouragement helped me to plow through what was an incredibly formidable task; and to my mother who inspired me to become a home economist in the first place.

V. T. H.

Preface

The Art of Homemaking is a one-of-its-kind book designed to help you run your home with ease and style. Almost everything you need to know about housekeeping is covered somewhere in the following pages.

In addition to the time-tested techniques for planning, cleaning and maintaining your home, we have made a special effort to incorporate the newest innovations and appliances that can really cut your work time and effort.

The speed with which technological advances are being made, as well as a growing ecological awareness constantly alter modern housekeeping techniques. Breakthroughs such as new formulations of home-care products, dishwashers, self-cleaning ovens, self-defrosting refrigerators, no-iron fabrics, microwave ovens, permanent-care labeling and all sorts of easy-to-use "everythings" have unbelievably lightened our housekeeping tasks. In this book we have made a constant attempt to show you how you can use these devices to your advantage.

Hand in hand with these rapid changes in technology are dramatic changes in our life-styles and values. As we go to press we realize that managing a home today is both easier and more complex than it was in the past. To get the most out of our suggestions, always keep in mind:

Housework—There will always be some work around the house.

Techniques—All techniques can be adapted to optimum or minimum standards of housework. The level of perfection you choose to aim for depends entirely on your life-style and personal priorities.

Products—There is a product on the market for doing almost any task that needs to be done around the house. Some save time, some save effort, some save money. Again the choice will depend upon your own particular needs and priorities.

Ecology and the Environment—Product designs and/or formulations are currently under both private and public scrutiny as to their effect on life and environment. We have attempted to define their use generically, though because of the nature of some products it has been necessary at times to be more specific. These products will continue to change as more and more research is developed—some, no doubt, this very minute. We urge you as responsible citizens to keep up with these changes and be guided in your use of home-care products with good judgment. To make it easy for you, we have included several blank pages at the end of this book for you to note current changes in methods and products. There is also space for you to list the page reference for your convenience.

And always remember. If properly organized according to specific family and personal needs, housework no longer need be a chore. A well-run home often requires less work than a poorly run one.

—Gini Habeeb

Contents

CHAPTER ONE

Managing Time, Motion, and Money

Homemaking is a very real game of juggling people, activities, and clutter. Finding an easier way to cope and still find time for the grace notes is perhaps the major goal. How we do it depends on following *some* of the rules *some* of the time and *making up some of our own* as we go.

A FACT OF LIFE

Let us decide right at the outset that housekeeping is a fact of life. You don't have to *like* it—but you do have to *face* it. And since we do have to do it, we might as well go about it in an organized fashion. For without question, keeping a family and home running smoothly, to say nothing of fulfilling our own needs, is the toughest management problem that exists.

If we can learn to view housekeeping in its proper perspective, we'll soon find out that about 50 percent of the work disappears. Suddenly "coping" becomes merely a matter of "doing."

As for the mechanics of approaching it properly, here are the four steps we regard as musts.

- Put yourself in a positive frame of mind.
- Analyze your housekeeping needs.

1

- Organize the tasks into a meaningful sequence according to priorities.
- Schedule your priorities into a workable routine.

Now make up your mind that:

- Housekeeping is never done. It only solves temporary goals—making the beds until you sleep in them again, washing the dishes until the next meal.
- It must be faced daily. Accept it as a matter of fact.
- Resolve to do the work as quickly and easily as possible.
- Develop respect for the job.
- Remember that the results you obtain from following any directions will depend largely upon your personal judgment and technique. Think before you act, whether it is following the instructions on a package label, in a use and care manual, or in this book.

WHAT ARE YOUR STANDARDS?

Only you can decide whether or not you are striving for an antiseptically clean house or one that is just reasonably clean and orderly. Whatever your goal, *set your standards early on* so that you can determine how you like to keep house and hence decide on how you will achieve this goal.

Curious ourselves to see how many homemakers rated themselves as housekeepers, we took an unofficial poll and came up with what we have called *The Homemaker's Barometer*. Actually no one person will fall into a single category. Most will overlap into the one above *and* below it. But it might be fun to rate yourself (or your friends) as you set about to determine your own standards. And if you take it tongue-in-cheek, you'll find that your own sense of humor will get you through practically anything.

The Perfectionist—This is the person who does everything by the book. She'll dot every "i" and cross every "t," spending hours completing a project, or doing a single chore, regardless of its priority. She could be her own worst enemy, a bore to friends, and a drag on the family. She makes "work out of work," forgetting that placing a value on personal time is also important.

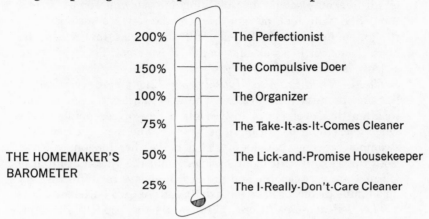

	200%	The Perfectionist
	150%	The Compulsive Doer
	100%	The Organizer
	75%	The Take-It-as-It-Comes Cleaner
THE HOMEMAKER'S BAROMETER	50%	The Lick-and-Promise Housekeeper
	25%	The I-Really-Don't-Care Cleaner

The Compulsive Doer—This is the one who constantly cleans the silver and rearranges closets, bakes cakes from scratch, loves to make draperies, knows the latest "point" in needlepoint, manages to have the house clean by some unbelievably early hour and is off to "wherever." She may give some friends guilt complexes and occasionally has a few herself when she can't accomplish more. Her goal is one of personal satisfaction as well as that of accomplishing what has to be done. If this is her "bag," why should anyone else complain?

The Organizer—She knows she is swamped and will never get her housework done without a schedule. She sifts essentials from unessentials by planning ahead. She structures her housekeeping in an organized way. Sometimes she doesn't live within the allotted schedule because she hasn't allowed time for interruptions, but she's learned over a period of time how to build some flexibility into her schedule. She is a short-cut thinker and skips steps where they don't really matter. She has learned to analyze her way through housekeeping. Follows the daily-weekly, monthly, and seasonal routine.

The Take-It-as-It-Comes Cleaner—No schedule-maker this one, she does what has to be done as it comes up, sometimes making mental schedules that work out very well. Some flexible cleaners use their time as efficiently as organizers just by doing what

3

comes naturally. Such a housekeeper cleans the living room when it seems dusty and washes the kitchen floor when it seems spattered. She may scatter her cleaning into several rooms at one time. She will feel no guilt when she opts occasionally to straighten up instead of clean, for she thinks that when the house is neat it looks clean, whether it is or not. She may make a "loose" schedule occasionally.

The Lick-and-Promise Housekeeper—She gives everything a lick and promise to return, but she may short-cut so much and so often that every once in a while a day of reckoning comes when everything has to be done at once. She may get that "I'm swamped" feeling, but doesn't let it bother her for long. (*Note:* Both the Take-It-as-It Comes Cleaner and the Lick-and-Promise Cleaner are very flexible and are nearly always ready to rush off on a family picnic, or have the kids' friends in for a barbecue.

The I-Really-Don't-Care Cleaner—If the slouch functions within a family unit she may be in trouble, particularly if anyone else in the household has higher housekeeping expectations. Our only recommendation to such homemakers is to jump in and swim. If possible try a schedule, even if it is a very simple one.

PLACING A VALUE ON TIME

We are of the opinion that even the most well-equipped and perfectly designed house will not, of itself, provide a homemaker with more free time. Even with all our invaluable labor-saving devices, we still place the responsibility for saving time squarely on the shoulders of the person doing the job. For it is that person who can place the proper value on the *time that is saved*.

Learn from the guidelines established by industry and management. Become an efficiency expert around your own home. Decide how you can utilize your time most productively. Time is one of the best resources we have available to us, and perhaps the first step is to *develop a healthy respect for it*. We have been taught to evaluate time in terms of money. Well, that's one way, but not the only one. How about the hour spent in the garden or the afternoon at the piano or easel?

Then, the second step is to *never take time for granted*. It is doled out to us on a 24-hour basis, and try as we may, we cannot accumulate it as we can money. There are only 1440 minutes in a day. Subtract 8 hours for sleeping and we've only 960 left to use as we will. And these 960 minutes must be reckoned with daily.

As for evaluating time in terms of money, even housekeeping has its price tag. It would cost $11,680 a year to replace a home-maker, based on an arbitrary "wage and hour" rate of $2.00 for various household services, such as a maid, cook, laundry services, baby sitter, accountant, etcetera.

For our purposes we believe the best way to make the most of our time is to follow some kind of schedule or routine.

What this really amounts to is time budgeting.

What Will a Schedule Accomplish?

A schedule simply helps you to:

1. Cut down on confusion and disorder.
2. Avoid duplication (like cleaning the same area again before it needs it).
3. Determine your priorities or decide what is more important to you.
4. See exactly what has to be done.
5. Gain a sense of accomplishment because you *will* get things done.

TIME BUDGETING

How much time should one spend on certain jobs? At what point does the amount of time it takes you to clean a living room, for instance, become ridiculous? There is also the big question on how clean is clean? No one can really set a hard and fast rule as there are so many variables to consider—how fast you work, the other demands on your time, your life-style, your standards of perfection. For example, take cleaning alone. You have to consider the size of your house, how many people live in it, whether you live in the city or the country, what kind of cleaning equipment you have, whether or not you have help.

A good rule of thumb to follow in budgeting time is based upon your own work patterns. As you study your own methods of working, you will begin to settle into some kind of routine and allot your time as you feel will be reasonable. Compare the averages over a certain period. As you relate them to your personal standards, you may determine that 10 minutes is long enough, for instance, to tidy up the bathroom, or that 15 minutes is long enough to spend getting breakfast ready in the morning.

As you begin to budget your time, keep in mind that all jobs have three time periods: preparation time, doing time, and cleaning-up time. This following list may be of some help to you in planning.

Making breakfast	15 to 30 minutes
Cleaning up children's room	20 minutes
Cleaning up kitchen, straightening house	45 minutes to 1½ hours
Making beds, tidying bathroom	30 to 45 minutes
Making dinner	30 minutes to 1 hour

PLANNING A SCHEDULE

Now that you have analyzed your housekeeping life-style and have determined your priorities, it's time to work out a schedule. It's easier than you might think.

For the most part household activities separate into four segments: *daily, weekly, monthly,* and *seasonal.* Weekly tasks are added to daily activities as they seem best to fit your life-style and monthly jobs are added to the weekly schedule one or two at a time. Seasonally, adjunct to these daily and weekly jobs, there are necessary shifts in household routine: clothes, furniture and activities, holidays, and general maintenance. In general, these jobs include:

DAILY   Cooking, serving and dishwashing; once-over surface cleaning; family care; individual care

WEEKLY   Complete cleaning of each room; laundering; meal planning; food purchasing and preparation

MONTHLY OR
PERIODIC   Hostessing; outside activities; care of clothing and home furnishings (sewing and mending); letter writing and finances; specific cleaning jobs such as refrigerator, range, freezer (unless weekly)

SEASONAL   Cleaning of major items such as shutters or porch furniture; changing house and clothes from season to season; special activities such as holidays and food preservation

KEEPING TRACK OF YOUR TIME

If you feel so inclined, before you make any work schedules, try keeping a detailed log of your time for at least a week. That's the way time and motion experts tackle their jobs and it will enable you to budget your time more efficiently if you know where it goes.

In *Management in the Home* (Dodd, Mead and Company, 1959) time and motion experts Lillian M. Gilbreth, Orpha Mae Thomas, and Eleanor Clymer suggest that keeping an account of your time will help you to see what you do with your day. In order to chart results, get yourself a pad and make a note of the time you begin each new job during the day. This, too, is easier than you think. Just don't make a big "production" out of doing it.

SOME TYPICAL SCHEDULES

At Home—with Children

7:30   Up and dress
7:45   Begin breakfast
8:00 to 9:00   Get family off to school, work
9:00   Projects, telephoning
                Put load of children's clothes in washer
10:00   Straighten kitchen

7

10:30	Clean living room (weekly job)
	Finish laundry
	Straighten bathroom
11:15	Mix cake and bake
11:30	Check market order
	Look at mail, pay bills
12:00	Baby's lunch
1:00	Baby's nap
1:15	Make casserole supper
Afternoon	Outside project

Single Person or a Working Couple—No Children

7:00	Up and dress
7:30	Start coffee
7:45	Set out fruit and cereal
	Breakfast and once over the house lightly

Office 9:00–5:00

5:30	Return home
5:45	Change clothes for dinner and organize for guests
6:15	Wash potatoes and put in portable oven (turn on when guests arrive)
	Cut vegetables for dip
6:30	Jim home
	Set steak on broiler rack
	Set out dip, vegetables, and nibbles for drinks
	Open can of vegetables (brown almonds to go with green beans)
	Toss salad (set out bottle of dressing to add last minute)
7:00	Guests supposed to arrive (they actually come at 7:30!)

Doing this is just like staying on a diet for several weeks. Just as you keep track of what you eat when you are counting calories, here you are keeping track of the time you spend while doing your work. Soon you will begin to see a pattern of how you spend your time. You will note that there are certain activities such as sleeping, personal care, cooking, cleaning up after meals, care of children, laundry, and housecleaning that never change. Then there are certain changeable activities, such as entertaining, hobbies, community work. There are unexpected chores resulting from illness, meetings, visits by relatives or friends, etcetera. Somewhere between the unchangeable and unexpected time slots, you can begin to juggle your day to accomplish your plans.

Now you are ready to make your own schedule based on your priorities and tailored to suit you and your family's own special needs. The daily, weekly, and seasonal guides in this chapter may help you in planning, as will our suggestions as to the average length of time it takes to do certain household tasks.

To fill in your schedule on the following chart:

1. List the jobs you have to do *daily*.
2. List those you want to accomplish *weekly,* then work them into the weekly plan wherever they seem best to fit.
3. List the ones you want to get around to at least once a *month*. Scatter them throughout the various weeks of the month, being careful to balance the work load. Try not to do too many special jobs in any one day.
4. List the important *seasonal* jobs that are necessary, such as those required as the seasons change from summer to winter, or yearly maintenance jobs such as cleaning the screens or washing slipcovers. Work them into a weekly schedule as the season or time dictates.

Here is a list of daily, weekly, monthly and seasonal tasks that we feel offer a reasonable breakdown of everyone's cleaning chores. Even if you follow this guide quite loosely you should find your housework less troublesome and your home a more comfortable place in which to live.

Daily:
- Wash dishes and straighten up kitchen after breakfast. Wipe off tables, counters, range, refrigerator. Clean floor as necessary. Clean sink. Empty trash and garbage.
- Make beds.
- Straighten up house. Tidy up rooms. Hang up clothes. Put soiled ones in hamper. Put away toys, stray objects. Empty ash trays. Fluff up pillows. Straighten window shades. Dust surfaces as necessary.

9

DAILY List your priorities in order of importance	WEEKLY Fill in special jobs you wish to do monthly or on seasonal basis
MONDAY	
TUESDAY	
WEDNESDAY	
THURSDAY	
FRIDAY	
SATURDAY	
SUNDAY	

- Tidy up bathroom. Clean bathtub, basin and toilet. Put soiled towels into hamper. Set out fresh linen. Clean floor as necessary.
- Do weekly projects scheduled for today.
- Straighten up kitchen after lunch and dinner. Follow breakfast order above.
- Empty all trash or garbage.

Weekly:
- Damp mop kitchen floor.
- Clean range and refrigerator (unless you opt to do them monthly). Check contents of refrigerator.
- Dust all surfaces—furniture, floors.
- Clean one or two rooms thoroughly each week. Follow instructions for cleaning specific rooms given in Chapter Three.
- Vacuum rugs, floors, and baseboards. Vacuum or brush lampshades. Open closet doors for airing.
- Clean bathrooms thoroughly—sink, tub, shower stalls, and toilet. Scrub floor.
- Change linen in bathroom and bedroom. Replenish soap and supplies.
- Polish metals as necessary.
- Wipe off doorknobs, switch plates, clean mirrors, glass surface, lamp cords, picture frames, picture cords.
- Do mending, laundering, ironing as needed.
- Do marketing.
- Special activities, engagements, projects.
- Children's activities.
- Parents' activities.

Monthly or Periodically:
- Polish furniture and other surfaces.
- Scrub and/or wax floors.
- Vacuum walls, ceilings, woodwork. Wash if necessary.
- Wash windows.
- Dust or vacuum venetian blinds and/or window shades.
- Vacuum upholstery, draperies.
- Straighten closets; dust shelves, floors, and contents.
- Empty and clean kitchen cabinets, medicine chests, and contents. Rearrange, if necessary.
- Detach and wash light bulbs.

11

- Air blankets, comforters.
- Turn mattresses.
- Clean flower pots and leaves of household plants.

SEASONAL CLEANING

There seem to be two schools of thought on seasonal cleaning. Many people feel that spring and fall cleaning is passé—that there is really no need to tear the house up twice a year. Such housewives believe that a thorough and consistent job of cleaning daily, weekly, and monthly is sufficient. We subscribe to this theory, except there *does* come a time—every two or three years—when you will *have* to do more than a good daily, weekly or monthly job. Perhaps when you paint the inside of your apartment or house.

On the other hand, regardless of whether or not they have done a consistent job of cleaning throughout the year, there are those homemakers who once or twice a year derive enormous satisfaction from knowing "everything is clean"—all at one time. Or simply out of sheer necessity they *have* to do it in spite of themselves, just to clear out the excess clutter, before they can settle in for the winter or summer. And it probably is good for the *soul!*

The seasonal cleaning routine is also an ideal one to follow if you have been away on an extended leave or vacation or if you own a vacation house.

Seasonal Chores to be undertaken as needed, in some cases three or four times a year:
- Cleaning and/or washing curtains and draperies.
- Washing or cleaning walls, ceilings, and woodwork (unless you have a paint job).
- Cleaning window shades and blinds.
- Cleaning and/or shampooing upholstery.
- Cleaning and/or shampooing carpets and rugs.
- Cleaning and waxing floors.
- Cleaning out closets.
- Sorting, mending, cleaning, and storing seasonal clothing and special gear.

⊙ Repairing, washing and/or cleaning of blankets and comforters.

*Seasonal Chores to be undertaken according to the time of
year:*

Spring   Inspect and clean self-storing storm windows,
doors, screens, etc. or take down storm windows
and storm doors. Wash and store. Brush screens
and put up. Clean and/or put away winter
clothes, blankets. Take out summer ones. Put on
clean slipcovers if used.

Summer   Brush awnings and put up. Change curtains, take
up rugs, if desired.

Fall   Take down screens and awnings, wash and store.
Clean and/or launder, put away summer clothes,
blankets. Take out winter ones. Remove and
clean slipcovers if used.

Winter   Put up storm windows and storm doors. Hang
winter curtains and draperies. Re-lay rugs.

How to Schedule Seasonal Cleaning

Set aside at least two weeks and schedule the work over this
period. Clean one room at a time, finishing it completely before
tackling another.

Before you begin your cleaning, check throughout the house
for any special jobs you wish to accomplish, repairs you want to
make, items you wish to replace.

If you don't have help with your seasonal cleaning, then follow the sequence for seasonal cleaning below. You will have to
stretch it out over a longer period of time, for it will take you
longer. Take one week to go through the house, reorganizing
where necessary, throwing out all the "junk" that always accumulates. Then follow the directions for thoroughly cleaning
rooms given in Chapter Three.

If you do have help, make certain that you use their time to
your best advantage. Let a handyman do some of the heavy
cleaning, such as taking down storm windows, washing the
windows, putting up screens, etcetera. Work with your cleaning

woman or service on one room until it is entirely finished. It is a good idea to make sure all closets, drawers, and other areas that might need reorganization are completed before the cleaning begins. The work will go faster if you do. List the things you wish to accomplish, then divide the tasks between you and your help, delegating the chores you can't or do not want to do.

If you expect your cleaning help to do *all* the work, then the little time you spend in the *pre*-organization of the cleaning and the *re*-organization of your household will pay huge dividends in how well the job gets done.

The Sequence for Seasonal Cleaning

Closets and drawers:
Sort according to: things to be cleaned or repaired,
                      things to be used currently,
                      things to be stored.
Clean and rearrange articles to be returned to drawers.
> *Tip:* When cutting new linings for dresser drawers, turn the drawer upside down, cut several at one time, then lay several sheets of lining paper over the bottom of the drawer. When one is rumpled, remove it and find a fresh one underneath.
> *Tip:* Cover a vacuum cleaner nozzle with cheesecloth, held in place with a rubber band. Then clean button boxes, dresser drawers, and sewing kits without removing all the items.

Cleaning furniture, draperies, rugs and carpets, blankets, slipcovers:
Collect things to be cleaned and repaired.
Send out things requiring professional care.
Launder or repair articles to be done at home.

Cleaning special rooms—basements, attics, garages, other workrooms:
Sort the things you want to keep, throw out trash, give away items no longer needed.
Clean ceiling, walls, woodwork, floors.

General housekeeping:
Follow instructions in Chapter Three on sequence of cleaning rooms and cleaning techniques.

How to Keep Your Schedule Working for You

Now that you have actually devised a workable schedule and you feel that you are beginning to accomplish a good day's work, try to keep it working *for* you rather than against you.

If you decide to do something at the last minute, don't just add that to your day's work. Change your schedule. Remember if you add motion, you add time! Make sure that whatever you spend your time on is necessary and relevant to your schedule, desires, and life-style. Otherwise, *don't do it!*

All this may sound very inflexible, but there is simply no use of making a schedule and creating some discipline in your life unless you plan to stick to it.

As you keep working, study your surroundings and methods. What are your work patterns? Are you wasting any time at all? Is there an easier method? Is there some appliance or utensil that would make the job easier, quicker? Do you need help? Is your equipment in proper working order? Are supplies readily accessible? Would it be more economical to tackle a big cleaning or repair job on a favorite item or would it be better to toss it out and buy a new one? Are you wearing comfortable clothes? (See section on Dressing for the Job in Chapter Three.) Do you have enough light? Is the temperature comfortable? Is your schedule too ambitious? Are you trying to be a perfectionist? What is your mental attitude? Are you duplicating effort? Are you doing a job more often than necessary? Are you working through your schedule all at one time, which is the best method, or are you jumping from one thing to the other? Are you rationalizing your interruptions? (We wager that at least 25 to 35 percent of daily interruptions are self-made and unnecessary.)

As you work you may find that some major structural or physical change in your surroundings may be worth the cost in the time and energy you will save. For example, if time is a big factor and you've a large family, a freezer may be an excellent investment. When you do have time, fill it with freeze-ahead foods, both for family meals and entertaining. Or a dishwasher may save you hours of work. Or a second vacuum cleaner in the bedroom area of your ranch or two-story house may save energy and time

15

moving the one you do have from place to place. Or a pass-through cut into a wall between the kitchen and dining room may save miles of walking over a year's time.

Or you may find that simplifying your methods is all you need:

- Change your body motion and position.
- Change your tools or equipment and working arrangement or sequence.
- Change your product—use unironed sheets instead of ironed ones, or change to the no-iron type.

Now that you have all the basic facts on managing time and motion, study them, practice them regularly, then *forget* them. Soon you'll find how fast they become second nature to you as you go about your daily chores.

Learning to Think in Short-Cut Terms

As you go about your daily, weekly, monthly, or seasonal routines, do everything you can to use your time most efficiently. Here are some examples:

- If your oven is particularly soiled, soak a cloth with ammonia, place it over the soiled area, and let it set while you are doing something else in the kitchen.
- Use a cotton swab to clean crevices, dials on ranges. Store them where you can reach one quickly.
- Instead of the familiar method of rotating sheets and linens to distribute wear, marking for identification, and worrying about storing an ample supply, why not just remove the sheets from the beds and towels from the kitchen and bath, launder them, and reuse, pronto. When they wear out, buy new ones! It does save time—and money—because you buy fewer at a time, and can replenish during annual white sales.
- Painted windowsills, woodwork, and similar surfaces will be easier to clean if they have a coat of white liquid cream wax.
- When you have a lot of plastic items to wash, fill the bathtub with hot, sudsy water and throw in all the washable items to soak. Swish clean, rinse, and dry.

Some short-cuts can have their drawbacks, though. For example, take shelf-liners. Shelf-liners are excellent for helping to keep shelves clean. However, there are several theories to consider regarding time-saving and sanitation. Several layers of paper shelf-lining can be a help. When you are ready to straighten the shelves, remove the top soiled layer and you've a clean one at the ready. On the other hand, if crumbs and soil collect under the bottom of kitchen shelf-liners, this becomes a breeding place for kitchen pests. In this case it might be wise to eliminate them altogether.

Rubber liners are more permanent and washable, although if you store oil cruets or salad oil in jars, be sure to keep a plastic liner under the jar as oily substances can cause rubber surfaces to deteriorate. If your shelves are metal or made of laminated plastic, you really could get along without any liners at all; this way the shelves are much easier to keep clean!

Learning to Do Two Things at Once

Here are some examples:

- If you are planning to bake a cake—do it after breakfast and before you straighten up the kitchen. It can be baking while you straighten up the house.
- Soak broiler pans while you eat dessert. After dinner, a swish with a sudsy steel wool pad should do the trick. Otherwise, you may have to scrub twice as hard later.
- Put laundry in the machine before you begin your morning routine, or the minute you come home from work.
- Fold diapers while you are watching TV.
- Be sure the dishwasher is empty before you begin cooking. Load it with dirty pots and pans as you finish with them. Or fill the sink with hot sudsy water and throw in pots and pans as you cook.
- Make the beds in the morning while coffee is perking.
- A wall phone with a long cord in the kitchen can be a great time-saver—there are many things you can do around the kitchen while you are talking on the phone.
- Keep a small carpet sweeper near the dining area for daily crumb pickup.

MANAGING YOUR FINANCIAL AFFAIRS

Money management is a very real part of keeping a house and family running smoothly. The best money managers are ones who have goals and keep on working toward them. Of course, everyone's budget and how one executes it will vary from family to family, person to person . . . and in a very large part with one's own sense of values. It is true that planning ahead always looks good on paper.

It's easier said than done. That is also true. However, there are certain guidelines to executing and planning a budget wisely. You'll achieve your goals better, whether things work out perfectly or not, *with* a plan than with *none* at all!

ATTEMPTING A BUDGET

- Determine your goals—things you want *now, soon,* and *in the future.*
- Analyze your income—determine how much money you have to work with and what your current resources are.
- Determine how you will execute your budget—weekly, semi weekly or monthly. Then divide your net annual income accordingly.
- List the everyday living costs. These may be some or all of the following:

Food	Automobile and transportation
Shelter	
Household maintenance and operating expenses	Family personal and incidental expenses
Entertainment	Allowances
Clothing care and laundry	Household help and services
Utilities	

- Subtract your everyday living costs from your net income. For a while keep track of all you spend in a notebook to determine a practical figure for everyday living expenses.

- Now, set up a list of your fixed obligations and expenses. These include those of a present (monthly, quarterly, semi-annually, and yearly) nature and those for the near future.

Present fixed expenses may include:

Pledges	Retirement and pension
Federal and state	Dues
income taxes	Payments on charge ac-
Insurance payments	counts, car, savings, home
Tuition	furnishings, mortgage
Licenses	

Near future fixed expenses may include:

Home improvement	Donations and
Medical and dental	contributions
Travel	Magazine, book, and
Special gifts	newspaper expenses

- Subtract all your fixed expenses from rest of income after everyday expenses have been deducted.
- Plan for an emergency. Set aside an amount for unexpected expenses—care of a parent, unexpected travel, illness, death.
- Plan your savings and investment program:
  Stocks and bonds
  Bank savings
  Insurance (life, annuity, endowment, health, homeowners)
  Home
  Other investments

The lists above have been suggested only as a guide to help you think about proper money management. Get the best advice you can from a sound financial adviser. Refer to the Bibliography at the end of this book for more information. Of course, plans must be adjusted to meet the specific needs of your family. Money management takes a good deal of juggling as we are sure you have already found out, and budgeting may be more theoretical than realistic at times.

ESTATE PLANNING

When should it begin? After one accumulates a great deal of wealth? (Highly unlikely in today's economic structure.) Actually, according to money-management experts, if you own anything at all you have an estate in the true sense of the word. It's not how much but how you handle it and how you arrange to dispose of it that makes your estate significant during your own lifetime and to your heirs. Real property, money, stocks, bonds, and personal possessions all put an obligation on you to plan ahead. The alternative—automatic disposal of whatever the head of the household leaves according to state laws—robs you of the decision.

Young families tend to shy away from the term "estate planning"—even as it applies to assessing their ownings. It sounds complicated and applicable only to real wealth. But sound planning is needed even for modest amounts, and must always be done step by step. First steps should be taken at the start of a marriage, when there may be little besides a modest home and budding bank account to consider.

Actually, there's more than a practical aspect to estate planning. The feeling of building a life and future for the people you love lends a sense of direction to what can so easily come to seem merely a daily struggle to make another dollar.

Estate planning should take into consideration:

Savings and investments	Personal property
Real estate	Tax savings through gifts
Life insurance	and contributions
Wills	

How Important Is a Will?

It is very important. "A man's dying is more the survivors' affair than his own," so goes a familiar quotation. The very thought of making a will is often a touchy subject. Many otherwise responsible people are diffident about accepting the fact that a will is merely good business sense. Legally, there is no consideration of your personal wishes, unless you indicate what they are in an officially drawn will. Get the best legal advice you can from a lawyer or the trust officer of a bank on the following:

- Value of joint ownership.
- Necessity of naming a guardian for your children.
- How disaster clauses should be worked if both husband and wife die in a common disaster.
- Review of a will and the advisability of changing it from time to time. Changes in the case of birth, death, marriage, divorce will necessitate the need for checking it periodically. Check it in any case when you move from one state to another.
- When an executor should be named—most likely when your estate grows large enough to direct a bank or trust company to act as executors. Your best executor is a bank. In any case, it should be someone who can *objectively* gather, maintain, and distribute your assets properly—someone of competence and ability. A family member or good friend may be too emotionally involved to exercise objective judgment.
- Advisability of setting up a trust while you are still alive to accomplish the purposes of your will, thus avoiding probate or the cost of administrative handling of a will after death.

CHAPTER TWO

Decorating for Easier Care

Just as managing your time wisely allows you to adjust your cleaning schedule to your own personal needs, so decorating with an eye to later housekeeping allows you to furnish a home compatible with your life-style.

If you really dislike doing much cleaning, then select furnishings that require very little care, or that have protective finishes that resist dirt and damage. Permanent-press curtains that come out of the washing machine and dryer ready to hang and laminated plastic table tops are two good examples. Using wipable vinyl fabrics that resemble silk for upholstery is another example.

If you can't bear to keep wiping up fingerprints, give up using glass-top tables, no matter how much you love them. If you hate to wax floors, select flooring that does not require waxing, or cover your kitchen with carpeting. You may find vacuuming infinitely easier than mopping and waxing, even if you do have to clean the carpet occasionally. Housekeeping soon becomes a relative thing, based upon your personal preferences in selecting materials and furnishings. The trick is to know how to achieve the look you like with materials compatible with your housekeeping priorities. Consider ease of housekeeping before you make any decorating decision.

COMFORT AND EASE—WITHOUT SACRIFICING APPEARANCE

Analyze your housekeeping dislikes first. Jot down all your chores: daily, weekly, monthly. Then classify them as follows: those you hate the most, those you merely dislike, and finally, those you mind the least. Next, look over the following list of decorating tips and follow those that will help make *your* housekeeping as easy as possible:

- One-surface floors are easiest to take care of—wall-to-wall carpeting is probably the easiest of all, if you don't mind vacuuming and if you are in a fairly permanent home. If you are apt to move frequently, a room-size rug is a better solution, as it can be more easily transferred to a new home.
- Hardwood floors with area rugs look lovely if kept in good shape, but if you hate polishing and regular maintenance you might try another solution. Rugs plus floor are harder to take care of and clean than wall-to-wall carpeting.
- Vinyl tile or other similar floors need scrubbing and waxing, so don't have them if you hate swabbing the decks. Some of the newer ones claim no need for waxing. Ask about them and their durability over a period of time without waxing.
- Analyze your storage needs. Make sure you have plenty of storage space so that your nondecorative possessions can be put away as neatly as possible. If there is too much clutter, housekeeping is twice as difficult. (See Chapter Eight, About Storage and Stashing.)
- When buying new furniture and accessories, consider color and finish in relation to upkeep. Dark furniture tones show dust and fingerprints. Rough or carved wood pieces also gather dust and are harder to clean. Clean, simple lines are easiest to clean.
- When selecting carpeting, remember that plush, velvet-finish, one-color carpeting, particularly in a very light or very dark shade, shows lint and spots the most and is

23

difficult to keep clean. Tweedy, patterned, and twist carpeting is more practical in terms of easy care, especially in areas of heavy traffic.

- Cut down on knickknacks. One important piece looks better, cuts down on moving many aside for dusting. If you have additional decorative pieces you want to display, alternate with pieces from storage. This will cut down on clutter and give you an occasional change of scenery.

- When choosing a home or apartment to rent or buy, keep in mind that older, elaborate architectural styles with paneled doors, baseboards, many-paneled double-hung windows involve more housekeeping. If you love Victorian architecture, by all means this is what you should have—but just remember, you will have a little more work.

- Magazines don't have to be fanned out à la dentist's reception room. Stack them neatly instead; same goes for books that don't fit on shelves.

- Pewter, copper, brass, and silver are lovely and fun to collect—but don't do it unless you're prepared to polish.

- Don't buy a marble-top table thinking it needs no care. Marble looks stain-resistant and people tend to put drinks down on it without thinking. If you hate to rush coasters under your guests' glasses, you may end up with a ruined table. Removing glass rings and stain from marble is next to impossible. For care of marble, see section on Marble Furniture in Chapter Three.

- Use laminated plastic surfaces, vinyl plastics, fabrics, wallpapers, and wall panels that have been especially treated to resist stains.

- Plants are wonderful to have around, but they require a lot of care—think of this when you start collecting them. One big palm in an entranceway or living room is easier to keep healthy and looking nice than a whole lot of little plants.

- Glass shelves, mirrors, etcetera, are dust collectors and need frequent cleaning.

- Look for washable fabrics and those in darker colors or prints that don't show every little spot. Use light colors in places where they will not soil easily; for instance, off-white draperies are great, but an off-white sofa—watch out!

Furniture Arrangements

The way furniture is arranged will certainly affect housekeeping and comfort. Place furniture to make the best use of the space you have:

- Group furniture according to use—conversation, eating, entertainment, reading.
- Consider traffic flow in relation to placement.
- Consider ease of cleaning, vacuuming in relation to placement. You'll be more apt to clean properly if it is easy than if you have to move a lot of furniture.
- Think about easy access to tables, television, bookshelves, heating, and air-conditioning.

BUYING HOME FURNISHINGS

If you are newly married and just beginning to decorate an apartment or home, and if you're living on a limited budget, you have to decide what to buy first and how best to spend your money. Obviously you can't go out and furnish your dream house just the way you want it—and even if you did have the money to do this, it's not a good idea as your tastes may still change and develop.

We suggest buying just one or two really good pieces and using cast-offs and other second-hand furniture bought inexpensively to fill your temporary needs. For example, if you want a beautiful king-size bed and a wonderful sofa or a dining set, put your money there, and use cushions, canvas chairs, and "finds" from your mother's attic or thrift shops to furnish the rest of your place.

Gradually you'll replace these temporary pieces with furnishings you really want. Good decoration takes time and thought and experimentation. Study the current magazines, clip out "dream" pictures, keep up with the current designer trends. Then when you are ready to buy, you will be well prepared.

Impulse buying is never a good idea. And in the case of furniture it could result in an expensive error. Even though so much

25

of the furniture you buy is underneath the surface, it will help to know some of the facts about its construction in order to answer two basic questions. Always consider these questions before starting to decorate:

1. How will a particular room be used—and the furniture in it?
2. Is the furniture you are considering suitable for these activities?

WOOD FURNITURE

When buying wood furniture, you will often hear the term "case goods." This is the name that the home-furnishings industry has given all wood furniture that is not upholstered. This includes everything from china cabinets to chests of drawers to tables.

You will find "case goods" in both solid types and in veneers. Solid furniture means that all the wood parts are made of solid wood. With the possible exception of Early American and Colonial furniture, most wood furniture is made from plywood or chip-core panels (pieces of wood particles bound together in a man-made composition) and faced with wood veneers on exposed surfaces.

There is a wide selection of wood used in furniture. Walnut, mahogany, oak, cherry, pecan, and chestnut are among the most widely used. There are also many exotic woods with highly patterned designs. Patterns may come from the wood itself, such as teak. Or they may result from the way a tree is cut, such as "crotch mahogany," cut from the crotch of the mahogany tree.

FINISHES

Finishing not only improves the natural beauty of the wood but also protects it against moisture and wear. Finishes often vary from the true color of the wood. The only way to be sure of what you are buying is to read labels carefully and ask questions. With the variety of finishes available today, you may find one wood in both light and dark tones, to suit individual preference.

Finish is also an indication of quality. Any decorative finish should be used to bring out the best characteristics of the wood. The most common finishes are as follows:

Oil-rubbed. A dry, close-to-the-grain finish that's most often used on teak and walnut.

Distressed. A speckled antique-look finish, found most often on antique reproductions and some contemporary pieces. When you are considering this finish, make sure it looks irregular and not too mechanical.

Polished. While there are certain pieces that may look best in a polished high-gloss finish, depending upon fad and fashion, even the most formal pieces are now done primarily in a subtle low-luster gloss. And the lower the gloss the easier the furniture is to take care of. (See Chapter Three.)

Special finishes are available for furniture that gets hard use. Laminated plastic tops resist stains, scratches, acids, moisture, and even burns that result from contact with food and smoking materials. These plastics may be applied as clear coats to let the beauty of the wood show through or they may be colored and designed to resemble wood. When selecting furniture with plastic coatings, read the labels carefully and know what to expect from the protective finish.

CONSTRUCTION

A piece of furniture is only as strong as its joints. Good joinery is an expensive, often hidden, hand operation that requires the skill of an expert craftsman. More than any other phase of furniture construction, joinery determines the worth of the item. Some of the most popular methods of joinery include:

Mortise and Tenon forms a strong union by fitting a notch made in a solid piece of wood tightly into a hole cut in an adjoining piece of wood. No nails or screws are used, only glue, to achieve one of the best methods of joining. It is most frequently used to join stretchers to leg posts or top rails to backposts, as on a chair or headboard.

Double Dowel joinery is the most commonly used and the second best type of construction. Dowels are wooden pins that are fitted into holes drilled into both adjoining pieces of wood and

27

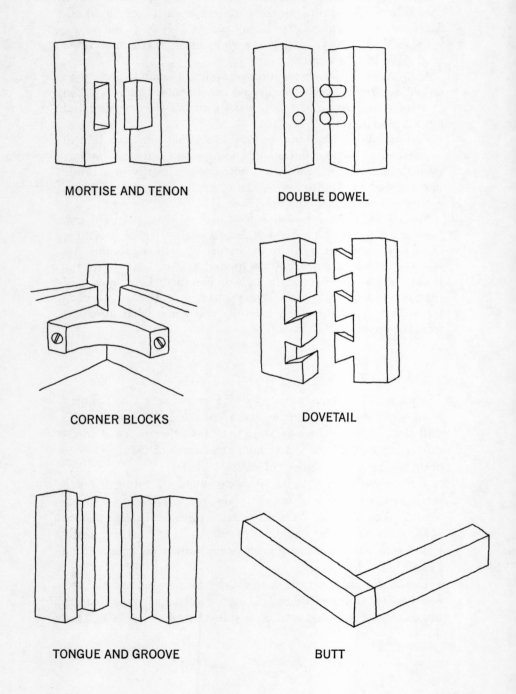

MORTISE AND TENON

DOUBLE DOWEL

CORNER BLOCKS

DOVETAIL

TONGUE AND GROOVE

BUTT

glued. Dowels were developed many years ago, before nails or screws were invented, and are a characteristic and decorative feature of Early American furniture. Dowels can also be used invisibly, as in joining stretchers to chair legs.

Corner Blocks are triangular pieces of wood, screwed and glued to support and reinforce the frame. They are used in the construction of tables, in most other case goods, and in seating pieces to keep one side from pulling away from the other. Corner blocks are usually made of wood that is different and stronger than that used in the exposed wood parts.

Dovetail joinery is a method of attaching boards at right angles, as in the sides of a drawer. Each board has interlocking tenons that are cut in the form of a dovetail. It is almost standard construction for all drawers. This provides a rigid construction.

Tongue and Groove Joints, if done skillfully, will be invisible. An example is where several boards are joined to form a table top. One board will have a projecting tongue that fits into a groove on a corresponding board.

Butt Joint construction is one in which one board is glued or nailed flush to another board. It is the least desirable of all joint constructions.

Gluing is required on all joints. Today's glues have been so developed and improved that there are glues so strong they can actually outlast the wood!

ANTIQUE REPRODUCTIONS

Reproductions of antiques are machine-made by blunting corners and softening hard edges by hitting them with metal chains. Such reproductions should be executed ever so subtly so as to avoid any obvious look of mechanical "aging." Otherwise the buying considerations for reproductions are the same as those for other wood furniture and upholstered pieces.

How to Determine Quality—Questions to Consider

- Does the piece wobble when it is rocked? If so, it is cheaply made.
- Are the tops of drawers and doors properly aligned? Any gaps along the edges?

29

- How do the doors hang when opened? Do they rub or drag the bottom of the chest?
- Do drawers glide out freely? If they bind or screech, they are improperly installed.
- Are the insides of drawers, backs of chests, and undersides of tables and chairs smoothly sanded and finished?
- Are joints in drawers made with interlocking dovetailing? This provides rigid construction.
- Are corner blocks used to reinforce the frame?
- Do doors stick when they are shut? Are they easy to open?
- How are legs attached—with mortise and tenon (best) or dowel joinery (also good)?
- Are leveling legs provided to counterbalance the possibility of uneven floors?
- Are surfaces smoothly finished and free from defects? Look at them in good light and rub your fingertips over them lightly.
- Has a protective finish been used on surfaces that will receive hard wear?
- Is hardware heavy and solid, securely attached? The more solid and heavy it is, the better the hardware.
- Have you read the label carefully to determine the materials used and any other pertinent information as to construction and care?
- Are there extra leaves for dining tables? How do they store—separately or within the table itself? Are the leaves finished exactly as the table is?
- Do large and heavy storage pieces come with casters for easier moving?

  Note: Always make these same buying checks on furniture that is delivered to your home, as you do not generally receive the floor sample you looked at when you purchased it.

UPHOLSTERED FURNITURE

The second major furniture category is upholstered furniture. Upholstered furniture should be judged not only on the basis of quality and style but also on comfort. Most furniture is designed for people with an average height of 5 feet, 8 inches. Sit down and try the piece before buying.

CONSTRUCTION

The Framework. A good sturdy frame is the backbone for any upholstered piece. If a frame is cheaply constructed, legs and arms will loosen and require repairs. Joints should be securely doweled or mortised, braced and glued. Nails are not satisfactory for this purpose. They tend to work loose from the frame. Legs should be sturdily attached. The "weight" test is important. When you sit in an upholstered piece and it sags or gives, beware!

Many of these points are difficult to check because of the outer covering on upholstered furniture. Therefore, it is most important to deal with a reliable store, read labels and hangtags carefully, and talk to a knowledgeable salesman who is willing to answer your questions.

Springs. The seat construction most often used is the S-type spring. *Flat springs* are nailed to the frame at equal points and are linked together with tiny coiled springs. This type of construction is used when a minimum of bulk or a flat appearance is desired. The *coil spring* has springs generally placed on and attached to webbing crosses. A double-cone spring is more comfortable than a single-cone, which is often used in moderately priced furniture. An average-size chair should have anywhere from nine to twelve springs per seat. (Feel or look underneath to find out how many there are.) Check the labels to find out how many times the springs have been tied. Quality construction has springs tied eight times. Less expensive pieces may have springs tied only four times. This is not sufficient to keep springs in place and prevent them from poking up and marring or possibly tearing the cover with hard use.

CUSHION FILLERS

A label, required by law and usually attached to the muslin dust cover, will identify the cushioning materials used. Urethane or polyfoam are used frequently in seating, backs, and arms of

31

upholstered pieces. They are nonallergenic, and mildew-, fungus-, and moth-proof.

Urethane Foam may be used as a solid unit or may serve as core that is wrapped with a light, fluffy polyester material or down.

Foam Rubber is another foam filling which offers many of the same characteristics as the plastic foam. However, it has better resiliency and is extremely comfortable for sitting. It is also more expensive than plastic foams.

Other types of cushion fillers include: *Spring-filled cushions* with Dacron or Fortrel wrap; *Down,* the most expensive and most luxurious, but which requires the most care in plumping or refluffing; and *Down and feathers,* the less expensive version of the all-down filler.

THE OUTER FABRIC

The outer fabric of upholstered furniture is one of the few areas where you can easily determine quality. Good workmanship in stretching, fitting, and attaching the covering is important to both appearance and durability. Check for a well-tailored look, straight welting on all major seam constructions, a zipper closing on foam cushions for a neat fit, hem and pleats that hang straight, and reversible cushions to distribute wear.

How to Determine Quality—Questions to Consider

- Are the legs and joints securely attached?
- Have you studied the labels or asked about the kind of springs which have been used and how they are attached?
- What are the cushion fillings and how have they been constructed?
- Do the cushions have zipper closings? (Zippers give a neat fit and provide ease in removing covers when cleaning.)
- Will the fiber and construction of the fabric provide long wearability?
- Does the fabric have a soil-retardant, flame-resistant finish?
- Is it comfortable to sit in?

- If a sleep sofa, is it comfortable for both sitting and sleeping? Can you move it comfortably?
- What standards exist as to fabric flammability and durability?

When selecting any furniture, either wood or upholstered, keep these important points in mind if easy care is your goal:

1. Single surfaces are always easier to clean than a combination of wood and upholstery.
2. Low-luster surfaces on wood pieces are easier to clean than highly polished ones.
3. Darker fabrics show less soil than lighter ones.
4. Foam-filled cushions always keep their shape and don't require plumping.
5. Lightweight pieces or those on furniture casters are easier to move out for cleaning than heavy ones.
6. Soil-retardant finishes on fabrics help to keep them cleaner longer.
7. Plastic laminated surfaces are virtually damage-proof, easy to clean.

MOLDED PLASTIC FURNITURE

Furniture made from molded plastics has recently become extremely popular.

It has the advantage of not being susceptible to moisture or dryness, so it does not warp. It is very light in weight, providing ease in moving.

Inflatable vinyl chairs are extremely lightweight. You deflate them when you are on the move and blow them up again when you arrive. Wipe them with lukewarm sudsy water and dry thoroughly. Be sure they are thoroughly dry before deflating.

ANTIQUES

If you really have your heart set on antiques, then there are a few cautions that are important to note.

Unless you have unlimited funds or are fortunate enough to

33

have acquired some old pieces from parents, relatives, or friends, then concentrate on your "hunting" at auctions, Good Will and Salvation Army stores, thrift shops, or attics. And then do your own restoring.

Most pieces found in the better antique shops have been refinished, sold from dealer to dealer, and have very little repairing or restoring, if any, to be done on them. Consequently prices are set accordingly. Keep in mind that unless you plan to become an avid collector and acquire antiques for an investment, which in itself requires a great deal of time and money, you may want to consider buying fine reproductions.

The definition of an antique used to be something that was manufactured prior to 1830; today, however, the less restrictive definition is an article made at least 100 years ago. This very fact alone means that the piece, depending upon its age and condition, may require special care in cleaning and maintenance and in the general indoor environmental conditions of your home.

Another important consideration in buying an antique is how it will be used. Tables, desks, and some chests do not usually get hard wear; consequently, any fragile quality would not be as much of a concern with these as it would be with a chair, for example. If you plan to use a chair frequently for general use, then an antique might not be a wise choice.

As for cleaning, generally the regular care is just about the same as for other fine furniture. If much repairing or restoring is necessary, or if very special care is necessary, it is wise to consult a professional, or read a few good books on the subject. (See Bibliography at the back of this book.)

CHILDREN'S ROOMS

BABY'S ROOM

A baby's room is easy to furnish because you pretty much know what you need—crib, chest of drawers, dressing table with shelves below. It's also easy to keep looking neat and clean because your little one is not getting around yet to create confusion.

Furniture. You no longer need stick to white for a baby's furniture. Now it comes in natural wood and bright colors, which are practical, easy to care for, and cheerful. Junior beds are available—the sides come off when a child no longer needs them. But most mothers still seem to prefer using a crib first, then a regular bed. Cradles are great for newborns because you can rock the baby to sleep in his bed. A rocking chair is a good alternative to this in a new baby's room.

A good chest of drawers should last till the child is older—don't invest much in a small, babyish one. Changing tables are a must to save your back—don't try to do all a baby's dressing and changing on a bed. Shelves underneath a dressing table are convenient for keeping all a baby's changing needs right where you need them.

Bathinets that serve as changing tables are still available, but small plastic tubs and plastic dishpans are just as good for tiny babies, and easier to handle and care for.

Decorating. When planning colors for a nursery there's no need to stick to pink for a girl's room and blue for a boy's, unless you happen to have a passion for pink and blue. If you want to decorate the room before the baby's arrival, some great color schemes we have found for either boy or girl include blue-and-white, red-white-and-blue, yellow-orange-and-red, and blue-green-and-white, or yellow-and-green. A friend did a nursery in lively mixed patterns of red and white stripes and polka dots—it turned out to be a little girl's room but would have been great for a boy too.

Decorate with toys, dolls, and stuffed animals—they don't have to be stowed away. They look great lined up on a shelf, chest, or bed.

As They Grow Older

Furniture. As a child grows from infant to toddler to schoolchild, his room will have to be more carefully organized to contain all his things, for his collection will grow and grow with him until you don't know what on earth to do with all the toys, stuffed animals, books, records, games, train and car sets, crayons and paints, and so on (see Chapter Eight).

35

Furniture made with plastic finishes or plastic laminate are easy to care for and take the brunt of active youngsters.

Chest of Drawers. Get a roomy one—a child's clothes get bigger as fast as he does. He should be able to reach all the drawers, to encourage him to dress himself when he's able.

Beds. Bunk beds are great space-savers and especially fun for boys or when two children are sharing a not-too-large room. A canopy bed with ruffles looks lovely and feminine in a little girl's room. There are bunk beds with chests and drawers built in to serve as a footboard. They are convenient, compact, and attractive.

Decorating. Remember, nothing fancy or fragile in furniture, walls or floors—they'll all take a beating. Bright vinyl tiles are practical for a child's floor; they're easy to put down and easy to keep clean *if* you select the kind that requires no waxing. A small rug by the child's bed will do—carpeting isn't too good an idea for a child's room because building blocks and mechanical toys work much better on a hard surface.

If you're artistically talented (or if you're not!) try painting a mural on a child's wall. One young mother copied the cover of her son's favorite book on one wall—a bold red-white-and-blue toy soldier. It looked terrific and the little boy was delighted.

Make sure wall surfaces, whether painted or papered, are washable—small children love to "paint" the walls with Magic Marker or your favorite lipstick.

A pint-size table and chairs are a great asset in a child's room —here they can paint and draw, have a snack, etcetera. Saw the legs to a lower height on an old card table or piano bench. These make ideal play tables. When sawing, measure very accurately the first time. Need we say why?

CURTAINS AND DRAPERIES

There is a wide variety of fabrics, colors, patterns, and styles in both curtains and draperies. Price will depend upon the type and amount of fabric you need and whether or not you buy ready-mades, have them custom-made, or make them yourself.

In selecting curtains and draperies, keep these things in mind:

Size. There are usually three widths from which to choose—extended draperies, regular mounting, and inside mounting. These are available in four lengths—sill, apron, floor, and ceiling-to-floor.

Style. There are shirred glass curtains (referring to sheers that cover the "glass"), traverse curtains and draperies, straight panels, shirred draperies, cafe curtains, and crisscross or ruffled curtains.

Construction. Consider whether or not the seams are straight, the corners squared, the stitching neat, and the hems doubled and ample, which will allow for proper hanging and possible lengthening. Fibers include the natural ones as well as synthetics and blends. Check for labels that indicate fiber content and instruction for proper care. Weaves are available in plain, twill, satin, or a variation of one of these. All fabrics may have certain finishes which will improve or change the appearance. For more about fabric finishes, see Chapter Four.

If you are buying ready-mades, or if you are making or having the curtains made, these points in quality construction will make for easier care and longer wear:

- Hems on each side should be at least 1 inch; bottom hem 4 inches. If they are blind-stitched (see Chapter Seven) there will be less chance of puckering.
- In draperies using more than one width, seams should be overlocked and hemmed without puckering. This will let them hang smoothly.
- Pleats should be at least 4 inches deep and spaced not more than 5 inches apart. There should be at least three folds to each pleat to provide ample fullness for hanging. Fabric width should be almost twice the width of the window to provide minimum fullness. Make sure buckram is "trained" to assure even folding.
- To line or not to line is an important question. If you have lots of soot and smog in your area, linings will provide the protection your draperies need from dirt and grime. They will also help to cut down on both heat and cold coming into the room if linings are insulated.
- Plain curtains and draperies are easier to take care of than those with flounces and ruffles.

- If your curtains are washable, make sure any trimming, such as embroidery, fringe, tape, or appliqués, is also washable. Single panels are easier to launder in a machine than widths of attached panels, though they are not as handsome at the windows.
- Using decorative window shades and NO curtains or draperies requires the least care. They need only be wiped if wipable or dusted with a vacuum cleaner attachment, and washed only when necessary. Dark shades disguise soil.
- What standards exist as to fabric flammability?

SOFT-SURFACE FLOOR COVERINGS

RUGS AND CARPETS

When purchasing rugs and carpets, it is wise to consider first which type you prefer or which will meet your specific needs: *wall-to-wall*, which is cut and fit to the size and shape of the room and permanently installed; *room-size,* which come in standard sizes or can be seamed to make room-size, leaving anywhere from a 3- to 12-inch border of flooring exposed; *room-fit,* which gives the illusion of wall-to-wall carpeting without permanent installation because it is cut from standard lengths to fit the room; *area rugs,* which vary in size and shape, covering only part of the room.

Generally the price of carpeting will depend upon style and quality of construction as well as the fiber. Wool fibers are usually found in higher price ranges, acrylic and polyester fibers in medium price ranges, while nylons, polypropylenes, cottons, and rayons are lower in cost.

Construction. Carpeting is constructed in one of five ways:

1. Woven
2. Knitted
3. Tufted
4. Flocked
5. Needlepunched

Each construction will vary; however, one is not necessarily better than the other. In woven types, the weaves—named for the loom on which they are made—include *axminster,* which is likely to have intricate patterns with many colors; *velvet,* which may be cut pile or tightly twisted yarn of uncut loop, usually solid in color although tweeds are available; and *wilton,* which can be woven in a variety of multicolored patterns with both loop and cut pile. Ninety-five percent of today's carpeting, however, is of the knitted and tufted variety.

In *knitted types,* the backing and surface yarns are interlocked simultaneously, as they are in woven carpets. Rows of chain stitches lock pile yarns securely into the backing. The backing usually has a latex coating to give the carpet more body. They are available in solid color or tweed and a variety of textures.

The largest percentage of carpeting and rugs manufactured today are actually made by the *tufting* process. In tufting the pile is sewn into a pre-woven backing material. The tufts are then locked in place by a latex adhesive. A secondary backing is added for extra tuft bind and offers more dimensional stability. They are available in cut or loop pile, textured, carved, twist and plush styles and in plain or multicolor combinations. As for the term *broadloom,* many have construed it to mean a kind of carpet. Not true. It means that the carpet was woven on a broad loom— in widths wider than six feet. It is simply a term of measurement.

The *quality* does not depend on fiber and construction alone, since various qualities are available in each fiber and by each construction method. Your best guides to judging quality are the density or the thickness of the pile and the depth of the pile. Actually the deeper and denser the pile, the better the quality. Density is the number of lengthwise and crosswise units of yarn. Test it by bending back a corner of the carpet. If there are wide spaces between tufts it is usually of lower quality.

For carpet padding, see Chapter Three.

Check also to see what standards exist as to fabric flammability.

When selecting a rug or carpet, keep these points in mind with reference to easy care:
- *Color.* The medium shades are usually the most practical. Colors that show the most soil are those in very dark or very light shades. Patterned designs, such as tweeds, stripes, and florals, disguise soil better than solid colors.

39

If you do want light colors, use them in lightly used areas or plan on cleaning them often.

- *Style*. There are several different styles from which you can choose and some will require more care than others. While plain and luxurious carpets are elegant, they do require care, especially if they are not thick and are in a light color.

Those carpets requiring less care include:
- *Twists*. The flat, carefree surface does not soil readily under normal use. The yarn has been given a permanent "twist," which makes it more durable, easier to keep clean.
- *Textured*. These are usually embossed, sculptured, carved or sheared to give them a cut "high-low" look. These varying degrees of levels help to disguise soil, footprints, and shading.
- *Tweeds and Patterns*. Because of their multicolored designs, soil is readily disguised.
- *Shags*. Since the loops lap over each other they may not show soil as readily. Soil buries itself deeply and is hard to remove with a regular vacuum cleaner. They will require a special shag cleaner or "rake," some of which are available as vacuum cleaner attachments.

Those fibers requiring less care include:
- *Wool* is abrasion- and soil-resistant, and will clean well when necessary.
- *Acrylics* are the most similar to wool in man-made fibers. While acrylics do not hide soil as readily as wool, they are easier to clean.
- *Nylon* is the strongest of the man-made fibers. While it characteristically shows soil readily, it does clean well. There are some newer types of nylon that do look cleaner longer. Ask about them. The *continuous filament* type was created to eliminate the fuzzing and pilling normally associated with the *staple* type nylon.
- *Polypropylene*, like continuous filament nylon, is tough and durable, resists soil, and cleans well. It is virtually static-free. Because its color is "built-in" or solution-dyed, color will not fade.

For more about rugs and carpets and for information on hard-surface floor coverings, see Chapter Three.

ORIENTAL RUGS

An Oriental rug is a hand-knotted rug made anywhere in the Orient. Some of the countries include Pakistan, China, Japan, India, and Iran.

Authentic Oriental rugs must be hand-knotted. While there are some very good-looking reproductions, those made on machines do not have the same "appreciative value." They are primarily functional, decorative and less expensive.

The most familiar types are those made in Iran and surrounding countries. You'll recognize them by such names as Sarouk, Tabriz, Kasvin, Kashan, Kerman, Ardabil, Hamadan, Heriz, Mehriban, and Shiraz.

If you are in the market for an Oriental rug it is important to buy from a reliable dealer. Unless you are an expert on the subject, in which case the information here would be extremely elementary, it is not a good idea to buy at an auction, as glamorous as it seems. A good dealer, many of whom are found in leading department stores as well as private shops, can help guide you into a wise choice.

As for the value of Oriental rugs, you will find both new and old ones on the market. Officially, according to the United States Customs, an "antique" rug is one made before 1701. In general, however, the industry calls an antique any rug over 100 years old.

Buying an Oriental rug requires more information than we can cover in this book. To learn more about them, check with your library for a good book on the subject. There are several good ones listed in the Bibliography at the back of this book.

For care of Oriental rugs, see Chapter Three.

SHEETS, PILLOWCASES, MATTRESS PADS

A good inventory normally calls for six sheets for each bed—two on the bed, two in the hamper, and two in the linen closet. With today's permanent-press, no-iron fabrics, it is conceivably possible to get along with four sheets per bed. Some people we know actually remove the sheets from the bed, wash and dry them and put them back. When they wear out, they buy new

41

ones! Pillowcases soil more quickly and wrinkle more readily; therefore it is good to change them weekly, regardless of how often you change your sheets.

Always check the size of your mattresses before buying sheets. A good rule is to figure about 20 inches more than the mattress size (length and width) in determining the size sheet to buy. This will let you tuck 10 inches in on each side and at the foot with a 10-inch fold over the blanket or comforter at the top.

Sheets are available in both flat and contoured styles. It is especially important to know the exact measurements of your mattress when buying contoured sheets. If they don't fit well you will save virtually nothing in time and energy.

Sizes are available as follows:

SHEETS	MATTRESSES/BEDS**	
72" × 108" (cotton) 72" × 104" (polyester/ cotton)* × 120" (extra long)	Twin Bed	39" × 75" × 80" (extra long)
81" × 108" (cotton) 81" × 104" (polyester/ cotton)* × 120" (extra long)	Double Bed	54" × 75" × 80" (extra long)
90" × 120"	Queen-Size Bed	60" × 80"
108" × 120"	King-Size Bed (Some are available in extra long 78")	72" × 80/84"
63" × 108"	Bunk Beds, Cots, and Single Daybeds	30/36" × 72/76"
Same as conventional sizes above	Sofa Beds—same as conventional sizes above	

* Polyester sheets shrink less than all-cotton sheets; therefore sizes are smaller.

** Beds are available in various sizes beginning with a width of 29 or 30". Fitted sheets are made for standard mattress sizes and are

PILLOWCASES

These are generally available in 42- to 45-inch widths, and from 36 to 48 inches in length, depending upon the size and bulkiness of the pillow.

STANDARD SIZE
> 42″ × 36″ (pillow size 20″ × 26″)

KING SIZE
> 42″ × 46″ (pillow size 20″ × 36″)

QUEEN SIZE
> 42″ × 40″ (pillow size 20″ × 30″)

BOLSTER SIZE
> 42″ × 46″, 42″ × 54″, 42″ × 72″

Thread Count. This refers to the number of lengthwise threads plus the number of crosswise threads per inch. The higher the count, the smoother the sheet. A higher thread count may also mean greater durability.

The prices of sheets and pillowcases are influenced by high thread counts, designer styles, trims, and convenience features such as permanent press, fitted corners, or special sizes.

Sizing. Some manufacturers add a sizing to the finishing process to add body. This is only a cover-up for poor quality. Rub two pieces together. If a powdery substance appears, don't buy it.

For easy care, your most carefree decision would be to buy no-iron sheets.

---

preshrunk. When the mattresses are not standard sizes, add approximately 20″ to the width of the mattress for turning under and approximately 30″ to the length for folding down and tucking under the mattress.

FIBERS AND THREAD COUNT

FIBER	SHEET	CHARACTERISTICS	THREAD COUNT
Cotton	Muslin	Heavier, longer-wearing, coarser than percale.	Has a lower thread count than percale—128-139 threads per inch.
Cotton	Percale	Soft, luxurious, fine texture.	Has a higher thread count than muslin—180-188 threads per inch.
Polyester cotton	Muslin	Long-wearing, stays smooth on the bed. No-iron finish eliminates ironing if tumble-dried.	Thread count depends upon whether sheet is muslin or percale.
Polyester cotton	Percale	Luxurious, long-wearing, soft, wrinkle-free appearance. No-iron finish eliminates ironing if tumble-dried.	

MATTRESS PADS

You will need mattress measurements to assure proper fit. Pads are usually available in white, with quilted cotton surfaces and cotton or acetate fillings.

There are some foam-rubber-type pads which will give added resiliency to old mattresses; also plastic zip-on types that can cover a mattress completely.

For care of mattress pads, see Chapter Four.

BEDS AND MATTRESSES

According to *Consumers All,* The Yearbook of Agriculture, United States Department of Agriculture, if you live to be 75 and sleep 8 hours a day, you will spend about 25 years of your life sleeping or resting. Seems like an incredible waste of time, doesn't it? But if we are going to spend 25 years in bed, it makes sense to buy the best mattress and bed we can find! As with kitchen work heights (see Chapter Five), there are certain bed measurements that will assure personal comfort.

A mattress should fit your bed and for maximum comfort that bed should be 10 inches longer than its tallest occupant. This leaves 5 inches free at both ends. A person 5' 6" or more needs a longer bed than the old 75-inch length. Every sleeper should have at least 38 inches of width for comfortable sleeping. Therefore, the old 54"-wide double bed (for two people) is gradually giving way to extra-sized bedding. The standard double size gives each occupant only 27 inches of width—the same amount of room as a baby's crib.

There are, of course, oversize beds and twin beds on swing-away frames attached (or not) to one headboard, which provide more sleep area and comfort in width and length.

A chart of the usual mattress and bed sizes and the sheet sizes they require is given in the preceding section.

The test of a good mattress with regard to support is whether or not you feel well-supported at the vital pressure points and that your spine is straight. We are told that 85 percent of the body's weight is centered between the shoulders and hips; therefore, a mattress should give enough support in this area so your hips don't sink and thus leave the head higher than the torso.

It is best to try out any mattress, spring or foam, before you buy one. Lie down on it and test its buoyancy. It should support every part of your body equally and not sag at points of greatest weight.

As to firmness, most mattresses are available in soft, firm, extra-firm, and special orthopedic types. As we said above, firmness will vary with competing brands. (Using a bedboard between the mattress and innerspring helps to add to mattress support. Have one cut to size at your nearest lumber dealer, or buy one from a department store if you need one.)

There are three basic types of mattresses: innerspring; solid; and latex or urethane foam.

Innerspring mattresses may have anywhere from 180 to 850 coiled springs enclosed between two layers of insulating materials, such as sisal, and padding, usually of cotton. Most manufacturers feel that if the number of springs ranges from 200 to over 300, a mattress can be considered of good construction. Strangely enough, more springs will not necessarily mean a more comfortable or longer-lasting mattress. Actually, the quality of steel and the shape and size of the coils are more important than number. Above and below the coils is an insulator which supports the filling. Fillings are usually cotton felt, though sometimes they may be made of hair, without foam or latex.

When mattresses are *solidly* filled they may contain hair, cotton, or kapok, though such are usually not preferred in this country.

Mattresses made of *urethane foam* (plastic) or *latex* (rubber) are usually about half as heavy as innerspring mattresses. Urethane foam is the lightest. If they are from 4 to 6 inches thick and made of high-density foam, they should be just as comfortable as an innerspring. If they are too soft, you might as well not buy them.

Check these features when buying a mattress:
- Prebuilt or reinforced borders help to prevent sagging or breakdown from sitting on the edge of the bed (which should not be done but which will be done in any case!).
- Securely fastened handles.
- Enough padding so that innersprings will not be felt through the padding.
- Ventilators on the border panels for air circulation.
- Well-secured stitching.
- Well-secured filling, whether tufted or tuftless, to prevent shifting of filling.
- Heavy, twill-weave ticking; 8 ounces is best for durability.
- Personal preference is the only factor in selecting a plain, tufted, or quilted top.

BOX SPRINGS

The box spring does serve a functional purpose: it acts as a shock absorber and literally supports your weight. Usually these wear out at about the same rate as the mattress and should be replaced at the same time. It is a good idea to lie down and test the box spring as well as the mattress. You should not feel the coils. Also feel the bottom of it—the better box springs will have a wood slat supporting every row on springs. Again, if it is firmness you are looking for, look for a 72-to-80-coil box spring. This is also the best type for a foam mattress.

TABLEWARE

DINNERWARE

It helps to know the types of dinnerware in order to choose a set that will meet your needs. There are several kinds available.

China or *Porcelain* is vitreous, clear, and translucent, with a nonporous body. Firing at high temperatures during manufacture "vitrifies" or hardens, adding strength. It is thin, highly glazed, lightweight, and strong. Tap china or porcelain and its resonance has a bell-like sound.

Fine China. This is the finest of all china. Made of highly refined clay, it is fired at a very high heat for long periods. It is a strong durable ceramic.

Bone China. This is a fine china, virtually "bone-" or chalk-white since it contains a mixture of animal bone ash along with the clay.

Casual China. This is more informal and often quite durable, even more so than porcelain. Often ovenproof from refrigerator to oven, it resists chipping and cracking. Most likely decorated with decals under the glaze.

Earthenware and *Pottery* are semi-vitreous. They are thick and heavy—heavier than china—and generally opaque. Firing temperatures are lower than those used for china, resulting in a product that is quite porous and less resistant to chipping and breaking, and also less expensive. Pottery is made of a crude clay and fired at a low heat. Earthenware is made of white clay and fired at higher temperatures than pottery, thus making the body less porous. It is more durable and chip-resistant, thinner and stronger than pottery.

Stoneware is heavy, often colorful ware, with a hard finish that resists oven heat. It is suitable for casseroles as well as dishes.

Ironstone is a refined form of earthenware with better heat resistance. It is usually casual in appearance.

Plastic dinnerware is popular for everyday family use. One of the hardest, most durable plastics is Melamine. Molded under heat and pressure, it is very lightweight, with high resistance to breaking, cracking, and chipping. It is dishwasher washable.

Other types of dinnerware include heat-resistant glass that is also break- and chip-resistant. Interesting and useful serving pieces can also be found of wood, stainless steel, silver plate, and sterling.

Buying Dinnerware

The quantity of dinnerware you need is in direct ratio to the number of people you will feed daily. Consider also the types of entertaining you plan to do and allow extra dishes for party use. Dinnerware is purchased in one of several ways:

- A *starter set* may have as few as 16 pieces, as many as 45. Most basic sets include 4 each of dinner plates, salad plates, cups, and saucers. Quantities are doubled and serving pieces are added for a 45-piece set to serve eight. Additional dishes or even sets can be added to bring the dinnerware to the traditional 98-piece service for 12.
- *Open stock* means that you can purchase individual items of a particular pattern. Usually open stock indicates that the patterns will be available for some years (5 to 10 years) but not forever! Plan to replace or increase the number of dishes within a reasonable length of time. Some companies may guarantee patterns for replacement for a specific number of years.
- *Place settings* are a popular way of giving or acquiring expensive china. A place setting is a complete service for one person and includes four to six pieces. The place setting method of purchase, while convenient, usually costs more than buying the same dishes as part of a set.

Keep these points in mind if easy care is your objective:
- China is more durable and chip-resistant than earthenware, pottery, or ironstone.

48

- If you dislike washing dishes by hand, do not select gold-encrusted china or hand-painted designs. Smooth surfaces and borders, simple designs are easier to store and are generally dishwasher washable.
- Avoid designs with raised lips and edges as they are harder to store and more susceptible to breakage and chipping.
- For care of china, see Chapter Five.

FLATWARE AND HOLLOWWARE

The utensils used for eating and serving are often those pieces you have acquired as gifts for special occasions, and thus you may not have the opportunity to exercise any judgment in their selection. On the other hand, many brides do pick out certain patterns and list them in bridal registers for the convenience of friends and relatives who are looking for gift ideas. In this case, it is a good idea to keep certain facts in mind when selecting patterns.

Analyze your life-style and determine how you will use certain pieces. Coordinate your tableware—a very simple and tasteful design of china allows the use of a more ornate pattern of flatware.

Give flatware the balance and weight test before you select a pattern. Lift and hold each piece. Is it comfortable to hold? Is it properly balanced? Is the shape pleasing to you? Weight and thickness should always concentrate in the handle and in the areas where pressure is necessary—the bowls of spoons, the tines of forks.

Flatware describes the utensils used for eating and serving. All sizes of knives, forks, and spoons belong to the flatware family.

Hollowware includes all the metal pieces for table and decorative use that are not classified as flatware.

What Do You Need?

25-piece service for 4

8 teaspoons	4 knives
4 forks	4 soup spoons
4 salad forks	1 serving spoon

50-piece service for 8

16 teaspoons	8 knives
8 forks	8 soup spoons
8 salad forks	2 serving spoons

75-piece service for 12

24 teaspoons	12 knives
12 forks	12 soup spoons
12 salad forks	3 serving spoons

A basic 6-piece place setting includes:
Place knife all-purpose size for any occasion.
Place fork all-purpose fork for any entree.
Place spoon all-purpose spoon, slightly larger than a teaspoon, used for soups, cereals, some desserts.
Teaspoon used for hot beverages, fruits and desserts.
Spreader individual butter knife.

Of the many metals used in flat- and hollowware, the most common are as follows:

Sterling silver is a combination of 92.5 percent solid silver reinforced with 7.5 percent copper to give it strength for use.

Silver plate is made from a base metal—either "nickel silver," copper, or brass—which is plated with pure silver for added beauty. Quality ranges from "quad plate," which will give a lifetime of service, to "A-1 plate" for limited years of use. Fine plated flatware is reinforced with extra silver at points of greatest wear—the bottom of a spoon or the tines of forks.

Stainless steel ranges from expensive to very inexpensive, depending on manufacture, finish, and design.

Dirilyte combines several metals in alloy—aluminum, copper, and nickel—which gives it a characteristic golden color.

If easy care is your goal, keep these tips in mind:
- Stainless steel, now available in formal patterns as well as casual designs, does not tarnish and need not be polished as sterling silver, silver plate, or dirilyte.
- The plainer silver patterns are easier to keep clean than those with more ornate designs.
- Sets purchased in simply designed tarnish-proof cases

are often easier to store and use. The flatware stays cleaner longer.

Tip: While we don't recommend dip-it silver cleaners for long-time use, it is a good idea to keep some of it near the sink for quickie cleanups, such as the darkened tines of forks, etcetera.

For care of silverware and flatware, see Chapter Five.

GLASSWARE

Lead glass is the "royalty" of glassware. The expensive materials used in manufacture give it brilliant luster and when the edge is tapped it has a bell-like ring. Such glass is usually hand-blown and is suitable for "cut" decorations.

Lime or potash glass was the first glassware to be manufactured and it is the most economical and popular for daily use. Lime glass has a soft sheen and a hard, brittle surface which gives a dull sound when tapped. It is formed by pouring liquid glass into molds or presses which solidify it into desired shapes. It is used for inexpensive glassware such as tumblers, plates, bottles, and light bulbs.

"Crystal" refers to "clear" rather than cost when we talk about glassware. Unintentional off-color tints or a cloudy look are the result of improper mixing of materials and impurities in the ingredients. Check for quality by holding the glass to the light: lead glass will reflect light brilliantly and have a slight blue cast; good lime glass will have a softer, slightly yellow cast. In general usage, crystal usually means *lead glass* to most people.

Milk glass is white and produced from a special combination of aluminum fluorides for opaqueness, then hand-crafted under fire-polish control for a smooth finish. All *colored* glass is made by adding various kinds of mineral salts to the basic glass. Milk glass is an example.

Colored glassware can be tested for quality by looking for luster and evenness of tint. In glassware of dark colors, check depth of color and sparkle as well as clearness.

Glassware designs include: Goblet, All-Purpose Wine, Dessert Champagne, Cocktail, Snifter, Cordial.

Seconds

When buying seconds you may actually be getting a very high-quality product for quite a saving. They contain slight flaws which can hardly be noticed in many cases.

If easy care is your goal, consider these pointers:
- Stemware is more fragile, harder to handle than tumblers.
- Gold-banded glassware is generally *not* dishwasher washable.
- Lime glass, though less expensive and brilliant, resists scratches and marks.

SECURING GOOD LIGHTING FOR YOUR HOME

Good lighting makes a home comfortable to live in and much easier to maintain. Decorative or "mood" lighting is important at times, but adequate lighting, well-planned and properly placed, is essential to maintaining a well-ordered household.

WHERE EYES DO THEIR WORK

It is important that the lighting in your house makes seeing easy wherever eyes do their work. It has been estimated that there are fifty or more seeing jobs that need specific lighting in order to accomplish work effectively and safely. Some of these jobs include:

Prolonged reading or studying
Television
Setting the table
Dining
Reading recipes and measuring ingredients
Reading labels and following directions

Inspecting and sorting foods
Reading dials and cooking
Washing dishes and cleaning equipment
Sorting and pretreating laundry
Ironing and pressing
Sewing and mending
Workshop activities and repairs
Housekeeping (dusting, vacuuming, waxing, washing walls, woodwork)
Deskwork
Closet organization
Dressing
Caring for children

There are many others, but these seem most pertinent to maintaining an efficient and comfortable home.

Minimum Levels of Illumination

According to experts at the Illuminating Engineering Society, there are minimum amounts of light needed to do certain tasks. How much light you need is measured in foot-candles. This can be checked with a light meter. Ask your local utility company lighting specialist or an extension agent to give you some assistance with this. Check your light levels with the following chart and adjust your light accordingly.

Light Bulbs and Fluorescent Tubes

Light bulbs and fluorescent tubes do not insure good lighting by themselves. You must select the right bulb or tube for the purpose you have in mind. Then the bulb or tube has to be placed in an appropriately designed lamp or fixture. And finally, the lamp or fixture must be correctly placed in the room.

Incandescent Bulbs

The incandescent bulb comes in a wide assortment of shapes, colors, sizes, and wattages.

53

MINIMUM LEVELS OF ILLUMINATION*
[*Recommended by Illuminating Engineering Society*]

SPECIFIC VISUAL TASK	AMOUNT OF LIGHT ON TASK** (FOOT-CANDLES)†
Reading and writing:	
Handwriting, indistinct print, or poor copies	70
Books, magazines, newspapers	30
Music scores, advanced	70
Music scores, simple	30
Studying at desk	70
Recreation:	
Playing cards, table games, billiards	30
Table tennis	20
Grooming:	
Shaving, combing hair, applying makeup	50
Kitchen work:	
At sink	70
At range	50
At work counters	50
Laundering jobs:	
At washer	50
At ironing board	50
At ironer	50
Sewing:	
Dark fabrics (fine detail, low contrast)	200
Prolonged periods (light-to-medium fabrics)	100
Occasional (light-colored fabrics)	50
Occasional (coarse thread, large stitches, high contrast of thread to fabric)	30

* *Planning Your Home Lighting*, Home and Garden Bulletin No. 138, United States Department of Agriculture [Data—Illuminating Engineering Society].

** Average of light measured over the task area.

Handicraft:
Close work (reading diagrams and
blueprints, fine finishing)   100
Cabinetmaking, planing, sanding,
gluing   50
Measuring, sawing, assembling,
repairing   50

GENERAL LIGHTING	AVERAGE LIGHT THROUGHOUT AREA‡ (FOOT-CANDLES) †
Any area involving a visual task	30
For safety in passage areas	10
Areas used mostly for relaxation, recreation, and conversation	10

General household bulbs, the most commonly used type, range from 15 to 300 watts. They are available in three finishes—inside frost, inside white (silica-coated), and clear.

Inside frost is the older bulb finish, still in general use. Use bulbs of this type in well-shielded fixtures.

Bulbs with inside white finish (a milky-white coating) are preferred for many home uses. They produce diffused, soft light and help reduce bright spots in thin shielding materials.

Decoratively shaped *clear bulbs* add sparkle to chandeliers or dimmer-controlled simulated candles.

Three-way bulbs have two filaments and require three-way sockets. Each filament can be operated separately or in combination. Make sure that a three-way bulb is tightened in the socket so both contacts in the screw-in base are touching firmly.

The three lighting levels offered by these bulbs are particularly nice in portable lamps and pull-down fixtures. You can turn the lamp high for reading and sewing, on medium for televiewing, conversation, or entertaining, and on low for a night light or a soft, subdued atmosphere.

Dimmer switches are available on some lamps. They make it

† A foot-candle is the amount of light falling on a surface one foot away from a standard candle (ordinary 1½-inch-diameter candle).

‡ Average of light measured on a horizontal plane 30 inches above the floor.

SELECTION GUIDE FOR INCANDESCENT BULBS*

ACTIVITY	MINIMUM RECOMMENDED WATTAGE**
Reading, writing, sewing:	
Occasional periods	150
Prolonged periods	200 or 300
Grooming:	
Bathroom mirror:	
1 fixture each side of mirror	1–75 or 2–40's
1 cup-type fixture over mirror	100
1 fixture over mirror	150
Bathroom ceiling fixture	150
Vanity table lamps, in pairs (person seated)	100 each
Dresser lamps, in pairs (person standing)	150 each
Kitchen work:	
Ceiling fixture (2 or more in a large area)	150 or 200
Fixture over sink	150
Fixture for eating area (separate from workspace)	150
Shopwork:	
Fixture for workbench (2 or more for long bench)	150

possible to light from very low to the maximum output of the bulb.

Tinted bulbs create decorative effects indoors and outdoors. Silica coatings inside these bulbs produce delicate tints of colored light—pink, aqua, yellow, blue, and green. Home uses of these bulbs are best limited to lighting plants, flowers, or art objects. You'll need to buy tinted bulbs of higher wattage because they give less light than white bulbs.

Silver-bowl bulbs are standard household bulbs with a silver coating applied to the outside of the rounded end. They are used

* *Planning Your Home Lighting*, Home and Garden Bulletin No. 138, United States Department of Agriculture.
** White bulbs preferred.

SIZES AND USES FOR THREE-WAY BULBS

SOCKET AND WATTAGE	DESCRIPTION	WHERE TO USE
Medium:		
30/70/100	Inside frost or white	Dressing table or dresser lamps, decorative lamps, small pin-up lamps
50/100/150	Inside frost or white	End table or small floor and swing-arm lamps
50/100/150	White or indirect bulb with "built-in" diffusing bowl (R–40)	End table lamps and floor lamps with large, wide harps
50/200/250	White or frosted bulb	End table or small floor and swing-arm lamps, study lamps with diffusing bowls
Mogul (large):		
50/100/150	Inside frost	Small floor and swing-arm lamps and torcheres
100/200/300	White or frosted bulb	Table and floor lamps, torcheres

base up, and direct light upward onto the ceiling or into a reflector. You can get them in 60-, 100-, 150-, and 200-watt sizes. They are generally used with reflectors in basements, garages, or other work areas. Fixtures for silver-bowl bulbs are widely available.

Reflector bulbs are available with silver coatings either on the inside or outside of the bulbs. The spotlight bulbs direct light in a narrow beam and generally accent objects. The floodlight bulbs spread light over a larger area, and are suitable for flood-lighting horizontal or vertical surfaces. Typical floodlight sizes include 30, 50, 75 and 150 watt.

Heat-resistant bulbs, called PAR bulbs because of their para-bolic shape, are used outdoors. They are resistant to rain and snow. Common sizes are 75 watts, 150 watts, and up.

Bulbs in decorative shapes are designed to replace bare bulbs in older fixtures and sockets. Some shapes and sizes are made for traditional fixtures (chandeliers and wall sconces); others combine contemporary styling and function. Bulb shapes include globe, flame, cone, mushroom, and tubular.

Some of these bulbs are made of diffusing-type glass and are tinted to produce colored lighting effects. Clear bulbs may be needed to produce sparkle in crystal chandeliers. When selected to harmonize with fixtures and room decor, these decorative bulbs may offer a pleasing, low-cost solution to a lighting prob-lem.

Colored floodlight bulbs are available for indoor or outdoor use. The tints—particularly pink and blue-white—create nice ef-fects on plants or flowers, and are acceptable for lighting people and furnishings. Strong colors—blue, green, and red—are best reserved for holiday and party decorations.

Fluorescent Tubes

Most households use fluorescent lighting in some form. Al-though know-how is needed to select and use this light source correctly, it does offer advantages in home lighting. For guid-ance in selecting fluorescent tubes and fixtures, see the following table.

Fluorescent tubes must be used in fixtures that contain the nec-essary electrical accessories.

White fluorescent tubes are labeled "standard" and "deluxe." The whiteness of a standard tube is indicated by letters, WW for warm white; CW for cool white. The addition of an "X" to these letters indicates a deluxe tube.

A deluxe warm white (WWX) tube gives a flattering light, can be used with incandescent light, and does not distort colors any more than incandescent light does. A deluxe cool white (CWX) tube simulates daylight and goes nicely with cool color

SELECTION GUIDE FOR FLUORESCENT TUBES*
[All are T12 (1½-inch diameter) tubes]

USE	WATTAGE AND COLOR**
Reading, writing, sewing:	
Occasional	1 40w or 2 20w, WWX or CWX
Prolonged	2 40w or 2 30w, WWX or CWX
Wall lighting (valances, brackets, cornices):	
Small living area (8-foot minimum)	2 40w, WWX or CWX
Large living area (16-foot minimum)	4 40w, WWX or CWX
Grooming:	
Bathroom mirror:	
One fixture each side of mirror	2 20w or 2 30w, WWX
One fixture over mirror	1 40w, WWX or CWX
Bathroom ceiling fixture	1 40w, WWX
Luminous ceiling	For 2-foot squares, 4 20w, WWX or CWX
	3-foot squares, 4 30w, WWX or CWX
	4-foot squares, 4 40w, WWX or CWX
	6-foot squares, 6 to 8 40w, WWX or CWX
Kitchen work:	
Ceiling fixture	2 40w or 2 30w, WWX
Over sink	2 40w or 2 30w, WWX or CWX
Counter-top lighting	20w or 40w to fill length, WWX
Dining area (separate from kitchen)	15 or 20 watts for each 30 inches of longest dimension of room area, WWX
Home workshop	2 40w, CW, CWX, or WWX

* *Planning Your Home Lighting*, Home and Garden Bulletin No. 138, United States Department of Agriculture.

** WWX = warm white deluxe; CWX = cool white deluxe; CW = cool white.

schemes of blue and green. Deluxe tubes are the only fluorescent tubes recommended for home use. They are worth waiting for if your dealer has to order them for you.

As we have determined thus far, the ease with which you can accomplish your housekeeping chores is dependent upon the degree of maintenance your furnishings require. It is our primary objective in this book to offer suggestions on how almost every task can be done with as little effort as possible. With easy care in mind, you will find purchasing hints throughout this book in almost every chapter. These, of course, are in addition and supplemental to those found in this chapter. The following topics are specific examples:

Vacuum cleaners, Chapter Three
Hard-surface flooring, Chapter Three
Laundry equipment, Chapter Four
Pots and pans, Chapter Five
Cutlery, Chapter Five
Major appliances, see Index for specific products
Small appliances, see Index for specific products
(See Index for topics not listed here.)

While we are aware that there are all these specific easy-care features which will help to cut down on the degree of work you have to do, nevertheless the job of cleaning the house and establishing order requires a constant daily, weekly, and monthly routine. No matter how many easy-care furnishings you may choose, housework must still go on. As you read the following chapter, Cleaning the House, you will find that the specific routines suggested will help you do your work with a great deal of ease and with very little effort.

CHAPTER THREE

Cleaning the House

STORAGE OF CLEANING SUPPLIES

Most up-to-date apartments and new homes have allotted at least minimum space for the storage of cleaning equipment and supplies. In some instances special utility cabinets have been designed to help organize your cleaning equipment. There are also many metal and plastic storage units and organizers which can make the use of your cupboards, closets, and drawers more effective. Systematic storage will make housecleaning quicker and easier. Supplies are easier to locate and there is definitely less wear and tear on large equipment (vacuum cleaners, floor polishers, etcetera) when everything has a special place of its own.

If you don't have a good cleaning closet, make a creative study of the space around you. There must be some minimal but workable area that will do the trick. For example:

- Try unused corner space. A folding screen can camouflage equipment, or you can build an old-fashioned corner cupboard with louvered doors.
- Utilize empty wall space in a storeroom, laundry room, or back hall. Hang equipment on appropriate hooks. Put up a shelf for small tools, cleaning aids.

THE CLEANING CLOSET

What to Store Where? All cleaning equipment and supplies, of course, should not be necessarily stored in your general cleaning closet. Special equipment belongs in specific areas around the house, such as in the bathroom, laundry, and kitchen. Duplication of equipment and cleaning aids in strategic areas can make housework easier, helping to save steps, especially if you live in a two-story house or a rambling ranch-type house.

The General Cleaning Closet. Assuming you do have a good cleaning closet, arrange it so that everything has a specific niche and that all things are easily accessible. Hang such things as brooms, dust mops, and wet mops, working ends down to avoid matting. Store vacuum cleaner tools in a hanging container of their own or in a shoebag. Store supplies on shelves above. Some upright vacuum cleaners also can be wall-hung. Or set them along with buckets and pails on the floor.

Cover the wall with perforated hardboard and hang up as much of your equipment as you can on convenient, easy-to-use hooks. Be sure to keep a basket there, for carrying small cleaning equipment and general supplies as you move about the house.

In Your General Cleaning Closet

Basic Tools and Cleaning Aids:
- Vacuum cleaner and attachments
- Broom
- Dustpan and brush
- Dust mop
    Untreated for bare and waxed floors
    Treated for oiled floors
- Dust cloths and/or brush, cleaning cloths, scrub brushes
- Pail
- Wet mop
- Floor wax applicator and polisher
- Sponges
- Whisk broom or fabric brush
- Paper towels
- Rubber and household gloves

- Step stool
- All-purpose household cleaner (spray or liquid is easier to use than powdered or crystalline, but all are good)
- Window and glass cleaners
- Furniture polish (wax or oil or both, depending upon furniture)
- Floor wax

"Nice to Have" Tools and Cleaning Aids:
- Carpet sweeper and/or lightweight stick-type vacuum cleaner
- Hand vacuum cleaner
- Floor scrubber/waxer/polisher/rug cleaner
- Art gum eraser
- Lemon oil used for polishing furniture, if desired*
- Boiled linseed oil (bought as "boiled"—do not attempt to boil "raw" linseed oil—and used for wood surfaces such as wood chopping blocks)
- Kneeling pads
- Turpentine or solvents for removing wax from floors, also paint stains and grease*
- Fuller's earth, French chalk, for removing light or freshly made stains and grease stains*
- Spray-on spot remover
- Rottenstone for removing white spots and other light blemishes from furniture*
- Whiting powder moistened with ammonia, excellent for cleaning fine silver*
- Blemish and scratch remover
- Wallpaper cleaner (dough type, available in wallpaper stores) if you have nonwashable wallpaper or covering

In Your Kitchen

- Appliance wax
- Cellulose sponges
- Scouring powder or cleaners
- Scouring pads
- Oven cleaner
- All-purpose detergent (liquid and granular)

* There are commercial cleaning aids available which contain these products and often do the job more quickly, giving explicit directions.

- All-purpose household cleaner
- Dishwasher detergent
- Metal cleaners or polishes—copper, silver, brass
- Household disinfectant
- Insecticides
- Drain cleaner
- Ammonia
- Baking soda
- Rubber gloves
- Paper towels

In Your Bathroom

- Household disinfectant
- Scouring powder or cleaner
- Toilet bowl cleaner
- Toilet bowl brush
- Spray bathroom cleaner
- Drain cleaner
- Packaged water softener or conditioner
- Tile cleaner
- Liquid detergent
- Cellulose sponges
- Toilet tissue
- Rubber gloves

In Your Laundry Area

- Necessary laundry products (see Chapter Four)
- Scouring powder or cleanser
- Cellulose sponges

If you do not have a washer and dryer in your house or apartment, you might wish to keep your laundry products in the general cleaning closet or bathroom.

Upstairs in a multiple-story house or a bedroom wing of a ranch-style house:
- Second vacuum cleaner, brooms, mops, dust cloths, sponges, pails, cleaning supplies, etcetera.

A Cleaning Basket—The Movable Cleaning Closet

A small deep basket with a carrying handle, light enough to be carried from room to room, makes a fine cleaning basket. Such a simple way of organizing cleaning equipment and supplies will save many steps to and from the cleaning closet. Use it mainly for your small cleaning equipment and supplies. A cleaning basket should include:

- Whisk broom, upholstery brush
- Dust cloths and polishing cloths
- Duster
- Scrub cloths
- Sponges
- Furniture polish or wax
- Scouring powder or cleanser if not duplicated in kitchen or bathroom
- Spot and stain remover
- All-purpose household cleaner
- Window and glass cleaner

WHAT'S IN A CLEANING AID?*

When you think of cleaning, the first thing that comes to mind is, cleaning what? But the object deserves only about 25 percent of your consideration. The *what* that is so important is the *soil* itself, and for our purposes we define soil simply as matter in the wrong place.

In an ordinary house you will have to deal with *three* types:

Dust, which can be removed by vacuuming or wiping.

Soot and grime, which require moisture to remove, provided by either water or chemical solutions. *Water-soluble* soils include

* Extension Division, Virginia Polytechnic Institute and State University, Publication 359, "What's in Home Cleaning Products and Why"—Janice Woodard, Extension Specialist, Home Management. Reprint 1972.

65

sugar, fruit juices, and starch. *Water-insoluble* soils are oily substances, combined with solid soil.

Clutter, accumulation of objects which you throw out or put back in their proper place.

While we don't expect anyone to become a chemist or laboratory technician, it is helpful to know something about the cleaning and laundering products which are required to remove soot and grime and embedded soil. It would certainly help to clear up the mystery of the "cleaning-product maze" in the supermarket. And as more discussions arise on the chemical compositions of products and their effect on our environment, you will at least have a working knowledge of some of the terms and what they mean. With facts comes the ability to make proper value judgments on the use of products.

Almost all soaps, detergents, and cleaning compounds are formulated from a combination of only a *few* chemicals. This means that you need only a few good cleaning aids to do most household cleaning jobs well.

The most common ingredients in home-cleaning products are:

Alkalis	Bleaches
Acids	Sanitizers
Detergents	Spirit Solvents
Abrasives	

ALKALIS

Alkalis are chemicals that help dissolve dirt. The most familiar ones are baking soda and ammonia. Others include borax, trisodium phosphate (TSP), washing soda (sal soda), and lye. Alkalis allow you to remove a concentrated accumulation of dirt and grime without too much rubbing. They are especially effective in removing *grease,* as they react with it to form an emulsion. This means that these greasy particles will be held in suspension in the liquid and will not be redeposited again on the surface you are cleaning.

It is a good idea to wear waterproof gloves, since alkalis remove oily dirt and could also take oil from your hands as you work with them. They may also remove oil from linoleum and oil-base paints, causing them to crack or peel. Concentrated doses of these cleaners can loosen paint surfaces or darken aluminum surfaces. You can prevent some of these harmful results if you use a mild alkaline solution and rinse the surfaces thoroughly with clear water after cleaning, to remove all the cleaner.

Baking soda (very mild) is sodium bicarbonate. Mixed with water, it can remove coffee and tea stains from china and plastic dishes. Baking soda can also clean glass, wall tile, and porcelain enamel.

Household ammonia (moderately mild) is a dilute mixture of 5 to 10 percent ammonia gas in water. It can be used in cleaning kitchen range burners and greasy ovens, windows, and mirrors. The sudsy type of household ammonia, which looks slightly cloudy or milky, contains a small amount of soap or detergent. This type of ammonia can be used in cleaning garbage pails, kitchen range burners, and sinks.

Borax (moderately mild) is a white crystalline powder. You can use it in a variety of household cleaning jobs, such as washing walls, woodwork, and sinks.

Trisodium phosphate (TSP, moderately mild) is also a crystalline powder. It is an effective cleaner for walls, woodwork, and resilient floors, except linoleum.

Washing soda (very strong), also called sal soda, is sodium carbonate. See nonphosphate detergents, Chapter Four.

Lye (very strong) is sodium hydroxide, also called caustic soda. It can severely burn your skin. It effectively contributes to some drain and oven cleaners.

ACIDS

The two most familiar acids for cleaning jobs at home are *vinegar* and *lemon juice*. Other acids may be found in a variety of cleaning products and may include oxalic, hydrochloric and sulfuric.

Two dry substances that form acids after they are dissolved in liquid are cream of tartar, familiar to cooks, and sodium bisulphate, also known as sodium acid sulphate. You can use cream of tartar for several cleaning jobs such as sweetening coffeemakers and brightening aluminum ware. Sodium bisulphate can be one of the main ingredients in some toilet bowl cleaners.

Some acids help remove hard-water deposits. Some aid in removing discoloration from aluminum, brass, bronze, and copper. Other acids remove iron rust stains without a lot of rubbing.

When they are too strong, acids eat away clothing, leather, and some metals. Strong acids can also irritate and injure the skin and eyes. *Check product labels for potential hazards and follow directions for use.*

Vinegar, a weak acid, is about 5 percent acetic acid. It will remove hard-water deposits from glassware, rust stains from sinks, and tarnish from brass and copper. It will also counteract alkaline oven cleaners.

Lemon juice contains citric acid, also a weak acid, and can be used in much the same way as vinegar.

Oxalic acid is especially effective as a rust remover, but is also very poisonous.

Hydrochloric and sulfuric are strong acids even though they are used in dilute concentrations. They are used in some toilet bowl cleaners. *Follow directions carefully for products containing strong acids. They are extremely hazardous.*

Some cleaning products in which acids are generally found include toilet bowl cleaners, rust removers, and metal cleaners.

DETERGENTS

While some laundry detergents may be used for housecleaning jobs, detergents are also one of the ingredients in many home-cleaning products.

You can usually tell that a product contains a detergent when some suds appear.

Detergents found in cleaning products help loosen dirt from surfaces. When "builders" have been added to a detergent, it has greater ability to remove oily dirt. These products are marked "heavy duty" or "all-purpose." See more about detergents for laundering in Chapter Four.

ABRASIVES

Abrasives are materials that scour off dirt by rubbing. Rottenstone, whiting, pumice, quartz, marble, feldspar, and silica are some of these materials. Such abrasive materials are used in scouring powders and pads. Sandpaper, plastic and nylon meshes, and steel wool are considered abrasives too.

Avoid the use of harsh or coarse abrasives on plastic ware, glass and nonstick finishes on cookware, painted woodwork, silverware and highly polished metals. These surfaces are easily scratched.

A good general rule to follow when abrasives are recommended is to use the least amount that does the job well, after making sure you can't wash the soil away with soap or detergent and water. If you insist on being a "fussy Bridget" every time you clean the tub and sink, use a mild abrasive. Very harsh ones feel extremely gritty.

If surfaces on which harsh abrasives have been used too frequently become dull and rough, they may soil faster and stain deeper.

BLEACHES

The bleach used in household cleaning products is generally the chlorine type. This bleach contains sodium hypochlorite as its active ingredient, which helps remove stains.

Because this type of bleach is an alkali, it will darken aluminum and make linoleum brittle.

Liquid chlorine bleach reacts with strongly acidic products such as toilet bowl cleaners and rust removers to form an irritating or dangerous gas. Chlorine bleach plus ammonia also produces an irritating gas.

Because of the benefits (and, in some cases, hazards) of bleach, manufacturers usually call attention to its presence in their products. For more about bleach, see Chapter Four.

SANITIZERS

Sanitizers are chemicals that reduce the number of bacteria to a safe level. The words "sanitizer" and "disinfectant" are used interchangeably, although, technically, *disinfect* means to reduce the number of infectious agents, while *sanitize* means to reduce the number of all bacteria.

Common sanitizers and their trade names are:

liquid chlorine bleach .... Clorox
Purex
A&P Laundry
Bleach

solutions of quaternary ammonium
compounds such as alkyl,
dimethyl benzyl ammonium
chloride .... Lysol Basin/Tub/Tile
Cleaner
Roccal
Glade Spray
Disinfectant

solutions of phenolic compounds
such as ortho-benzyl-para-
chlorophenol .... Lysol Cleaner
Pine-Sol
Dow Bathroom
Cleaner

You may want to use these chemicals when cleaning bathtubs, shower stalls, toilet bowls, bathroom sinks, and plastic or ceramic tile floors in the bathroom. Follow directions carefully when using products containing a sanitizer. For types, examples, and use of sanitizers in laundering, see Chapter Four.

SPIRIT SOLVENTS

Most polishes and waxes for wood furniture and floors contain a spirit solvent. A few all-purpose cleaners, sanitizers, and drain cleaners may contain these solvents. These chemicals are similar to the fluids used in dry-cleaning or spot removal, and they are added to products to help them remove oily dirt. In wood-care products, spirit solvents are necessary because water is harmful.

Some spirit solvents are flammable but others are not. For example, one liquid drain cleaner contains trichloroethane; this is nonflammable.

If the product is one containing a spirit solvent and will catch fire at a temperature between 20° and 80° F., the label must say,

"CAUTION: Flammable. Keep away from heat, sparks and open flame."

If the product is extremely flammable, the signal words will be "DANGER: Extremely flammable." In addition, the label might say, "Harmful or fatal if swallowed. . . . If swallowed, do not induce vomiting. Call a physician immediately."

LABELING

Products which are toxic, corrosive, irritating, strongly sensitizing, flammable, or which generate pressure and may cause substantial personal injury or illness during or as a result of any customary handling and use of the product come under the regulations of the Federal Hazardous Substances Act. Depending upon the degree of toxicity, they may be labeled, "Caution," "Warning," "Poison," "Danger." Read your labels carefully before using a product, and follow specific instructions.

PACKAGING

Household cleaning aids are usually available in powders, liquids, or sprays. Many are in aerosol containers.

The packaging of household cleaners undergoes frequent changes to improve their storage life in the supermarket and at home and to improve their convenience and safety in use. Plastic bottles and lightweight cans are common where once only glass and heavy metal were used.

Cleaners in aerosol containers and spray bottles are more convenient to use than liquid or powdered cleaners that must be mixed with water. They often cost more than powdered products or liquids that do not come with a spray attachment, because of this added convenience. Observe the cautions that accompany aerosol containers.

For Safe Use of Products:
- Always read the label before using household cleaning products, insecticides, and medicines.
- Return products to safe storage areas after use.
- Keep poisonous products in their original containers with labels intact—always out of reach of small children.

71

- Do not combine cleaning agents unless label directions indicate that it is safe to do so.
- Never set aerosol cans near any kind of heat, and never spray them near an open flame.
- Before discarding an aerosol container, hold the valve open until all contents and gas have escaped. Place empty container in the trash, never in a fire or incinerator.

TO GET THE MOST OUT OF YOUR CLEANING EQUIPMENT

To get the most mileage out of your household tools and equipment, read all your instruction books before the initial use and refer to them periodically to refresh your memory. Manufacturers will tell you the best way to obtain optimum performance from your equipment. It is important in exercising your responsibility as a good consumer to follow them accurately. Above all, use your own good judgment on use and care. Try to clean each piece of equipment before putting it away, or at least periodically, to assure continued maintenance. Check all equipment occasionally to make sure it is in good working order.

CLEANING TOOLS AND TECHNIQUES

VACUUM CLEANERS

The vacuum cleaner is the most useful piece of cleaning equipment you will own since it literally breathes in the dust that might otherwise just be pushed around. There are several types, ranging from very inexpensive models which are really not very satisfactory to those that cost over a hundred dollars. A good quality, moderately priced model with features to meet *your* needs is ample. With such a range it would pay you to do your homework before you purchase a new one.

There are two types of vacuum cleaners:

Upright cleaners are best for cleaning rugs and carpets and for pulling out deep-down dirt and embedded soil. They operate with a motor-driven rotating brush which combines suction with a brushing and/or beating action to clean both surface and below. They have convenient disposable dust bags and filters. Uprights have cleaning attachments, though they are not usually as efficient as those on the canister type because the suction is not as high. The motor that creates the cleaning suction is designed mainly to operate the carpet-cleaning brushes and beaters. Some newer models may have special design features to make the attachments work more efficiently. Ask about this when purchasing an upright.

Canister or tank cleaners are lighter in weight, easy to carry, and usually have a powerful motor with a strong suction. They operate with a motor-driven fan that suctions in air and dirt up through a nozzle and hollow wand. They are especially good for bare floors and for cotton loop and loose pile carpeting. Attachments usually operate more efficiently with canister cleaners, because of their direct suction. You may find a special carpet-cleaning attachment for the canister cleaner with a separate electric motor-driven brush to make rug and carpet cleaning more efficient.

Which to Buy?—In general, while both upright and canister cleaners have been designed for both rug and carpet cleaning and to use with attachments, if you have an active household, with children, and have a great deal of pile or twist carpeting, a hard-working upright is your best choice. (Pair it with a strong-suction hand vacuum cleaner or a canister type for above-the-floor cleaning, if possible.)

If you have more bare floors and area rugs than carpeting, or if your carpets are loose pile or loop types, and if you need your cleaner mainly for above-the-floor cleaning, a canister or tank type is your best choice.

If you have a small home or apartment with not much area to clean, a good lightweight upright cleaner or stick-type vacuum will be a good start.

If you have many shag rugs, look for special shag rug cleaners or attachments. Regular vacuum cleaners are not adequate for these types.

73

Cleaner Attachments and How to Use Them

These will be your best dust chasers. Learn to depend on them, for as we said, the vacuum actually "breathes in the dust." Use the handy storage kit that comes with some vacuum cleaners or devise a method of your own to keep the attachments readily accessible. A shoebag hung on the back of a cleaning closet is an excellent idea, and should contain the following:

Wand—when you require extra length for cleaning bare floors, or hard-to-reach places.

Dusting Brush—for furniture, table tops, books, bookcases, fireplace screens, venetian blinds, lamps, light fixtures, registers, baseboards.

Floor Brush—for hard-surfaced polished or waxed floors, kitchen and bathroom floors, carpeted stairs.

Shag Rake—for cleaning shag rugs.

Upholstery Nozzle—upholstered furniture—sofas and chairs, draperies, tapestries, mattresses, suits, coats, automobile interiors, stairs.

VACUUM CLEANER ATTACHMENTS

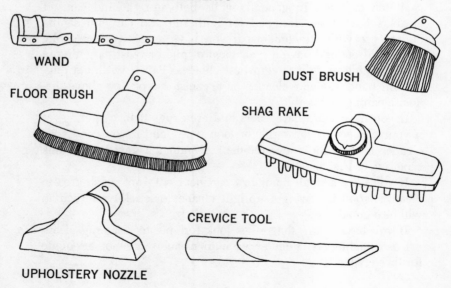

WAND

DUST BRUSH

FLOOR BRUSH

SHAG RAKE

CREVICE TOOL

UPHOLSTERY NOZZLE

Crevice Tool—for upholstered furniture, edge of wall-to-wall carpeting, radiators, dresser drawers, refrigerator condensers, all hard-to-get-at places.

Spraying Attachments (may be available for some cleaners)—for quick, convenient spraying or blowing of insecticides, moth crystals, etcetera. (Follow directions with caution.)

Disposable Bags—most bags on new cleaners are of the throw-away type, and it is wise to use the type made especially for your cleaner.

Supplementary Cleaners

In addition to the upright and canister models, there are supplementary cleaners that lend major support for special cleaning.

Lightweight Upright Cleaners—They are excellent for quick surface cleanup for floors and carpets. A suction cleaner, they resemble a heavy-duty upright in styling and design, and are especially good for small apartments.

Stick-Type Vacuum Cleaners—These cylindrical-shaped suction cleaners are very light in weight and are good for daily cleaning and quick pickups or as duplicate equipment in a two or more level house. They store easily, hanging in a minimum of space. A good "stick" vacuum cleaner can hold off a thorough cleaning for several weeks.

Hand Vacuum Cleaners—These are used for above-the-floor cleaning. They are small, portable, easy to handle. They can be used in place of attachments when a basic vacuum cleaner is used for floors. Excellent paired with an upright, or for boats, trailers, cars. Make sure you buy one with strong suction power, otherwise it will only go through the motions of picking up dust. The suction is usually inadequate for heavy cleanings.

Heavy-duty Vacuum Cleaners (sometimes called shop vacuum cleaners)—These are used for heavy-duty cleaning in garage, basement, workshop, on the patio, or for fireplaces. They are large tank or canister types and are ideal for picking up pebbles, wood shavings, nails, ashes, grass, etcetera. Newer ones for outdoor use will compress large quantities of leaves or outdoor scraps into compact shape for easy disposal, or to be used as fertilizer or in compost heaps.

Built-in Central Vacuum Cleaning System—Similar to commercial units in hotels and industrial areas, this is a heavy-duty built-in system with a central motor, fan, filter, and installation. Baseboard inlets, like convenience outlets, are located in strategic areas around the house. The hose is plugged into these inlets which suction the dust to a central receiving area in basement or garage or wherever. These systems are best installed in new homes while they are under construction. Otherwise the long hose and high cost of equipment and installation especially in a house that is already built could be prohibitive.

How to Use the Vacuum Cleaner:

*   Set the control according to the kind of surface you are cleaning and the degree of suction you desire, unless the adjustment is automatic.
*   Push the vacuum cleaner slowly in straight strokes—lengthwise on a rug—going over each section several times to remove deeply embedded soil.
*   As you work be sure to keep the cleaner cord out of the way to avoid running over it or tangling it with other loose cords.
*   Before vacuuming, check floor or carpet for hard, sharp objects such as pins, tacks, and hairpins that may cut the belt of your vacuum cleaner or puncture the dust bag. Also pick up objects such as twine, socks, or cellophane that might wrap around the brushes or clog the tube. We have been trying for years to get manufacturers to design some kind of magnet on the "masthead" of the vacuum cleaner to pick up metal objects that might damage the cleaner. Since we have been unsuccessful thus far, we would suggest that you tape one onto the end of a yardstick and carry it around with you while vacuuming, unless you need the exercise of stooping and bending.
*   Empty or replace the dust bag, according to the directions for your vacuum cleaner. If yours is not disposable, shake the dirt into a large moistened paper bag to keep the dust from scattering. Most vacuum cleaners today have disposable dust bags which filter out dust while allowing air to flow through freely. When a bag is full, replace it. You can purchase these bags at your local dealer or generally in any hardware store or housewares

department. Be sure to take the name and model number of your vacuum cleaner with you when you shop.

• Check secondary filters which protect motor from dirt (see your instruction book) to see if they need cleaning or replacement. To clean, tap against a hard surface or rinse with warm water and dry.

If the vacuum cleaner does not pick up as it should, check to see if the bag needs to be changed or emptied. Check the filters also. Check to see if the bristles on an upright are worn down and need to be changed. Check to see if hose connections are tight on a canister cleaner. Any leakage reduces suction.

If the bag is empty and the action still isn't good, check the belt on an upright cleaner. It may be loose, crooked, or have slipped off the pulley. Belts need changing every six to twelve months, depending on use. Check the suction opening on a tank-type cleaner. The hose may be clogged.

Tip: If clogging is the problem, pass a long handle through the hose to remove the obstacle. Or if you can, reverse the suction and blow it out.

Make sure vacuum cleaner is unplugged before checking any area.

CARPET SWEEPERS

They may be electric or nonelectric, and are used, as are lightweight cleaners, for quick cleanups in heavily used areas. They operate by moving brushes which pick up soil. They do give carpeting a fluffed-up look and remove dirt before it gets into the pile.

We like the idea of keeping a carpet sweeper close by halls, fireplaces, and dining rooms where heavy soil is a problem, for emergency cleanups.

How to Use a Carpet Sweeper:
• Push the carpet sweeper firmly and rapidly back and forth over the carpet, being careful not to use too much pressure.
• Set any adjustable controls, but keep in mind that some sweepers adjust automatically to the thickness of the pile.

Check your instructions carefully.

Tip: Moisten the brushes slightly with warm water before using and they will pick up dust and dirt more efficiently.

Care:
- Clean the dustpan in the sweeper after each use. If you don't, the sweeper will redeposit soil on the carpet.
- Remove the brush and clean it periodically. Cut threads, hair, and lint and remove them with a brush or sturdy comb. Use a cleaning fluid to clean sticky or gummy brushes. If badly soiled, soak them briefly in a sudsy solution using an all-purpose household cleaner and warm water.
- If you have done all these things and the sweeper still doesn't operate efficiently, check to see if the brushes are badly worn; they may need replacing.

BROOMS

Is there a home without a broom? Despite what some might say, there actually is an art to buying a broom and a technique to using one properly. They come in a variety of sizes and shapes. The least desirable one is made of those pretty, lush-looking colored synthetic fibers. They are hard to control and simply flip the dirt from one spot to another, unless you find one with the bristles "ruffled" at the tips, to control the sweepings. In natural bristles, you'll find brooms made from broom corn, Chinese palm, or Tampico fibers.

Broom corn are the least expensive, but don't last long. Those made of *Chinese palm fiber* are better, last longer, and cost more than broom corn. When sweeping, palm-fiber brooms wear down evenly and do not flip up dirt and dust. The best and most durable brooms are those made of *Tampico*—tough vegetable fibers. They are the most expensive. Shellacked, varnished, lacquered, or enameled maple handles are the best.

DUSTPANS

Brooms almost always call for a dustpan, and if you buy one with a long handle it will save stooping.

There are some commercial combination dustpan/broom sets which have been adapted for home use. The dustpan itself is a long-handled implement with a flip-over cover. Its broom is also long-handled with short bristles—just long enough to sweep up stray dirt and clutter.

How to Sweep (Fiber Brooms):
- Keeping the broom firmly on the surface, sweep slowly, in one direction only, to avoid spreading dust. Direct sweeping to one central section of the floor.
- Sweep soil into the dustpan.

Care:
- To store, always hang a broom. If it doesn't have a ring for hanging, insert a screw eye in the handle top. Resting the bristles on the floor will break them.
- To clean badly soiled palm and Tampico fiber brooms, dip them up and down in lukewarm sudsy water and rinse thoroughly. Hang to dry.
- Dip occasionally in clear water to soften and prevent brittleness.
- When a broom starts to lose its bristles, it's time to get a new one.
     Tip: If you clean your bathroom floor with your broom, it will help to soften it while cleaning the floor.

MOPS

Dry Mops

You need a *dust* mop to dust bare floors, unless, of course, you use the bare floor attachment of your vacuum cleaner, which is not always convenient for quickie cleanups.

You will find dust mops made of cotton, wool, or synthetic yarn. Those made of synthetic or wool fibers are best, as they generate a static electricity which helps dust "cling." You can buy a special spray conditioner or a "treated" mop which will accomplish the same thing. *Caution:* Some "treated" mops may contain oil and should be used only on oiled surfaces. Using them on wax may cause the wax to soften.

79

How to Use a Dry Mop:
- Dust the floor without raising the mop to avoid spreading dust. On wood follow the grain.
- Follow specific manufacturer's directions for using and cleaning anti-static or "treated" mops.

Care:
- To store, always hang a dust mop. Resting the mop head on the floor will mat it.
- Shake the mop into a large moistened paper bag after each use, to avoid spreading dust. Or use the suction tool attachment of your vacuum cleaner to clean it. Try never to store without cleaning first.
- When dust mop is badly soiled, remove thread and hairs, then wash mop head in hot sudsy water. Wash several times, using fresh sudsy water each time until it is clean. Rinse in clear lukewarm water until all trace of suds have disappeared. (Many mops are machine washable. Slip them, along with soiled dust cloths, into a nylon mesh bag and wash in your automatic washer. See Chapter Four.) Wash wool mops in lukewarm sudsy water, rinse thoroughly in lukewarm water, squeeze gently, shake out, and dry in a breezy, shady place. Shake thoroughly until all strands have separated. Hang up to dry in a breezy place.
- To treat a mop for dusting oiled floors, add a few drops of oil polish to the mop head and store in a metal container.

Wet Mops

You need a wet mop for cleaning up dirt and grime from washable smooth- and hard-surfaced floors, such as vinyl, rubber, linoleum, asphalt, ceramic, marble, and the like. Wet mops are used with all-purpose cleaners, soaps, and detergents in a water-based solution and are usually made of cotton yarn or string, cellulose sponge, chamois, and synthetic fibers. Lightweight mops made of synthetic fibers, sponge, or chamois are really the best as they are easier to push around, clean, wring out, and will dry more quickly than cotton string, thus preventing mildew and an unpleasant odor. We would also suggest using a mop with its own wringing attachment, as there should be no need in this day and age to put your hands in such dirty water!

How to Use a Wet Mop:
- Sweep or vacuum floor, if necessary, to pick up loose soil.
- Dip mop in sudsy solution and squeeze until just damp, then rub mop over floor until you need to dampen again. Repeat process until the entire floor is clean. Follow specific directions for the household cleaner you are using.

    Caution: It hardly seems necessary but we'll mention it anyway. Always begin mopping from the inside corner, toward the door!

    Tip: If you find that your floors are not clean after you wet mop, use a more *concentrated* solution of the cleaner you are using. Be sure to rinse thoroughly, unless cleaning product does not require rinsing.

Care:
- Wash and rinse string, synthetic, or chamois mops in hot sudsy water after each use, rinse thoroughly, and squeeze to dry, shaking it to separate strings. Hang or turn upside down to dry (dry in sun if possible), hang to store. Never store while damp or wet in a pail or on the floor; wet mops may mildew and develop unpleasant odors. Trim frayed ends occasionally.
- Wash sponge rubber mops in warm sudsy water and rinse thoroughly. Squeeze out excess water and return to frame. Squeeze again with squeegee lever. Store in a cool, dry place. Harsh chemicals, such as grease, acids, gasoline, and oils, can damage sponge rubber.

Dust Cloths, Polishing Cloths, Scrub Cloths

There is an abundance of dust and cleaning cloths on the market: untreated, lintless ones; treated types for special jobs; and paper "cloths" reinforced with heavy-duty fibers. They are quick, efficient and inexpensive. And a supply of good dusters can do more to speed up your chores than almost anything else we can think of. On the other hand, using the wrong cloth for a job can do more harm than good.

81

You will need a good *lintless cloth* for dusting and polishing.

Lintless cloths you will find at home include: old diapers, undershirts, soft "scratchless" wool, and flannel. Soft wool is excellent as it creates its own "cling" feature, through the static electricity it generates while you're using it. *Note:* When using old clothes be sure to remove all hooks, buttons, etcetera, which will scratch surfaces.

Cloths you may buy include: cheesecloth and treated cloths. Buy *cheesecloth* by the roll and cut off the length you need—shake the threads out after cutting. *Treated cloths* have been given a special conditioner to attract and hold the dust. Follow specific instructions. *Caution:* Some contain oil and should be used for oiled surfaces only, as oil may soften some waxed surfaces.

Dry Dusting

Use lintless cloths for *dry dusting.* Surfaces which should be dry dusted include: all polished and lacquered finishes, furniture and surfaces in general which are lightly soiled with dust.

Damp Dusting

Use barely dampened, absorbent items such as knitted cotton, diapers, undershirts, cellulose sponge for *damp dusting.* There are times when damp dusting is necessary to remove stubborn soil. Surfaces which may be damp dusted include: plastic, laminated plastic, and some oiled finishes, such as teak. Lacquered finishes and polished surfaces (waxed or oiled) may occasionally be damp dusted to remove smears and fingerprints, as may painted gloss or semi-gloss surfaces like windowsills, to remove heavy smudges or soot. Dry thoroughly after each damp dusting. Dry dusting over soot and greasy stains will only serve to streak the surfaces. For special cleaning jobs, see Index for particular item.

How to Use a Dusting and Polishing Cloth:
- Make sure the dust cloth is clean. Dirty ones scratch surfaces.

- Follow the grain of the wood and gather the dust into the cloth to avoid spreading it.

  Tip: Spray a little of the polish (oil or wax, depending upon the surface) you are using into the dust cloth to keep dust particles from scattering.

Care:
- When soiled, wash in hot sudsy water; rinse thoroughly in clear lukewarm water. Dry. (Scrub heavily soiled ones and use bleach, if necessary.)
- For home treatment of dust cloths to be used on oil finishes and surfaces (never on waxed surfaces) dip in a lemon oil solution:

  1 pint hot water   ¼ cup lemon oil

  Combine hot water and lemon oil. Dip fine cheesecloth squares, about 2 feet square, in solution. Squeeze out all excess moisture. Dry thoroughly. Store in a tightly covered container.

- To wash commercial chemically treated cloths, soak in warm sudsy water; rinse thoroughly in clear lukewarm water. Dry.

  Note: Rags and cloths that have been used for cleaning, waxing and polishing, should never be placed in a washer or dryer unless *all* traces of the flammable fluids or solids and their fumes have been removed.

Chamois (Leather Cloths)

These polishers are excellent for silver, brass, other metals and other smooth surfaces such as glass, glossy enamel, etcetera.

Care:
- Wash in lukewarm sudsy water. Squeeze suds through it gently, as it may tear easily when wet.
- Rinse in lukewarm water and squeeze out excess water. Do not wring or twist.
- Dry in shade.
- Pull gently into shape while drying to avoid stiffness.

Scrub Cloths

If you use a cloth instead of a sponge make sure it is highly absorbent. Diapers, undershirts, soft turkish toweling are all excellent.

How to Use:
- Dip in hot (or warm—depending on surface) sudsy water and squeeze thoroughly so it isn't dripping.
- Rub in firm straight vertical or horizontal strokes (depending upon area) until surface is clean and cloth is lightly soiled. Redip in sudsy water and repeat process until surface is clean.
- If household cleaner you are using requires rinsing, repeat process using a clean cloth and warm clear water.

SCRUB BRUSHES

These are made of stiff natural fiber or synthetic bristles with natural wood or plastic handles. Some have long handles to eliminate stooping or bending. Scrub brushes are excellent for outdoor porches, and ceramic and tile floors. Flat-handled ones come in various shapes to fit your hand and are good for cleaning cracks and crevices.

How to Use:
- Scrub in firm long strokes with hot sudsy water, using an all-purpose household cleaner. Use according to package directions.

Care:
- Wash scrub brushes in hot sudsy water after each use, until the bristles are clean. Rinse thoroughly in clear warm water. Shake and let them dry, bristles down, at room temperature. Never store until completely dry.

SPONGES

These may be used in place of scrub cloths or damp dust cloths. There are three types—*natural sponges* are the skeletons of small sea or marine animals which grow like plant life attached to rocks and craggy surfaces. They are dried, cleaned, and bleached before marketing. They vary in size and the smaller ones are less expensive. Oddly enough, natural sponges are even less expensive than cellulose ones.

Cellulose sponges (and mops), made of the woody parts of plants (used also for paper and rayon), come in fashion colors and are the most popular type—probably because of their color selection and variety of sizes. They are not affected by regular household cleaners; however, strong concentrated solutions and bleaches may damage them. They are more expensive than natural sponges.

Synthetic (plastic) and *foam rubber sponges* and mops may be damaged by strong solutions, harsh chemicals, grease, oil, and acid. They, too, are available in colors, but are not as effective a cleaning tool as either the natural or cellulose types. We really don't recommend them. They are too soft and pliable, slippery and nonabsorbent.

Which to Use—A Sponge or a Scrub Cloth?

Use sponges for general and all-purpose cleaning—either natural or cellulose. We prefer *cellulose* because they feel better "in the hand" and are more absorbing, and look better because they are colorful. They should *not*, however, be used on rough surfaces, as they split and tear. A scrub cloth or rag is preferable for rough surfaces. For applying suds as a cleaning solution to fabrics and upholstery, use only a *sponge* or a *soft brush*.

How to Use:
- Follow the directions given previously for using a scrub cloth.

Care:
Natural:
- Wash in clean lukewarm sudsy water. If heavily soiled soak in sudsy ammonia and water solution—1 tablespoon to 1 quart of water.
- Rinse thoroughly in clear water, squeeze, and dry in a breezy, shady place.

- Hang them by a string run through them, when not in use.

    Note: Sterlize by boiling 10 to 12 minutes.

Cellulose:
- Wash in hot sudsy water. Rinse after each use. They may be washed occasionally in the washing machine along with a general load of dish towels, etcetera.
- Bleach them occasionally (when they begin to "smell"), in a mild solution of household bleach. Do not soak too long.
- Hang up sponge mops after washing and avoid letting them "dry hard" between using. Moisten them occasionally.

Foam Rubber and Plastic Sponges:
- Wash in lukewarm sudsy water. Rinse, dry, and store in a cool place.

    Tip: Keep a sponge near every sink in the house for quick cleanups.

Paper Towels

Well, what can we say? They're great and they're disposable. They'll do everything a scrub rag or sponge will do for light-duty and general-purpose cleaning—wipe up spills, clean off smudges, fingermarks, clean windows, etcetera. They are more expensive, however, than a reusable sponge or rag. Personally we could write a book on paper towels alone—but we'll spare you that here! Suffice it to say, how could we live without them? A roll mounted in the bathroom, kitchen, or laundry is virtually an indispensable luxury!

Dusters and Dust Brushes

There are several good types of dusters which you may prefer using for furniture and surfaces in lieu of cloths.

Wool Duster—These resemble giant posies. They pick up dust gently from furniture and help it to cling through the static electricity generated from friction while dusting. Wash them when soiled in lukewarm sudsy water, rinse and hang "head" down to dry.

Yarn Furniture Duster—These dusters have an opening in the center to let furniture legs slip through, dusting all sides at once. Wash as wool duster above.

Feather Dusters—The new, smaller ones, treated for helping dust to cling, are excellent for quick surface dusting. *Do not use* a feather duster unless it is treated as above.

Venetian Blind Brush—There are two-, three-, or four-fingered soft bristled brushes for cleaning dust from the slots of venetian blinds—cleaning several at one time. They are especially good for removing soil from around the tapes and cords. Wash as wool duster above.

Duster Brush—These are small and have soft bristles, ideal for dusting carved furniture and frames.

You can find a special brush for every possible job you have around the house. We've discussed dusting and scrub brushes above as they are basic cleaning tools. However, there are these others too.

A Brush for Every Job

Selecting and buying a brush deserves more than a casual plucking off a rack as you check out of the supermarket. A good brush should have enough bristles to do the job it's supposed to do, and they should be firmly attached. Bristles vary in softness or stiffness depending on the type of brush. While each brush is designed for a specific job, you'll find its talents will grow with your imagination . . . and you can save hours of work.

A *Wall Brush* with soft bristles is excellent to keep painted, papered, or paneled walls free from dust and soot.

Silver Polishing Brush reaches into the design and between fork tines. Bristles are soft nylon, won't scratch silver.

Window Brush is a handy tool for washing windows from the outside without climbing on a ladder. Handles vary in length.

Radiator Brush has a long handle to reach those hard-to-get-at dust catchers.

Lampshade Brush is soft as a feather and gently curved to dust the contours of various shades. Comes in pastel colors.

Tub Brush is shaped to clean all areas of the bathtub. Nylon bristles come in several colors.

Toilet Bowl Brush is curved to clean the hidden areas of the bowl. Always hang up after use to keep bristles from flattening.

Floor Brush with its 14″ width sweeps all hard-surface floors in a hurry. Colorful plastic bristles are sturdy but flexible.

Whisk Brooms chase lint, dust, and loose hairs from clothes and upholstery. It is a good idea to keep one hanging in every closet. They come in natural fiber or soft wire bristles. The natural bristle ones are best as they are more flexible and gentle on fabrics—and they are easier to clean.

How to Use a Whisk Broom:
- Whisk the broom firmly enough over the surface to raise the dust. Whisk it all the way so the dust doesn't resettle on the fabric.

Care:
- To clean, wash in warm sudsy water, rinse in clear cool water. Hang, bristles down, to dry.

RUBBER AND SYNTHETIC RUBBER GLOVES

Use household gloves for heavy-duty cleaning and to protect your hands from harsh chemicals. Use them especially if you wash dishes by hand, to allow you to use water hotter than your hands can stand. Some people feel that they are not comfortable in household gloves, and, of course, this is a matter of personal preference. Personally, we think it is a good idea to have two pairs of rubber gloves. For light washing you can use surgical gloves, which are less clumsy.

Care:
- Do not allow rubber gloves to remain in cleaning fluid, acid, or alkaline solutions longer than half an hour. Follow specific instructions when using gloves in special solutions.

- Soak used gloves in lukewarm sudsy water 10 to 20 minutes; rinse thoroughly in clear lukewarm water; hang up to dry. Sprinkle inside with talcum powder. Never put away until thoroughly dry.
- Store rubber gloves in a cool dark place.
- Newer synthetic rubber gloves are not affected by solutions that injure genuine rubber. They hold their shape and may be stored in any convenient place.

   Note: Prevent fingertip puncture in rubber gloves caused by long pointed nails by placing bits of cotton in each glove finger.

WAX APPLICATORS

There are three ways to apply wax to floors:

1. Scrub cloth or rag, in which case you also need your "knees."
2. Manually operated wax applicator.
3. Specially designed electric floor scrubber, waxer, polisher, rug shampooer.

If your only smooth-surface flooring is in the kitchen (and you occasionally opt to wax the tile floor in the bathroom), then all you need is a good heavy-duty rag like a piece of terry toweling.

If your home has smooth-surface flooring, vinyl, rubber linoleum, etcetera, in the kitchen, family room, and hall (lots of floors you wax often) you'll no doubt find a manually operated wax applicator handy. They are either a chenille or lamb's wool pad covering a base on a long stick (some are hollow-handled plastic types which dispense liquid wax). They allow you to apply wax without bending or stooping.

If you have primarily resilient smooth-surface flooring (floors that need scrubbing and/or waxing and polishing), such as vinyl, rubber, ceramic tile, or marble, then you'll find that an electric waxer and polisher would be a worthwhile investment if you do it often. If not, you can *rent* these machines from your hardware or flooring dealer or a supermarket.

For detailed instructions on how to scrub and wax floors, see the later section on hard-surface floorings in this chapter.

How to Apply Wax Manually:
• Pour a little wax on a clean dry floor, spread evenly in a *thin* coat using straight strokes in one direction only.

Care:
• Wash nylon chenille pads immediately after using in warm sudsy water, before the wax has time to harden.
• Rinse in clear lukewarm water, until all trace of suds has disappeared.
• Hang up to dry. Fluff occasionally during drying to revive texture.
• Replace on frame, if you have the detachable type.
• To store, hang the applicator. Resting the pad on the floor will mat it.
• For care of applicators depending upon type of wax used, see section on floor care.

HOW TO CLEAN

We are assuming that you are reading this chapter for one of two reasons. Either you

1. Are looking for a way to create some system and organization to your cleaning routine because you are dissatisfied with the way you are doing it, *or*
2. Are just beginning to keep house and would like to start doing it the right way from the very beginning.

There are times when *all* of us have that beautiful feeling that comes from knowing our house is completely organized and thoroughly clean. We usually enjoy this state of mind after repainting closets, moving into a new home, or finishing a seasonal cleaning. Unfortunately, the house doesn't stay that way for long. Soon the papers and magazines pile up, toys are out of place, sweaters and shirts get in the wrong drawers. Suddenly the whole purpose for the preceding section on scheduling and reorganization becomes a reality.

That "I'm Swamped" Feeling—If someday you have that feeling, make up your mind that you are going through your house like a wild tornado and toss out everything you don't need or want. Put everything else back where it should or does belong and start out anew with a freshly organized house.

DRESSING FOR THE JOB

What Will You Wear?

It is desirable, of course, to look as attractive as possible but not at the expense of your working comfort and safety. There are some very handsome shifts and pants outfits that combine good style with practical design. You can feel secure regardless of who rings the doorbell! Here are a few tips to keep in mind:

- Wear flat-soled shoes or ones with low rubber heels. Don't work all day in slippers.
- If you wear a skirt, make sure it is wide enough for action, but not so wide it will get in your way or make you trip on stairs or a ladder. If you look well in pants, there are some very handsome jeans and slacks that are ideal for working around the house. Some of the high-fashion apron-smocks with large pockets are ideal for collecting stray objects as you move from room to room.
- Wear something that lets your arms move freely and comfortably. Avoid wearing full sleeves or loose ties when you are cooking.
- Needless to say, it is desirable that all clothes should be washable.
- To protect your hands, try wearing rubber gloves.
- Those great triangular scarves will keep the hair out of your eyes and the dust out of your hair. Besides, they are good-looking!
  Tip: For those of you who like to get down on your knees to scrub the floor, there are colorful foam rubber pillows or kneeling pads on the market to keep your knees from getting sore!

For some tips on working comfort—how to stoop, reach, lift, and push for good exercise and safety, using your energy—see Chapter Ten.

THE ORDER OF CLEANING

As we suggested earlier, it is almost impossible to make hard and fast rules. There are so many variables that influence the frequency with which you have to do a job and the amount of work involved. Much depends on the quantity of dust or soot in the air, whether or not your home is air-conditioned, your personal attitudes about housecleaning, the size of your family, and the age of the children.

Family habits also influence the kind and amount of cleaning that you have to do. If your family cooperates in tidying up, keeping their own clothes and belongings in order, avoiding bringing outdoor dirt inside, you will have a lot less work.

Whatever amount of work there is, having a *system* to follow will make your job easier and faster. *Before you begin to clean,* it helps to collect all the cleaning supplies and equipment you will need for each room. A cleaning basket, mentioned earlier, will help you to organize this task. Use another container to collect small objects such as toys and scissors that have become displaced. This will save a lot of time running back and forth. Set aside a large container for collecting trash you want to throw away. When you have finished cleaning, take it all to the incinerator or garbage pail.

Where to Start Cleaning

At best, we can only suggest a guide to help you establish the system that works best for you. As for the amount of time it will take to perform each task, this will depend upon how fast you work, how many interruptions you may have, and how large your home is.

WAYS TO CLEAN

Quick Touch-Up Cleaning

There are times when you simply *have* to get the house in order in practically no time at all. According to a law developed by the brilliant British economist, Mr. C. Northcote Parkinson, "work expands to fill the time allotted." In this instance only tackle what shows. Leave any thorough cleaning for a day when you are not under pressure.

1. Make the beds, if they have not been made.
2. Wipe up any visible dust or grime.
3. Lightly vacuum or carpet sweep the rugs.
4. Rinse and stack the dishes or load the dishwasher. (That's why we *love* dishwashers. They hide dirty dishes, as well as washing them. If you don't have a dishwasher, you can rinse pots and pans and put them in the oven until later.) Or fill the laundry tub with sudsy water if it is close to the kitchen and give the pots and pans a quick swish. Don't soak, as some metals may discolor.
5. Close the door to any untidy room that you can and make it off limits. Keep a corner of a room or closet as a "stash away" area—until you can get time to put things back in place. (Don't forget and leave them there!)

Honest-to-Goodness Cleaning

The routine that follows is based on the premise that the daily straightening-up is simply to re-establish order in the house and clean up the dirt that shows. You can do this sort of cleaning any time you want things to look straight, but not necessarily clean. Weekly, monthly, and seasonal cleaning involve the serious jobs that keep your house really clean.

Start the Daily Once-Over the Night Before—If you can or would take ten minutes before going to bed to put the house in order, you'll find the house a lot more pleasant to face in the early hours:

- Straighten furniture.
- Fluff up the pillows.
- Return any stray objects such as cards, games, toys, to their places.
- Throw out trash.

In the Morning—If you have opted not to straighten up the night before, then try to do it as quickly as you can. Creating order in the entire house before you begin a daily routine—

93

whether you stay home or go off to work—will make you feel much more comfortable about your home. It will leave you ready to face any unexpected situation and it makes daily cleaning easier, too.

> *To create order in the morning:*
> - Airing a room is important. Open the bedroom windows (and other rooms as you get to them) when you get up, unless your home is air-conditioned or you live in an area where soot and pollution are major problems. If so, try using window filters or special screens which can be purchased at the hardware store.
> - Fold back the bed covers to air the beds.
> - Clear away obvious clutter like breakfast dishes and other articles from kitchen, breakfast room, or dining room.
> - Load dishwasher or rinse and stack dishes, pots and pans. (The first five steps should take no more than 30 minutes.)
> - Straighten living room and/or family room.
> - Give all rooms the daily once-over as outlined for specific rooms in the following section.

Once you have done the morning straighten-up you will be free to go on to the individual rooms/or daily cleaning.

Then, move into the major project you have set aside for the day, that is, marketing, doing the laundry, cleaning one room thoroughly or leaving the house for a personal, community, or social engagement, or your job.

GENERAL DIRECTIONS FOR CLEANING ALL ROOMS

Don't forget to vacuum, carpet clean, or dust under the bed. Live kittens are cuddly, but "dust kittens" are not! *Don't forget* to wipe the picture frames and backs, lamp bulbs, and tops of the wall cabinets in the kitchen. Oh yes, remember the inside strip of the swinging door, that faces the door frame! These areas are the telltale keys to once-over-lightly housekeeping which someday can catch up with us.

The Order of Cleaning

We have often been asked, "Is it better to make all the beds at one time, then go back to clean, or is it faster to finish one room at a time, then proceed to the next?" That's an easy one for us to answer since you simply do too much running about when you do parts of each room, then return to finish the job. In addition, finishing one room completely gives us a feeling of satisfaction.

A Few Ground Rules and Definitions

1. *Do the dust-raising things first.* That means that you do any whisk-brooming of furniture or dusting of ceilings, walls, draperies before you *dust* the furniture or vacuum the carpet. It is really best to dust in this sequence: ceiling, walls, windows, doors, blinds, draperies, lampshades, radiator, bookshelves, decorative shelves, upholstery, furniture surfaces, floors, carpets.

2. When you damp dust, make sure your cloth or sponge is wrung dry to avoid drips.

3. After straightening or cleaning each room, adjust shades and blinds and add some special touch if desired, like flowers, plants, etcetera.

4. Learn the *language of housekeeping. Warm sudsy water* means water that feels moderately hot or more hot than cool to the touch and which contains liquid or powdered soap, detergent, or a household cleaner. Follow specific directions on whether the soap or detergent you use is light-duty or all-purpose or heavy-duty.

Lukewarm sudsy water means water that feels tepid to the touch or more cool than hot, and which contains powdered or liquid soap, detergent, or a household cleaner. In general, liquid detergents dissolve more effectively than powdered detergents in lukewarm or warm water.

Hot sudsy water means water that feels hotter than the hands can stand (that's why rubber gloves are important) and which

95

contains liquid or powdered soap, detergent, or a household cleaner.

Rub, pat or sponge lightly—apply gentle pressure to avoid abrasive action.

Apply generously—use enough mixture or solution to provide sufficient cleansing power.

Long, even strokes—push cloth or applicator forward or backward in straight, clean strokes so surface dries without streaks. (Usually refers to furniture or floor wax or polish.)

Foam—¼ cup of light-duty detergent and 1 cup warm water beaten together to form a thick, solid mass of suds for cleaning carpet or fabric surfaces.

DIRECTIONS FOR CLEANING SPECIFIC ROOMS

Here is our suggested guide for cleaning the various rooms in your apartment or house. After you have cleaned a room for a while you will find little short-cuts of your own that will make your work easier.

LIVING ROOM, DINING ROOM, DEN, LIBRARY, RECREATION AND/OR FAMILY ROOM

Daily

Supplies:
- Sponge or rag for damp dusting.
- Soft cloths or paper towels for drying.
- Piece of knitted undershirt or diaper for dusting.
- Piece of flannel or cheesecloth for polishing.
- Special duster treated for dust-clinging feature (optional).
- Whisk broom.
- Spray cleaner for cleaning up smudges and fingerprints.
- Household cleanser or scouring powder.
- Window and glass cleaner.

- Carpet sweeper or lightweight vacuum cleaner (if floors need a "pickup").

- Empty wastebaskets, ash trays, throw out dead flowers. Remove articles that don't belong in the room. Sort newspapers, magazines and discard old ones. Clean desk tops and throw away "junk mail." If you have a fireplace, brush up hearth and empty ashes, if necessary.
- Put things away where they belong, fluff pillows, straighten up furniture, and clean off table tops, mantels, etcetera.
- Whisk furniture and dust surfaces *only* if necessary. See preceding section for kinds of dusting.
- Dry mop bare floors, if necessary.
- Vacuum or use carpet sweeper *only* if necessary.
- Adjust shades, draperies, and close windows, if you've opened them.

Weekly

In addition to daily supplies:
- Dust mop.
- Vacuum cleaner with attachments.
- Warm sudsy all-purpose detergent solution.
- 2 pails—one for detergent solution, one for clear warm water.

- Open windows unless you have air-conditioning.
- Clean fireplace and hearth. Brush up ashes with a broom or special brush.
- Create order in the room.
- Empty wastebaskets, ash trays, remove any wilted flowers, sort newspapers, magazines, discard old ones.
- Clear off tables, desks, mantels and throw away "junk mail," unnecessary clutter.
- Wipe up smudges from walls, areas near light switches, doorknobs with spray cleaner or liquid household cleaner and dampened cloth or sponge. Spot-clean serious spots on upholstery, rugs, etcetera.
- Spray-clean telephone with disinfectant cleaner.
- Damp dust windowsills and frames inside only.

97

- Vacuum upholstered furniture or use a whisk broom.
- Dust surfaces of furniture with dusting or polishing cloth.
- Dust woodwork, baseboards, wipe off all bric-a-brac, lamp bulbs, lamps and bases with a damp sponge, wrung out in warm sudsy detergent solution. (Make sure lamp is disconnected and bulb is cool before wiping.)
- Clean windows inside, mirrors, all glass, and chrome with window cleaner.
- Wipe painted (and waxed), lacquered or plastic furniture with damp cloth or sponge wrung out in warm sudsy detergent solution. Dry and polish with a soft dry cloth.
- Dust or vacuum radiator.
- Dust any visible bare floor area with dust mop or bare floor attachment of vacuum cleaner.
- Vacuum carpet or rug.
- If you have any smooth-surface or vinyl flooring, damp mop with floor cleaner solution or special cleaner. See later section on hard-surface floors.
- Groom and freshen plants, if any.

Monthly

Set aside one day of the month in lieu of your weekly cleaning and add the following to your daily and weekly routine—or do one or two of these jobs each week, spreading them out over the month. We prefer setting aside one day and getting the job over with.

- Wipe windowsills on the outside.
- Vacuum carpets and rugs thoroughly. Move furniture and clean floors under and behind it.
- Clean windows inside, mirrors and glass of pictures with window cleaner.
- Dust tops and around books. Remove from shelves *only* for seasonal cleaning. Use vacuum cleaner attachment.
- Polish furniture, if necessary.
- Clean out and straighten any drawers, shelves, cabinets.

- Clean and polish metals—brass, copper, silver—if necessary.
- Spot-clean upholstery, if necessary.

Seasonal

- If necessary remove and clean or wash draperies, curtains.

  Caution: If curtains or draperies are subjected to hot sun it may be better to vacuum often and clean or wash as infrequently as possible since sun can weaken fiber so fabric disintegrates upon cleaning. There are new glass tints just on the market to prevent sun damage but they are still very expensive.
- Clean wood furniture according to gloss desired. Clean other furniture according to type. (See Index.)
- Clean carpets and rugs, if necessary. Reverse direction for equalizing wear.
- Clean and wax wood and/or hard-surface floors.
- Clean and wax vinyl, rubber, and smooth-surface flooring.
- Clean closets and cupboards.
- If you hang fresh curtains or draperies and use summer slipcovers, change as appropriate.

BEDROOMS

Daily

Supplies:
- Same as for living room.

- Air beds.
- Put away clothes, shoes, small articles.
- Collect all articles belonging in other rooms; soiled clothing.
- Collect trash in wastebasket; empty ash trays.
- Make beds. (See following section on bedmaking.)
- Dust furniture, windowsills, all surfaces, as necessary.
- Dust exposed floors with mop, as necessary.
- Vacuum rugs or carpets.

99

Weekly

In addition to daily supplies:
• Clean linen for beds.

• Straighten up as above.
• Remove bedding from beds.
• Change sheets and pillowcases. Make beds.
• Don't forget to wipe off perfume bottles and other containers.
• Clean and dust all surfaces.
• Wipe off smudges and fingerprints from walls and surfaces. Spray-clean telephone with disinfectant cleaner.
• Dust woodwork and baseboards.
• Dust exposed wood floors with the vacuum cleaner attachment or dry mop. Don't forget to dust or vacuum clean the closet floor occasionally. (By the way, keep the closet door closed while cleaning the bedroom to keep out excess dust.)
• Whisk curtains, draperies and window shades.
• Use whisk broom on upholstery.
• Wipe or brush lampshades, if necessary.
• Dust mop the floor or use floor attachment after vacuuming the rugs.
• Vacuum carpeting or area rugs. *Don't forget* to vacuum under the beds and dressers. Most vacuum cleaners will adjust low enough to slide under tight areas; however, some may not. If yours doesn't, move furniture from time to time.

Monthly

In addition to weekly routine:
• When beds are changed, vacuum or brush mattress and bed frame with upholstery attachment.
• For stuffed mattresses, turn end to end one month, side to side the next, turning completely over to distribute wear. (No need to turn foam rubber mattresses.) Vacuum box springs.
• Vacuum furniture with upholstery attachment.

- Vacuum curtains, draperies, window shades, blinds using drapery attachment.
- Vacuum walls, woodwork, paying special attention to corners and crevices.
- Straighten out drawers and closets.
- Clean windows inside and on the outside when necessary. (See directions for outside washing later in this chapter.)

How to Make a Bed

There are several methods for making beds. Many suggest the hospital technique of doing first one side then the other to save steps. Even though a few steps may be saved, we feel the following method is infinitely easier and more practical:

- Straighten mattress pad.
- Spread bottom sheet right side up with center crease in center of bed and wide hem at top. If you are using contour sheets, they virtually make themselves.
- Tuck in sheet at head and foot of bed.
- Make "hospital" or mitered corners on all four corners. Be sure sheet is smooth. To make "hospital" or mitered corners:

    1. Pick up edge of sheet about 15 inches from foot of bed. Lift up into diagonal fold; lay fold on mattress.
    2. Tuck the part of the sheet that is left hanging under the mattress.
    3. Drop the fold, pull smooth, tuck under mattress.
    4. Repeat for top of bed.

- Spread top sheet right side down with wide hem at top.
- Tuck sheet in at foot. Make mitered corners at foot only, to secure corners. Cover with blanket. Tuck in at foot, miter corners, and turn top sheet down over blanket.
- Plump up pillows and place at head of bed.
- Cover with bedspread.

Seasonal

- Remove everything that you are not going to leave in the room—blankets, quilts, curtains, slipcovers, pillows, etcetera, to be laundered, dry-cleaned or aired.
- Clean and rearrange contents of drawers.
- Clean closets (see Chapter Eight). Remove all clothing and other items. Wash walls, ceilings, and clean floors. Closets should be disinfected by adding a household disinfectant to the wash water or using an all-purpose disinfectant household cleanser. Follow by hanging a moth-preventive container or using moth crystals or balls.
- Take care of clothes. Separate into three piles: those to be laundered or dry-cleaned and stored; used currently; discarded or given away. See Chapter Eight for general storage of clothing and home furnishings; for mothproofing blankets, quilts to be stored, see Chapter Four.
- Clean or brush walls and ceiling.
- Wash windows inside and out and sills.
- Wash or clean window shades, blinds.
- Dry-clean, shampoo, or vacuum upholstery, if necessary.
- Clean and polish furniture.
- Clean rugs and carpeting.
- Clean exposed wood floors.
- Vacuum mattress box springs. Remove springs and clean bed frames. (See special section following.) Turn box spring end to end to distribute wear.
- Clean all other accessories, such as lampshades, etcetera.
- Polish or wash accessories and return these and all other items removed from room.

SPECIAL CARE FOR BEDS AND BEDDING

Mattresses

Protect these with a muslin, cotton, or plastic preshrunk, zipper-fastened cover which is easy to remove, launder and replace. Quilted mattress pads, which come in several different styles, should be used between the mattress and sheets for additional protection. Launder both the cover and mattress pad about every three months, giving the mattress itself a thorough cleaning at that time, if you have decided not to do it monthly. Use the upholstery attachment of the vacuum cleaner or a whisk broom. During the weekly change of bedding it is not necessary to remove the muslin cover if you wish to vacuum the mattress. But vacuum the pad, then remove it to vacuum the mattress with cover. Air and sun (set them near the window, if possible) periodically will help to freshen them. To clean soiled mattresses follow directions for upholstered furniture, given later in this chapter. To launder mattress pads, see Chapter Four.

Innerspring Mattresses—When an innerspring mattress is new it should be turned monthly. After six months, when the inside is firmly packed down, turning it every other month is sufficient. *Avoid* bending, rolling, or standing mattress on end, as this will damage the springs.

Foam Rubber and Latex Mattresses—Turning is unnecessary and rolling or bending it will not injure a foam rubber or latex mattress. However, foam rubber should never be exposed to the sun as this will dry it out, making it hard and brittle. A zipper-fastened cover may be removed for washing; a permanently attached one should be cleaned with the vacuum cleaner attachment. The mattress itself may be cleaned occasionally with the dusting brush attachment of the vacuum cleaner, although the "breathing" action of the mattress prevents such accumulation of dust. Foam rubber mattresses generally do not need washing. If extremely soiled, wipe with a damp cloth, but *do not allow to get wet*. It is slow drying.

Hair Mattresses—Turn at least once a month (some insist on a weekly turn for hair mattresses) from end to end and side to side. Follow general directions for cleaning and care.

Kapok Mattresses (related to the cotton family and silky in texture)—Turn frequently from end to end and side to side. Kapok mattresses should have frequent sunning to prevent deterioration. Follow general directions for cleaning and care. Do not wash. Raise window shades for sunning, if possible.

Mattress Repair and Restoration—If you wish to have a mattress restored, there are specialty shops that will do it, although it may be less expensive in the long run, and a lot less trouble, to buy a new one.

103

Springs and Bed Frames

Box Springs—Should be cleaned at least on the top and sides about once a month or every time the mattress is turned. Using the upholstery attachment of the vacuum cleaner, clean it more thoroughly on all sides during the seasonal cleaning or at least twice a year. The box spring, too, should be turned around at least twice a year to distribute wear.

Coil Springs—Should be dusted with the dusting brush attachment of the vacuum cleaner and wiped occasionally with a few drops of lemon oil for protection and to prevent squeaking. When cleaning a coil bedspring, try a long-handled dish mop that has been treated with a little furniture polish. You will find it does a good job of cleaning those hard-to-get-at places.

Dust bed frames thoroughly, being careful to get at corners and turns, with the dusting brush attachment of the vacuum cleaner. If the frame is metal, wash exposed areas as for painted metal furniture (see later section in this chapter).

Pillows

Fluff pillows daily and air them at least once a month near a window or outdoors. Pillows should be protected with a pillow cover slipped over the ticking and under the pillowcase. Wash these covers periodically, when they become soiled. Wash pillows every two or three years.

Feather and Down Pillows—They should be washed and restored every few years. Underneath a crisply laundered pillowcase are, all too often, crushed, lifeless feathers, dirt, soil, and dust! You may wash them at home (see Chapter Four) or send them to a commercial laundry, who will not only wash and recondition them, but will fill them with additional feathers at your request. Or you may buy feathers or down by the pound and refill them at home. To tell if a pillow needs reconditioning, lay it flat and press down the center with your hand. If it springs back, there is still life in it. If not, then it's time to do something about it.

Synthetic and Foam Rubber Pillows—Check manufacturer's

instructions first to see if they are washable. If so follow specific directions. Machine wash outer casings on *synthetic pillows*. To refresh and restore life to Dacron pillows, refluff several times yearly (remove washable cover) by tumbling in a dryer on regular heat setting for about 10 to 15 minutes. To launder foam rubber pillows, see Chapter Four.

Kapok Pillows—Do not machine wash or dry kapok pillows. Use dusting brush attachment of your vacuum cleaner.

For laundering blankets, bedspreads, bedding, see Index.

Nursery or Baby's Room

Follow same procedure as for cleaning of bedrooms, adding the following:

Weekly

- Clean the crib and mattresses with a damp sponge wrung out of a warm sudsy detergent solution to which a disinfectant has been added, or use a disinfectant household cleaner or spray with a disinfectant.
- Wash washable toys. As a general rule, babies should not be given toys that are not easily washed.

Monthly

- Clean other toys (particularly those used mostly for decoration) with a dry or powder cleaner or brush white cornmeal onto lightly soiled stuffed animals (remove from room to clean), then brush out.

  Caution: Be absolutely certain to remove every grain of commercial cleaner as it is very dangerous if inhaled. If you have doubts, throw toy away or use only cornmeal and vacuum with upholstery tool or open wand before returning.

Children's Bedrooms

Follow same procedure as for cleaning of bedrooms, adding the following:

105

Monthly

- Sort through toys, school supplies, collections. Cull and keep the essentials.
- Repair broken toys.
- Clean washable toys with a sponge wrung out of warm sudsy water.

Generally:

- Let the child be responsible for picking up his room after play, as soon as he is old enough—and start him on the idea when he's very young. Also let a child make his bed when he can manage—a little five-year-old youngster we know is very proud of her bedmaking skills.
- If you have a toy box, cabinets, and shelves and still have a toy overflow, there are bright-colored canvas and terry cloth bags for hanging on a wall or in a closet which make good catchalls for loose toys or may be used as a child's laundry bag.
- Shoes can be a problem with a child—somehow one of them always gets lost. A shoebag in a child's closet and a reminder to put them there will help.
- Hangers in a child's closet that are low enough for him to reach will encourage him to hang up his own clothes.
- Have an occasional "weeding out" of toys that have been outgrown and are old and broken. There are a few treasured possessions, such as a shabby old teddy bear, an armless doll, or a hairless Cuddles or Raggedy Ann worn out with loving, which a child won't want to (and shouldn't have to) part with, but if you let him participate in the "weeding out" he'll help you choose. Separate them into broken toys for throwing away and others that are still good but outgrown—these can be donated to organizations along with outgrown clothes.

CHILDREN'S PLAYROOMS

If your child has a large enough room, let him have a little place in it to call all his own—a playhouse or tent he can crawl into and hide his treasures in—a place so private that sometimes grownups aren't even allowed there. And let it be one place where he doesn't have to pick up his toys—after all, you can't see them.

Trash and clutter seem to accumulate at a rapid rate in playrooms. A *large* wastebasket can be a big help. One family we know uses a bright-colored plastic one with a swinging lid. Call it the "playroom litter basket" instead of a wastebasket.

Washable walls and resilient floors make cleanup easy.

Plenty of drawer storage, both large and deep, will be a big help, too.

BATHROOMS

If each person using the bathroom assumes his own responsibility for keeping it neat, the *daily* cleaning becomes much easier. Try and get everyone in your family who is old enough to wash out the bathtub, flush the toilet, put down the toilet seat, pull the shower curtain out to dry, put the soap back in its dish, hang up towels and washcloths. It is a good idea to keep the following supplies in the bathroom, out of children's reach:

scouring powder or cleanser	toilet tissue
liquid detergent	spray bathroom cleaner
toilet bowl cleaner	toilet bowl brush
household disinfectant	cellulose sponges
tile cleaner	packaged water softener
drain cleaner	rubber gloves

Daily

Supplies listed above, plus:
- A wet mop and a pail of hot water.
- All-purpose household cleaner.
- Vacuum cleaner (if you have carpeting).
- Window and glass cleaner.

- Open the windows.
- Remove trash and empty ash trays.
- Straighten towels; put up fresh ones, if necessary.

107

- Put soiled towels and linen in hamper.
- Replace items such as comb, brush, toothpaste, etcetera, to cabinet or wherever you keep them.
- Clean wash basin, tub, mirrors, faucets, toilet seat, and toilet bowl.
- If necessary, sweep rug or clean floor; replace bath mat and/or rug.

Weekly

Supplies:
- Same as for daily cleaning.

- Clean toilet bowl with a toilet bowl cleaner and/or disinfectant and brush. Wash top, bottom, seat, seat hinges, tank, and base (using an all-purpose household cleaner) with a cloth or sponge reserved for that purpose.
- Use a drain cleaner, if necessary, in sink and bathtub drain.
- Clean wash basin, fixtures, bathtub outside and inside, with household cleaner or scouring powder and damp sponge.
- Clean shower stall.
- Wipe off other accessories—scales, hampers, etcetera.
- Dust cabinets, tables, shelves, pictures.
- Damp mop floor.
- Vacuum carpet, if you have carpeting; shake or vacuum rug.
- Hang up clean towels, washcloths, bath mat.
- Empty trash and return wastebasket.
- Replace rug or carpet.

Monthly

- Clean tile or marble walls with an all-purpose household cleaner or a special tile and grout cleaner.
- Wash loose washable carpeting or throw rugs.
- Mop or scrub the floor; wax, if desired. (See section on care of ceramic tile floors later in this chapter.)
- Wash windows inside and outside if necessary.
- Clean out and edit medicine cabinet—throw out clutter.

Seasonal

- Wash and rehang shower curtain, if necessary.
- Remove and launder or clean curtains.
- Clean hamper with hot sudsy water to which a disinfectant has been added. Or wipe out with a damp sudsy sponge and spray with a disinfectant. Air in the sun, if possible.
- Clean venetian blinds or window shades.
- Clean medicine cabinets thoroughly and cull or throw out old medicines. Reorganize and replace all items you plan to keep. For information on when to discard medicine and drugs and special tips for storing them, see Chapter Ten.

Bathroom Tips

- To dispel any unpleasant odors in the bathroom, keep a spray deodorant within arm's reach, or keep a room deodorizer open on shelf. Or if you don't have small children, keep your matchbook collection in the bathroom in a handsome dish. Striking a match is like magic! Or burn a candle.
- To keep mirrors and sliding glass doors from fogging up when running bath water, fill the tub first with cold water, then add the hot water.
- When cleaning a medicine chest and a wash basin, a pastry board or tray comes in handy. Place it across the basin, so you can put the items from the shelves on it. You will avoid breakage and save steps.

Bathtub, Wash Basin and Fixtures—Use a cellulose sponge or scrub cloth with a tub and basin cleaner or a mild scouring powder or cleanser; a long-handled brush will save stooping when cleaning the bathtub. Rinse fixtures thoroughly and shine with soft, dry cloth.

To avoid bathtub rings (soap curd deposits), use a water conditioner in the bath water, unless you have a water-softening system.

Toilet Bowl and Toilet Brushes—Daily care is important. Use a disinfectant bowl cleaner or chlorine bleach and a long-handled toilet bowl brush, or one of those disposable toilet cleaner mops. Or insert a brightly colored cleaner-freshener into the tank, which dispenses automatically each time the toilet is flushed.

Drain Traps—After each use of the bathtub or wash basin, run some clean, very hot water down the drain. This carries off accumulated grease and leaves the trap full of clean water. Dirty water left in the traps may create an unpleasant odor. Always clean any lint and hair which has collected in the basin before turning on the water. These lead to clogged drains. Most drain stoppers are removable with modern plumbing fixtures. Simply pull them out, wipe away hairs and lint, then replace. Use a drain cleaner periodically as directed. Avoid overuse of drain cleaners.

Shower Stalls—The base and walls of the stall should be thoroughly cleaned at least once a week, or even oftener in hot, humid weather. Pay special attention to crevices or cracks which may collect soil and harbor fungus bacteria. Use a disinfectant.

Shower Curtains—Leave the curtains fully stretched out after each use. Let them dry completely, especially in the summer when mildew is apt to ruin fabrics that remain damp for any time. Shower curtains come in a variety of colors and are made from a variety of fabrics. Wash shower curtains in a washing machine, if possible. Many are machine washable, particularly since the newer machines are so flexible as to water temperature, agitation, and spin speed. For machine washable curtains, follow the directions on the label as well as those provided by your machine's manufacturer. Otherwise follow instructions given below.

Canvas or duck shower curtains are generally water-resistant and mildew-proof. Machine wash in hot water and detergent like any heavy cotton fabric. If mildewed, however, soak first in chlorine bleach according to directions on the container, rinse, then launder. See Chapter Four for how to control mildew. Iron damp with a hot iron.

Plastic or waterproof silk curtains should be placed on a smooth flat surface and sponged gently with lukewarm sudsy water. Be sure to squeeze the sponge dry before rubbing curtains. Rinse with clear lukewarm water and hang on curtain hooks to dry, or follow machine instructions for laundering automatically.

Wash rubber curtains in lukewarm sudsy water, using mild or light-duty detergent. Immerse and move gently in the sudsy water to clean, being careful not to rub or squeeze the fabric. Rinse in cold water and hang on shower curtain hooks to dry.

Wash rubberized fabric, water-resistant cotton, rayon, and silk curtains as you do rubber ones. Press cotton, rayon, or silk while damp with a warm iron, and hang on shower hooks to dry completely.

Bath Mats—Wash them often. Select your colors wisely, for if they are not color-fast you may end up with a lovely pink when you really wanted red. Wash brightly colored mats separately, unless labeled as color-fast.

Clothes Hamper—A hamper for soiled clothes is often kept in the bathroom, but wherever it is kept it should be cleaned thoroughly several times a year. Use an all-purpose disinfectant cleaner, either liquid or spray. Wash, rinse, and dry thoroughly. Leave open to let it air, preferably in the sun.

Bathroom Accessories

To Clean Combs, Brushes, Personal Items—Everyone in your household who is old enough should really take care of his personal grooming aids. Combs and brushes should be cleaned frequently, at least each time you wash your hair. Swish nylon or plastic brushes through warm mild sudsy water. For those with natural bristles, add a little ammonia to the sudsy water. Do the same thing for combs. As you clean the comb, run it through the bristles of the hairbrush and you'll do a faster job of cleaning each one. After washing brushes, rinse them thoroughly in clear cool water until all traces of suds have disappeared. Shake to remove water and dry, bristles down, being careful they don't mat.

You can believe it or not, but an occasional cleaning of your toothbrush is in order. Use warm sudsy mild soap and water solution and wipe handle with a clean cloth or sponge. Or soak

111

occasionally in warm water with a little baking soda added to keep it clean and in good condition.

All the new bathroom accessories that we have acquired recently are susceptible to dust. These include water jets for the teeth, electric toothbrushes, manicure sets, facial saunas, massagers, just to mention a few. Wipe them off with a sponge squeezed out of warm sudsy all-purpose detergent solution and a cotton swab to clean in and around corners. Rinse and wipe dry. Follow the specific use and care instructions for the accessories you own.

HALLS AND STAIRS

- Follow general instructions for cleaning living rooms.
- Check special information for stairs in relation to safety, Chapter Ten.
- Dust uncarpeted stairways and railings as often as necessary, using floor brush attachment of the vacuum cleaner or a dry mop and dust cloth.
- Vacuum stair carpeting with rug-cleaning attachment of vacuum cleaner at least once a week.

CLEANING ALMOST EVERYTHING ELSE

When we are equipped with facts and know-how, cleaning is easier and goes faster. Using the correct method for a specific job will save time and effort. It will, in fact, guarantee good results and your furnishings will look better and last longer. The old axiom "do it right the first time" pays big dividends in housekeeping.

DUSTING WALLS AND CEILINGS

Cobwebs are super dust collectors. If they are a problem, vacuum them away in seconds with the open wand of your vacuum cleaner. Do not wipe them off as the dust and grease they seem to collect will smear the walls. If you remove them with a long-handled object, use an upward-lifting motion, to avoid streaking the walls.

How to Dust:
- Use the dusting brush attachment of your vacuum cleaner as this is the best method of dusting without scattering dust. Or use a long-handled duster, one that is treated to hold the dust.
- Push your furniture aside. Cover it with a plastic sheet or an old sheet, if your ceiling and walls are especially dirty.
- Dust the ceiling first, then work from the top down, paying special attention to moldings and corners. Be sure to dust all woodwork, cornices, ledges, shelves, and around windows and doors.

WASHING PAINTED WALLS OR CEILINGS

Washable Flat Paint and Glossy Enamel—If you do a fairly good job of dusting your walls and ceilings periodically, chances are that they will seldom need to be washed. And if they do, our best advice is to have someone else do it. If this is not possible, the following suggestions will help you make this horrendous task a bit easier.

If the walls are slightly soiled around light switches, doorknobs, near room and closet entrances, etcetera, use an ordinary spray or liquid household cleaner as it comes from the container, following specific directions. A warm sudsy all-purpose detergent solution for very light soil is also effective.

If the walls are heavily soiled and you want to wash down a complete wall of one room, tackle the job when you feel as if you could "beat the world." You will find that stamina is an essential requirement. In addition to that, you will need:

- A wall brush or two cellulose sponges.
- Two pails, one for cleaning solution, the other for rinse water.
- All-purpose household cleaner or special paint or wall cleaner.
- A step stool or ladder.

Use a powdered all-purpose wall cleaner or a special paint cleaner as directed on the container. Special paint cleaners may be purchased at your grocery, supermarket, or hardware store.

113

Caution: Always clean a small area first in an inconspicuous place to determine how well the wall will accept the washing. Some paints, especially those applied with a thin coating, may rub off with hard pressure. Or the cleaner itself, if it is too harsh, may take some of the paint off as you clean.

Note: If you plan to wash the ceiling, do it first so as not to streak the walls.

To Wash Ceilings

- Cover the furniture.
- Be sure to squeeze sponge or wall brush as dry as possible to avoid dripping.
- Clean one section at a time, using a circular motion, letting the cleaned areas overlap to avoid rings or streaks.
- Rinse with clean water and wipe dry.

To Wash Walls

- Dust thoroughly.
- Follow directions for the specific cleaner you are using.
- Work from the bottom up. If dirty water runs down over the soiled wall, streaking occurs that is hard to remove, but if the walls have been washed first, there should be no streaking.
- Squeeze sponge or cloth as dry as possible and wipe one section at a time (no more than three square feet), using a circular motion.
- As you work, let the cleaned areas overlap, to avoid rings or streaks.
- Rinse with clear water and wipe the area dry.
- Be sure to change the water in both pails as it gets dirty.
  Tip: Wind a clean strip of old cloth or washcloth around your wrist and use a rubber band to hold it on. This will catch dripping water as you work.

Wall Coverings—Washable
(Soap or Detergent Method)

Washable wall coverings include *wallpaper* (which is either water-resistant or plastic-treated), *vinyl-coated,* or *vinyl-processed coverings.* All are washable, but some are easier than others. The vinyls are the hardiest and will take the most wear and tear. Paper labeled water-sensitive cannot be washed.

- Before you begin to wash any covered surface, test-wash an inconspicuous area to determine results.
- *For thin paper,* use a cellulose sponge squeezed out of clear lukewarm water. Do not use soap or detergent. Overlap strokes and lightly pat dry. Do not rub.
- *For heavier washable papers and wall coverings,* wash gently, using a cellulose sponge squeezed out of a luke-warm sudsy all-purpose detergent solution. Clean a small area at a time. Rub gently. Rinse with a sponge squeezed out of clear cool water. Pat dry with a clean cellulose sponge. An all-purpose household cleaner or spray cleaner also may be used on some heavy vinyl or plastic-coated papers. Follow specific directions, however.
  Caution: Avoid using hot water and harsh cleaners.

Nonwashable Wall Coverings (Dough-like Method)

- For nonwashable papers use a commercial dough-like cleaner. You can buy it in paint and hardware stores.
- Knead dough-like cleaner into a large ball and use it like a soft eraser, following the directions on the container.
- Use firm, long strokes, and as you work, fold soiled surface of "dough" to inside, exposing clean surface.

Lacquered Paper—If you have lacquered paper, ask the dealer what he recommends. (If you can't reach him, you might try using a sponge squeezed out of a lukewarm mild sudsy detergent solution. Try in an inconspicuous place first to determine results.

Special Wall Stains

Walls are vulnerable to all sorts of smudges, stains, and brush-ups. Here are some of the most common problems.

Grease Spots—Use one of the new spray-spot removers. Try a small area first to be sure it doesn't leave a ring and follow instructions carefully. Or apply a thin coating of paste made of fuller's earth, French chalk, or any other absorbent powder and cleaning fluid. Let it dry, then remove by brushing it with a soft

115

brush or cloth. Or, apply a clean blotter to the spot and press with a warm iron. Repeat until the spot disappears.

Crayon Marks—Children love to use walls for blackboards. For washable wallpaper, sponge lightly, using a soft cloth, with cleaning fluid. Do not rub. If cleaning fluid leaves a ring on nonwashable paper, try the absorbent powder paste for grease stains.

Ink—Apply fuller's earth, French chalk, or other white powder, such as whiting or cornstarch—anything colorless and absorbent. As soon as it absorbs, brush off immediately with a soft brush. Be careful not to smear it. For washable coverings, blot quickly with the corner of a blotter, being careful not to spread; then touch stain very lightly with chlorine bleach on a bit of absorbent paper. Don't rub; rinse with clear cold water.

Caution: Test this method first in an inconspicuous place.

Smudges and Pencil Marks—Use an art gum eraser and rub out spot lightly.

Food Stains—Brush off as quickly as possible and use same method as for grease stains.

Wall Covering in the Kitchen

If you like paper or wall covering in the kitchen you may have a pesky problem with spotting and staining in areas behind the sink and around the range. Use vinyl coverings that are washable, wallpaper that is plastic-coated or stain-resistant and wipable. If you already have a nonwashable paper, cover problem areas with transparent plastic or purchase special plastic guards specifically designed for this purpose.

Other Wall Coverings

Grass Cloth—Dust often, using dusting brush attachment of vacuum cleaner. For heavy soil use dough-like cleaner as for nonwashable coverings.

Linoleum, Vinyl or Cork—Clean with a lukewarm sudsy all-purpose detergent solution. Rinse with clear lukewarm water. Dry thoroughly. Use same wax prescribed for specific flooring (see Index).

Tile: Ceramic, Aluminum or Steel—Wash with a warm sudsy

all-purpose detergent solution. Rinse with a sponge wrung out of clear water and dry with soft cloth. If a soap buildup on *ceramic tile* walls in the bathtub and shower area is difficult to remove, use an all-purpose household cleaner or a special ceramic tile cleaner. Or try washing them with a cloth dipped in white vinegar. A white liquid wax, often used for kitchen cabinets, will also do a good job on tile walls and will help to keep dirt from becoming embedded in the grout. If the grouting has become stained, or if there are light rust marks or mildew, you may use a commercial "grout" cleaner or a scouring powder that contains bleach. Use carefully to avoid scratching tiles.

For *metal tiles* (aluminum and steel), polish according to manufacturer's instructions, or clean them with a white liquid appliance-type wax.

Wood-Paneled Walls and Woodwork

Varnished Woodwork and Paneled Walls—Dust often. For periodic cleaning, dust, then apply a coat of creamy wax. Or use one of those special cleaning products made for paneled walls. Many are available in spray containers.

Painted Woodwork and Paneled Walls—Follow the same directions for painted walls. After cleaning, apply a coating of liquid or paste wax, then polish. This will keep them from soiling as easily and will make them easier to clean the next time.

Unvarnished Wood with Open Grains (Oak, Chestnut, Walnut, Teak, Etcetera)—These require an oil finish. Treat them occasionally with equal parts of boiled linseed oil and turpentine. Mix together thoroughly and apply with a soft cloth. Or use a recommended commercial oil polish.

Shellacked Wood—Clean and polish with liquid wax.

Caution: Do not use water. It may turn the surface white.

Note: All woodwork, windowsills, cupboard doors, and wood surfaces exposed to heavy soil should be coated and polished with a liquid cleaning or cream wax after cleaning. This helps to preserve the finish and makes cleaning easier. When the surface becomes soiled, a new application of wax will clean it.

Tip: To make the job easier, work with two clean cloths. Saturate one with cleaning wax and apply to wood; then dry and

117

polish with the second cloth. If you can, using two hands will save time!

WINDOWS

Today, windows seem harder than ever to clean because of increased smog, soot, smoke, and grime. Inside, inadequate kitchen ventilation can cause problems. Yet, while windows get dirty faster, there are more ways to clean them. And easier, too!

If you live in a house with lots of windows or an apartment several stories above the ground, we hasten to make the same suggestion as we did for washing walls—have someone else do the outside if you can. Admittedly, it is much more expensive, since they usually charge by the window, but if you do a consistent job of cleaning the windows on the inside, as we have suggested in the outline for cleaning rooms, then you may be able to get by with washing the outsides only once or twice a year.

To clean windows indoors (and outside if they are accessible) it is easiest to use one of the *commercial cleaners:* spray and liquid cleaners with ammonia are the quickest and easiest. They do an excellent job and make light work of an otherwise messy job. Other types available include creams and powder cleaners. There are also specially treated disposable window glass cleaner cloths for quick touch-ups. Buy them in housewares departments or grocery stores. Also absorbent paper towels are excellent for achieving a high shine, as are crushed newspapers (a component in the news ink helps polish the windows).

To use a spray cleaner, you will need just the spray cleaner and some paper towels. First, spray the cleaner on, then wipe the pane clean, using absorbent paper toweling. Keep wiping until the pane is dry and glistening.

Make Your Own Window-Cleaning Solution

The familiar home remedies are certainly more economical, but do require some work in preparation. They include ammonia or vinegar and water. To make the solution, use 4 tablespoons of household ammonia or vinegar to 1 quart of warm water.

Window washing supplies:
- Two pails—one for cleaner and one for rinse water.
- Window-cleaning solution, as described above.
- Ladder or step-stool.
- Two sponges or cloths for washing and rinsing.
- Lintless cloth, paper towels, newspaper, a rubber squeegee, or chamois cloth for drying.

Wet a sponge, chamois, or soft lintless cloth with the cleaning solution. Wash one pane at a time. Next, use a clean damp cloth or sponge to rinse that part of the window the same way. Rinse water should also contain a little vinegar or denatured alcohol. Dry immediately with a rubber squeegee, chamois or absorbent paper toweling.

Tip: If you are washing windows both inside and out, wash them from one side to the other indoors. Then wash from top to bottom outdoors. This allows you to check for streaks and areas you may have overlooked.

Change both the wash water and rinse water as soon as they are dirty.

To use a rubber squeegee, hold firmly, press downward and wipe the edge after each stroke.

A Few Special Tips

- If you wash windows when the weather is freezing, use 2 tablespoons of glycerine (buy it from the drugstore) or ½ cup denatured alcohol in 2 quarts of warm wash water and the same for rinse water. This will keep the water from freezing.
- Use a cotton swab, dipped in the wash water, to clean out the corners of window frames.
- Avoid washing windows when the sun is shining directly on them. The warm sun dries the glass so quickly that it will look streaked. Believe it or not, cloudy days are especially good for washing windows.
- Use a hose to wet the windows outside before washing them. If they are not too dirty, all you have to do after hosing them down is wipe dry. The long-handled squeegees are the most convenient. A clean floor mop, or a special window brush dipped in cleaner, makes quick

work of cleaning windows outside. You can then hose to rinse and dry with a rag tied about the end of a mop.

- If you are building a new home or remodeling one, consider installing the new kind of windows that can be snapped out of their frames for washing. Others pivot from the middle so that you can wash both sides from the inside, and are also good choices.
- Never lean out of a window. Most windows can be washed by pushing the bottom half up, and pushing the top half down. If you live in a two-story house you can wash a few first-floor windows by standing on a ladder outside. Be careful! But never use a high ladder or let it lean against the glass.
- Before washing windows, pull down the shades and dust them on both sides. Don't forget to dust the window frames and sills.
- On the days you wash windows, consider doing the curtains, if necessary. Don't forget to clean the frames.
- To clean aluminum window frames, use steel wool pads or a special aluminum window cleaner which you can buy in a hardware store.
- Clean any small inside panes, such as those in French doors or old kitchen cabinets, with liquid spray cleaner.

WINDOW AND DOOR SCREENS

Many people simply vacuum occasionally and let it go at that, but if *you* want to really clean them, here is the way to do it.

The only way you can do a thorough job is to take the screens down (once a year is sufficient). It is a good idea to write a number in each window or door frame and write the same number on its screen. Put any screws or bolts in a bag and write the same number on it. You'll be glad you did when the season rolls around to put them back.

Dust mesh and frame with the dusting attachment of your vacuum cleaner or a brush and then *take outside to wash* if possible.

Supplies:
- A pail.
- Hot sudsy water.

- A hose.
- Several clean cloths.

- Fill pail with hot sudsy water.
- Lean screen against a wall, railing, or handy support and scrub both sides with a stiff brush dipped into the hot sudsy water.
- Hose down both sides of the screen with clean water.
- Let screen drip a little, then wipe with a clean cloth.
- Stand up to dry completely, in a breeze, if possible.

If washing screens indoors, follow same procedure as far as possible, using basement floor with a drain, bathtub, or washtub. Rinse by squeezing clean water out of a sponge or use a shampoo hose. Dry thoroughly.

Note: Before you put screens back, wash out the window or door grooves where the screens slide with a narrow brush or strip of cloth wrapped around a piece of wood. Or use the crevice tool attachment of vacuum cleaner to remove dust. Be sure to wash window and door frames and sills before putting in a clean screen. To store clean screens, put them in a dry, clean place. Cover with an old shower curtain or plastic tablecloth or one of the inexpensive plastic drop cloths sold in paint stores.

Copper wire screening may streak nearby surfaces. Aluminum screens cause less discoloration. Fiberglas screens will not cause streaks at all. Polish aluminum screens with a fine steel wool before you put them up. Paint steel frames every few years with metal paint to prevent rusting. Wipe out tracks of roll-up screens and wax them for easier maneuverability.

WINDOW SHADES

Regular dusting and an occasional spot-cleaning will satisfy most people. Always handle them gently when pulling up or down. Operate them often to keep them in top working order. Most shades are washable, except those made of paper.

Regular Care:
- Dust often, using a soft cloth or the dusting attachment of your vacuum cleaner. Pull all the way down and dust

121

both sides, especially at the top of the roller and the hem. If washable, wipe off fingermarks with a damp sponge and all-purpose household cleaner.

- If shade is not washable, it may be cleaned as for non-washable wallpaper.

To Wash:
Supplies:
- Large plastic drop cloth.
- Two cellulose sponges.
- Two pails—one for warm sudsy water, one for clean water.
- Two clean soft cloths for drying.

- Clear off a large table, preferably near a sink.
- Cover table with a plastic cloth or old shower curtain.
- Remove shade from window and unroll flat on the table or counter. Dust both sides.
- Use a cellulose sponge wrung out in warm sudsy water, rubbing lightly. Rinse with clear water, using as little water as possible. Take care not to wet the fabric too deeply.
- Wash a small section at a time and overlap the strokes.
- Wipe dry with a clean soft cloth.
- Turn and repeat on other side.
- If shade has a rough finish, scrub lightly with a soft brush.
- Roll up, tighten springs, and hang shade back in the window. Then, unroll and let dry completely. Do not dry in the sun. When thoroughly dry, roll back into position.
- Wash the pull cord in warm suds and rinse. Let it dry and put back on the shade.

Venetian Blinds

Regular Care:
- To dust, start by closing the blind and letting it hang all the way down.
- Dust both sides with the vacuum cleaner dusting brush or a special "pronged" venetian blind brush. You can also use a soft cloth.

To Wax-Clean:
- A satisfactory method of cleaning is to use a cleaner-wax which will be easy to apply and will leave a finish that will not soil quickly.

To Wash a Blind at the Window:
Supplies:
- Rubber gloves.
- Two sponges or cloths, one for washing, one for rinsing.
- Two pails—one for cleaner, one for clear water.
- Scrub brush.

- Use rubber gloves to protect your hands.
- Open the blind and let it hang all the way down. Wash slats with a sponge or cloth wrung out of a mixture of warm sudsy water or use an all-purpose household cleaner.
  Tip: Some have used a spray window cleaner successfully and find that it is faster. When cleaning windows, do the venetian blind at the same time, if you have time.
- Start at the top and wash one or two slats at a time. Fold the cloth or sponge around the slat and slide it from side to side; or cut halfway through a thick flat sponge and use it the same way. A pair of thick cotton work gloves are ideal, also.
- Rinse the slats the same way and wipe them dry.
- Scrub the tapes on both sides with a brush covered with thick suds or with an all-purpose household cleaner. Rinse them with a clean damp sponge or cloth.
  Tip: Touch up especially soiled areas on the tapes with white shoe polish.
- Wipe each pull cord with a folded sponge or cloth, first with suds or cleaner, then with clean water.
- Let the blind hang open and dropped all the way down until it is dry and the tapes are stretched smooth. Put old cloths or newspapers under it to catch any dripping water.
  Tip: To keep the tapes from puckering or shrinking, secure them at the top and bottom with adhesive-backed tape while drying.

123

To Wash a Blind in the Bathtub:
Supplies:
- An old shower curtain.
- Scrub brush.
- Sponge.
- Soap, detergent, or all-purpose household cleaner.

- Take the blind off the window and pull the cord so that the slats are open.
  Tip: To protect your tub, line it with an old shower curtain or a plastic drop cloth, being careful not to cover the drain.
- Fill the tub halfway with warm water.
- Add an all-purpose household cleaner or detergent and swish up suds.
- Put blind in the tub and spread it out. Wash both sides with a sponge or cloth. Scrub the tapes and cords with a sudsy brush.
- Drain the sudsy water out of the tub. If the blind was very dirty, start again with clean suds and wash a second time. Drain tub.
- Half-fill the tub with clean water to rinse away the dirt and suds. Repeat if necessary.
- Or, if there is a shower over the tub, turn it on and rinse the blind under the running water, or attach the hose of a shampoo spray to the bathtub faucet, and use this to rinse the blind.
- Leave the blind in the tub until it stops dripping. Then wipe with a cloth or towel.
- Put it back on the window and let it hang open and dropped all the way down until it is dry and the tapes are stretched smooth. Put old cloths or newspaper under it to catch any dripping water.
  Note: If you want to dry it outdoors you may need help in carrying it, since most blinds are very heavy. However, if you decide to, wait until the blind finishes dripping, then carry it outside in a dishpan or bucket to protect your floors. Hang over a clothesline, fence, or porch railing. When it is dry, put it back on the window. Our own feeling is that if you have enough energy to carry the blind out to dry, you might as well wash it outdoors, too.

To Wash Outdoors:
Additional supplies:
- A hose.

- Hang over a clothesline. If there are hooks on the side of the house or garage, you can hang the blind from them.
- Wash exactly as you would if the blind was on the windows.
- Rinse on both sides with a hose, or as you would at the window.
- Let dry outdoors. If still slightly damp when you put back on window, let it hang open and dropped all the way down until dry.

Other Shades and Blinds

Note: Do not wash any novelty shades unless directed to do so by the manufacturer. If they are vinyl-coated and guaranteed washable, follow specific instructions, if they are available. Be sure to ask the dealer, decorator, or company from whom the shades are purchased, if and how they are washable.

Bamboo Blinds—Should be dusted frequently with the dusting attachment of your vacuum cleaner. When they become heavily soiled wash both sides with a sponge dipped in warm sudsy water and rinse with clear water. Squeeze the sponge dry and rub blind gently. If you want to tackle a man-size job, you can take them outdoors and hose them down. Hang by the top to the clothesline and direct the spray of the hose through the slats. Do them on a day when they will dry quickly. When you rehang them, leave them rolled down until they are completely dry.

Awnings

Awnings made of canvas and similar material really cannot be cleaned effectively, but there are some tips that can help to guarantee longer life and improved appearance:

- Dry them thoroughly after a rainstorm. Do not raise them until completely dry. If they are up during a rainstorm, lower them to drain off water that has collected.

125

Water allowed to remain in the folds will cause staining and eventually rot the fabric.
- Store during the winter months in a cool, dry place.
- Awnings can be treated for mildew resistance with a special conditioner. Ask for it in the hardware store.
- Special "plastic-based" paints can be applied to awnings and outdoor fabrics that have faded and have become generally worn. Ask about them at your paint store.

Newer awnings made of synthetic materials and plastic are practically maintenance- and mildew-free. To clean, just hose down or follow specific instructions that came with your awning.

RADIATORS AND REGISTERS

One of the best ways to help keep dust and dirt to a minimum all over the house is to keep your radiators as clean as possible. Since heat carries dust and dirt upward, it deposits quickly on walls, ceiling, and woodwork. The radiator also works more efficiently if cleaned frequently. If you find that your room is not as warm as it should be, check the radiator first to see if dust has accumulated on the pipes.

- Clean radiators as often as possible with the crevice tool of your vacuum cleaner or a radiator brush. If once a week is asking too much (and we rather suspect it is), never let the job go longer than once a month.
- Place a dampened newspaper under the radiator (or a damp cloth on top and one on the floor) and brush the dust and dirt downward between the coils.

If you are planning to build in a radiator, or conceal it in some way, don't forget to make some provision for getting at it to clean and service when necessary.

Clean hot-air registers once a week for as long as they are in operation.

- Slip out the grating and put it on a dampened newspaper to keep dust from spreading.
- Clean with the dusting brush of your vacuum cleaner or any good household brush.

- Don't forget to clean the register opening before replacing the grate.

FIREPLACES

Fireplaces are to be enjoyed and a few ashes will not hurt anything if not allowed to accumulate to an unsightly degree. Brush the hearth daily or as often as possible. Empty the ashes as frequently as necessary. Keep a metal container nearby to dispose of hot ashes.

In large fireplaces you may want to leave a bed of ashes, since fires are easier to light and will burn better if built on ashes from the previous fire. Never use your fireplace as an incinerator for trash. Not only is it unsightly, but a fire hazard as well.

Removing Smoke Stains from Around Fireplace

- *Wash slate or tile* with an all-purpose household cleaner and rinse thoroughly.
- *Wash marble* with warm sudsy water, using a mild detergent. Rinse thoroughly. If marble is rough or scratched, buff with a putty powder (available in a paint store) on a damp cloth or use a felt buffing pad with an electric hand drill. If marble is particularly rough, you may need to sand it first with a fine sandpaper (000 or 0000), then buff it with a buffing pad.
- *Scour stone* surfaces with a scouring powder and a stiff brush. Or mix ½ cup of detergent with a quart of hot water. Add ½ pound powdered pumice stone and ½ cup household ammonia; mix thoroughly. Brush off as much excess smoky stain as possible with a stiff brush, then coat with the pumice solution and let it absorb for about a half hour. Scrub off and rinse thoroughly with warm water.
- *Clean brick* with a strong solution of washing soda (follow directions on package) or a mixture of warm water and an all-purpose household cleaner. Rinse thoroughly with clear warm water.
- *Clean painted brick* as painted walls.
- *Clean iron tools* and accessories with a cloth dipped in kerosene. Keep away from fire until totally dry. Ask also about commercial preparations recommended. If

127

they become rusty, scour first with a fine steel wool (000 or 0000), then treat with kerosene.

- *Clean brass andirons,* fender and tools with a metal or brass cleaner. If brass areas become fire-blackened or sticky with wood resins, you might try rubbing with a fine steel wool or a fine emery cloth. Polish afterward. For lacquered brass, see section on care of metals at the end of this chapter.
- *Check woodboxes* occasionally for insects and ants. Clean out frequently.
- *Iron tools* can be treated with heat-resistant paint. Ask paint dealer for advice.

MIRRORS, PICTURES, FRAMES

- Dust picture frames and don't forget to wipe off the backs and wall area. This helps to prevent wall soil around the picture, inevitable though it may be.
- Handle gilt picture frames gently. Clean periodically with a soft cloth moistened with a little dry-cleaning fluid. Rub gently, then pat dry. If desired, you may coat them ever so lightly with a soft cloth moistened with a little lemon oil, being careful not to touch the painting. Wipe dry.
- Use a window cleaner to wash mirrors and glass on pictures. Apply the window cleaner to the cloth, rather than spraying it directly on the picture glass or mirror. This is to protect valuable frames and to prevent the solution from running between frame and mirror or painting, causing possible damage to the picture underneath or to the mirror backing. Or clean with a sponge squeezed out of a lukewarm water and ammonia solution. Dry and polish with a lintless cloth, chamois, or paper toweling.
- Do not expose mirrors to direct sunlight or a concentrated source of heat, as the silvery backing may be harmed.

OIL PAINTINGS, WATERCOLORS, SCULPTURE

- It is best to leave valuable oil paintings in the care of a professional restorer, except for an occasional dusting. To dust, brush lightly with a very soft brush. Avoid any method of cleaning unless directed by a professional. No care at all is better than the wrong method used by an inexperienced person. Good housekeeping methods and well-controlled indoor ventilation can do more to protect fine objects of art than almost anything else.

- Watercolor paintings cannot be cleaned under any circumstances. If you have any questions about them, see a professional.
- To clean sculpture, dust very gently and follow the specific instructions given to you by the sculptor or gallery from whom it was purchased.

LAMPS

Bases

Regular Care:
- Dust lamp bases with a soft cloth or the dusting tool of your vacuum cleaner. Wipe off bulbs occasionally with a damp sponge to maintain adequate light. Be sure they are cool and lamp is disconnected before wiping off bulbs.
- Damp dust pottery, porcelain or metal bases with a sponge or cloth wrung out of clear warm water. Dry carefully with clean cloth.
- Clean glass or plastic bases with a window cleaner.
  Caution: Never immerse base in water as it will damage the wiring. Be sure base is totally dry before replacing on wood furniture.

Seasonal Care:
- Clean and wax wood bases as for wood furniture.
- Wash pottery or porcelain bases with a sponge or cloth wrung out in warm sudsy water and rinse with a clean damp one. Dry with clean cloth.
- Wash glass and plastic reflectors and globes in warm sudsy water. Rinse and dry carefully.
- Metal bases and fixtures may be polished following directions for specific metal. (See section at end of this chapter.) If they are lacquered, dust and wax occasionally with a cream wax. Polish to a luster with a soft cloth.

129

- Painted metal lamps (tole) should be dusted, then wiped with a sudsy sponge or soft cloth and rinsed with a clean damp one. Dry carefully.
- Crystal lamps and transparent plastic lamps can be cleaned with a window cleaner. If at all possible, try to clean the underside of clear plastic or crystal bases. A warm sudsy all-purpose detergent solution is also effective. Rinse with clear warm water using a soft cloth or sponge squeezed dry. A few drops of ammonia or vinegar in the rinse water will make transparent plastic and crystal fixtures sparkle.

Shades

Regular Care:
- Always remove cellophane wrapping from new shades as the heat will shrink the cellophane and warp the shade.
- Use a clean soft brush or dusting brush of your vacuum cleaner to dust the lampshade inside and outside.

Seasonal Care:
Fabric Shades—Silk, Rayon or Metallic Fiber:
> *Note:* Unless linen or cotton shades have been treated for shrink-resistance, have them dry-cleaned. Silk and rayon shades that are glued together should also be dry-cleaned. If shades are too fragile or if they are old and frayed, it may be worth your time and money to buy new ones instead of trying to clean them.

- Take off any nonwashable trim. If the cloth is glued to the frame, sew it on with thread of the same color. Then you will be able to wash it more satisfactorily. Test-wash in an inconspicuous place to determine results.
- Fill a deep pan, washtub, or bathtub with enough warm water to cover the shade. Add an all-purpose detergent and swish up a light solution.
- Rub any spots lightly with suds on a soft brush.
- Dip the shade up and down.
- As the water gets dirty, change to clean sudsy water. Repeat.
- Rinse by dipping up and down through two or three changes of clean water.

- Don't worry if the cloth stretches and sags while it is wet. It will tighten up for a snug fit when it gets dry. Shape as it dries.
- To dry a fabric shade, tie a string to the middle of the frame. Then hang it over the bathtub or from a clothesline outdoors. Do not hang in the sun. Or you can wipe the shade with a bath towel until it is almost dry. Or you can put it in a breeze or in front of a fan to dry. Fast drying is important to keep metal frames from rusting.
- If the lampshade has ruffles, "press" them with your fingers.

To Clean Plastic, Plastic-Coated, Laminated, Parchment, or Fiberglas Shades:

- Put ½ cup of detergent into a bowl. Add 2 cups of warm water just to moisten. Whip this mixture with an egg beater or an electric mixer to make stiff "dry" suds that look like whipped cream.
- Put some of the thick suds on a cloth or sponge. Use this to wash the shade, inside and outside. If the binding around the edge is glued on, don't rub it or let it get very wet. It may loosen.
- Rinse the shade right away by going over it with a clean damp sponge, then wipe dry.

Condition real parchment shades periodically with neat's-foot oil or castor oil to prevent leather from drying out. Clean imitation parchment shades periodically with a creamy wax.

Dust metallic shades. Remove an occasional smudge with a damp sponge. Dry quickly with a clean soft cloth. To clean paper shades, dust regularly. Condition metallic paper shades with a mixture of one part turpentine and ten parts mineral oil. Rub on shade gently with a clean soft cloth, then wipe dry.

LIGHT FIXTURES AND CHANDELIERS

If you don't have too many chandeliers (and we assume you don't these days), a window cleaner makes quick work of this pesky job. Cover one side with a large piece of plastic and spray toward that area, to keep spray from scattering. Wipe each piece carefully.

Or, the latest method is a spray cleaner formulated expressly to clean crystal chandeliers. You simply spray it onto the fixture—and that's it!

To clean a crystal chandelier in the more familiar tradition, take out all bulbs and set aside. Lay a folded towel over the bottom of sink or a pan. Fill half full with medium hot water. Add detergent and swish up suds. Fill a large pan with clear hot water and a little ammonia for rinsing. Also pad this pan with a towel, to keep glass from breaking. Remove crystal drops and saucers a few at a time. Wipe the frame or "arm" of the chandelier with a soft cloth wrung out of the sudsy water. Wash the parts in the sudsy water. Rinse and wipe dry. Then put crystal drops back right away to make sure that they go in the right places. If any pins or wire look weak or rusty, put in new ones. Repeat until the chandelier is all clean. Sponge off bulbs, rinse and wipe dry. Return them to the chandelier.

To Clean Light Fixtures:
- Be sure to turn off the current before cleaning.
- Clean any shades according to directions for lampshades.
- Dust the fixture itself with the dusting tool of your vacuum cleaner.
- Wash heavily soiled areas, globes, and bulbs with a damp sudsy sponge; rinse with a clean damp one and dry with a clean soft cloth.

CURTAINS AND DRAPERIES

Curtains and draperies can always be counted on to collect dust.

- Dust them frequently (once a month if possible) using the vacuum cleaner attachment.
- Work from top to bottom with firm but gentle strokes. If you do not have attachments, use a long-handled brush of medium stiffness, or shake them gently.
- For laundering, see Chapter Four.

Cornices and Valances

Clean cloth-covered boards as you do curtains and draperies above. Shampoo as for upholstered furniture or dry clean. If they are made of wood, treat as for wood finishes; if they are wallpaper, as for wallpaper.

Books

If you or your family are avid readers, no doubt you'll see to it that your books are kept clean. Even if they are there just for show, don't forget to clean them occasionally, as they are real dust collectors.

- Avoid crowding bookshelves; bindings are damaged easily that way.
- Stand books near the front ends of the shelf, allowing enough air circulation behind them so they can "breathe."
- For monthly dusting, use the dusting brush attachment of your vacuum cleaner, running it gently over the entire shelf of books, tops, backs, and sides.
- For seasonal cleaning (or once a year), remove each book from the shelf and dust each separately. Run the brush or cloth gently over the edges and cover of each book. Do not put the books back on the shelf until you have cleaned all the books on one shelf and have cleaned the shelf itself. Wipe it with a damp cloth and make sure it is dry before returning books.
- Never hit the books together to remove dust.
- Flip the pages to remove the dust from inside.

Special Care of Books

To condition leather books, start when they are new. Once a year (or year and a half) apply white petroleum jelly, lanolin, or saddle soap with a small piece of cheesecloth. Spread quickly and lightly over the leather being careful not to touch the end papers or pages.

133

- Mend torn pages with gummed tissue, rice paper, or onionskin.
- Secure loose pages with a piece of folded paper glued to the edge.
- When repairs have been made, protect the other pages by inserting a piece of wax paper until the mended places have dried.
- If pages are wrinkled, cover with a clean sheet of bond paper and press with a warm iron.
- Indoor environment and "weather" control are especially important to the long life of books and fine furnishings. Heat and humidity, if not controlled, can cause serious damage. Heat dries books out and takes the oil out of leather bindings; moisture causes mildew. Year-round air-conditioning is important to a good library.
- To prevent mildew, it is important that you control the humidity. Turn on the furnace or space heater and dry out the air if mildew is apparent.
- To remove mildew, try *one* of these methods:

    1. Wipe bindings and pages with a clean soft cloth.
    2. Wipe with a soft cloth slightly dampened with alcohol and spread the pages open.
    3. Sprinkle mildewed pages with cornstarch. Close pages for several days, then open and brush powder away. *Note:* If book is badly mildewed, you may not be able to renew it.

- Careless handling can be as damaging to books as poor atmospheric conditions. It is important to open a new book properly. Lay the book on its back and open a few pages at a time, first on one side then the other, until you reach the center of the book. Press lightly along the bound edge as you open the pages. This technique will prevent the back from breaking at the binding.
- Never use a book as a coaster!
- Never mark pages with pencils or other thick objects. Use a bookmark.
- For insect damage to books, see Index.
- Do not attempt to repair valuable books yourself. Seek professional advice. It is not a good idea to have a rare

book rebound, as its value depreciates if it is a first edition.

- To clean cloth bindings use an art gum eraser.

RECORDS

Some players have a built-in brush attached alongside the needle, which dusts the records automatically. If you do not have one of these, use a record brush regularly. The use of a static remover which you can purchase at the record store will help to reduce static, which attracts dust.

For additional information on music and record storage, see Chapter Eight.

- Store records in their wrappers. Stand them vertically.
- Do not leave them stacked in the player. Put them away immediately.
- Handle records by their edges. Fingermarks and oily smudges are harmful to them.
- Avoid excessive heat from heat sources and sun. Records may warp.
- Devise a system for indexing if you are an avid collector.

PIANOS

Large though it is, a piano is really a very delicate object. It must be handled carefully if it is to continue to give you long service and good tone. A piano should last a family for a lifetime of growing up, piano lessons, entertainment, and pleasure. Professionals say it should last for at least forty years.

- Like books, a piano is susceptible to temperature and humidity. If you are comfortable in a room, so is your piano. If you are too hot or too cold, adjust the temperature.
- Do not stand a piano near a window, or against an outside wall, unless you are reasonably sure your home is very well insulated.
- Avoid placing it near a radiator, register, or heat source of any kind. Too much heat will dry out the sounding

135

board. A humidifier, fish bowl, or open source of water can help to correct a room which is too dry.

- Extreme and abrupt changes of temperature will cause the wood parts to expand and contract. This makes the piano go out of tune.

To clean a piano:
- Dust lacquer finishes frequently with a clean soft cloth. Newer finishes are treated in such a way that home polishing is rarely necessary—in fact it is not recommended by many piano manufacturers.
- Clean varnished finishes by wiping with a dampened soft cloth, either cheesecloth or chamois. Dry with a clean soft cloth or chamois. Apply a light film of paste wax and buff with a soft polishing cloth.
- For old pianos, soiled from age and poor care, follow directions for wood furniture care.
- To clean keys, wipe them gently with a slightly dampened cloth (no soap or detergent, please). Dry thoroughly with a soft cloth. Be sure no moisture is left on the keys as it may loosen the ivory or plastic tops of the keys.

    Tip: To whiten *slightly* yellowed piano keys use a piece of flannel saturated with lemon juice. Badly yellowed keys can be removed and sent to the factory for scraping and repolishing.

  - New pianos should be tuned at least three or four times the first year, though they seldom are. After that, at least once a year is enough, unless you have a budding concert pianist in the house!
  - Have pianos professionally cleaned inside and out; check the mechanical parts; check for moth damage, though the felt on newer pianos is generally moth-proof. If not, treat with gum camphor or mothballs on the inside of the piano where it will not interfere with the action.
  - If you leave home for an extended period, place the camphor or mothballs as suggested above, where it will not affect the finish of any metal or wooden parts. Place newspapers inside carefully to absorb any moisture. Cover the tops with a soft blanket.

Organs

Follow the same instructions for pianos above.

FURNITURE CARE

Furniture, perhaps more than anything else, takes the brunt of everyday living. We set a glass down on a wood table without thinking or allow dust to accumulate without regard to the potential damage that casual treatment can cause. Of course we believe that rooms should be used and enjoyed, but a little care is important.

It is important to know at the outset that furniture requires three types of attention.

1. Dusting.
2. Creaming, polishing, or waxing.
3. Special treatment such as periodic cleaning or "washing" and repair of blemishes, scratches, etcetera.

It is also important to know just a little about how furniture is finished so that we can determine the correct method of care.

Dusting, of course, is something we do regularly, so it is good to determine the best method early on how to keep pieces in good condition. Dusting sometimes may be *dry* or *damp.* See section on techniques of dusting in the beginning part of this chapter, then check each type of furniture for its specific method of care.

Wood Furniture and Wood Laminates (Plastic)

How It Is Finished

Furniture care relates more to the finish applied to the wood and its appearance than to wood itself. These finishes can impart a high, shiny gloss or a smooth, dull patina. The kind of polish

137

you choose depends upon the luster you want. Finishes include *shellac, varnish, lacquer,* or *oil.*

Shellac, varnish, or *lacquer* may be polished to a very high mirrorlike finish or a low luster.

Surfaces which have a low luster with a *matte* or very dull appearance and a porous surface usually have an oil finish. Many modern and contemporary designs in furniture made of teak, rosewood, and even walnut have *oil-rubbed finishes.* Antique oak is also similarly treated.

Shellac is the high-luster finish usually applied to custom-made furniture. It is usually waxed, then finely polished, and is often referred to as a French hand-rubbed finish.

The *varnish* and *lacquer* finishes are less expensive and are used primarily on competitively priced furniture. The newer synthetic resin finishes are particularly resistant to heat, alcohol, and water.

Plastic laminates used widely for table and counter tops and wall paneling are virtually mar-proof and damage-resistant. Many furniture pieces are now given an entire wood-grained plastic veneer. They, too, may have a high or shiny gloss or a dull matte finish and can often pass for real wood.

SPECIAL NOTE: The finishes applied to contemporary furniture by manufacturers are as varied as those found on contemporary fabrics; often little is known about their performance and their care. Many of the newer wood finishes are difficult or impossible to identify and may be damaged by traditional cleaning methods and products. Therefore, if possible, get directions for the care of new furniture from the manufacturer or dealer. Otherwise, proceed with caution, first testing your polish or cleaner on an inconspicuous spot.

To Wax or Oil?

Even among the furniture experts there are many varying opinions on whether to oil or wax furniture. Some insist on linseed or lemon oil for all finishes; others insist on wax, either paste, liquid, or cream, followed by a buffing. Actually, there are so many excellent polishes on the market that clean and polish in one operation that furniture care often boils down to what seems easiest for you to use. You may wish to follow the guidelines for the gloss desired, on the following chart. Whatever your choice, make it and stick to it. Do not change from one polish to the other. Mixing oil with wax or silicones or using a wax on an oil finish may cause damage.

If you have antiques the use of paste wax, a fine furniture cream, or a cream wax is best. These are recommendations of some fine museums. If, on the other hand, your antiques have been oil-polished, stick to that method. In any case, consult with an authority on antiques for specific information as to regular care, polishing and refurbishing. See Bibliography at the back of this book for further reference to antiques.

Selecting the Correct Wax or Polish

In our opinion, the best protection for wood furniture is wax (either a liquid, cream, or paste), unless it has an oil-rubbed finish. To achieve a high luster and gloss and provide maximum protection, of course, *paste* wax is the best, but it requires the most work. It should be applied once or twice a year and buffed immediately following application. Regular dusting and hand buffing between waxing should help maintain a shine. A *liquid* or *creamy wax* is easier to apply and it too provides excellent protection.

Spray or self-polishing waxes are the quickest to apply. Many of these, however, contain silicones which, while helping to bolster their protective quality, may have a tendency to build up if not rubbed in thoroughly.

Cream waxes or polish are excellent for surfaces that have a low luster. May be used on teak or rosewood.

Boiled linseed oil or lemon oil are the best for oil-rubbed surfaces, such as teak or rosewood. Some people, however, may prefer to use the creamy polish described above. It won't really harm the surface, but it may produce an unwanted shine. There are cleaners or foams designed especially for these oil-rubbed finishes.

After considerable research, and tests of our own, here are our suggestions as to which polishes to choose and how to use them:

SURFACE FINISH	CARE (IN ORDER OF PREFERENCE)
Wood—Shiny Gloss (*Non-oil-base wax or polish*)	*Paste Wax*—Harder to apply but provides maximum protection. Requires rubbing and buffing. Apply once or twice a year, following container directions. Dust regularly with a soft, lintless cloth. (Examples: Butcher's, Johnson's, Goddard's Cabinet Makers' Wax.) *Liquid Wax*—Easier to apply. Provides adequate protection, but not as much as paste wax. Requires little rubbing. Cleans and waxes. Apply about three times a year. Dust regularly with a soft lintless cloth. (Example: Pride.) *Spray or Self-polishing Wax*—Convenient, easy to use, excellent for quick cleanups. Cleans and waxes in one operation. Contains silicones to provide extra protection. May need to be removed occasionally if they build up. (Examples: Pledge, Simoniz.)
Wood—Low Luster (*or for regular care of all furniture if you prefer, regardless of gloss*) (*Non-abrasive, non-oil wax or polish*)	*Creamy Wax or Polish*—Apply about two or three times yearly. Dust regularly with a soft lintless cloth. (Examples: Johnson's Cream Polish, Weiman's Furniture Cream, Hagerty's Vernax, Goddard's Cabinet Makers' Polish [aerosol].)
Antiques (*See also Index for other references*)	*Paste Wax*—(See instructions above for wood—shiny gloss.) *Furniture Cream or Polish*—(See instruction above for wood—low luster.) *Boiled Linseed Oil*—If antiques have been oiled for years, continue to do it.
Wood—Painted or Antiqued (*Non-oil base*)	*Creamy Wax*—Apply about two or three times yearly. Dust regularly with a soft lintless cloth. Clean or dust occasionally with a dampened sponge.

	Dry quickly and thoroughly. (Examples: Johnson's Cream Polish, Parker's Perfect Polish.)
Wood—Lacquered (*Non-oil base*)	Follow manufacturer's directions. Or damp dust and wipe dry with a clean soft cloth. *If a dull finish,* use a creamy wax and follow directions above for painted or antiqued finishes. (Examples: Johnson's Cream Polish, Parker's Perfect Polish.) *If shiny,* use a liquid wax. (See instructions above for wood—shiny gloss.)
Wood—Oil-rubbed, Porous (*Never wax*)	*Special Oil Polishes or Foam*—Designed expressly for oil-rubbed finishes. *Boiled Linseed Oil.* Buy it in a hardware store or use *lemon oil.* Apply twice yearly. Dust regularly with dry soft cloth or a treated duster.* Damp dust occasionally with a dampened sponge. Dry quickly. (Examples: Sani-Wax Lemon Oil Polish, Trewax Lemon Oil Creme, Wilbert Dri-Finish Lemon Oil.) *Commercially purchased treated dusters* usually contain oil. Do not use on any surfaces which have been waxed as it will make them gummy or sticky. Use *Creamy Polish or Special Teak Cleaner.* Use one of the creamy type polishes or a preparation made specifically for oil-rubbed finishes.

* *Treated duster.* You may buy these in a hardware store or make some of your own using the following recipe: 2 cups hot water, ½ cup lemon oil. Mix together and dip cloths into the solution. Squeeze thoroughly and dry. Store in a covered metal can.

141

Laminated Plastic —High Gloss	Wipe or damp dust with a dampened sponge. To clean spots, dirt, smudges, etcetera, use a dampened sponge wrung out in warm sudsy water. Rinse and wipe dry. Clean and wax occasionally with a liquid wax.
Laminated Plastic —Matte Finish	Same as above only use a creamy wax or polish or cleaner recommended by manufacturer.

Waxing or Polishing Furniture

Remove the old coat of wax, if necessary, by cleaning or "washing." See below. Follow the chart to determine the types of wax to use. Then follow the manufacturer's directions.

Regardless of the kind of polish you choose, these few guidelines are important:

- In general, polish or wax about three times a year.
- Use polish sparingly and apply with a clean, soft cloth.
- Follow the specific directions for the polish you are using.
- Always rub with the grain of the wood until all of it is absorbed and you have achieved the gloss desired.
- Rub periodically between polishings to revive luster.

Caution: Unabsorbed polish will collect dust and scratch the surface. To test, run your finger over the surface. It should leave no trace.

Cleaning or "Washing" Furniture

With the newer self-cleaning waxes, it should not be necessary to "wash" or clean your furniture. However, some waxes and polishes tend to gradually build up until a thick film is left on the furniture surfaces. Additional waxing can add to this residue and you wind up polishing the old wax instead of the finish. The thick film streaks, smudges, hides the beauty of the wood. If this happens, "wash" your furniture.

One of the easiest methods we know is to use a white liquid wax (which contains solvents). The type that you use in the kitchen on your appliances is excellent.

Take a clean cloth and dip it in cold water, wringing it as dry as possible. Then fold it into a pad to fit the hand. Shake the wax thoroughly and pour a little on the pad (never on the furniture), working it into the cloth. Apply a light, even coat in a circular washing motion to a small area. While the wax is still slightly moist, polish with a dry cloth, in this way working around the surface.

You can also purchase a special wax remover and cleaner especially for furniture.

Another good method that can be used to thoroughly clean furniture is to wash it with a good household dry-cleaning naphtha or mineral spirits. Fold a soft cloth to fit your hand and then saturate the cloth with a generous amount of the solvent. Work the saturated cloth around the furniture in a circular washing motion cleaning the surface thoroughly. Wipe off with a dry cloth. Use plenty of solvent and plenty of clean cloths to wash and wipe. Because cleaning solvents are flammable, be sure to observe the manufacturer's cautions. Guard against all possible fire hazards and don't smoke or operate electrical appliances during or immediately after use.

Some furniture experts recommend cleaning your furniture with *warm sudsy water*. We have found that this really will not do much to remove a heavy wax or oil buildup and it could soften the finish if you don't work quickly. We would recommend this method only for the very oldest and finest of *antiques,* or to remove grime or encrusted soil from any furniture surface. When using this method, work quickly and dry thoroughly so as not to let water stand on the surface. To do so may harm the finish. In the case of antiques, do check with a restorer as to specific recommendations.

You can purchase "furniture soaps" designed especially for furniture washing.

To Wash with Water:
- Use warm sudsy water. Dip a cellulose sponge (soft toweling is also excellent) in the sudsy water, squeeze dry.

143

- Wash a section at a time, rinsing the cloth or sponge often; dry thoroughly with a clean soft cloth. Then polish according to furniture finish.

FIRST AID FOR FURNITURE

When wood furniture accumulates scratches and other blemishes, some say only complete refinishing can be guaranteed to restore the original appearance. Before going to the expense of a professional job, or before starting such a big do-it-yourself project, try some first aid. These treatments have been recommended by professional restorers and other furniture authorities. Remember that there are so many different types of finishes that no one remedy can work for every problem.

Caution: For *repairing antiques* always check with a professional.

Note: You can buy some excellent furniture touch-up kits which can be handy in case of emergencies.

Minor Scratches and Blemishes

When the blemish has not penetrated the finish on the wood, an extra application of your regular polish will sometimes hide the mark. If not, try applying a paste wax with 3/0 or 4/0 steel wool (000 or 0000), rubbing gently with the grain; then polish. If the blemish still shows, here are some other tips to try, but first remove wax (which prevents absorption of coloring matter) by rubbing the area with a cloth saturated with naphtha, then wipe dry with a clean cloth. To remove blemishes:

Nut Meats, Linseed Oil—The oil from a Brazil nut or walnut (black, preferably) may provide enough coloring to hide a minor scratch. Break the nut meat in half and rub well into the blemish. Rubbing the mark with linseed oil may help, also, but *don't use crude oil—this could soften the finish on the wood.*

Coloring Crayon, Wax Sticks—Try coloring the blemish with brown crayon. Or use wax sticks—these are made especially for furniture in wood tones. They are softer than ordinary crayon and easier to work with. Fill the scratch with wax and rub in well with your finger. Wipe with a soft, dry cloth.

Shoe Polish—Use a paste shoe polish in the brown shade for walnut, the cordovan shade for mahogany, and the tan shade for light finishes. Apply with a cotton-tipped toothpick, rubbing carefully on the blemish; then buff dry. If the color is darker than the wood tone, erase with naphtha. Black paste shoe polish can be used to touch up scratches on black lacquered wood. Remember that the polish will provide a shine when it is buffed, so the repaired area could be noticeable if the furniture has a dull finish.

Iodine—To conceal scratches on red-finished mahogany, use new iodine; for brown or cherry mahogany, iodine that has turned dark brown with age. For maple, dilute iodine about 50 percent with denatured alcohol.

Rottenstone and Oil—Get an ounce of rottenstone from a paint or hardware store and keep it in an old salt shaker. Put a few drops of lubricating or salad oil on the blemish and shake on some rottenstone—enough to make a paste. Rub briskly with the grain of the wood, using a clean, soft cloth. Wipe frequently in order to compare and match the gloss of the damaged area with the original finish.

Medium Scratches and Blemishes

When damage is too conspicuous to be hidden by simple remedies, try this more professional method. First clean the area with naphtha to remove all wax or oil.

Caution: Check first with a professional before repairing antiques.

Step 1—Stain. Get ¼ pint oil stain of the proper color. Don't use spirit stain; this could soften the finish on the wood. For light wood dilute ¼ teaspoon stain with a few drops of naphtha or turpentine—mix in the cover of the stain can. Apply with a small brush or cotton-tipped toothpick, wiping with a cloth and reapplying until stain matches the original finish. Let dry at least 12 hours.

Step 2—Seal. Fill scratch with white or orange shellac to seal in the stain, using a toothpick or fine watercolor brush. (On some maple, orange shellac will match the shade of the wood and Step 1 can be eliminated.) Let dry at least four hours. Repeat until scratch is filled, allowing four-hour drying time between treatments.

145

Step 3—Sand. To even off the surface, sand with very fine sandpaper (8/0). Rub lightly with the grain of the wood until the scratch is even with the finish.

Step 4—Rub Down. Finish by rubbing with rottenstone and oil, as described in the preceding section. Use paste wax for final polish and subsequent protection.

Note: If there is any doubt in your mind, consult a professional furniture repair service.

Cigarette Burns, Severe Burns, and Blemishes

The deeper the damage on wood finishes, the more difficult the treatment. The following method requires care and patience, but it may save complete refinishing by a professional.

Step 1—Clean. Scrape the blemish clean with a sharp knife or razor blade (taped for safe handling). Remove all loose dirt or charred wood, and clean with naphtha on a cotton-tipped toothpick.

Step 2—Prepare. Smooth damaged area with 3/0 steel wool wrapped around the point of a wooden skewer or orange stick. Clean as before. Then rub with the grain of the wood, using 6/0 or 7/0 sandpaper or fine emery board.

Step 3—Stain. Follow directions in Step 1 under Medium Scratches and Blemishes.

Step 4—Fill. Fill damaged area with stick shellac to match wood finish. (This is preferred to plastic wood, which may damage lacquer.) Heat spatula with alcohol flame or electric burner. Do not use gas or candle; soot may discolor shellac. Have the blade just hot enough to melt shellac. Scrape off a bit and press into the blemish with the edge of the blade. Repeat until filled.

Step 5—Level. Heat blade of spatula, wipe it clean, and scrape across patch to level. Shave off excess shellac with razor blade.

Steps 6 and 7—Sand and Rub Down. Follow Steps 3 and 4 under Medium Scratches and Blemishes.

White Spots and Rings

Many white spots or rings on wood furniture can be removed, but the success of the treatment depends on the amount of damage and the cause. Try these tips:

- Rub a little mayonnaise on the ring. *OR*
- Rub blemish with cigarette or cigar ashes, using cloth dipped in liquid wax, lubricating oil, vegetable shortening, lard, or salad oil. Wipe off immediately and re-wax. *OR*
- Rub rottenstone or table salt on blemish with cloth dipped in any of the lubricants listed above. *OR*
- For varnish or shellac (do not use on lacquer)—dampen cloth with spirits of camphor or essence of peppermint and daub on spot. Do not wipe; let dry undisturbed at least 30 minutes. Rub down with rottenstone and oil. *OR*
- With a cloth, rub on a thick paste of powdered pumice and linseed oil. Use cloth wet with naphtha to wipe surface often for inspection. Finish with rubdown of rottenstone and oil.

Alcohol Spots

Perfumes, medicines and beverages containing alcohol can quickly cause irreparable damage because alcohol has a tendency to dissolve any finish. Always wipe up spills as quickly as possible. If the finish has been protected with wax, there may be no spot. If there is one, try these suggestions:

- Rub with finger dipped in liquid wax, paste wax, silver polish, linseed oil, or moistened cigar ash. Rewax. *OR*
- On some finishes a quick application of ammonia will do the trick. Put a few drops on a damp cloth and rub the spot. Follow immediately with an application of wax. *OR*
- For alcohol spots on which treatment has been delayed, a more complicated remedy, with rottenstone, is necessary. Mix rottenstone into a creamy paste with a few drops of linseed oil or salad oil. Apply the paste to the spot with a soft cloth, rubbing the grain of the wood. If necessary, substitute powdered pumice for rottenstone. (Pumice is a harder abrasive.) Finish with rottenstone treatment.

Heat Marks

White blemishes caused by heat are usually very difficult to remove without complete refinishing. If the damage has not penetrated too deeply into the finish, the following suggestions may prove effective:

- Stroke spot lightly with cloth moistened with camphorated oil. Do not use a linty cloth as fuzz may stick to the wood. Wipe immediately with a clean cloth. If rough, rub with 3/0 steel wool dipped in paste wax or lubricating oil. *OR*
- Try rottenstone and oil treatment, as described in the preceding. *OR*
- Salt and salad oil.

Bloom or Fog

When the humidity is high, glazed finishes often look gray or "fuzzy." First, try removing fog with an application of the furniture polish you use regularly. If that does not remove it, try a mixture of one tablespoon of cider vinegar to one quart of water. Moisten a soft cloth, squeeze dry, rub, wipe dry, then polish.

Water Marks

Marks or rings from wet glasses, vases or plants are common on tables, especially if these surfaces have not been waxed. Wax cannot prevent damage when liquids are allowed to stand on the finish indefinitely. However, it will keep them from being absorbed immediately, thus giving you time to wipe up the liquid before it damages the finish. If water marks appear, here are some tips to try:

- Apply paste wax with 3/0 steel wool. *OR*
- Place a clean, thick blotter over the ring and press with a warm (not hot) iron. Repeat until ring disappears. *OR*
- Try rottenstone and oil treatment. *OR*

- Try camphorated oil (see Heat Marks section, preceding).

Ink Stains

If the finish is worn or damaged so unsealed wood is exposed, ink stain will penetrate deeply and will be almost impossible to remove. When finish has been protected with wax, ink often can be blotted up immediately without leaving a spot. If a mark does show, try the following:

- A white liquid cream wax often does a remarkable job of removing spots which remain after ink has been thoroughly blotted. Apply according to directions on container. *OR*
- Pat spot with damp cloth. Do not rub but keep turning cloth to a clean area. Repeat as many times as necessary. *OR*
- Rub down with rottenstone and oil.

Paint Stains

- If the paint is fresh, remove with a cloth saturated with liquid self-polishing wax or rub with 3/0 steel wool dipped in liquid polishing wax.
- For old paint stains, cover spots with linseed oil and let stand until paint is softened. Wipe with cloth wet with linseed oil. Remove remaining paint with rottenstone and oil.

Nail Polish Stains

If surface has been waxed, polish may not have penetrated into the finish. Try rubbing with fine (3/0) steel wool dipped in liquid wax.

Candle Wax

Scrape up as much as you can carefully using your fingernails, a stiff card or very blunt blade, such as a plastic spatula. Polish or rub the remaining wax into the surface with a soft clean cloth.

Milk Spots

When milk or foods containing milk or cream (ice cream, custard, etcetera) are allowed to remain on furniture, the effect of the lactic acid is like that of a mild paint or varnish remover. Therefore, always wipe up this spilled food as quickly as possible. If spots show, clean with a white liquid wax. Then follow the tips under Alcohol Spots section.

Yellow Spots on Light Wood

The aging of bleached or blond furniture is accompanied by a change in color. With time, the chemicals used to bleach out the natural wood color begin to lose their effect. The wood darkens so gradually you are not aware of it until you purchase a new piece of the same shade. When light furniture is exposed to direct sunlight, however, the change may occur in just a few days and could result in ugly yellow spots. Nothing can be done to remove these yellow spots or change of color.

Checking or Cracking

These very fine "cracks" which cross each other over the entire surface are usually caused from excessive drying, lack of proper humidity, or long exposure to sunlight and heat. Without completely refinishing, this situation cannot be corrected. Polishing it with a wax similar to the wood finish can help its appearance.

UPHOLSTERED FURNITURE

The best method for cleaning upholstered furniture is "preventive" cleaning. If upholstered pieces are not kept clean, dust and soil eventually seep into the fabric and stuffing, and encourage fibers to disintegrate.

Protective Finishes

Many of the newer fabrics are treated with protective finishes. If they are not, you can either have the fabric treated before sewing by companies who do just that (ask your dealer or decorator about it) or you can spray finished pieces with soil-resistant finishes available at hardware stores or supermarkets. Treated fabrics resist soil and stay cleaner longer than untreated ones, though they are not soil-proof and should be cared for properly.

Regular Care of Upholstered Furniture

It is a good idea to brush all exposed areas with an upholstery brush or whisk broom. For more thorough cleaning, remove cushions and clean on all sides with the upholstery attachment of the vacuum cleaner. If they are down-filled, be careful that the suction does not pull the down through the fabric. The dusting attachment should be used for all napped fabrics (velvets, velours, etcetera) and the upholstery nozzle for smoother fabrics.

- Move the nozzle slowly over the entire surface of the chair or sofa. Don't forget to clean the backs and the fabric areas underneath.
- Use the crevice tool to clean all crevices and hard-to-get-at areas such as tufted surfaces and welted areas.
- Replace the cushions.
  Caution: Remove spots and stains as soon as possible after they occur. See below.

Spot and Stain Removal from Upholstered Furniture

Frequent spot and stain removal as these occur will help to prolong the necessity for complete shampooing.

Always dust the furniture before removing stains. In general, keep in mind that:

- Absorbent powders remove fresh grease spots.
- Dry-cleaning fluids remove greasy soil. (If there is a layer of soil over the entire surface it might be best to dry-clean the entire piece.)
- Detergent and water solutions remove most food spills. (See General Stain Removal section.)

151

Always test the fabrics for color-fastness.

Caution: Never use dry-cleaning fluids on furniture padded with foam rubber, as they will soften and damage the rubber.

Stains from freshly spilled food can often be removed with a warm sudsy water made from one part light-duty detergent and four parts warm water, or a commercial shampoo product, described below. Apply sparingly with a soft cloth or sponge, using a clean section for each application. Work from the outside of the stain toward the center to avoid spreading it. Rinse with a sponge or cloth wrung dry from clean warm water.

Selecting a Cleaner

The product you choose is dependent upon the kind of upholstery to be cleaned. In general a light-duty detergent mixed with warm water is suitable for most fabrics. Avoid the use of a soap or soap jelly. Soap is harder to rinse, and if used with hard water, it could form a sticky film which will attract and hold soil and dirt. There are also excellent commercial cleaners on the market, but make sure you buy the type that is recommended for the upholstery you want to clean. Below is a chart listing the upholstery material and the recommended cleaner. Use it as a guide.

FABRIC	CLEANER
Cotton and synthetic fibers	Detergent or commercial cleaner for general upholstery cleaning. (All-purpose detergents are efficient soil removers, but may dull colors.)
Silk and wool	Light-duty detergent or commercial cleaner made for these fibers.
Leather	Saddle soap and leather conditioner.
Plastics	Detergent and water solution.
Fabrics over foam rubber	Foamy or liquid cleaner. Never use spirit-solvent cleaning fluids, as they damage rubber padding.

General Directions for Shampooing

If you have cleaned and dusted your upholstered furniture regularly, shampooing may not be necessary for a long time.

A few cautions are in order before you begin shampooing. Some fabrics may not be color-fast; others may have glued-on trim which could be removed by the moisture from shampooing. Shrinkage could be a problem with some fabrics. It is a good idea to test the fabric in an inconspicuous area first to determine its washability.

If your fabric is velvet or a similar pile fabric, or if it is extremely fragile, *do not shampoo it yourself.* This requires professional care.

There are three do-it-yourself methods:

1. Home and commercial foam
2. Dry-cleaning fluid
3. Powder

Whichever shampoo you select, use as little moisture as possible to avoid wetting the furniture padding. You should actually be cleaning only the top side of the fabric. Always pay particular attention to the back and armrests and areas where greasy soil from hair and skin settles. Try to wash your furniture evenly so it will be evenly clean. Dry it as quickly as possible, though it could feel damp for 12 to 15 hours after cleaning, depending upon your indoor conditions.

Commercial Foam Cleaners—You can buy commercially prepared foam or liquid shampoo cleaners which you may find more convenient than making your own suds. Look for them in the supermarket, hardware store, or housewares department. Follow the directions exactly for the particular cleaner you have chosen.

Foam Method—Before washing vacuum the upholstery thoroughly as directed in regular care.

You will need:

A bowl or pan for thick suds	An eggbeater or electric
A bowl or pan for rinse water	mixer
	Soft cloths for rinsing

A sponge or soft brush   Soft cloths for drying
A rubber or plastic scraper Light-duty detergent
 or a metal spatula

RECIPE

1 cup of light-duty detergent 1 quart of warm water
Mix detergent and water together and beat it into a stiff
lather with a hand mixer or eggbeater until all liquid has
disappeared. Beat again as often as foam disappears during
use.

- With a cellulose sponge or soft brush, using a circular
  motion, apply suds evenly to fabric doing a small area
  at a time. Be careful not to get filling too damp.
   Note: If fabric is a sturdy one, you may use a stiffer
  brush for better cleaning power.
- When the lather begins to look soiled, scrape off suds
  with a rubber spatula and drop on a newspaper. Repeat
  suds cleaning if chair or sofa is heavily soiled. Wipe
  away excess suds with a clean sponge dipped in clear
  lukewarm water and wrung dry.
- Repeat process, overlapping previously cleaned areas,
  changing rinse water as often as necessary.
   Caution: Use only *clean suds, clean water,* and *clean
  sponges* or *cloths.*
- Hasten drying by using an electric fan. Do not use furniture until it is completely dry.
- If greasy spots remain, sponge with cleaning fluid.
- If furniture has a hazy or dull appearance after cleaning,
  brush thoroughly or use dusting attachment of vacuum
  cleaner.

Dry-Cleaning Method

If you feel that your fabric is not color-fast, cleaning with a
dry-cleaner which contains cleaning fluids may be your best
method. There are several on the market. Look for them where
household supplies are sold.

Follow this procedure:

You will need:
- A dry-cleaner or naphtha (follow directions on the container and observe warnings).
- Several pieces of clean turkish toweling.
- A container for the solution.

- Open all windows or move piece of furniture outdoors. Observe label directions carefully.
- Dust thoroughly with the vacuum cleaner attachment.
- Take a piece of clean turkish toweling and dip into dry-cleaning solution. Wring almost dry.
- Using a circular motion, clean a small area at a time, rinsing and wringing the cloth dry each time it becomes soiled. Overlap cleaned areas as you complete the entire surface.
- If when the chair or sofa is completely dry, any grease spots remain, go over them again with a little more of the cleaner.

The Powder Method

You will need:
- Newspapers.
- Cleaning powder.
- Brush.
- Vacuum cleaner attachment.

- Spread newspapers on floor around base of furniture.
- Sprinkle cleaning powder (any good commercially prepared cleaner, or French chalk, fuller's earth, cornstarch) on upholstered furniture.
- Apply liberally and leave for several hours or overnight.
- Brush off with a clean soft brush, then vacuum with vacuum cleaner attachment.

    Note: This method is especially good for removal of fresh grease stains or for overall greasy soil.
    Caution: Powder is sometimes hard to remove from deeply textured fabrics, so use this method with extreme caution.

Professional Cleaning Services

There are many good professional cleaning services available. Look for them in the yellow pages. They will come to your home and clean the furniture there or remove the furniture to their own workshop.

OTHER FURNITURE

Bamboo, Cane, Reed, and Wicker Furniture

Dust with a clean cloth, a duster treated to attract dust, or use the dusting attachment of your vacuum cleaner. To clean, wash with a sponge or cloth squeezed out in warm sudsy water, rinse immediately, then dry carefully. If heavily soiled, wash with lukewarm sudsy water to which a little ammonia has been added, rinse with clear water and dry thoroughly. An occasional treatment with a liquid wax is desirable, especially if the furniture is exposed to the elements.

To remedy a sagging cane seat, dampen it and let it dry slowly. Repeat process until it returns to shape.

Wet all bamboo, cane, reed, rattan, or wicker furniture about once a year to prevent drying out or splitting. Take it outside if possible, and use the fine spray of a garden hose or wet it down under a shower, if possible.

If furniture is enameled or painted, follow directions for cleaning painted furniture.

Do not use water if the finish can be damaged by it.

Chrome and Stainless Steel

Dust with a soft clean cloth.

To remove smudges and fingerprints, wipe with a soft damp cloth or sponge and polish with a dry soft cloth. If heavily soiled, use hot sudsy water or a spray glass and window cleaner. Avoid the use of harsh abrasives, scouring powder, steel wool.

For combination glass and chrome or stainless steel furniture, use spray glass and window cleaner on entire surface.

Avoid the use of chrome near the seashore, as salty air is apt to corrode it. Stainless steel is a more durable material and will not corrode. To clean it, use a little ammonia and water, a spray glass cleaner, or a special stainless steel cleaner.

Tip: Leftover carbonated water or club soda is excellent for cleaning chrome and stainless steel. We learned this trick from a friendly bartender!

Leather

Extremes in temperature can damage leather furniture. Too much dryness will cause it to crack; too much dampness will cause it to mildew. Avoid placing it near radiators or open windows. During the winter months, when there is heat on in the house, leather should be given a conditioning treatment often. You can purchase commercial preparations for conditioning in a hardware store or leather goods shop.

For regular care of leather furniture wipe with a dampened sponge or soft cloth and dry with a clean soft cloth.

For heavily soiled leather furniture, use a special leather soap or saddle soap following manufacturer's instructions. Rinse thoroughly and dry with soft cloth.

Condition periodically as suggested above. Or rub once or twice a year with castor oil or neat's-foot oil.* On light colors use a white conditioner or white petroleum jelly, since most oils tend to darken leathers.

Note: Neat's-foot oil will leave a dull rather than glossy finish, because it is readily absorbed.

For cleaning and polishing sealed leather table tops, spray polishes and non-oil-base waxes are recommended for high-luster finishes.

Marble Furniture, Table Tops, Mantels, Etcetera

Dust with a clean, soft cloth. Damp dust marble surfaces occasionally with a sponge squeezed from warm sudsy water. Rinse and polish dry with a soft cloth.

* *Neat's-foot oil,* available in hardware stores, is a pale-yellow oil made by boiling the feet and shinbones of cattle. It is used chiefly as a dressing for leather.

157

Many people think marble is unusually durable because of its hardness and weight. Actually, it is really very porous and should not be abused. Marble is a type of limestone, and acids, vinegar, wine, and fruit juices will stain and etch the surface. Coffee, tea, tobacco, oily and organic substances also stain marble surfaces. Alkali and acids break down the walls of the tiny pores. Continued use of harsh cleaners may result in rough spots. To protect its surface, wax occasionally with a self-polishing wax.

To prevent damage, make sure decorative objects, ash trays, etcetera, have felt on the bottom to avoid scratching; clean up spills immediately; use coasters for beverages.

Ask your hardware store about special preparations for cleaning marble.

For acid stains (tea, coffee, etcetera) clean surface with lukewarm to cool water. Dry, then apply a mixture of peroxide and a little ammonia. Let stand until stain disappears. Rinse and polish with a soft cloth.

For rust, apply a special rust remover, following package directions.

For grease, oil, wipe off with a sponge dipped in ammonia and water, then treat as for acid stains above.

To repolish etched surfaces really requires professional care. Or try using a felt buffing pad with an electric hand polisher or drill.

Plastic Furniture

*Laminated Plastic—*Dust with a dampened sponge. Rinse with clear water. Use warm sudsy water to remove encrusted soil. To polish, if desired, see chart on furniture polishes, given earlier in this chapter.

*Plastic and Vinyl Upholstery—*Dust with a clean, soft cloth. Wash periodically with warm sudsy water, rinse thoroughly, and wipe dry. Wax occasionally with a creamy polish.

*Translucent Plastic—*Dust with a clean, soft, lintless cloth. To clean, wash with lukewarm sudsy water. Rinse thoroughly and wipe dry. Or, on Lucite and Plexiglas use a commercial spray window and glass cleaner.

Painted or Enameled Furniture (Wood or Metal)

Dust with a clean, soft cloth. Clean periodically with a damp sponge and wipe dry with a clean, soft cloth. Wax occasionally with a liquid or paste wax; this will help to give it a protective coating and a rich patina.

Note: To remove scuff marks from chair and table legs, use a light application of liquid wax, being careful not to soil rug or carpeting.

Rustic Wood Furniture

While outdoor furniture is hardy and durable, it does need periodic care.

Treat once a year with varnish to protect it from weather and insects.

Store it in a dry, cool place. Treat base of legs with a little creosote or any good preparation recommended by a lumber or hardware dealer. Cover legs carefully with aluminum foil to keep insects from getting to it.

Wrought-Iron Furniture

Wrought iron purchased in the last few years most likely has been treated for rust-resistance. If not, follow this procedure:

- Keep it well painted.
- If rusting does occur, remove all traces with a wire brush, steel wool, or emery cloth.
- Coat it first with red lead or aluminum paint. Let dry.
- Paint with two or more coats of outdoor ornamental paint.
- A light coat of paste or liquid wax will give it additional protection.

TIPS FOR FURNITURE CARE

- Do not place furniture where strong sunlight will fall on it. Excessive exposure will bleach finishes and may cause them to check or crack.

159

- Use felt under table lamps, ash trays, and decorative objects.
- Never place furniture too close to heat sources or near open windows or doors.
- Use both hands when you clean with wax. Saturate one cloth with the wax and clean a small area. Using the dry cloth in the other hand, wipe off the wax immediately while wax is moist and dirt loosened.
- If you are unsure of your furniture finish, test the polish or cleaner first in an inconspicuous spot.
- Never leave a damp cloth on a wood surface. The moisture which is trapped under the cloth could easily damage the finish.
- To remove excess polish from carved areas of furniture, use a small, soft-bristle brush or cotton swab.
- Read and follow the instructions on label of waxes, polishes and other furniture-care products.
- Use pads on your dining table to prevent damage from heat.
- Do not use rubber or plastic mats or coasters without placing a pad of felt beneath them. Some rubber compounds and vinyl films will stain, etch, or soften finishes.

A shoe buffer makes an excellent tool for polishing table tops to a high luster. It is a good idea to set aside an extra buffing pad for this purpose.

Men's discarded cotton socks make excellent dust cloths to clean hard-to-reach corners and grooves. Slip the sock over your hand and go to work. Chair rungs are easier to clean if you spray wax on the sock.

When fitting slipcovers on furniture, use a rubber spatula to push the material into the corners and sides. It really is much faster and certainly easier on the nails.

HOW TO DEAL WITH HOUSEHOLD PESTS

The best way not to entertain any kind of household pest is to avoid inviting them in the first place. Here are some tips for preventive housekeeping:

- Scrub all parts of the house often where they might breed: water pipes, sinks, toilets, behind kitchen drawers, shelves (especially in the kitchen and bathroom), storage places (especially those not opened often), around baseboards and window frames, cracks and openings (in cupboards, walls and floors).
- Pests need food and they need places to hide. Get rid of garbage, bits of food, scraps of cloth and other wastes that they thrive on.
- Keep food in covered containers. Wash containers thoroughly with hot sudsy water, inside and out.
- Never leave greasy dishes or pans around. Wash as soon as possible.
- When you are marketing, make sure the boxes and bags of dry food are sealed and unbroken. You can bring pests into the house in shopping bags and boxes used to carry groceries and other supplies. Check them carefully.
- Air bedding and mattresses in the sun, if and as often as you can. Wash blankets, quilts, comforters, and sheets often.
- Tack down pieces of wood or tin to close up places where pests can enter.
- Use modeling clay to seal openings and cracks around sinks, toilet bowls, water pipes, radiator pipes, and to fill in cracks around baseboards and between floorboards.
- Make sure windows and doors fit tight, and use screens to keep out flying insects.

How to Choose and Use Insecticides

Preventive housekeeping will help immeasurably to keep out unwanted pests, but if they do get in treat them immediately.

You will need some special insecticides with which to treat them. They are available in drugstores, hardware stores, and grocery stores. Check on the latest, safest and most recommended types through local pest control sources.

Products will vary with the type of household pests you wish to kill. Some are sprays for the air; others are sprays for flat surfaces. Then there are liquids, creams, pastes, dusts, powders, traps, and poisoned bait.

161

When you buy an insecticide, make sure that you get just the right kind for your special problem and that it has been approved and tested under federal regulations. Read the labels on the packages or containers carefully for type of pest and how best to use the product.

Safety Rules for Using Insecticides

- Use and store insecticides with caution. Some may be injurious to people and pets and they may cause other serious damage. Some are extremely poisonous and hazardous.
- Keep these chemicals in a safe place, away from children and pets.
- Do not keep them near food, under the sink, or in the medicine chest. Some should be kept away from heat. Check label directions.
- Be careful not to get insecticide on food, dishes, or cooking equipment.
- Keep children, birds, fish, and pets out of the room when using an insecticide. Never leave any on the floor if you have pets or young children who may later enter the room.
- Wash your face and hands with soap and water after using any insecticide. If it spills on your clothes, remove those clothes and wash or have them dry-cleaned as soon as possible.
- Read the label each time you use an insecticide, no matter how well you remember the directions.

COMMON PESTS AND THEIR REMOVAL

Ants—There are many species of ants. Some like sweets. Others prefer meat and can spoil it, so keep food in tightly covered containers.

Find out where the ants are coming from by following their line of march from the food to their nests. When you find the nest, treat it with a liquid insecticide or a nonflammable spot remover. If the nest is outdoors, destroy it by pouring on boiling water, ashes, insecticide, or spot remover.

To keep ants from coming into the house, use an insecticide spray on the outside walls, from the ground up to the windows. Also spray any cracks and openings in the house, and indoor surfaces where you see the ants crawling. In the kitchen, it is best to put the insecticide on with a small paintbrush so it will go just where you want it to be. *Never use insecticide where it can get into food or on dishes.*

If the trouble is really bad, set the legs of tables and food storage units in containers of water, then pour a little oil over the water to trap the ants.

Bedbugs—They may be brought in with luggage, or visit you from next door, or come in on clothing. They are hard to find because they hide to avoid the light. You can detect them by a crushed bug, diasagreeable odor, or streaks of blood.

If there are signs of bedbugs, air and brush bedding *every day*—out in the sunlight, if possible.

The best way to kill bedbugs is with a special spray. Use enough of it to wet the bed frames—also the baseboards and cracks in walls and between floorboards. Spray mattresses all over, but do not soak them.

If you still find bedbugs after a few weeks, use the spray treatment a second time—and a third time, if necessary. Or call an exterminator.

Book Lice—These are small, grayish-white insects, often called psocids. They thrive in homes, libraries, museums. They feed on mold growing on wood and on feathers, books, photographs, and wallpaper. Warmth, dampness, or newly plastered rooms attract them. Cold kills them, but eggs hatch in spring. Clean and air room thoroughly, and let the sunshine in! Use a spray insecticide.

Carpet Beetles (sometimes called a Buffalo Moth)—They love fabrics of all kinds from wool carpets to clothing. Today most wool carpets have been chemically treated to prevent attacks from carpet beetles. The best method of prevention in carpets is thorough and regular vacuuming. Fill any cracks in floors or baseboards as the female lays its egg in these areas. The larvae are the most destructive. As eggs hatch, the larvae begin to feed on the wool. When fully grown, adult beetles will fly and enjoy day and sunlight. Look for them then.

Treat them as for moths.

Cockroaches—They may be carried in with groceries, laundry, and from nearby homes or apartments. They crawl along water pipes and are often called water beetles.

They like to hide during the day in warm, moist, dark, dirty places. At night they come out to get food. Never leave food exposed on shelves or counters. Clean up all crumbs. Watch where children eat and warn them not to leave snacks around.

To kill roaches, use a surface spray or dust. If there are a lot of roaches, use both spray *and* dust. First apply the spray. After it dries, apply the dust. Pour it into cracks and openings where the roaches hide.

Do not use any chemical inside of drawers where you keep food and dishes. Empty the drawers and scrub them with hot sudsy water. Then use the insecticide on the backs, sides and bottoms of these drawers—also on the inside of cabinets. Regular visits from the exterminator are the best medicine.

Crickets (house)—They like warmth and will inhabit kitchens, basements, fireplaces and chimneys in cold weather. They can damage fabrics of all kinds. Using a powder or spray insecticide in places where they hide is most effective.

Fleas—Fleas attack both dogs and cats—and can live on all kinds of other animals. If animals are given free rein of the house and beds, fleas can become a real problem. Treat the animals and their sleeping areas with special flea powders. Avoid the use of a powder, however, on cats, as they will lick it off. Wash all pets with a special shampoo to kill fleas. If pet's bedding has become infested, burn it. Spray new bedding, dog houses, baskets, etcetera.

Houseflies—Flies, flies, flies—all kinds and varieties and literally thousands of species. A few varieties of them can be very troublesome. The most common ones we should be concerned about are the common houseflies, fruit flies, bluebottle flies, and cluster flies. *Houseflies* can survive and feed on almost anything—therefore they are the most dangerous transmitters of germs and disease. The *fruit fly* is bred and hatched around decaying overripe fruit.

The *bottle fly* is large, noisy, and has a metallic or blue-green sheen to its wings. They are most commonly seen in the spring and summer and feed on meat. They won't hesitate to lay their eggs on any uncovered meat. The *cluster fly* lives outdoors in summer, but when cool weather is at hand it finds its way inside and clusters in dark areas. They are not food lovers, but they are noisy buzzers around bright windows or burning light bulbs. They will soil woodwork and wallpaper.

Make sure garbage cans have tight covers, as this seems to be their best breeding area. Line garbage cans with plastic liners and keep cans clean. Avoid the piling up of garbage both in and out of doors.

If you see just a few flies once in a while, try to kill them with a swatter. If you need to control a lot of flies, apply a spray that is made for flying insects. If it is in the kitchen, make sure all food and utensils are protected from the spray. There are also treated fly ribbons which attract a number of flies over a period of time, if left hanging for them to feed on.

Food-Loving Insects—It is always a surprise when we open a package and find a few unwanted creatures inhabiting what we thought was perfectly good food. They particularly like grain and grain foods. These are the most common of them:

- *Grain beetles* that bore holes in dried peas or beans.
- *Flour moth larvae* form weblike matter in flour and cereal.
- *Mites* are any of a number of minute insects that feed on stored food and look very much like masses of dust moving about.
- *Larder beetle bugs* feed on pork and cheese.
- *Cheese skippers* feed on pork.

Mosquitoes—They lay their eggs in water or in damp places, so don't keep open bowls or cans of water around the house. Water in vases and in saucers under potted plants should be changed every day to destroy mosquito eggs.

Clothes Moths—They like to feed on woolens and this leaves holes. Moths cause more trouble by laying their eggs in seams, pockets, and folds of clothes, blankets, and other things made from wool. Preventive medicine is best. Look for woolen articles that are moth-proof or moth-resistant.

One good way to get rid of moths and their eggs is to hang

165

woolen articles out in the sunshine. Then brush them on both sides. Be sure to brush out pockets, seams, and folds.

A second way to get rid of moths and moth eggs is to wash woolens (if they are washable). Otherwise, have them dry-cleaned. When woolen things are clean, treat them with an insecticide before you store them away.

To protect woolens from more moths, hang them on a clothesline and spray them with insecticide or a moth-proof spray until the cloth is just damp. Do not let it get really wet.

When you want to store away woolen things, make sure they are clean and sprayed. Put them in a clean cardboard box and seal the edges with sticky tape. Keep the boxes or bundles of clean woolens in a cool place until you are ready to use them again.

To prepare a closet or chest for storage, clean thoroughly with a vacuum cleaner and/or attachment. If you suspect a closet is inhabited with moths, treat with paradichlorbenzene crystals, following container directions. Wool upholstery and rugs and certain draperies which are not moth-proofed should be. Cold storage is a must for furs and fur pieces. If you use them in the summer they should be sprayed with a residual or long-lasting spray, shaking and airing often.

Meal Moth or Meal Worms—These are the larvae of certain beetles that infest granaries, bakeries, etcetera, and are injurious to flour and meal. Discard any food which is contaminated with any of the above insects and clean shelves, liners, bins, drawers, and cupboards where food is stored. Spray the entire area with a special insecticide, being careful not to spray other food and utensils.

Silverfish—These fast-moving silvery insects thrive in damp, warm areas, breed in particularly damp places such as basements, then use water pipes as highways to infest other damp areas of the house. Sinks in bathrooms, kitchens, and laundries are particularly vulnerable. Silverfish eat paper and will attack books, rayon and some starchy cotton fabrics. Spray vulnerable areas with a residual insecticide. Avoid the use of sprays near open heaters. Use powders instead.

Spiders—Your best protection against spiders is to keep your house free of other insects upon which they feed. Keep your ceilings and walls clean, especially in the corners where they spin their webs. Actually, if it were not for their unsightliness, spiders are functional little creatures, for they eat the very insects you are trying to get rid of. Keep doors and windows well screened.

Squirrels—Like chipmunks and rats, squirrels are rodents. If you have ever had a squirrel pay you an unexpected visit, you'll be sure to put screening over the tops of your chimneys from there on in. They are usually destructive, and if you ever hear a thumping noise in the chimney and it's not Christmas eve, you can be pretty certain that it's a squirrel and not Santa Claus.

Termites—Termites could be confused with ants in appearance though they are a little straighter. Since some ants have wings at one time in their development, what may look like swarms of small flying ants could really be adult termites on their way to breed new families. The ones that do the damage are actually sightless and wingless. You can recognize them by their light-gray color and the tubes or tunnels they make in wood structures. They are slowly destructive, eating away at the house foundation secretly until all of a sudden you detect these small tunnels and little piles of sawdust which become telltale symptoms. Sometimes while a wooden beam looks solidly intact, you have only to touch it and see it crumble before your very eyes. Preventive treatment of wood is your best protection against termites. Otherwise, call in the exterminators.

FLOOR CARE

Since floors seem to highlight the complexion of any room, it is important to take care of them properly. Preserving the beauty and finish is a matter of knowing what the material is, how to treat it, and following a program of continuing preventive care.

How well you take care of your floors will determine how easy they will be to clean.

Preventive care entails wiping up spills as they occur, keeping entrances clean to avoid tracked-in dust, using doormats and scrapers, covering up areas temporarily if you are doing a messy

167

job. This and a regular schedule of *routine maintenance* can help to take the "chore" out of keeping floors clean.

Daily:
• Dust mop or sweep with a soft broom or vacuum cleaner.

Weekly (or as necessary):
• Sweep, then clean floors with a mild detergent or special solution recommended for your particular flooring material. Recommendations will differ among specific floors and they will vary even among flooring authorities. In general, however, weekly care for all floors but wood involves mopping and rinsing with an occasional waxing. Your method of care should be dependent upon the flooring you have.
• Always follow container directions for the products you use.

Periodically:
• Remove old wax buildup with a wax remover; then re-wax and buff, if needed.

WAXING

Wax does provide some important advantages to your floors. It protects the surface, which will help to reduce wear. Wax makes floors easier to clean, helps them to resist spots and stain, and gives them a finished appearance.

Which Wax for Which Floor?

There is a growing profusion of floor waxes and finishes on the shelves of the supermarket and in housewares and hardware stores. Selecting the proper one can be a real source of confusion, unless you have the facts about your own flooring.

Basically, all floor products will fall into one of three groups:

Polishing waxes—either paste or liquid—which must be buffed to a shine.

Self-polishing waxes, which dry to a bright, shiny finish.

Vinyl or acrylic finishes (mainly synthetic ingredients), which also dry to a high luster and are essentially the same as self-polishing waxes.

Despite the profusion of brands, there are essentially only two types of waxes, depending upon their basic ingredient: Water Base and Solvent Base. Identifying them should be easy by simply reading the label.

Those of the *water-base type,* because they are recommended especially for linoleum, asphalt, rubber tile, vinyl, and vinyl asbestos floors, will say "for asphalt, rubber and vinyl . . .," "Keep from freezing," "Do not shake."

Solvent-base types, recommended especially for wood and cork floors, will read "Caution: Combustible mixture," "Do not use on asphalt or rubber."

Either spirit-solvent-base or water-base waxes may be used for ceramic tile, concrete, flagstone, slate, and terrazzo floors.

In addition to cleaning and waxing and self-polishing properties, waxes have other special qualities, such as buffability, ability not to darken light colors, resistance to slipping, water-spotting, or scuffing. Read the labels to determine these characteristics.

To Help You Choose

Because there is such a confusion between types and brand names, here is a list of examples:

Water-Base Waxes:

PASTE POLISHING	LIQUID SELF-POLISHING *(cleans and waxes)*
Butcher's Tile Wax	Dri-brite
Staples Tile Wax	Simoniz Vinyl Wax
Ultra-Gloss Paste Wax	

LIQUID SELF-POLISHING

Johnson's	Formica Floor Shine
Bravo	Aerowax
Glo-Coat	Simoniz Permacrylic
Klear	Stanley Floor Finish

Stride   Kentile Vinyl Floor Finish
Future   Armstrong's Mirasheen
Butcher's   Armstrong's Durelle
Bright
Green Stripe
White Stripe

Solvent-Base Waxes:

LIQUID SELF-POLISHING   LIQUID POLISHING

Johnson's Wood Klear   Bruce
     Butcher's Flo Paste
     Johnson's Beautiflor
     Simoniz
     Stanley
     Wood Preen

PASTE POLISHING

Aerowax Clear Paste Wax   Preen
Beacon White Paste Wax   Simoniz
Bruce   Stanley
Butcher's   Trewax
Johnson's   Ultra-Gloss

CARE OF SPECIFIC FLOORING

Asphalt Tile

Wash with warm mild sudsy solution, using either alkaline or nonalkaline cleaners, and rinse with clear water. Dry thoroughly.

Avoid the use of waxes, polishes, or cleaners that contain solvents or oils. Avoid grease. They may soften the surface of the tile. Always use a water-based wax.

To restore pitted, rough asphalt tile, use steel wool (grades 1 and 2) to smooth out the roughened surface. Wash with a mild cleaning solution, using a light-duty detergent, then apply a self-polishing, water-base product. If pitting is severe, try applying several coats to the clean surface. Pitting is often caused by the use of harsh cleaners or solvents.

Ceramic Tile, Slate, Marble, Terrazzo, Quarry Tile

Seal concrete or grouting between tiles or stones with penetrating sealer. Use floor-brush attachment of vacuum cleaner for regular care if flooring is cracked, as a mop will leave soil embedded in the cracks. Wash with a powdered floor cleaner and water, such as Spic and Span or Oakite. Rinse and dry thoroughly, then wax. A water- or solvent-base liquid or paste wax followed by a buffing operation will give it a mellow gloss. A self-polishing wax will give it a higher shine.

To remove wax use a combination wax remover and floor cleaner.

Caution: Never use steel wool or acids on terrazzo, marble or quarry tile.

Brick, Cement, Unglazed Tile, Flagstone

Seal with penetrating sealer to avoid wax penetration of pores. To wash, scrub with all-purpose powdered floor cleaner. Rinse, and dry thoroughly. Use either a water-base paste, liquid, or self-polishing wax. Liquid is the easiest to apply.

Cork Tile

Clean when soiled with a wax remover and floor cleaner.

Keep well waxed to prevent dust and soil penetration. Cork tile has a low resistance to oil and grease and stains easily. Avoid the use of caustic or alkaline cleaners or floor oils; avoid flooding. Use fine sandpaper on cigarette burns. Use only a solvent-base paste or liquid wax. Very little cork tile is manufactured today.

Linoleum

Keep well waxed. Frequent washing or scrubbing may cause it to harden.

Dust frequently. Damp mop weekly using only a nonalkaline cleaner such as light-duty detergent made for fine fabrics and dishes. Alkali removes the linseed oil, making it brittle.

171

Use either a water-base or solvent paste, liquid or self-polishing wax.

Rubber

Avoid contact with grease, oil or solvents. Not usually recommended for kitchens. Wash with a warm, mild, sudsy solution using a light-duty detergent, rinse in clear water, and mop dry. Use a water-base wax only. Very little rubber tile is used in homes today.

To restore pitted, rough rubber tile, follow same procedure as for asphalt tile.

Vinyl Plastic

Vinyl plastic, both sheet and tile, is the most durable of all resilient flooring and requires minimum care. It resists grease, oil and dirt. It is therefore excellent for kitchen use. Vinyl asbestos contains vinyl resins and asbestos fibers. *Dust* frequently and damp mop occasionally. Clean when heavily soiled with a powdered floor cleaner and warm water. Rinse with clear water and dry thoroughly. Apply a water-base wax or vinyl floor finish. A self-polishing type will dry to a high luster.

Wood

Unfinished wood—Apply a coat of penetrating sealer, then wax. This protects floor from absorbing soil. Use floor brush attachment of vacuum cleaner for sweeping. Wash, when badly soiled, with lukewarm sudsy water and powdered floor cleaner, rinse with clear water, using as little as possible. If you wish to darken an unfinished wood floor, use a strong alkali cleaner; chlorine bleach will lighten it.

Shellacked wood floors—Wipe up spills immediately as liquid will leave white spots. To wax, use a paste or liquid polishing wax following container instructions. Wipe up black heel marks with liquid wax.

Dust *varnished wood* floors with an untreated mop. Wax as for shellacked floors.

Dust *oiled wood* floors with a chemically treated or lightly oiled mop. Scrub or mop heavily soiled floor with warm sudsy water and rinse well. Let it dry thoroughly, then re-oil, with linseed oil or one recommended by your hardware dealer.

SPECIAL CARE FOR WOOD FLOORS

Dust regularly with a *dry* mop. See preceding sections on preventive care and routine maintenance.

One of the basic rules in floor care is *never use water on wood*. While sealing a wood floor will make it less susceptible to water damage, it is still best to avoid using water on it.

To clean wooden floors—Use either a solvent* (turpentine, nontoxic dry-cleaning fluid, etcetera) or a liquid cleaning wax which contains both solvent to clean the floor and a wax to provide the same protection to the floor as a paste wax. This single-step operation is time- and energy-saving and recommended over the solvent cleaning. (See section on solvent-base waxes.) Go over the floor with a cheesecloth moistened with the cleaner, turning out a clean part of the cloth frequently. Cleaning the floor actually involves removing encrusted dirt and old wax buildup, but as we have said before, if you have used a paste or liquid polishing wax properly, you should not have a wax buildup.

After you have cleaned the floor it should be protected with a wax coating. If you have used a liquid cleaning wax, all you need to do is follow it with a buffing operation using an electric polishing machine or a weighted floor brush on an old piece of carpet. If you have used a solvent only to clean it, then you will need to wax the floor with either a paste or liquid polishing wax, then buff according to directions. *In either case, buff occasionally after dry dusting and between waxings to maintain a glossy finish.*

Waxing only, without cleaning—At intervals, depending on traffic and wear, wax the entire floor with a paste or liquid polishing wax, after first dusting the floor thoroughly. Follow container directions.

* *Caution:* When using a solvent or a solvent-base product, be sure the room is well ventilated and that the cleaning cloths are disposed of carefully.

173

To remove water marks—Polish area with a little paste or liquid polishing wax.

To restore a neglected floor—Remove all surface dirt. Saturate a pad of fine steel wool with liquid polishing wax and rub the surface until the embedded dirt is loosened, or use an electric polishing machine designed to use steel wool pads, which should also be saturated with liquid wax. Wipe clean immediately with dry rags. After 30 minutes polish by hand or with an electric polisher.

To remove worn spots—Dip a pad of fine steel wool in a flat finisher such as Minwax Flat Finish (use the same type and color as originally used) and apply it to the worn spot. Have the pad wet, not dripping, to give the area a good coat. Rub in well and let it soak for about 15 minutes. Wipe thoroughly with dry cloths. Wax and polish the next day.

To remove dark spots—1) remove all wax with naphtha; 2) thoroughly wash spotted areas with household vinegar, allowing it to remain on spots for three or four minutes; 3) wipe dry with a clean cloth. If repeated applications of vinegar do not remove spots, apply 4% oxalic acid solution—1 tablespon oxalic acid crystals in 1 cup of water. Allow to stand two or three minutes or until spots disappear. Wipe up with damp cloth. If wood looks lighter after spots are removed, touch up with shellac or penetrating floor sealer. Re-wax after thoroughly dry.

To restore original color of wood surfaces (mainly floors and furniture), use a tinted paste wax. Select a color that closely approximates the color of the wood. Clean any soiled areas using a dampened cloth dipped in warm sudsy water. Working quickly, rinse and dry thoroughly. Apply a thin, even coat of wax. Let it dry, then polish or buff by hand or by machine. If the surface is new, a second coat may be necessary to provide more protection.

GENERAL CARE OF RESILIENT FLOORS

These include: linoleum, rubber, cork, vinyl.

This may come as a shock to many of you, but in our opinion the average person spends more time cleaning and waxing floors than is really necessary. This theory, strangely enough, is shared by some of the leading wax manufacturers too. Too much waxing, too much mopping can cause more harm than good. Many new resilient floorings do not require waxing. Actually care of resilient flooring can be one of the easiest jobs there is, if you follow a few *basic* rules. Of course, selecting the right floor in the first place is the first rule. Then use the proper cleaners and waxes. Let us hope you have taken the time to read some of the foregoing on the various waxes and how they are made. This, in itself, can be a great time-saver.

Sweep waxed floors as often as necessary with a floor brush or broom to remove loose soil and dirt particles. *Dust* with an untreated dust mop. (Treated ones which contain oil may soften the wax and leave an unabsorbed film of grease which will attract dust. Those mops designed to pull up dust like a magnet are excellent.) Wipe up spills as they occur, especially grease, fats, and oils. *Damp mop* occasionally to remove fine dirt.

Clean or wash the floor as needed, using regularly powdered floor cleaners, such as Spic and Span or Soilax or a mild detergent solution. Always rinse the floor after mopping and let it dry thoroughly. A light-duty cleaning every three to six weeks, depending upon traffic, is usually sufficient, except in areas where there is hard wear and tear and it is needed more often. A more thorough cleaning, once or twice a year, to remove old wax films should then be ample.

Special Tips:
- Wipe up water and spills immediately on floors waxed with liquid wax or they may make white spots that will require rewaxing.
- Remove soil spots and black marks (including asphalt tile) by rubbing with a fine steel wool dipped in a liquid water-base wax. Then buff or let dry according to directions on label.

    Caution: Do *not* use steel wool on "no-wax" floors and some "valley-printed" embossed tiles.
- Scratches may be removed by using liquid self-polishing wax (depending on type of floor—see above) and fine steel wool, rubbing with the grain.
- *To remove chewing gum, candle wax or tar,* do it when the material is hard. An ice cube in a plastic bag, placed on the area, will hasten setting. Scrape up excess with a

dull-edged tool. Except on floors that are not resistant to solvents, apply a household solvent (mineral spirits or naphtha) with a cloth or very fine steel wool, and rub clean. Wipe dry with a clean cloth and repolish the area if necessary. For asphalt and rubber tile floors that are not solvent-resistant, clean them by rubbing with a very fine steel wool dipped in a detergent solution. Rinse, then dry and apply polish.

APPLYING WAX

How often you wax will vary, depending on the type of floor, the amount of traffic, type of wax used. A new coat of wax should be applied after a thorough washing and removal of wax, but coats may also be applied to traffic lanes between light-duty washings, provided the floor is clean and dry.

A heavy buildup of wax films on light floors can be avoided by using light-colored waxes and applying in very thin coats.

Tip: It is also wise to stay approximately six inches away from the baseboards when applying wax. This prevents wax accumulation at the juncture of floor and wall.

Surely it isn't necessary for us to say it (but we will)—be careful not to wax yourself into an inside corner! It *has* been done. Always work from the inside out, toward the door.

Tip: When waxing the floor around an area rug, you can protect it by inserting several wooden blocks under the edge at intervals. This helps to elevate the rug from the freshly waxed floor.

Follow any specific directions for the wax you are using, observing these general rules:

- Before applying any wax, be sure the floor is clean and dry. (Unless you are using a wax that cleans as it waxes.)
- For *paste wax,* dampen and wring out a pad or soft cloth or a lamb's wool applicator. Coat it with wax and apply a thin film, using long, even strokes. Let it dry from 30 to 45 minutes. Then buff with a hand buffer or an electric polisher. See information on electric polishers in the following section.

- For *liquid wax* (cleans and waxes), do not shake the container. This will cause the wax to foam. Pour wax on the floor and work it thoroughly into a clean dry cloth or applicator. Push the applicator (or the cloth with the applicator) on the floor in straight even strokes, turning the cloth as it becomes soiled (if you have not cleaned the floor first). Change applicators or cloths if your floor is heavily soiled. Let it dry, then buff as for paste wax above.
- For *self-polishing waxes,* do not shake the can. The tiny bubbles that form will show when the floor dries. Pour the wax on the floor and spread a thin film in long, even strokes with a dampened cloth or applicator. Never push back and forth over the waxed area, as it will not dry smoothly. Wax over an area just *once.* Let it dry at least 30 minutes. Floors with self-polishing waxes can be detergent washed between waxing, but if you use a wax remover to wash, be sure to apply a new coat of wax afterwards.
- *Carnauba-based "waxy" waxes* can be slippery when highly buffed or if not buffed properly. However, the self-polishing vinyl finishes are no more slippery than the floor surface itself, no matter how many coats are used. Regardless of the kind of wax you use waxing floors properly does *NOT* make them slippery. However, observe *all* directions carefully.
- *If a polished floor seems sticky after the suggested drying time,* the humidity may be too high. Let it dry a little longer than the recommended time. If polish still feels tacky after additional time has been allowed, it may be due to: 1) incomplete removal of old polish; 2) insufficient rinsing; 3) applying polish too generously or re-coating too soon.

To Remove a Wax Buildup

If you have used a paste or liquid solvent wax properly, you should actually have no wax buildup.

For liquid or paste wax, use a commercially prepared wax remover or turpentine.

177

Make sure room is well ventilated, keep solvents away from flame, and observe the manufacturer's directions and cautions. Apply with a soft clean cloth to a small area and work until all wax is removed before moving on to a new area. Throw cloths away as they become saturated with wax.

After removing the wax, you may wish to mop the floor with a powdered floor cleaner, although it is not really necessary.

For self-polishing wax, mop with a hot sudsy solution of 1 to 2 cups of ammonia, ¼ to ½ cup powdered floor cleaner like Spic and Span or Soilax to each gallon of cool water. Use the higher concentration of floor cleaner if your floor is badly soiled.

Note: Some wax products now have manufacturer's directions for removal on the label—follow these instructions for best results.

EQUIPMENT FOR FLOOR CARE

Wax Applicators

These are long-handled manual applicators with removable applicator pads that come in chenille and nylon. Applicators should be removed immediately after use, washed, and rinsed thoroughly. Rinse applicator with self-polishing wax under warm running water. For those with liquid or paste wax, soak in warm sudsy water, then wash in hot sudsy water; rinse thoroughly to remove all soap or detergents, since any that remains will mix with the next application of wax. Hang applicators to dry, and fluff occasionally during drying.

Electric Floor Scrubber/Polisher/ Waxer/Rug Shampooer

You may either buy or rent these from specialty shops or supermarkets. If you have a good deal of bare floor area to take care of, it would be a worthwhile investment for you to own one. Otherwise, it may be more economical to rent. Standard accessories include brushes for scrubbing and polishing, felt buffing pads, and steel wool pads, and brushes for rug cleaning.

RUG AND CARPET CARE

Learn to depend on your best friend, the vacuum cleaner. For that reason, it is well to choose one suited to your flooring. (See earlier section on vacuum cleaners.) Your rugs and carpets will look better and last longer if you keep them free of lint, greasy surface soil, and embedded grit. Grit in particular can work its way down into the base of the nap and cut off small pieces of the pile, as people step on it.

KNOW YOUR CARPET FIBERS

Find out as much as you can about the weave, fiber, backing, and cushion of the floor covering you own or are about to purchase. This will help you know how to care for it more effectively. It is also a good idea, if you have a major investment in fine rugs and carpeting, to keep accurate records as to the date of purchase, dealer, carpet mechanic, cost, laying charges. Such records will be useful if you ever decide to sell these items.

There was a time when wool was the major source of carpet fibers. Now, in addition to the natural fibers, *wool* and *cotton*, there is a bright and growing world of synthetic fibers being used for all kinds and types of rugs and carpets, both indoors and out.

In synthetics there are the *nylons, acrylics, polyester,* and *polypropylene olefins.* Most of these should be given the same care and attention given to wool. The one exception, of course, is polypropylene, which is more durable. It is hard and nonabsorbent, not easily damaged by water, and is often used for kitchen and outdoor carpeting. The acrylics and nylons are particularly good for kitchen carpeting as they, too, are easy to care for.

RUG AND CARPET PADDING

Padding, often referred to as cushions, underlay, or lining, helps to reduce wear and tear and adds a luxurious resiliency

179

underfoot. Padding is available in a variety of materials—hair, hair and jute, jute and foam, or sponge rubber.

Foam or sponge rubber is the most expensive, most resilient, noncrushable and moth-resistant; hair is durable and resilient; hair and jute mixture is long-wearing but the jute tends to mat eventually; jute alone is not really very good. There are also thin sheets of rubber with a gripping surface and some of the rubberized hair. Be sure to lay padding with the textured side down, so it will grip the surface.

Taking care of the padding is as important as the proper care of your rug or carpet. To do so:

- It is well to vacuum the padding and the floor under it about every six months.
- If the carpeting is tacked to the floor, the only thing you can do is to be diligent about vacuuming the carpet regularly to keep grime from settling into and through the backing.
- If and when the carpeting is removed for professional cleaning, you can vacuum the pad.
- If a pad is made of hair, jute, or soft rubber, avoid agitation that could damage the surface. Use the hard-surface cleaning attachment or, if yours is an upright vacuum cleaner, remove the revolving brush.

How to Take Care of Rugs and Carpets

Rug and carpet care is threefold: a *daily pickup*, a *more thorough weekly cleaning*, and an *occasional shampooing* when necessary if fabric and age allow.

Vacuum slowly and do a thorough job, paying particular attention to edges, dark places under furniture, and under furniture legs. See How to Use the Vacuum Cleaner section earlier in this chapter. Use the crevice tool attachment of your vacuum cleaner or a whisk broom to clean and fluff up areas under furniture legs or hard-to-move pieces. (Don't give moths a chance to begin their campaign.) Use doormats at outside entrances; they help to prevent tracked-in soil.

Distribute wear evenly. Turn rugs in the opposite direction at least once a year. (Twice is better for delicate rugs.) Or, rearrange furniture to create new traffic patterns. Lay rugs and carpets on smooth floors. Rough ones, loose boards, protruding nails, or knots in the wood will create wear ridges. Use padding underneath carpets and rugs to reduce wear, help make them more resilient.

Use smooth steel guides or "carpet casters" on movable chairs, where necessary, to prevent permanent indentations; use rubber or plastic cups under legs of stationary chairs to keep pile from crushing. Remove spots and stains immediately.

Some Tips on Vacuuming

There are several theories about *dampening carpets* before cleaning or vacuuming them. If you sprinkle carpets with water before using a carpet sweeper, this helps to brighten the carpet and hold down dust. Another idea suggests using a vacuum cleaner first, then giving rugs and carpets a once-over-lightly with a damp sponge mop that has been dipped into a mixture of one pint of water and a half cup of ammonia, then squeezed dry. This helps to freshen them and add a sparkle.

If a room is comparatively free of traffic for certain periods, it is a good idea to sprinkle moth flakes or crystals on rugs and carpeting a few hours before using a vacuum cleaner. This will protect the carpeting and help to keep the moths out of the vacuum cleaner.

Observe These Don'ts:
- Don't shake small rugs; this can break threads, loosen knots, fray fringe, damage backing and tear binding.
- Don't hang rugs over the clothesline; it will bend the fibers and break the backing.
- Don't beat a rug.
- Don't run lamp cords underneath rugs or carpets; not only is this a fire hazard but it will create wear ridges.
- Don't shove furniture across rugs or carpeting; lift it (with help, of course).

181

- Don't dry-clean rugs with rubber backing or use a solvent for grease spots—it will damage the rubber.

WHAT TO DO FOR SPECIAL PROBLEMS

Cigarette Burns—Snip off fiber ends singed by the cigarette, and sponge area with a detergent solution. (See Formula 1 for rug spots and stains in the section on stain removal, later in this chapter.) If the hole is large, fill in with a piece of tuft or fiber taken from a sample or similar pile. If burn is serious, seek professional advice.

Crushing or Matting—All carpet fibers will crush when subjected to heavy loads, such as furniture, for prolonged periods of time. When furniture is to be removed, "matting" may be corrected by the following procedure:

- Moisten the matted areas with water and cover with a clean, white, dry cloth.
- Place a hot iron very lightly on the cloth, or use the spray setting over the cloth to moisten it.
- Brush the tufts erect with your fingertips or a dull, blunt knife or spatula.

Curling—Apply a hot iron to a damp cloth (see Crushing, above) on both back and front of rug and flatten with your fingertips. Repeat if situation is not corrected the first time. Or dampen the carpet and roll on a broomstick or baseball bat and pound curled surface repeatedly.

Loose Edges on Wall-to-Wall Carpets (Stretching)—If newly installed carpeting loosens or stretches near the edges, it needs restretching. Call the carpet mechanic who laid the carpeting and have him restretch or cut it to make it taut. Carpeting may have a tendency to loosen and ripple during the hot humid months. This rippling may correct itself as the fall season approaches.

Moths, Carpet Beetles, Silverfish—If you have purchased your carpeting within the last 18 to 24 months and it was made in the United States, you can be fairly sure it is permanently protected against moths, carpet beetles, and silverfish. An older rug or carpet should be checked now and then for insect damage, especially in dark corners and greasy areas. You can have moth-proofing done professionally or you can do it yourself with products made especially for carpets. Some come in aerosol sprays, and some can be applied with an ordinary spray gun. If you have a moth-proofing attachment for your vacuum cleaner, by all means use it according to instructions. Whichever method or product you use, be sure to treat the entire carpet, not just the area where you found insect damage.

Pilling—Pilling is characterized by small fuzzy balls of fiber, held to the pile by longer fibers which are too strong to break. Regular and thorough vacuuming and occasional shearing will minimize this problem. There are "pill-removing" gadgets available, usually in notions departments.

Shading—Continued or prolonged traffic wear will flatten pile carpet and tend to slant it in one direction or the other. This creates light and dark reflections, called shading. Turning a rug from side to side to distribute wear will help prevent this situation. If you place rugs so the light goes into the pile, the rug will look darker as the light is absorbed; if you turn the pile away from the light, it will take on a bright sheen. This is especially true with Orientals.

Shedding—During the first few months of use, even the best wool pile carpets will "shed" short pieces of fiber. This is due to short ends of fiber which are caught in the pile during the shearing operation or to loose ends of the staple fibers which are not anchored in the backing or to loss of moisture during the storage (which returns upon use). Normal shedding does not represent a significant loss of fiber. Regular vacuuming will end the shedding problem within a few weeks after installation, if the carpet gets normal wear.

Sprouting—Sometimes ladies' heels, pets' claws, sharp projections on floor-care equipment, or a child's toy will snag the carpet and pull up or "sprout" a tuft. These sprouts should be clipped off with small sharp shears, *never pulled!* If the condition persists, check one of the above sources.

Static—Most fabrics are susceptible to static electricity, but in carpeting the problem is more severe. It is caused by low humidity

183

when moisture is removed from the air by heat. You may get a "shock" by walking across the carpeting and touching metal or another human being. It is remedied by adding moisture to the air or by applying anti-static materials.

SPECIFIC CARE OF RUG AND CARPET TYPES

Wool Rugs and Carpet—Follow the general rules given. Most of them apply to both wool pile and twist wall-to-wall carpeting or area and room-size rugs. An *upright vacuum cleaner* is best for wool carpeting.

Oriental Rugs—Contrary to popular opinion, Oriental rugs may be and should be cleaned with a vacuum cleaner. Because of the often fragile quality of these fine masterpieces and particularly if they are old and worn, a tank or canister-type vacuum is recommended. If they are new, sturdy, and of thick pile, an upright vacuum cleaner may be used. Never attempt to clean an Oriental rug by the do-it-yourself method. Professional cleaning is recommended. (If you insist on doing it yourself, use the shampoo method. Many like to add a little ammonia to the solution to help give the rug sparkle.)

Take care of imitation Oriental rugs according to fiber used.

Cotton Rugs and Carpet—Follow the general rules given. You will find that a canister or tank-type vacuum cleaner is more effective for cotton, especially loop and shag rugs. Small area rugs can be washed and dried automatically, but be sure to follow specific instructions given on the label for your particular rugs and the directions for your washer and dryer. Use cold water for rugs with rubber backing. See How to Launder Just About Everything, Chapter Four. For professional or do-it-yourself washing or cleaning of larger ones, see the following instructions. Do not dry-clean or use solvents on rugs with rubber backing. This may damage the rubber and eventually stain the pile.

Synthetic Rugs and Carpets—Nylon, rayon, acrylic, polyester, polypropylene olefins have decided advantages when it comes to everyday care. They are not attacked by moths, carpet beetles, or mildew. They are soil- and stain-resistant and spills can be easily wiped off them. Nylon, especially, being one of the toughest fibers, is particularly resistant to abrasion and scuffing. Vacuum clean and remove spots and stains immediately, following the general rules given. It is especially important to follow the manufacturer's instructions that come with synthetic carpets. If spot-cleaning seems to mat the pile, blot the spot in the same direction of the pile. Small rugs may be laundered automatically.

Some synthetics may not be dryer dried. Follow label instructions for specific care.

Fur Rugs—Clean regularly with the suction tool of your vacuum cleaner or a stiff brush or broom. How you clean the fur surface is essentially dependent upon the kind of backing on the rug. If it has a flannel or wool backing, it can be cleaned with an absorbent, such as cornmeal. Spread the meal over the rug, then brush it out as for regular cleaning. Keep repeating the process until the rug is clean.

If your rug has any other backing, or none at all, except the pelt or skin, wipe the surface carefully with a firm cloth (clean piece of turkish toweling) wrung out in a solution of lukewarm suds, whipped up with an all-purpose detergent. Be careful not to wet the pelt. Rinse with a cloth wrung out of clear lukewarm water until all the detergent has been removed. Use a little bluing, following package instructions, in the last rinse water if the rug is white. Let it dry flat on the floor.

For professional cleaning and glazing (and this is recommended for valuable furs) send to a furrier or cleaner just as you would a fur coat, once a year. The same applies to storage.

Fiber, Rush, Grass, and Sisal Rugs—Vacuum clean or brush on both sides regularly. Since these rugs are loosely woven, dirt and grit will sift through to the floor beneath them, so be sure to pick up the rugs and clean the floor as well.

For cleaning heavy soil you may shampoo them yourself or send out for professional cleaning. To shampoo, see the instructions in the following section.

Hooked and Braided Rugs—Follow the general directions for regular rug and carpet care. It is never a good idea to beat or shake hooked rugs, as this will loosen the loops and break the backing. "Sprouts," which may appear occasionally, may be clipped if the rug is firmly loomed, but be very careful not to clip into the chain of loops or backing.

Treat hooked or braided rugs according to fiber. If yours are all-wool, you may be able to clean them successfully yourself, as any other wool carpet, but do it gently to avoid snagging loops or breaking stitches. If you have dyed the materials and made your own rugs, they may be safer in the hands of a reliable professional cleaner.

Crocheted Rugs—If these rugs are small they may be washed or laundered at home. (See Chapter Four.) Room-size rugs or those too large to handle by hand should be sent to a professional cleaner.

Stair Carpeting—Stair carpeting receives heavy wear and tear and will last longer if it has padding underneath. Because stair carpeting is especially susceptible to wear it is a good idea to fold an extra length at one or both ends to provide an extra measure of unworn carpetry. This will allow you to shift the carpeting when it begins to wear.

To vacuum, use the rug attachment of your vacuum cleaner, a lightweight stick cleaner, or a hand vacuum cleaner.

Scatter Rugs—Run the vacuum cleaner diagonally across the rug forward and off the edge, so that the suction will not lift or roll up the rug. Be careful not to let the edges "suction" into the vacuum alone. This could damage the rug and the vacuum cleaner.

Fringe—Face the vacuum cleaner toward the edge of the rug. Raise the nozzle so that the cleaner will glide over the fringe up to the edge of the rug. Lower the nozzle and pull it back toward you, over the fringe. This will "comb" the fringe straight and remove tangled dust and litter.

REGULAR CARE OF RUGS AND CARPETS

Various cleaning procedures in the regular care of rugs and carpets are necessary to prevent unnecessary wear and maintain the appearance:

1. Constant pickup of crumbs, dust, and surface litter.
2. Regular vacuuming to remove grit and sharp dirt particles.
3. Periodic cleaning.

Cleaning Carpets

Regardless of how faithfully you vacuum and spot-clean, every rug or carpet eventually needs a more thorough cleaning. Depending on the type of carpeting and the soil problems you have, this could be every 12 to 18 months or every few years. Remember, though, that cleaning results are better on carpets and rugs that are not too heavily soiled.

There are two ways to clean carpets and rugs:

1. Do-it-yourself.
2. Professional cleaning *at home* or *in a plant.*

In deciding which is best for you, consider cost, time, and the value of the rug.

Do-It-Yourself

Periodic home shampooing or dry-cleaning, recommended between professional cleanings, will help to brighten a rug that has become dulled by an accumulation of greasy film and soil. You may use either a liquid foam cleaner or a dry-cleaning compound, depending on the carpet fibers. Read labels carefully before you buy, as your product should be recommended for the carpet fibers you wish to clean.

Liquids, for example, should be used only for color-fast carpets. You can test yours by rubbing the pile with a damp white cloth. If any color comes off, avoid wet cleaning.

On the other hand, the solvents used in certain dry-cleaner compounds may damage the latex backing used on some carpets. Or the compounds may be hard to remove from certain types of pile. Select a do-it-yourself cleaner with utmost care. Ask a professional cleaner his advice on the selection of a cleaner. Some chemicals used improperly can do untold damage.

Liquid Cleaners for Shampooing

Commercial liquid or foam cleaners are suitable for cotton, wool and blends of man-made fibers. Of course many small throw or scatter rugs can be machine washed and dryer dried.

187

If you use a liquid cleaner, take care to moisten only the surface. Overwetting and slow drying can cause mildew in the backing and, eventually, brownish stains on the pile. Some special applicators or machines are designed for use with liquid cleaners. They automatically dispense just the right amount of solution and convert it into foam that loosens and absorbs deep-down dirt without actually wetting carpet fibers. You'll find it faster and safer to use equipment and products which are designed to be used together.

If you use a home shampoo product, *never* use a soap or soap jelly. Soaps cannot be removed as easily as detergents. If any trace is left it may damage the fiber or leave a sticky film which attracts soil.

A light-duty detergent is recommended. *Never* use an all-purpose or heavy-duty detergent or chlorine bleach on wool, as alkaline substances may harm animal fiber. In fact, any colored fibers may be damaged by these substances.

Directions for Home Shampooing

You will need:
- Liquid shampoo.
- Two pails or containers—one for shampoo, one for clear rinse water.
- Sponge or brush.
- Rotary beater or hand mixer.
- Spatula.

- Vacuum rug or carpet.
- Know your carpet fibers, then read labels carefully on any commercial product you have chosen.
- Test rug for color-fastness in an inconspicuous area.
- Mix the commercial product or homemade solution. You can make a home shampoo as follows:

  ¼ cup light-duty detergent (the kind for delicate fibers or hand dishwashing)
  1 cup warm water

  Mix detergent and water and beat into a stiff foam with beater or mixer. Repeat beating as foam disappears.

- Apply foam to a small area of carpet with a circular motion, using a sponge or brush. A long-handled one is convenient. A sponge will clean the surface while a brush will make a deeper penetration of pile.
- Remove surface foam with a spatula. Check the surface. It should not feel "wet" to the hand. Too much wetting can cause mildew, shrinkage, or brown stains, which appear on the surface from the backing.
- Rinse with a sponge dipped in clear water and wrung dry. Repeat until all foam has been removed.
- Repeat foam application and rinsing until entire rug or carpet is cleaned.
- Brush "up" the pile, against the nap and dry quickly with the help of a fan. Plan on several hours for the carpet to dry.
- Place folds of aluminum foil under chair and furniture legs if they *must* be replaced before carpet is completely dry. This will help to prevent most stains.

Dry Cleaners

Dry cleaners may be made of either sawdust or powder, moistened with solvent. You simply sprinkle the compound on the carpet, then work it into the pile with a long-handled brush or an electric rug cleaner. (If you have a good deal of carpeting and want to do it yourself, it may pay you to invest in a rug cleaner/floor polisher. Or you may rent them from some hardware stores and supermarkets where they sell the cleaning products.)

In dry cleaners solvent loosens soil, and the sawdust or powder absorbs it. Some cleaners may be vacuumed up as soon as the solvent evaporates and the carpet feels dry to the touch. With others you must wait for a longer period before vacuuming.

Caution: If any of the ingredients are flammable or toxic, avoid fire hazards and keep windows open for good ventilation. All of this information, plus directions for proper use, is printed on the product labels. Follow them closely.

Caution: Do not attempt do-it-yourself home cleaning for valuable Oriental rugs. Take them to a professional. If you have any doubt about do-it-yourself cleaning of any rug or carpet, either consult a professional before doing it or don't do it at all.

Professional Cleaning

If you decide on professional cleaning, either to supplement your own efforts occasionally or because you'd rather not do it yourself, you'll have a choice of plant or on-location cleaning.

Plant cleaning is more thorough and also more economical for rugs that can be removed and sent out. They are given a thorough washing and rinsing so that even ground-in soil is removed, then dried scientifically to prevent mildew or brown staining. Wall-to-wall carpeting can be plant-cleaned too. If you are moving to a home or apartment with smaller size rooms, for example, it may be practical to have carpeting taken up, cleaned thoroughly, cut to new size, and relaid in your new home.

Plant cleaning is also better for many of the imported rugs, as they may not be color-fast. When you send a rug out for cleaning, provide as much information as you can as to fiber content and dyeing.

On-location cleaning is usually more economical for wall-to-wall carpeting, to avoid the expense of having it taken up and refitted. A trained operator will come into your home with special equipment.

Even though you do your own rugs or carpeting regularly, occasional professional cleaning is a good idea, if only to handle special problems such as stains you cannot remove yourself.

How to Treat Carpet Spots and Stains

We highly recommend that you take a few minutes to read through this entire section on stain removal, as we give you several alternatives for many specific stains.

Your best guarantee against serious stains is prompt attention to spills or accidents and a brief knowledge of stain-removal techniques:

- Always blot up liquids before they can soak into the carpet pile and spread through the backing. A simple spill may cause such problems as mildew, deterioration of the backing material, and even a larger stain as the liquid works its way back to the carpet surface.

- Blot with clean white cloth, white absorbent tissues, or white paper towels.

Spotting

Have you ever noticed those mysterious spots on carpets? These may be water stains or what professional cleaners call "delayed-action" stains. Either may be invisible for a time, often until the rug is thoroughly cleaned, and both are nearly impossible to erase once they develop. However, you *can* prevent them.

Water stains occur when moisture seeps down to the rug backing, works its way back to the surface in the process of evaporation. As the water reaches the fiber tips, it leaves any impurities that have been dissolved out of the backing material. To avoid water stains, blot wet spots thoroughly. Then cover them with a thick pad of clean cloth or tissues, weighted down with a book or brick. An electric heater, hair dryer, or fan can be used to hasten drying. When the carpet is completely dry, you'll find the brownish stain on the blotter instead of in the carpet pile.

"Delayed-action" stains can also be caused by a certain type of sugar in fruit juices, wines, soft drinks, and other beverages. You may blot up a spill and sigh with relief because you don't see any stain. But the sugar is still there, and the combined action of air and sunlight eventually turns it into a hopeless brown spot. So, whether you see a stain or not, at least sponge the area with cool clean water, blot well, and cover with a weighted pad to dry.

Another "mystery spot" is the tiny black fleck that appears here and there on new carpeting, particularly wool velvet pile. These are particles of oil, quite natural in some fibers, working their way to the surface. Simply sponge them away with cleaning fluid or use tweezers to pull out the burrs that sometimes form. However, if you see a steady line of oil spots or streaks, don't try to remove them. Instead, call your carpet dealer to have a representative check for possible manufacturing defects.

Stain Removal

To Remove Stains—Keep a ready kit of stain-removing materials. You can buy one, complete with instructions and bottled formulas, or you can assemble your own. Be sure it includes:

191

Clean, white unstarched cloths for absorbing
(Or white absorbent tissues or paper towels)
Spatula
Cellulose sponge

Light-duty liquid detergent
White vinegar
Household ammonia
Dry-cleaning fluid
Measuring cup and spoons

You may want to add rubber gloves, a medicine dropper, and a brush to raise carpet pile after it dries.

To prevent permanent stains follow these basic rules for spills and spot removal:

- Immediately blot up spills, using clean white absorbent material.
- Pretest your spotting formula in an inconspicuous place to be sure it doesn't affect the carpet dyes.
- Be patient. Some spots take considerable time and even repeated treatments.
- Try to wet only the carpet pile, using small amounts of formula.
- In applying formula, always work from the edge toward the center. Blot or sponge, but don't rub. Blot frequently.
- Dry dampened areas as much as you can by blotting; then the final step is to place a ½-inch layer of absorbent material over the dampened area and use a weighted pad to absorb any remaining moisture.

Stain-Removal Guide

The following simple remedies, formerly recommended by the National Institute of Rug Cleaning (NIRC), now called AIDS—Association of Interior Decor Specialists, Inc. (of which the National Institute of Rug Cleaning is a division)—and which we have used with success for a number of years, are safe for any carpet and effective for most stains. See the spot and stain list for specific uses.

Formula 1—Mix one teaspoon of mild or light-duty liquid detergent (the kind you use for delicate fabrics or hand dishwashing) with one cup lukewarm water. Saturate a cloth or sponge or use a medicine dropper to apply solution. Apply small amounts. Blot with a damp cloth or cellulose sponge. Then apply clean lukewarm water and blot again. Repeat until the spot is gone. Finish by blotting and drying with a weighted absorbent pad, as explained above.

Formula 2—Mix ½ cup of white vinegar with 1½ cups of lukewarm water. Apply the same as first formula, but allow the solution to remain for two or three minutes before blotting and using fresh water. Repeat several times, blot, and dry.

Formula 3—(Use very cautiously, to make certain it does not affect carpet dye.) Mix one tablespoon of household ammonia with ¾ cup water. Apply liquid to stain and work it in with a spatula. Apply a little clear water to rinse. Blot and dry.

Cleaning Fluid

Use a nontoxic, nonflammable type, if possible. Check the label for proper use and safety precautions. Apply it lightly to moisten only the carpet pile. Using too much may leave a ring or damage the backing. *Do not use gasoline, lighter fluid, or carbon tetrachloride.*

Specific Spots and Stains

Acids, Wine, Etcetera—Use Formula 3 promptly.
Ammonia—Use Formula 2 immediately.
Beverages, Fruits—Use Formula 1 several times. Then apply a little Formula 2.
Bleaches—Spots may form so quickly you cannot prevent them. Just rinse with cool, clean water and blot immediately.
Blood, Egg, Gelatin, Mucilage—If still wet, scrape away, then apply Formula 1. If stain remains, apply Formula 3, leave it on for two or three minutes, then rinse and dry. A dried stain will need professional treatment.
Butter, Oils, Fat—Use a cloth or sponge saturated with cleaning fluid and sponge gently from edge toward center.
Chewing Gum—Moisten with cleaning fluid and scrape off. Then sponge spot with cleaning fluid.
Cigarette Burns—Clip off blackened tuft ends with fine

193

sharp scissors. Apply Formulas 1 and 2 as directed. Only reweaving can remedy a deep burn.

Cosmetics—Lipstick: apply cleaning fluid and blot with paper towels. Repeat until color is removed, then use Formula 1. *Nail polish:* use amyl acetate (from drugstore). Apply a few drops, wait several minutes, then blot with tissues. Don't use nail-polish remover! *Rouge:* apply cleaning fluid, then wipe with dry cloth. Repeat until color disappears. If any remains, use Formula 1, then blot and dry.

*Dyes—*May not come out at all, but prompt treatment and patience may help. Use Formula 1 with medicine dropper, blotting and rinsing as directed. Repeat about every half hour for eight or ten hours, blotting well each time. Then blot and dry the dampened area thoroughly. *Or* test area with some of Formula 2, then Formula 3.

*Food Stains (greasy)—*Sponge with cleaning fluid, then with Formula 1. Follow with more Formula 1, plus Formula 3.

*Furniture Leg Stains—*Need professional attention.

*Furniture Polish, Wax Shoe Polish—*Sponge with cleaning fluid.

*Glue (animal type)—*If treated while soft, may respond to method given for bloodstains. Only a professional cleaner can safely remove hardened glue.

*Grease—*Sponge with cleaning fluid, then rub with dry towel to absorb.

*Ice Cream, Milk—*Sponge with clear, lukewarm water, then treat with Formula 1.

*Inks—*Blot as quickly as possible. Then apply cleaning fluid to a small area and absorb at once. Continue over entire spot. When cleaning fluid ceases to remove color, use Formula 1 the same way. Repeat until you can no longer see any improvement. Formula 3 removes some ink. Test it on a small area. It may take professional cleaning to remove the stain completely. Be sure to advise professionals what treatments have been used.

*Medicines—*Need professional treatment. Ask physician or druggist about ingredients and advise cleaner.

*Mercurochrome—*Call a professional.

*Mustard—*Apply Formula 1 as directed. However, yellow stain may be permanent.

Paint—If fresh, scrape up and apply cleaning fluid to spot. Blot well. Dry paint calls for professional treatment.

Rust—Call a professional cleaner.

Shoe Dye—Sponge with cleaning fluid. Spot may need professional treatment.

Sugar, Chocolate, Candy—Treat with Formula 1. Rinse well to remove all sugar.

Tar—Scrape off, sponge with cleaning fluid.

Varnish, Shellac, Lacquer—Need professional attention.

Vomit—Scrape up as much as possible. Apply Formula 1, then Formula 3.

Water—Formula 1 may remove brown stains if not too old.

Wine—Formula 3 followed by Formula 2. Absorb as much moisture as possible by placing absorbent material over remedied area.

Wax—Sponge with cleaning fluid.

Urine—Chemical action may affect carpet color, particularly in wool, but prompt action helps. First saturate area repeatedly with clean lukewarm water, blotting well. Then use Formula 2. It may take spot-dyeing to restore color.

Unknown—Try cleaning fluid, Formula 1 and Formula 2. If these do not work, try some of Formula 3. If unsuccessful, call for professional help.

CARE AND USE OF METALS, PLASTICS, AND OTHER HOUSEHOLD MATERIALS

A household is made up of so many materials that it would be difficult to count all the different ones we use each day. What's more, it seems that one must be something of a chemist to take care of them with a degree of technique. There are the familiar ones—aluminum, brass, copper, iron, pewter, steel, and tin. And now we have the newer ones with their dual combinations and varying finishes—for example, anodized aluminum, chromium-plated steel, chromium-plated aluminum, porcelain on metal, and plastics of all kinds, such as the acrylics, Lucite and Plexiglas, and thermosetting Melamine used in dinnerware. In addition, there are the nonstick finishes. Is there a home without at least one Teflon utensil? And these are just a few.

These materials help to account for the staggering selection of cleaning products available in the supermarkets.

ALUMINUM

To clean aluminum utensils, wash in warm sudsy water, using a light-duty detergent, then rinse in hot scalding water. Dry immediately. As a safeguard against warping, be sure to let them cool before washing. Scour heavily soiled and greasy utensils with a soap-filled steel wool pad, rubbing back and forth in one direction only and not in a circular motion.

To remove heavily "burned on" food from the bottom of a pan, fill it with water, let it boil for a few minutes, then remove the softened food with a pot scraper or wooden spoon. Follow by scouring the pan with a soap-filled steel wool pad, if necessary.

To remove darkened stains, caused by minerals in water or certain alkaline foods such as eggs, cook acid foods such as tomatoes or rhubarb in the pot. This will brighten the utensil without harming the cooked food. (You may be surprised to know that you probably have eaten some aluminum every day of your life. Because this metal is so abundant in soil, plants absorb it as they grow, and animals that are raised for food absorb it from their feed.) Boiling a solution of 1 to 2 tablespoons of cream of tartar to each quart of water in the utensil for 5 to 10 minutes also removes darkened stains.

Minerals in water and/or dishwasher detergents, especially combined with the very hot water necessary for automatic dishwashing, can sometimes discolor aluminum. Certain finishes such as anodized aluminum ware and "brite" finishes are not recommended for dishwasher washing.

There are *commercial cleaners* for aluminum. Follow the specific directions given on the container, though they work best if the utensil is washed first in hot water and the cleaner is applied to the metal while it is hot and wet.

To remove lime scale, which forms in teakettles in hard-water areas, mix a solution of one-half water and one-half vinegar and let it stand in the kettle for several hours. Scrape out the deposit with steel wool if the opening of the tea kettle is large enough. If not, scrape with the handle of a long-handled wooden spoon.

Repeat, if necessary. Swish out an aluminum tea kettle occasionally with hot sudsy water to keep lime scale from forming.

Do not use aluminum pans for storing foods. Chemicals in certain foods such as tomatoes and fruit juices may cause pitting. These tiny prick marks are unsightly, unsanitary, and hard to clean.

Decorative objects such as trays, candlesticks, candy dishes, etcetera made of aluminum alloys should not stain or tarnish. To clean, use warm sudsy water, rinse thoroughly. Dry quickly with a soft, clean cloth.

Aluminum window frames which are stained, darkened, or corroded may be cleaned satisfactorily with a soap-filled steel wool pad (and a little "elbow grease") or special commercial aluminum cleaners.

BRASS

Decorative objects such as vases, trays, candlesticks, andirons, etcetera, tarnish rapidly and require frequent cleaning and polishing, unless they have a lacquered finish.

To clean lacquered brass, simply dust with a clean, soft cloth. Wash occasionally in lukewarm sudsy water, using a light-duty detergent; then rinse and dry. To relacquer, remove all remaining lacquer with lacquer thinner, acetone, or amyl acetate (banana oil) or dip all-brass pieces (those which have not been cemented together) into boiling water. This will help to soften the excess lacquer. Dry it thoroughly; then wipe it with acetone to remove all film. Spray on clear transparent metal lacquer.

Warning: This process is not as easy as it might sound, and unless feel you are fairly skilled in metal work, consult a professional metal craftsman.

To clean brightly finished brass, wash first in hot sudsy water, rinse, then apply a good-quality brass polish with a soft cloth, or use a soft brush on embossed or carved designs, following container directions. Let the polish dry thoroughly, then polish with a soft cloth.

To clean dull-finished brass, add linseed oil or salad oil to rottenstone until the mixture resembles heavy cream. Apply mixture with a soft cloth and rub until the tarnish disappears. Use a soft brush on embossed or carved designs. Wipe off with a soft cloth, dipped in linseed oil. Wipe off excess oil with a clean soft cloth and rub with a flannel polishing cloth.

To revitalize antique brass (for a warm antique finish) rub with lemon oil and polish gently with a soft, dry cloth.

To clean very old and neglected brass pieces such as trivets, andirons, etcetera, use a fine emery cloth similar to those used by metal workers. You can obtain them at a hardware store. Otherwise a fine steel wool pad (000) will work pretty well. Rub the surface back and forth in one direction. Do not use a circular motion. When it is clean, polish with a brass polish. Wash thoroughly after polishing in warm sudsy water to remove all film. Dry with a soft cloth.

To remove corrosion from brass, use a piece of lemon, dipped in salt or hot vinegar and salt.

BRONZE

Follow same general directions as for cleaning brass, both lacquered and unlacquered.

CHROMIUM

Chromium needs only warm sudsy water to keep it clean. Polishing with a soft dry cloth will restore the luster. Do not use harsh chemicals, cleaning powders, or metal polishes as they may be injurious to chromium. Salt, and acid, such as lemon juice and vinegar, is also injurious. Salt-containing foods should not be left to dry on chromium surfaces. Remove burned-on grease with a little silver polish.

COPPER

Copperware requires regular care. Keeping it clean and free of surface tarnish will help to prevent "green patina."

Cooking Utensils

To remove the protective film of lacquer often found on new copper cooking utensils, cover them with boiling water to which a little baking soda has been added, and let them stand until the water is cool. The lacquer should be easy to peel off. Follow manufacturer's specific instructions.

Contrary to some opinions, copper does not cook better if it is dull and tarnished. *Clean it!* It is true that copper is an excellent heat conductor. To assure consistent and even distribution, with no hot spots, it should be kept polished. Use the same method as for brightly finished brass. Only apply a good-quality copper cleaner, instead of brass cleaner, or polish with a mixture of flour, salt, lemon juice, and ammonia. Then wash in hot sudsy water, rinse thoroughly, and dry. A mixture of vinegar and flour will also work on utensils not too badly tarnished.

Important: Always be sure to wash copper thoroughly in hot sudsy water after cleaning with any polishing compound. Otherwise, copper utensils will retarnish quickly.

Watch for signs of corrosion. To remove corrosion, rub with a piece of lemon dipped in salt or hot vinegar with salt. An old-fashioned method calls for rubbing corroded areas with a little buttermilk. Whichever method you choose, rinse thoroughly, then dry.

Copper cooking utensils must be well lined with tin (some may be coated with nonstick finishes; others may have only a copper-clad bottom on a stainless steel pot). Cooking food directly on an uncoated copper surface is dangerous, as a potentially poisonous chemical reaction may take place. Tin lining will wear off eventually and pot should be retinned. Take it to a metalsmith.

To clean decorative lacquered copper, wash in lukewarm mild sudsy water, rinse thoroughly, and wipe dry. Do not polish. Using water too hot or soaking it in hot water will cause the lacquer to crack and the copper will begin to tarnish.

IRON

Wrought iron is made from the purest form of iron and decorative accessories made from it, such as chair and table legs, lampstands, ash trays, etcetera, resist rust to a greater degree than cast iron. A protective coat of liquid wax increases its resistance and makes it easier to dust. To remove rust from wrought iron, rub the surface with kerosene, then scour with steel wool. If the rust is hard to remove, repeat the kerosene treatment until the

199

rust is softened. For iron furniture, see the preceding section on care of furniture.

Cast iron utensils require slightly different care than do those made of other materials. Cast ironware usually is preseasoned. Use only hot sudsy water, rinse, and wipe dry. Because iron will rust very quickly if the least bit of moisture remains on it, dry thoroughly after washing. Rinsing is important, too. Detergent solutions used regularly can remove the seasoning which prevents rust. It need not be washed with strong detergents or scoured. Occasionally, after washing, coat the inside with unsalted shortening. Just before use again, wipe with a dry cloth or paper toweling. Treat exterior surfaces on porcelain-lined cast iron utensils the same.

Never store cast iron utensils with the cover on, as this might create moisture which will cause rust. Store these utensils in a dry place.

To preseason cast iron utensils which have not been treated or to reseason those which have, scour utensils thoroughly, wash in hot sudsy water (to remove any lacquer or surface coating), rinse and dry thoroughly. Coat the inside surfaces with unsalted fat and place in a moderate oven (350° F.) for about two hours. After removing from the oven, wipe off the excess grease.

This reminds us of the story our good friends told about their cast iron cookware. They came home from a busy day at the office only to find out that their new housekeeper, in her effort to please, had cleaned, scrubbed and scoured all their cast iron utensils, which had taken years to season. "Oh, look," she said, "no more grease!"

NONSTICK FINISHES

The most familiar one is Teflon, which is the trademark for Du Pont's fluorocarbon resins. Two kinds of Teflon are available: the *conventional* type which may be easily scratched and *scratch-resistant Teflon II,* a pebbly, more durable surface.

Other nonstick processes used by equipment manufacturers include the use of special silicones which offer similar qualities. To find out which of these or other special nonstick methods are used and how to care for them read the hangtags or labels that accompany them. Follow the manufacturer's directions for the particular utensils you are using. For the use and care of Teflon-lined cookware, follow these directions:

- Before using initially, wash in hot sudsy water, using a soft sponge or dishcloth, then rinse and wipe dry. Lightly grease or oil the nonstick surface prior to first use.
- Wash in hot sudsy water, using a soft sponge or dishcloth after every use, so that grease or residual food will not contribute to staining.
- Teflon cookware may be washed in the dishwasher. Be sure that the exterior is also dishwasher washable.
- Avoid the use of high heat, especially on skillets, griddles, and top-of-range cookware. This will reduce chances of stains and discoloration.
- Do not use steel wool pads or harsh abrasives, which may scratch the surface.
- To avoid scratching nonstick surfaces, use plastic or wooden tools, unless otherwise directed. Light scratches do not impair the finish.
- Avoid the buildup of stains as this may impair cooking results. To remove stubborn stains, use a special commercial cleaner made for nonstick finishes. If you do not have a special cleaner handy, try this method:

  Use 2 tablespoons baking soda and ½ cup of liquid household bleach in 1 cup water. Heat to boiling in utensil and simmer for 5 to 10 minutes. Wash thoroughly in hot sudsy water, rinse and recondition by rubbing with oil before using.
  Caution: Do not let solution boil over, as it may stain the exterior surface. Do not be alarmed if the solution lightens the interior lining.

- Clean non-Teflon-coated areas by the method recommended for the particular material in question.
- To grease or not to grease depends on the food being prepared. For general top-of-range cooking, light greasing seems to enhance both flavor and ease of cleaning. However, the use of no grease at all, especially for low-

201

fat cookery, is permissible. Tubed angel food cake pans should not be greased if used for angel food cakes, as the batter must cling to the sides of the pan during baking. For baking fragile desserts or cakes that contain fruit or a great deal of sugar, greasing usually is necessary to insure even browning and complete release of the products. Cake pans also should be floured. However, be sure to follow the specific directions for the recipe you are using.

PEWTER

Pewter is an alloy, the basis of which is tin. It is a favorite collector's item, and some understanding of its content is necessary in order to care for it properly. Old pewter is primarily composed of tin and lead; it is soft and pliable, but hardens with use. Modern pewter is a tarnish-resistant alloy comprised of tin, antimony, and copper. Generally the best grades contain no lead. The antimony helps to whiten the alloy and imparts a hardness unknown to old pewter. Modern pewter, which looks almost like silver, seems to retain its brightness indefinitely and lends itself to many types of finishes, from bright to satin.

There are special cleaners for pewter which are simple to use, although a good-quality silver polish may be used with some satisfaction. Your best method for regular care is to wash it in warm sudsy water, using a soft cloth. Rinse and dry thoroughly with a clean soft cloth.

If you have a great deal of pewter you may be interested in these special methods:

To clean a dull finish, gently rub it with a paste made of rottenstone and olive oil, using a soft clean cloth. Wash thoroughly, rinse, then dry with another clean soft cloth.

To clean a bright finish, mix whiting powder and denatured alcohol. Rub on gently, using a soft clean cloth and let it dry. Then polish, with a soft cloth. Wash, rinse thoroughly, and wipe dry.

To remove corrosion, use a very fine steel wool dipped in oil to prevent scratching. If the pewter is very black, send it to a professional metal cleaner who will restore the finish.

PLASTICS

Plastics used for most home furnishings are easy to care for. Wash them with warm sudsy water, using a soft cloth. Rinse with clear warm water, using a soft cloth. Then wipe dry. A soft cloth is preferable to a damp sponge or a dry cloth, as the dust particles may scratch the surface of highly polished plastic. Avoid the use of scouring powder and harsh abrasives. All-purpose household cleaners can be used for surfaces such as counter tops, tiles, switches, etcetera. Follow specific directions when using any commercial product. Wipe up spills of household cleaners promptly to avoid possible damage to surfaces.

In general, all plastics can be classified into two groups, depending upon the effect of *heat* upon them.

1. *Thermosetting plastics* are set into a firm shape when they are manufactured. They may warp or crack, but they do not become soft and pliable as they become warmer. They can be used in hot water and will withstand temperatures up to 300° F.
2. *Thermoplastics* become soft when heated and stiffen when cooled. This happens each time they are subjected to heat. These plastics are usually *not* dishwasher washable, though some may be able to take these temperatures (if so, place these items only in the top rack, away from the heating element). Thermoplastics include acrylics, nylon, polyethylene, polystyrene, and vinyl.

Acrylic (thermoplastic) Plastics (Lucite and Plexiglas) used for fine lamps, tables, hairbrushes, shelves, light fixtures, dresser sets, picture frames, furniture, etcetera, are best cleaned with warm sudsy water, rinsed, then wiped dry. Also a spray window and glass cleaner is most effective. If accidentally scratched, use a little cream wax to camouflage it.

Melamine Plastic (thermosetting) used for dinnerware, some table and counter tops, cutlery handles, and on certain appliances should be washed with hot sudsy water, rinsed, and wiped dry. Melamine dinnerware of top quality is dishwasher washable. Special commercial cleaners are available to remove stubborn stains. Sodium perborate is also effective for heavy stains; baking soda for light ones.

To prevent static electricity which attracts dust to plastic, add a little fabric softener to the wash and rinse water. Or you can buy special anti static preparations specifically designed for this problem. When using any of these liquid anti static agents, follow the directions on the container.

PORCELAIN ENAMEL

Handle enamelware as you would glass. It is made of glass and can crack or craze. To clean porcelain enamel utensils, wash in warm sudsy water, using a sponge or cloth. "Burned-on" foods or other stubborn stains can be removed by soaking in detergent and water or by using a nonabrasive "scrubber." If scouring is necessary, use a mild nonabrasive cleanser or baking soda. Cooking utensils may be dishwasher washed unless the exteriors are made of cast iron. Avoid high heat, rapid cooling, chipping, and scratching. Teflon-lined porcelain enamel may be washed in the dishwasher.

SILVER (STERLING AND SILVER PLATE)

To keep silver looking its best requires tender loving care. If you have a great deal of silver, try to organize a special schedule for keeping it clean. Regular care will help to prevent an excess accumulation of tarnish, which will be harder to clean. And it will not have to be polished as often.

Follow these tips for regular care:

- Use your silver as often as possible. This will help it to mellow with use, creating the soft patina associated with fine antiques.
- Wash immediately after use with hot sudsy water and a soft cloth. Rinse in hot water; dry immediately.
- Rotate your flat silver as you use it. This will balance the wear and help it to mellow evenly.
- Store your flat silver in a lined chest or in silver cloths.
- Dust decorative pieces regularly with a soft cloth, and wash often, as above.

- All flatware may be washed in the dishwasher except hollow-handled knives or forks with handles secured with cement. They may loosen. *Never* let them soak in water.
- *Do not* place silver next to or touching stainless steel in dishwasher silver basket. This can cause pitting of the stainless by electrolytic action. Remember, most silver knives have stainless steel blades.

Polishing Silver

There are some excellent commercial silver polishes on the market. Study them, read the directions, and decide on the one that seems easiest for you to use. Actually, you will soon learn, by trial and error, which is best for your silver. Tarnish-preventive polishes and finishes and polishing mitts are available which render silver tarnish-resistant for a longer period between polishings.

While *dip polishes* are convenient, especially kept near the sink for quickie cleanups of flatware, they really *should be avoided* as they may include harsh chemicals and acids which may damage certain finishes.

We also don't care for *electrolytic cleaning*, using aluminum foil, salt, and baking soda in a water base, as in our opinion it tends to dull the finish and remove any oxidation or dark decorations which you may want to retain. Besides, it's too complicated to our way of thinking. The best method is to use a good-quality polish.

When polishing silver, take the time to clean it properly.

Wash it first in hot sudsy water, using a soft cloth. Apply the polish, according to container directions, using a soft cloth or a sponge provided for the purpose. A chamois cloth is also excellent. Rub each piece gently but firmly (never hard). Do not rub in a circular motion or crosswise with the silver. Use straight, even strokes whenever possible. Use a silver brush for cleaning decorative trim and borders.

Caution: Rub gold linings and plated ware gently, as these finishes wear away quickly with harsh treatment. Wash again in hot sudsy water, being sure to remove all the polish. Watch that no polish clings to decorative areas. Polish left on the silver causes it to tarnish again rapidly.

205

Special Care of Silver

- Keep air away from silver. The reaction of certain gases in the air will cause it to tarnish.
- Wrap or store silver in specially treated tarnish-proof bags, paper tissues, or in plastic bags. Or place in tarnish-proof chests and cabinets. There are tarnish-preventing compounds available which, when opened and stored with the silver inside a cabinet, will help to cut down on tarnish. Read the directions carefully.
- *Caution:* Contrary to popular opinion, never wrap silver in plastic film. While this method does retard tarnishing, the plastic that adheres to the silver tightly may damage the finish, creating black spots that are next to impossible to remove. Never use rubber bands to hold wrappings on silver. Rubber can tarnish and corrode it quickly, despite several thicknesses of paper or cloth.
- Remove eggs, olives, table salt, salad dressings, vinegar, fruit juices immediately. Salt and sea air also are harmful to silver, as is leaking gas.
- When using silver bowls for flowers, always use an inner glass container.
- Do not leave fruit too long in silver bowls. When using fruit, slip a piece of paper toweling in the bottom of the bowl or use an inner glass bowl.

STAINLESS STEEL

Stainless steel is rustproof and one of the easiest materials to clean and keep clean. It may be pitted by salt and acid foods (fruits, fruit juices, vinegar, milk, etcetera) left in contact with it. Washing by hand in hot sudsy water, or in a dishwasher, usually is the only requirement for keeping stainless utensils bright and shiny. Prompt drying prevents water spots. Avoid placing stainless steel flatware next to silver in the silver basket of the dishwasher. This can cause pitting of stainless steel through electrolytic action.

To remove burned-on foods, soak and wash in hot sudsy water. Light scouring with a fibrous pad, stainless steel wool, or a stainless steel cleaner will remove stubborn burns. After much use, a mottled, rainbow-like discoloration, commonly called "heat tint," may develop on the interior stainless steel surfaces of a utensil. If it is not heavily "tinted" this can be removed with a good stainless steel cleaner. If heavily tinted, it is almost impossible to remove this heat tint.

With normal use, a stainless steel utensil will not dent, warp, or chip. It thrives on exposure to the air, so it is an attractive utensil to display in the kitchen.

Tin

Kitchen utensils made of tin will heat better if allowed to darken. Wash in hot sudsy water, rinse, and dry thoroughly. If not dried carefully, tin may rust. Remove burned-on foods by boiling them in a solution of two teaspoons of baking soda and one quart of water for about 5 minutes—no longer. To remove rust, use a mild abrasive or fine steel wool, dipped in oil. Avoid the use of harsh abrasives.

Zinc

Wash in hot sudsy water, rinse, and dry. Remove any tarnish with a fine scouring powder or by leaving vinegar or lemon juice standing on the surface for a few minutes. Rinse and wipe dry.

Woodenware

Woodenware will crack or warp easily if left in contact with water for long periods. Clean it quickly after each use by wiping with cold water, then washing quickly with a cloth or sponge dipped in lukewarm sudsy water. Rinse with cool water and dry quickly. Never soak in water. Certain pieces may be dishwasher washable, but check accompanying labels.

It is not a good idea to stand woodenware on edge to dry or to stack and store wooden bowls until they are completely dry.

As for the great debate of whether to wash salad bowls after each use or to just wipe them out, we prefer the former. Clean

207

them as directed above. It is our feeling that remaining oil contributes to the possibility of imparting a rancid taste to your next bowl of salad.

Wooden Chopping Blocks and Work Surfaces

To make these surfaces more durable and practical, remove any existing finish, then treat with boiled linseed oil, which you can purchase in that form from any good hardware store. Apply the oil to the surface and rub it down with steel wool. Let it set for several hours, then wipe with a sudsy sponge, rinse and dry quickly.

Clean after each use by wiping quickly with a sudsy sponge. Rinse and dry quickly. Periodically, scrub with a fine steel wool, then rub in heated vegetable shortening.

CHAPTER FOUR

Of Dirty Clothes
and the Laundry Basket

Almost everyone does some laundry each week. It could be anything from a handful of underwear to several wash loads of family laundry.

We are extremely lucky today to have such well-engineered automatic equipment that it practically does our thinking for us. For those who do very little laundry at home but want the advantage of automatic equipment, there are the portables or compacts that fit into minimum space. And, of course, there is a wide selection of standard-size washers and dryers that do everything from the smallest load of fragile lingerie to the largest family load imaginable.

While all this automation has made laundering quicker (compared to the laundry tub and washboard), it has also made it more scientific! These days it is necessary to understand a little more about fabric content, the varying effects of "hard" and "soft" water, the difference between a high-sudsing or low-sudsing detergent, and, indeed, the difference between a soap and a detergent, a fabric softener and a water softener. We also need to understand what is a bleach, an absorbent, an alkali, an acid, a color remover, an enzyme. Not to mention the confusing environmental dilemma of whether to use phosphate or nonphosphate detergents.

In her book *Male and Female,* Margaret Mead points out, "There was a time when in the first flush of laundries and bakeries, milk deliveries and canned goods . . . it did look as if

209

American life was being enormously simplified. . . . But just as the new medicines are creating new vulnerabilities and new disease states, so the new equipment has led not to more leisure, more time to play with babies, etcetera, but has merely combined with other trends in making the life of the American homemaker more exacting, not easier."

Even so, the world welcomes progress and indulges in it. Over 90 percent of all the homes in America have some kind of automatic washer and almost half of them have automatic dryers! And in these homes over *three quarters of a million tons* of clothes are washed each week.

Certainly if we are involved with any heavy wash load, we should give some consideration as to where we do the laundry. If all the laundering is done at home, it does not seem too extravagant to plan a separate laundry room, if space permits.

PLANNING THE LAUNDRY

Actually, it is easier to find space for a laundry than one might expect. As you make your own plans, keep in mind that the smallest overall area that can contain an adequate and complete laundry is 8 × 10 feet.

Some of the laundry rooms we have seen are the brightest and most cheerful areas in the house! And with all the colorful laundry equipment available, including such matching accessories as measuring cups, laundry sorters, and ironing board covers, laundries are actually fun to decorate!

Of course, for many of us who live in small homes or apartments, our main concern is simply getting the laundry done as efficiently as possible.

No matter where it's located, whether in a corner of the kitchen, a nook in the bath, or a separate room, a laundry can and should be *planned* to provide the most working convenience for the available space.

It is possible to have an adequate laundry area with very little space. If you are cramped for space, look to such space-savers as the compacts, portables, combination washer/dryers, and stackable laundry equipment. With these space-savers, you can have more work surface and room for storage.

Laundry facilities may be placed in any one of many locations from the tiniest closet to the largest room, as you will see.

LOCATIONS

In a Special Utility or Laundry Room—This should be as close to plumbing connections as possible. For many, the ideal laundry may be a separate room where you can leave the ironing board up, unironed laundry out until you are ready to iron it. If you can manage a really large area, we are in favor of a "planned-clutter" room—a place for "organized chaos," where you can close the door when you are not working and forget it. If you have the space, you may do well to include a children's hobby corner, or a flower-arranging or sewing area. These are all activities which are nice to put down without putting away.

Take sewing, for example. What a convenience it is to have all your sewing supplies handy and near the laundry area. Or at the very least, to keep a sewing box close by for mending rips and tears right on the spot. If space allows, having your sewing machine and ironing board in close proximity is both time-saving and efficient.

One major advantage to a *utility room* is that it usually offers ample storage space and can sometimes even house a water heater if you have a problem maintaining sufficient hot water.

Our only complaint is that utility rooms in newer homes are often too small.

In a Central Hall—A niche in a wall can be disguised with sliding or louvered doors.

In the Kitchen—Strawberries and dirty socks are not a compatible twosome. If, however, there is no other space, or if you enjoy the convenience of centering the bulk of your work in a single area, you can segregate the laundry and food, if plumbing permits, either by a peninsula divider or a separate wall. Plumbing costs in this instance are relatively low because you can hook up to existing pipes.

In a Closet—This arrangement is good for storing portable equipment. If you are considering this location for a permanent

211

installation, remember venting is an important consideration for the dryer and proximity to plumbing is a must for the washer.

In the Family Room—This is particularly convenient for families with small children. Disguise the equipment, if possible, by putting up a partition or a storage unit with sliding or louvered doors.

In the Garage or Carport—Such a location, often utilized in warmer climates, takes advantage of otherwise wasted space. It allows for indoor drying on rainy days if you don't have a dryer. One disadvantage is that your laundry and equipment can get dusty if left uncovered. It also is impractical in cold climates.

Near Kitchen-Powder Room Area—This arrangement is convenient to all plumbing facilities and major work areas.

In the Bedroom Area—Such a step-saving arrangement may be located in a passageway between bedrooms and bath, allowing you to collect the soiled laundry where the bulk of it accumulates. It can be economical if plumbing is backed up to the bathroom and if the area is convenient to major storage units. Some disadvantages may be difficulty in providing adequate venting and the fact that the noise may keep you from running the equipment if someone is napping or in bed.

In the Bathroom Area—Though compact, this arrangement may be ideal for some, as equipment can be hooked on to existing plumbing and it is the spot where most soiled laundry accumulates. It is often convenient to linen storage as well. Such a location may entail higher installation costs if structural changes are necessary.

In the Basement—Here, there is usually plenty of space, and plumbing and other utility outlets are usually available. Disadvantages are the fact that you may be too far from other major activities and the many extra steps involved.

In Apartments or Homes with Limited Space—An excellent laundry setup that's ideal for an apartment or small home is one with a washer-dryer combination arranged under a kitchen counter so counter top doubles for cooking or laundry. Newer apartments may provide optional plumbing facilities for tenants. Ask about it if having your own laundry equipment in an apartment is important to you. Otherwise, there are usually adequate laundry facilities, generally in the basement, or sometimes for the tenants on each floor.

Using a Public Coin-Operated Machine

If you do your laundry in a public coin-op, convenience is relative. Make up some kind of lightweight kit to hold a supply of detergent, bleach, and other laundry aids. Also, consider one of those laundry hamper bags that slip over a portable cart. You can use it to double as a hamper and as a tote to the coin-op.

Tip: When doing your clothes at the coin-op laundry, take several plastic bags to sort loads for each family member. If you don't get to the ironing right away, you won't have to dig through a big load to find something someone needs immediately.

Planning Checklist

If you plan to remodel, buy, or build a new home, go over this laundry checklist first:

- *Space to Work In.* Where will you sort your clothes . . . pretreat heavily soiled ones or remove stains . . . fold your clean laundry? A counter top or table and a sink are a must.
- *Storage Area.* What will you do with soiled clothes waiting to be washed and clean clothes waiting to be ironed? Where will you make room for detergents, laundry aids, and stain-removal supplies?
- *Drip-Dry Area.* Don't forget a place to hang those permanent-press items which should be removed and hung as soon as the dryer stops tumbling. Do you want to consider a niche over a drain for hanging drip-dry items?
- *Plumbing and Venting.* The availability of plumbing (for washer) and ventilating (for dryer) is important in laundry planning. And while you're thinking about plumbing, check the capacity of your water heater. Is it large enough to deliver an adequate supply of 140° to 160° F. water for laundry, plus other household needs? If your water is objectionably hard, consider installing a mechanical water-softening appliance. See page 445. For more about water and water hardness, see special sections in this chapter and the *Water Systems* section in Chapter Nine.

- *Electricity and Gas.* You'll need a 20-amp, 120-volt circuit for your washer, a 30-amp, 240-volt circuit (208 in some metropolitan areas like New York City, for example) for an electric dryer or a combination electric washer-dryer; a 20-amp, 120-volt circuit for a gas dryer in addition to a gas connection (you can use this same circuit for your iron); a 120-volt circuit for portable laundry equipment. Good overall lighting plus spot lighting for work areas.
- *Easy-Care Flooring and Wall Surfaces* should be kept in mind and attractive decor is always an added plus.

ORGANIZATION

To make your plans for a pleasant, efficient laundry, follow the same general "center" principle as you do for kitchen planning (see Chapter Five). For optimum efficiency, the laundry centers can be placed as you note them on the plans. However, the amount of space available greatly influences your arrangements. The centers provide for *soiled clothes storage, sorting and preparation, washing, drying, ironing, general storage, water heater.*

Each work center encompasses one particular step in the laundry process:

Preparation and Storage Center—This must include space and equipment necessary for storage of soiled laundry, sorting, pretreating, and general preparation. A flat work surface, sufficient storage for laundry supplies, a counter area for pretreatment, a sorting table, mending supplies, and a sink complete this center.

Washing Center—This should consist of the washer with sufficient storage for detergents and other laundry products, such as bleaches, bluing agents, starches, and conditioners. Drainage must be located here.

Drying Center—Your dryer is the major appliance in this center and is most convenient if placed on an outside wall to allow exhaust for moisture and warm air. Counter space should be available for folding.

Ironing Center—Space is essential for an ironing board to be left in place, plus storage space for items to be ironed at a later time. Automatic ironer, hand iron, some counter space, and all facilities for hanging ironed clothing should be included in this center. A chair, utility step-stool, and laundry cart might also be useful.

General Planning Pointers

- The same basic types of plans apply to the laundry as to the kitchen (see Chapter Five).
- For right-handed people, the smoothest flow of work will move from left to right, beginning with a clothes hamper and sorting counter. (Vice versa for left-handers.) To the left should be a sink, then washing and drying areas, and last the ironing and storage center.
- Transferring clothes from washer to dryer is easiest if the dryer door opens away from the washer.
- A water heater installed in or near the laundry area guarantees a constant supply of hot water.
- General floor drainage is wise in a laundering area.

MEASUREMENTS TO KEEP IN MIND

In planning, it is essential to allow adequate space for each appliance and/or work center.

- Most washers, dryers, and combination units are from 25 to 27 inches deep, 36 inches high, and approximately from 27 to 30 inches wide. For a standard washer and dryer you'll need about 30″ × 30″ of floor space for *each* unit. That should be ample.
- For an automatic washer, dryer, or combination and work areas adjoining, allow a space approximately 4 feet wide by 30 inches deep.
- For an automatic washer and dryer side by side, plus adjoining work space, allow about 5½ feet in width and 30 inches in depth.
- For a washer and dryer facing each other, allow a 4-foot aisle.

SUPPLIES TO KEEP IN MIND

Having all the necessary laundry supplies and small equipment near the laundry area will save time and unnecessary steps.

215

You will need:
- Soap and detergent.
- Bleach.
- Water softener (mechanical system or packaged).
- Fabric softener.
- Starch.
- Stain-removal supplies.

You may occasionally need:
- Presoakers.
- Bluing.
- Tints and dyes.

EQUIPMENT TO KEEP IN MIND

- Washing Machine and Dryer.
- Clothesline (indoors and/or out). There are simple plastic ones in varying lengths, which are easy to keep clean, or those that can be mounted on the wall, which are retractable. The outdoor portable ones that slip into a ground socket are excellent.
- Clothespins. We like the sturdy plastic ones, as they are smooth and won't snag or discolor as wooden ones sometimes do.
- Forms for Drying Pants (optional). These help to keep pants in shape and cut down on ironing.
- Brown Paper for Shaping and Drying Wet Garments (optional). Forms for drying knitwear are also available, which saves having to draw the shape on paper.
    Note: The necessity for using forms and paper is diminishing with the advent of permanent-press and washable knitwear.
- Fold-up Drying Racks. These come in metal, wood, and rubber- or plastic-coated designs. Great for small amounts of laundry.
- Hampers and Canvas Dividers for Sorting Loads. Make sure hampers are ventilated. Dividers make quick work of sorting loads.
- Measuring Cups and Spoons. A must for measuring detergent, bleach and other laundry products.

- Sprinkler. There are colorful plastic ones you buy, and some of us still cling to our old soda bottle and sprinkler top.
- Iron.
- Ironing Board.
- Sleeve Board (optional). Makes the job of ironing sleeves neater and quicker.
- Pressing Cloth. You'll need one for pressing wool.
- Brush. For pretreating heavily soiled areas.
- Mending Basket. A "stitch in time" still "saves nine."
- Device for Filing and Keeping Directional Tags. So many garments require different care that it is important to keep them for quick reference.
- Paper Towels.
- Stool or Chair. If you like to sit down while ironing.
- Hangers and Hanging Racks. These are convenient for hanging permanent-press clothes as they come out of the dryer and for all garments after ironing.
- Stain-Removal Supplies. See page 285.

WATER

Water is your main washing ingredient. The condition of your water—whether it is hard or soft and whether or not it is hot enough—will determine to a large degree how clean your laundry is. It may mean the difference between yellowed, grayed, or streaked laundry, and clean, bright loads.

A great many complaints about unsatisfactory washing results can be traced directly to water hardness. You may be surprised to know more than 65 percent of households have water hardness that ranges from medium to hard, with minerals that can cause "tattle-tale gray" when combined with soap or if detergents are underused.

Water hardness is usually expressed in "grains of hardness" or parts per million (ppm). You can discover the grains of hardness in your local water supply by calling the local water or utility company. In rural areas, ask your state university exten-

217

sion service or your home demonstration agent. Water may vary from soft to very hard.

If your water is hard it may be softened by installing a mechanical water-softening appliance, or through the use of a packaged water conditioner, most often referred to as a water softener.

How Hot the Water?

For general laundering, the best results will be obtained when the water in the washer is between 140° and 160° F. (Set water heater thermostat at 145°–160°.) Setting the washer control at HOT will not insure that the water will be hot. The incoming water temperature will depend on the temperature of the water as it comes from the water heater. If the pipe run is long from water heater to washer, the water will cool down. A cold washer and cold laundry load will also decrease the temperature of the water. Set the water heater high enough to allow for these conditions.

Cold- or Warm-Water Washing?

For most laundry loads, hot water is best. However, some fabrics will look better and give a more satisfactory appearance when washed in warm (100°–110° F.) or cold (80° F. or cooler) water. Check your hangtags for proper instructions. See page 256 for *What Makes a Good Laundry Load?*.

Water Conditioners

The key to best results is soft water. Conditioning it refers to treating the water in order for it to react properly with the various laundry products. Water may be conditioned or softened in one of two ways:

1. Use a mechanical water-softening appliance.
2. Use a packaged water softener or conditioner.

You may often hear the term "softener" used in connection

with packaged products, though the term is technically used in reference to a mechanical type described later in Chapter Nine. Actually, a packaged product does "soften" the water. (You may find the term used interchangeably throughout this book.) You will find two types in the supermarket:

- *Non-Precipitating*—These sequester or "tie up" the hardness minerals in solution so that soaps and detergents can do their best cleaning job. These are best for automatic washers. Examples include Calgon, Spring Rain, and Noctil.
- *Precipitating*—Removes water hardness by combining with hardness minerals and precipitating them out of the water. This frequently gives a cloudy or milky appearance to the water. These should not be used in automatic washers because they will form a residue which can cling to fabrics and which is hard to remove.

    Some of these products also carry warnings that they should not be used for soaking aluminum, and some washers have aluminum parts. Examples include Climalene, and washing soda.

Water should be soft enough to allow soaps and detergents to remove soil effectively. Water with a high mineral content is called "hard" water. Water in the home can range from 0 to 30 grains of hardness. Hard water will not remove soil as well as soft water and can result in grayed, dingy laundry. To get clothes clean in hard water, it is best to add extra detergent.

If you wash with a synthetic detergent, it is not necessary to use a water softener unless the water is very hard. Synthetic detergents do contain a water-softening agent. If, however, water hardness in your area is from 7 to 10.5 grains you may wish to increase the amount of detergent. Water over 10.5 grains should be softened. Follow package directions for recommended amounts, depending upon hardness.

If you wash with soap, you will have good results only if your water is soft (under 1 grain hardness). Otherwise, unless you have a mechanical water softener, use a packaged one so that hardness does not exceed 3.5 grains.

219

WATER-HARDNESS CHART*
(1 grain per gallon, GPG = 17.1 parts per million, PPM)

	GPG	PPM
Soft	0 to 1 grain	0 to 17.1
Slightly hard	1 to 3.5 grains	17.1 to 60
Moderately hard	3.5 to 7 grains	60 to 120
Hard	7 to 10.5 grains	120 to 180
Very hard	over 10.5 grains	180

* See also Water Systems, page 446.

LAUNDRY EQUIPMENT

As we said earlier on, we ask more of our laundry equipment today than ever before. Special finishes and fabrics demand special care, such as selective water and drying temperatures, variable wash, spin, and dry speeds, even special cycles to "iron" your clothes wrinkle-free. There are washers and dryers on the market today that will do just that. Here is a list of the major washer and dryer features that you'll want to consider. Keep in mind, however, that it is not always necessary to buy the top of the line to get quality performance. Even the economy-price models offer some flexibility for your wash load, and as convenience features increase, so does the price.

WASHERS

Washers are available in either top-loading or front-loading designs. A *top-loading* is one in which the wash basket is mounted and loaded from the top. The washing action in this machine is created by a central agitator which moves the water and flushes it through the clothes. Most washers are designed as top-loaders, with the exception of some which are designed with certain conveniences which require front-loading designs.

A *front-loading* model or tumbler washer is one in which the wash basket or tub is mounted horizontally and is loaded through a front opening. The washing action in a front-loading machine is accomplished by a tub or drum, equipped with fins that lift the wash load up and drop it into the water. Some tumble-type washers are designed as stackables with a matching dryer to fit into minimum space, or as a taller unit for waist-high loading. Front loaders also have the advantage of being able to fit underneath a counter when the controls are located on the front of the machine.

Automatic Washers—These machines have an assortment of push buttons and controls to individually regulate speeds, temperatures, time, etcetera. If you want the flexibility and the responsibility of making these decisions yourself, you will find many models of this type—from the very inexpensive machines with only basic components for good washing results to top-of-the-line models with every convenience for specialized washing.

If you have the money and do not wish to bother making these decisions, you might want to consider one of the machines that allow you to just set a single control for the type of load you are washing (such as normal, delicate, permanent-press, washable knits or wash-and-wear). These machines are preset to make the decisions about water temperatures, agitation, spin speeds, etcetera.

Wringer and Spinner Washers—Though these are somewhat old-fashioned in design and concept, there are many areas where they are still popular. Both are portable and movable as they are mounted on casters. They use less water than the automatics and cost less to operate. Most wringer washers are power-driven for both washing and wringing the water from the clothes. Two rollers which can be operated by a foot control on some models wring the clothes completely dry.

A spinner washer, also power-driven, is one in which the clothes are washed in one tub, then removed to another in the same machine for rinsing and spinning to extract the water.

Semi-automatic Washers—There are fewer and fewer of these types available. They look like a regular automatic machine, but you have to set the controls for each setting of the wash, rinse, and spin cycles.

Other Types—Because many homes have space limitations, there are combination washer/dryers; stackable (one on top of the other) washers and dryers; and compact or portable washers and dryers. Compact washers and dryers are pint-size versions of major designs which allow you to wash and dry your clothes automatically in very little space. They may be caster-mounted for portability and hideaway storage. Portable washers, whether mini- or standard-size, must be rolled to a sink or tub for filling and draining.

How Clean Your Clothes?

There are many pros and cons on the cleaning powers of the various designs of washer agitators and tub formations. Actually, they all do a satisfactory job of cleaning your clothes. The key lies in using the proper amount and kind of detergent, careful sorting, and adjusting the amount of clothes to the size of the tub, the temperature, and amount of work (the clothes should be able to move freely).

What About Size?

You can buy a washer that will launder from 1 to 18 pounds. (Who knows how much larger they'll get?) However, the weight of the dry load is not so important a consideration. The size of your load will depend on the kind of sorting you do, according to type of fabrics and how they should be laundered. If you have a large family and your properly sorted loads are large, then you should consider a large capacity washer and dryer. Otherwise, an average capacity machine should do an excellent job for you. Dryers are available in matching capacity. Those machines which do wash very small loads—from one to five pounds—usually have some sort of flexible adjustment in control setting and amount of water used.

Buying Your Washer

Look for these features:
- Water level and temperature controls to vary the amount of water and its temperature—cold, warm, or hot.
- Adjustable wash time to control the number of minutes you want to wash the load.

- Automatic stop and reset or specially designed tubs to offset unbalanced loads.
- Adequate lint removal (some filters are self-cleaning).
- Automatic bleach, fabric softener, and detergent dispensers.
- Variable wash and spin cycles (choose only those you will use).
- Multiple agitation and spin speeds. Slower agitation speeds are important for delicate fabrics, slower spin speeds for no-iron garments. Most washers with multiple speeds offer a selection of 2, 3, or 4 speeds. However, a few washers with solid-state controls (which have no moving parts) have an infinite range of speeds (very slow hand wash to regular wash speed).
- Special safety features for wringer models.
- Weighing lid or door.
- A safety lid switch that shuts off the spin cycle when lid is raised.
- Small, separate tubs or baskets for washing loads simultaneously.
- Programmed controls which allow temperature and cycles to be selected with one setting.
- Special cycles for permanent-press, washable knits, soak, prewash cycles, extra rinses.

These special cycles are offered as convenience features to perform specific functions automatically determined by the setting of the controls. Proper conditions regulating water temperature, agitation speed, and spin speeds are set up to launder delicate fabrics, permanent-press, washable knits. Or cycles may prewash or soak the clothes or add extra rinses if desired. See programmed controls above.

Getting the Most Out of Your Washer

Locate your washer as close as possible to the hot water source. Clean lint filter regularly. Use correct temperature for type of fabric. Use correct amount of detergent—depends on hardness of water, load size, and degree of soil. Do not overload the machine. Use low-sudsing detergent for front-loading models and high- or low-sudsing for top-loading models. Turn off both hot and cold faucets after washing to relieve pressure on hoses. Wipe out the interior and leave door open to dry. Never use dry-cleaning solvents in your washer. Run washer through an entire wash cycle if you do any dyeing in the machine or if colors have faded. Wipe outside surfaces with a special appliance wax occasionally. It is advisable to have a serviceman drain the washer completely before you leave for a winter vacation. Also, disconnect cord from outlet and hoses from faucets.

If you have problems with your machine, refer to your instruction book for possible causes before calling for a serviceman.

DRYERS

Like the washing machine, dryers have contributed enormously to cutting down on housework. In one laundering study, it was found that 57½ minutes and 625 steps were required to hang, remove, and fold an 8-pound load of clothes. Use of a dryer cut the time to 12 seconds and 3 steps to load, 15 seconds to remove, and about 10 minutes to fold the same quantity of clothes. Needless to say, ironing time was cut to half. Now with newer no-iron fabrics, ironing has *all* but disappeared.

Types

Automatic Sensor Controlled or Dryness Control—Electronic sensing controls actually feel the moisture in your clothes, turn off the dryer when they are dry. This takes guesswork out of drying—a good investment if your budget allows.

Thermostat or Temperature Controlled—This type provides a selection of different temperatures or heat levels—high, medium, or low—and are usually indicated by the type of fabric or load you are drying.

Time Controlled—A timer control turns the dryer off at the end of a specified length of time which you set. Good for limited budgets but does require more time and attention to get wash properly dried.

In selecting a dryer, study these buying considerations: Do you prefer a dryer with time control, thermostatic or temperature control, or sensor (dryness) control?

What are the special electrical or gas requirements? Most electric dryers require a separate 30-amp, 3-wire, 240-volt circuit. Some compact dryers can be plugged into standard household 115-volt receptacles if properly grounded. Gas dryers can be plugged into a standard 115-volt receptacle if properly grounded but require a gas supply line and a certified shut-off valve.

Inquire about installation costs.

Visualize where your dryer will be used in order to provide the best venting system. The hot, moist air given off by a dryer must be disposed of in some way. This is easiest done by venting it outdoors. If you cannot do this, there are no-vent models which condense the vapor with cold water. These dryers need a cold-water connection and a drain.

> *Look for these features:*
> - A lint trap that is easily accessible or removable for cleaning.
> - An automatic ignition on gas dryers.
> - A legible, well-lighted control panel.
> - An air-only cycle for fluffing pillows and special items.
> - An indicator light for end-of-cycle.
> - An automatic sensing device to automatically turn off the machine when clothes are dry.
> - Variable temperature settings for specific fabrics or loads.
> - A permanent-press cycle which incorporates a cool-down period (5 to 10 minutes of tumbling with no heat at the end of the drying cycle). This minimizes wrinkling.

Getting the Most Out of Your Dryer

Clean lint filter after each use. Check dryer ducts once or twice a year. Tie sashes, apron strings, etcetera, loosely before drying. Avoid overloading—this requires longer drying time and causes wrinkling. Remove clothes immediately at end of cycle to avoid overdrying and wrinkling. This is especially important for permanent-press items. When you have several loads to dry, dry those items first that take the least amount of time. If you are drying a mixed load, set the drying time for the lightest-weight fabric. Remove those clothes you plan to iron from the dryer

225

while they are damp. Use a damp dry setting if you have one. This eliminates wrinkling. If you cannot dry dampened clothes immediately, put them in the refrigerator or freezer to hold moisture. To dry starched items, you will need to use a heavier starch solution as some starch is lost in the tumbling process. Overdrying also causes starch loss. Dry starched items separately from other loads.

Turn dark articles inside out to avoid starch spots on the right side. For best ironing results, remove items from the dryer at ironing dampness, place in a plastic bag, and hold for at least 30 minutes before ironing to distribute moisture evenly. Do not dry items which have been cleaned at home with dry-cleaning solvents, knitted woolens, Fiberglas curtains, foam rubber, or sponge rubber. Always disconnect cords on dryers before leaving for vacation. On gas models, shut off gas valve.

Drying Tips:
- A tip we learned from a college gal who puts the hair dryer to dual-purpose use: to dry a small article in a short period of time, place it in the hood of the hair dryer (the part that fits over the head). It should dry completely within a few minutes (from 10 to 20), depending on the article.
- Some dryers have an "air" setting. This setting on your dryer provides tumbling in room temperature air to "fluff" bedding or shag rugs and to "air" or "dust" draperies and clothing. *Hint:* Put flat, matted pillows in your dryer and set for air—they'll fluff up plump as you please.

LAUNDRY AIDS

You'd think in this day of scientific miracles that selecting a laundry product would be a relatively simple job. But, just as the discovery of new fabrics has complicated washing directions, so the increasing availability of specific additives and aids has made our choice of a laundry product more confusing.

Consider, if you will, the enormous variety of soaps and detergents, low-sudsing compounds and high-sudsing ones, additives and rinse additives, vegetable starches and synthetic ones, agents to soften the water and agents to soften the fabrics. To help clear up this confusion, we've done some investigation on our own.

OF HOUSEHOLD PRODUCTS AND THEIR EFFECT ON THE ENVIRONMENT

One reason product use and selection have become more complicated is our recent awareness of some of the environmental problems that have resulted from both industrial and household waste and by-products.

We have all tried to rise to the occasion in helping to solve the problem and in so doing have come to realize that the solution is not that simple.

Producing chemical formulations to achieve safe and satisfactory results, both in performance and quality, takes a great deal of research and development by reliable professional and technical people and cannot be done overnight.

The safety of our families and the protection of the environment is a many-sided problem. If we are to face it responsibly, as good citizens, we must learn a little about some of the variables involved. It becomes difficult, in a book of this nature, not to editorialize to some degree, so with the indulgence of my editors, let me urge consumers, manufacturers, retailers, and the government as well to rise to the age of consumerism and the environment with tolerance and patience. Let us all work out the problems together.

The consumer has a right to the safety of both products and the environment. The manufacturer has his right to operate competitively within the free enterprise system. The government has a responsibility to establish whatever regulations are necessary for the protection of both the consumer and the manufacturer. We all have a responsibility to exercise good judgment.

In our work with both the government agencies and private industry, we are coming to realize that they are both aware of the needs for quality and good performance and the relationship of both to the safety of people and the environment.

227

As responsible purchasers and users of household products, we must get all the reliable facts and respond with good judgment to possible solutions. Here are a few suggestions:

- Before you buy, read package labels and understand as much as you can about the product. If you wish, write the manufacturer or the proper government agency for more information.
- Changes are constantly being made. Keep up to date by reading newspapers, magazines, government bulletins and newsletters dedicated to the environmental problem.
- Investigate your own local environmental problems, if any; then be guided accordingly.
- We all know that many chemicals are hazardous. Follow the directions exactly and keep the containers out of the reach of small children.

THE PHOSPHATE DEBATE

At this writing, there exists an intense controversy over the use of phosphates in detergents. Nonphosphate detergents now on the market are not really giving us the kind of laundering performance we desire. More and more studies are being made by both government and industry to find new formulations that will provide both satisfactory laundry performance and safety to humans and the environment. In the meantime, here are some suggestions on how to improve laundry results with the available nonphosphate powdered detergents.

1. Delay adding the clothes until after the detergent is mixed with the wash water. First add the detergent, then fill the washer with water; wait a minute or two, if possible, then add the clothes. (The longer you wait before adding the garments, the more time the detergent has to soften the water. Nonphosphate detergent powders are carbonate—washing soda—based and thus not as effective a softener as phosphate; they tend to form water hardness residues or scum which may cling to fabric surfaces.) Not only will the detergent be more effective in cleaning,

but colors will appear brighter, as the water hardness minerals will have been precipitated out before fabrics were added.

2. Use the hottest water suitable for the fabric—at least 140° F for colorfast cottons. Although hot water has always been important in helping to get clothes clean, it is especially important with nonphosphate powdered detergents. *Caution:* Not all fabrics should be washed in hot water. Check care labels and hang tags.

3. To keep towels and other fabrics soft follow steps 1 and 2 and, in addition, use a fabric softener in the last rinse.

Note: The above is true primarily for powdered nonphosphate detergents. Some liquids, however, because they are composed of citrates (which soften water similarly to phosphates) will show little or no difference in results from phosphate products.

We feel that we would be remiss not to say that the mere elimination of phosphates in detergents will not completely solve the problem of eutrophication in the areas where it exists, which is in roughly 15 percent of the country. If you personally want to do something about the situation, you can support the measures suggested for more adequate sewage treatment plants, which seems to us one logical way to achieve a marked improvement in the nation's water supply.

THE MAIN INGREDIENTS IN LAUNDRY DETERGENTS

Each cleaning product has its own special formulation. This is especially true with laundry detergents and laundry aids. While each brand may vary its formulation to certain degrees, each type of product designed to do a specific job is basically the same. Our main objective is to obtain maximum results from a laundry product in order to do a better job with fewer laundry problems.

Here is a cursory look at some of the ingredients that make up most laundry detergents: surface active agents (surfactants), builders, machine anti-corrosion agents, suds control agents, soil redeposition inhibitors, processing aids, fabric brighteners, perfumes, and occasionally other special ingredients.

Surfactants (Surface Active Agents)—A surfactant is one of the basic ingredients of synthetic detergents. Its function is to "make

229

water wetter" and therefore helps loosen and remove dirt more effectively. They perform in hard or soft water without combining with hard-water minerals to form insoluble curds. It is this portion of the detergent that is frequently referred to as a *biodegradable*. All surfactants today are biodegradable. Biodegradable simply means that the surfactant ultimately breaks down into harmless carbon dioxide and water. This is an important consideration, as it keeps foam and suds from floating on rivers and streams.

Builders—The function of a builder is to soften water and to add some alkalinity for more effective cleaning power. From the time heavy-duty laundry detergents were introduced until the late 1960's, the builders which were almost universally used were phosphate compounds. However, at this time the role of phosphorus, the basic element of phosphate, became controversial because some scientists believed that phosphorus is an important contributor to the excessive growth of algae in lakes and streams. As a result, a number of detergents were formulated without phosphates. The *nonphosphate builders* most commonly substituted are *sodium carbonates* (washing soda) and *citrates*. Undoubtedly, other builders will appear as more research continues to find effective ingredients for improved performance.

What, then, is the difference in the way these three types of builders soften the water? The *phosphates* sequester or "tie up" hardness minerals in a soluble material that readily rinses away. Citrates act similarly. On the other hand, sodium carbonate (washing soda) removes water-hardness minerals by combining with them and forcing them out of the water in the form of a fine granulate residue, which is primarily *calcium carbonate*.

Machine Anti-Corrosion Agents—These ingredients, such as sodium silicate, are added to protect washing machine parts from corrosion.

Suds Control Agents—These are the ingredients that help to control the amount of suds a detergent will make and which help establish the sudsing characteristics of a detergent.

Somewhere in the book we mention a tip that says, in effect, after hand laundering if you are left with a bowlful of suds, all you have to do is wash your hands with soap over the suds and they will disappear! This is the principle used in some low-sudsing formulations. For example, we were told about the wife of one chemical engineer who broke a large bottle of shampoo in the bathtub. When she couldn't rinse all these suds down the drain, she called her husband. Being busy, he hurriedly told her to add soap flakes. She thought he had lost his mind, so, probably out of spite, to prove him wrong, she did just that! To her surprise she found all the shampoo suds she couldn't rinse out collapsing right in front of her.

Soil Redeposition Inhibitors—These ingredients keep the soil from settling back on the fabric after it has been loosened and removed.

Processing Aids—These simply make the products easier to pour.

Brighteners and Whitening Agents—These are found in most soaps and detergents. When they are absorbed on fabrics during washing, they convert some of the invisible ultraviolet light in sunlight to visible blue light. The additional blue light from a fabric counteracts yellowness and makes the fabric appear brighter and whiter. Brighteners will vary in effectiveness depending upon the fabric. Finishes may reduce the effectiveness of some brighteners.

Perfume—Helps cover odor from soiled clothes during washing and leaves a clean fragrance on clothes after washing.

In addition to the above, one or more of the following may be found in a laundry product:

> *Oxygen bleach* to aid in whitening and cleaning to remove some soils and stains, *borax* to make clothes sweet and fresh and assist in stain removal, and *bacteriostats* to inhibit growth of bacteria on fabrics, especially diapers, *bluings* to counteract natural yellowing, and to leave a slight tint on fabrics.

Enzymes are included in some detergents to break down soils and stains composed of protein and starch, so they can be easily removed during laundering.

While enzymes have been confirmed as completely safe for

231

consumer use, safe for the environment, and effective in removing certain stains and soil by the National Academy of Sciences/National Research Council, they may irritate some people with sensitive skin. You will be the best judge as to their use for *you*.

DIFFERENCES BETWEEN SOAPS AND DETERGENTS

Technically, "detergent" refers to both pure *soap* and synthetic compounds. Essentially, a detergent is a product that acts as a cleansing agent, but in current usage it has come to mean synthetic detergents, not soap. When you walk through your local supermarket or grocery you will find that all laundry products that are labeled as "detergents" are in effect "synthetic detergents."

Throughout this book, when you see the term detergent, it means a synthetic detergent.

For naturally *soft* or *softened water* you may use either soap or a synthetic detergent. For *hard* water, you will get the best results with a synthetic detergent. If you feel you must use soap and you have hard water, be sure that you soften the water.

For more specific information on each type of product see below.

SOAPS

All-Purpose Soap (heavy-duty) is designed to remove soil from just about any fabric found in the family laundry. Moderately alkaline "builders" or chemical agents are added that improve cleaning power. Soap usually includes brighteners and is available in granular, flake, or bar form. For best results, *soap should be used only in water that is naturally soft or which has been softened;* otherwise it will combine with minerals in untreated hard water to form a soap curd, film or "lime" soap. (The same thing occurs to form "bathtub ring.") All-purpose soaps are recommended for normal to heavy soil and are suitable for general laundry purposes. Examples are Duz, Instant Fels, White King Soap.

Light-duty Soap (generally referred to as mild) is an essentially pure soap containing no builder, designed for the care of baby clothes, diapers, fine fabrics such as silks, rayons, woolens, and fine cottons and linens. They are most suitable for lightly soiled and delicate articles, usually those laundered by hand. Examples include Ivory Flakes, Ivory Snow, Lux Flakes.

DETERGENTS (SYNTHETIC)

Detergents are the most popular of the laundry products because they work well in either hard or soft water. They contain water softeners, alkaline builders, or special chemical agents to improve cleaning power, agents to prevent washed-out soil from redepositing onto clean fabrics, and brighteners to improve whiteness and brightness. Some also contain bleach, antibacterial agents, bluing, and enzymes. Unlike soap, they do not form a curd in hard water, and generally no water conditioner is needed, unless the water is extremely hard.

All-Purpose Detergents. These contain special agents to strengthen cleaning power and to improve heavy soil removal of family laundry as described above. They may be granular, liquid or tablet; high-sudsing or low-sudsing.

Examples include:

High-sudsing—Not generally recommended for front-loading tumble-type machines. If you do use this type, follow exact measurement on package or use even slightly less to avoid any chance of oversudsing. These are suitable for the entire wash, ranging from heavily soiled work clothes to diapers to lightly soiled delicate lingerie.

	GRANULAR		LIQUID
Tide	Duz	Surf (cold	Wisk
Fab	Bonus	water)	
Cheer	Breeze	Oxydol	
Dreft	Silverdust	Rinso	

Low- or Medium-sudsing—Produces fewer suds, which reduces the chance for too many suds to slow down or "cushion" the water action, thus producing poor washing results and possible damage to machine. Especially good for front-loading washers.

233

GRANULAR		LIQUID	TABLETS
All	Cold Water All	Cold Water All	Salvo
Dash	Cold Power	Cold Power	Vim
Ad	Drive		
Bold	Gain		
Ajax	Fluffy All		

Light-duty—Nonalkaline, these are generally recommended for washing fine fabrics, silk, hand washing, delicate cleaning, and dishwashing.

GRANULAR	LIQUID	
Trend	Chiffon	Oxydol
Vel	Dove	Trend
	Joy	Vel
	Fels	White King
	Lux	

Specialty Detergents. Those formulated for specific uses. Some include cold-water soaps for delicate woolens and woven fabrics, "special garment" detergents for elasticized fabrics, and "optical whiteners" and detergent for synthetic fabrics. Some have static inhibitors. Woolite is one example for woolen fabrics.

How Much Soap or Detergent to Use?

It is wise to follow both your laundry equipment instruction book and the detergent package instructions as to specific measurements. Soap or detergent is designed to loosen and remove soil and to hold the soil in the wash water until it is drained out of the machine. Therefore, *the proper amount must be used.*

Caution: If you do not use an adequate amount, the soil may be released, but since there is *not enough detergent to hold the soil in the wash water,* it is redeposited on the fabrics . . . and you have that common culprit called tattle-tale gray! To remove tattle-tale gray, see page 261.

Hints on using detergent:
• The harder the water, the more detergent required.
• The larger the load, the more detergent required.

- The heavier the soil, the more detergent required.
- Greasy soils require more detergent.
- Instructions on the detergent box are based on average washing conditions: a 5- to 7-pound load of clothes; moderate soil; moderate water hardness (4-9 grains per gallon); and average water volume (about 17 gallons of water for a top-loading washer, 8 gallons for a front-loading washer).
- If you are using a non-phosphate detergent, it is important to follow new package directions to assure proper results.

FABRIC SOFTENERS

If you like a soft, "cushy" feeling on bath towels, chenilles, corduroys, pants, T-shirts, socks or baby· clothes, use a fabric softener which lubricates the fibers. A fabric softener also reduces static electricity and that "cling" quality in certain permanent-press and wash-and-wear fabrics, reducing wrinkling, and improving appearance. Add the fabric softener to the last rinse, unless it is one designed for use in the wash cycle. If your washer has a fabric-softener dispenser it will release the fabric softener at the proper time, during the last rinse. Examples include: Downy, Final Touch, NuSoft, Sta-Puf, Rain Barrel.

Caution: Fabric softeners do not do their best job when combined with other laundry products. Do not add them to the wash water (unless directions so indicate) with detergent or bleach, and do not use other laundry aids such as a water conditioner in the same rinse that you use fabric softener. Avoid the use of too much fabric softener, as this can make fabrics nonabsorbent. If this does happen, either decrease the amount of fabric softener the next time, or leave it out for several washings.

ENZYME DETERGENTS AND PRESOAKERS

Enzymes are particularly effective in helping remove protein-type stains such as blood, baby formula, meat juice, and vegetable-protein stains such as grass and tomatoes. You will find two types of enzyme products on the laundry shelf:

1. *A laundry detergent* to which enzymes have been added. These include Ajax, Bold, Drive, Gain, and Fab.
2. *A presoaker* which is not intended to replace your present soap or detergent, but rather to be used as soaking agents prior to the regular wash. Some are: Biz, Axion, and Amaze. If you wish, you may add a presoaker to the wash cycle along with a regular laundry detergent to act as a cleaning booster.

BLEACHES

Remember that bleaching is not a substitute for good laundering. But it is a great help in removing stains, whitening clothes, and brightening fabrics. There are several kinds of bleach.

Chlorine—Chlorine bleaches are available in both liquid and powder. They are the most effective bleaches for heavy stain removal and especially helpful as a disinfectant. Using chlorine bleach improperly can harm fabrics, so *follow instructions carefully*. It is wise to observe these few *precautions:*

- Do not pour undiluted liquid chlorine bleach on any fabric. This can cause permanent damage which you may not detect until several washings later, when the item tears. Always dilute the bleach with water before adding to a load of clothes, unless you have a built-in bleach dispenser.
- Do not use chlorine bleach on silk, wool, or spandex fibers, or on resin-treated cotton fabrics, unless recommended by garment manufacturer. To do so may yellow fabrics or stain them permanently. (To remove these yellow stains, see Packaged Color Removers, page 237.

Examples include:

GRANULAR		LIQUID	
Action	Clorox	Fleecy White	
Hilex Heavy Duty	Purex	Roman	
Linco	Hilex	Linco	
Stardust			

To Use Bleach

If your machine has a bleach dispenser, follow your instruction manual. If you are adding bleach by hand, dilute in a quart of water before adding to the wash after the load. Detergents contain brighteners themselves and it is best to let them fasten to the fabric before adding the bleach. It will not hurt, however, to add it at the beginning of the cycle if it is more convenient.

Oxygen Bleaches—These are dry light-duty bleaches and safe for all fabrics. They are not designed for heavy stain removal and are used mainly to *maintain* whiteness and brightness, rather than *restore* it. Use these bleaches regularly for best results on silk and synthetics like orlon, nylon, spandex, and rayon. They work best on fresh stains and lightly soiled fabrics. A few colors may be sensitive to these bleaches, so do not pour them directly on colored clothes. Follow directions carefully.

Examples include:
Beads-o-Bleach, Daybrite, Clorox-2, Snowy, and Dexol.

Packaged Color Removers—These products are actually called "reducing bleaches." They have the capability to remove some stains and dyes. They are particularly effective in removing the yellowish color from aging nylon and from resin-treated cotton fabrics that have been harmed by chlorine bleaches. For proper use follow specific package directions.

Examples include:
Rit, Tintex.

BLUING

Bluing doesn't really make fabrics cleaner or brighter, but it does help to revive the "white" in fabrics dulled with age. It also acts as a fabric "cosmetic," to make things look whiter. Actually, bluing has largely been replaced by brighteners contained in laundry detergents, bleaches, and fabric softeners. If

237

you do use it, follow container directions. Some bluings should be added to the wash water, others to the rinse water.

Examples include:

La France, Little Boy Blue, Blu White, Bull Dog, Mrs. Stewart's.

STARCH

Starch gives a crispness and a firm body "finish" to fabrics that make them look perky and fresh. You may starch fabrics by hand and spin them in the washer, starch in the washer, or use one of the sprays. The last are easy to use and gaining in popularity. If you want to starch in the washer, follow the instructions for the machine you are using.

You can choose from liquid and dry vegetable starches as well as the spray fabric finishes and starches. After experimenting, you will soon know which gives you the best results and which is easiest for you to use.

Examples are:

VEGETABLE (LIQUID)	VEGETABLE (DRY)	SYNTHETIC
Linit	Argo Gloss	Gloss Tex
Sta-Flo	Faultless	Perma-Starch
	Niagara	

SPRAY STARCHES AND FABRIC FINISHES

Easy-on	Niagara	Bab-O	Pruf
Faultless	Sta-Flo	Magic Finish	

DISINFECTANTS

While the ideal wash water temperature ranges from 140° to 160° F., the water temperature in the average home is often lower. Therefore, you cannot be sure that just "doing the laundry" will disinfect and/or kill harmful bacteria. It is possible, unless water temperature is over 140°, to transfer germs from one family member to the other. Even some coin-ops have insufficiently hot water and there you are exposed to an even wider array of germs. In addition, if you are laundering clothes or bedding belonging to someone who has been ill with a cold, flu, or other contagious disease, it is a good idea to use a laundry disinfectant regardless of the water temperature.

Microbiologists at the U.S.D.A.'s Textile and Clothing Laboratory* did a study of the various effective and practical laundry sanitizers. They considered only those that met the following criteria:

- It must kill many kinds of bacteria.
- It must not injure or discolor fabrics.
- It must not leave a residue on clothes that is harmful to humans.
- If used in the wash cycle, it must be compatible with the detergent.
- It must be readily available and reasonable in cost.

They found four types of disinfectants that met these requirements:

Quaternary disinfectants. These are colorless and odorless.
Examples include:
Co-op Household Sanitizer and Roccal Brand Sanitizing Agent.

Liquid chlorine disinfectants. More commonly called chlorine bleaches.
Examples are:
Clorox, Purex, and Texize.

Pine oil disinfectants. These smell of pine oil.
Examples are:
Fyne Pyne, Fyne Tex, Pine-O-Pine, Texize Pine Oil.

Phenolic disinfectants. These have a distinctive phenol or carbolic acid odor.
Example are:
Pine-Sol, Lysol, Texize 83, Centex.

* Home and Garden Bulletin #97, U.S.D.A., "Sanitation in Home Laundering."

All of the above are effective for use as sanitizers in *hot* and *warm* water. Some may be effective in cold water—check labels.

DEODORANTS AND DIAPER PRODUCTS

These products, available in powder, liquid or tablet form, are formulated to control bacterial growth and to soften diapers. You can purchase a special diaper detergent or an additive for use in soaking, washing, or rinsing.

Examples are:

Diapersol, Diaper-Sweet, Ammorid, Diaperine Chloride, Diaper Soft, Borateem.

DYES

Dyeing will produce deep, lasting color in fabrics. Directions call for simmering in a dye-bath and it is usually impractical to attempt to dye any but small items at home. Tie-dyeing, which is achieved by twisting and immersing fabrics and garments in dye, has become a very popular hobby among fashion-conscious people. Since the items are usually no larger than a dress, shirt, or jeans, this can be quite successfully done at home.

Tip: If you have permanently damaged the color of an item during laundering by forgetting to remove a non-color-fast sock or the like, you might try dyeing it. Follow package directions.

TINTS

Tinting does not require high temperature or simmering but neither will it produce lasting color. After tinting, fabrics will have to be separately washed as tinted colors may fade and transfer to other items.

Tinting may be done in the washing machine. Follow manufacturer's directions. Whether tinting or dyeing, fabrics must be thoroughly rinsed of washing film and free of spots and stains to assure even dye distribution. Some tints and dyes are available in both liquid and powder types. Examples of tints and dyes are: Rit, Tintex.

Tip: Unless directions call for straining, it might be a good idea to add a water softener to the dye or tint bath to help disperse the dye thoroughly in the color bath. When tinting or dyeing an article, first tie the dye in a piece of cloth, then pour boiling water over the cloth until all dye is dissolved. This will help eliminate dry particles of powdered dye which could spot the article.

After you complete the tinting process in the machine, run it through a complete wash and rinse cycle, using detergent and bleach as you would for a normal wash load, to clean the machine.

A LOOK AT THE LAUNDRY BASKET

Doing the laundry today is not as simple as it was when only the natural fibers, cotton, linen, silk, and wool, were available. Now we are able to buy a wide variety of fabrics made from *synthetic fiber* or a blend of different synthetic fibers. Yet in many ways it is much quicker to do the laundry, because newer fabrics are lighter in weight and demand less care.

There are also fabrics which have been treated with *special finishes* to change their appearance, feel, and performance. As a matter of fact, sometimes even an expert cannot recognize a fabric just by its appearance. Rayon can look like linen, cotton may look like silk.

In purchasing clothes and home furnishings, it really is important to think first about their care. Anything you can launder at home will be much cheaper in the long run than an item requiring dry-cleaning. Of course there will always be some items that you want that must be dry-cleaned. Be sure never to try laundering these or you may cause permanent damage. It adds up to big dividends to understand a little about the different fabrics in your laundry basket (and those that should never be found there).

LABELING

Another factor to consider is labeling and what the manufacturers tell you about their products.

241

How many of us have carefully put away the care instructions for garments only to forget where we put them? Now the government has made the job of keeping track of these instructions easier for us by establishing *permanent care labeling*. On July 3, 1972, the Federal Trade Commission ruled that all wearing apparel, domestic and imported, manufactured after that date, must have a permanent label that carries care instructions. The care instructions must be clear and explicit enough to ensure the purchaser's ordinary use and enjoyment of a garment through regular maintenance such as washing, drying, ironing, and dry-cleaning.

Some care instructions may be pretty brief, but we have come of age and should know what to do when a label reads "dry-clean only" or "machine washable."

Because different fibers and fabrics require different wash water temperatures and other laundry conditions, it is more necessary than ever before to save the hangtags, labels and instructions that come with whatever you buy.

Hangtags and labels indicate brands, trade names, fiber content, and textile categories. A wise shopper will try to understand just what kind of performance can be expected of each textile family. Only then can you really evaluate just what to expect from the claims that are made on labels and hangtags. Labels also *provide information on finishes* and *supply use and care instructions*. Trade names can be identified by the trademark symbol, registered, such as Dacron®. The generic or family name usually follows.

Opposite are some of the most common terms to appear on these labels:

MEANING OF LABELS*

WHEN THE LABEL SAYS	WASHER SETTING	DRYER SETTING	LINE DRY
Machine Wash Hot	Regular** Cycle Hot Water	Regular**	Yes
Machine Wash Warm†	Regular Cycle Warm Water	Regular	Yes
Machine Wash Warm Line Dry	Regular Cycle Warm Water	No	Yes
Machine Wash Warm Gentle Tumble Dry Low	Gentle‡ Cycle Warm Water	Low	Yes
Hand Wash Separately Line Dry	No	No	Yes
Hand Wash Separately Dry Flat	No	No	No
Dry-Clean Only	No	No	No
Wipe with Damp Cloth Only	No	No	No

When the word "No" appears above, it indicates a prohibited procedure.

The above wash water settings are based on typical home conditions and approximate the following ranges:

Hot	130° to 150° F
Warm	90° to 110° F
Cold	Less than 75° F

* Prepared by a Joint Retail Apparel-Textile Industry Committee in Response to the F. T. C. Care Labeling Regulation of December 9, 1971. Courtesy of N. R. M. A. (National Retail Merchants Association).

** The term "Regular" as used above encompasses other terms that may appear on some washers and dryers such as, Automatic Dry, Timed Dry, Special Normal, etcetera.

† The term "Warm" as used above encompasses other terms that may appear on some labels or washing machines, such as medium, etcetera.

‡ Gentle or delicate cycle indicates low-speed agitation and shorter washing periods, or permanent-press cycles on dryer.

Additional terms that may be combined with any basic label when appropriate include:

1. Do not bleach
2. Do not use chlorine bleach
3. Do not twist or wring
4. Remove before full dry
5. Wash inside out
6. Do not iron
7. Use cool iron
8. Furrier clean only
9. Leather clean only
10. Do not dry-clean
11. Wash separately
12. Remove trim

Tip: To save loose hangtags, start a file box for quick reference, or use a small shoebag, hung near the laundry, for sorting the hangtags by categories.

Drip dry means drying fabrics by removing them from the rinse water without spinning, wringing, or squeezing, and hanging them freely in air, allowing the water to drip from the fabric.

Tumble-dry (machine dry) means to dry in an automatic dryer by evaporation and air through tumbling, with or without heat.

Flat dry means to dry fabrics on a clean, absorbent surface (such as a towel).

CONSTRUCTION

Always examine the construction of a garment or item before buying. The seams should be ample enough to prevent splitting during use or washing. Trim should be washable or easily removable. Linings of jackets, dresses, or blouses should be of a fabric heavy enough to stand the pull of the outer fabric during washing. Look for metal trim that will not rust, colors that will not bleed or fade. Make sure that the thread is color-fast and of the same quality and type as the item on which it is used.

Fabric Finishes

Not only are there many new kinds of fibers and blends, but there are also many new *finishes* applied to fabrics as well as new techniques to improve and widen the performance or use of the fabric. Several even change the care of the basic fiber itself.

Some finishes may last for the life of the product. Others may need to be restored after several launderings or cleanings.

Permanent-Press Finish—Perhaps the most exciting thing that has happened in the fabric world is permanent-press—the finish that allows home furnishings and clothing to be used after laundering with minimum or no ironing. What is even better is that they always look impeccably neat and pressed while being used! Permanent- or durable-press is really a refinement of the finish generally known as wash-and-wear. It is a heat treatment (baked in) finish which "locks" the shape, pleats, and creases into the item. Permanent-press items generally differ from other wash-and-wear fabrics in that the finish, or cure (heat treatment), is applied to the product *after* it has been made and pressed, so it is permanently pressed when it is made. Quality is important. To date, blends of 50 percent to 65 percent polyester with 35 percent to 50 percent cotton seem to have produced the best performance. Other blends are acrylic/rayon, rayon/acetate/nylon, and cotton/nylon. Spandex is used in products where stretch qualities are desired. A 100 percent cotton permanent-press, if not already here, is just around the corner.

When purchasing permanent-press items, look for unnecessarily pressed-in creases or wrinkles. If they are there when you buy them, they will be there forever!

Alterations which require letting out or exposing previous seams or creases are next to impossible with permanent-press fabrics.

Because permanent-press and wash-and-wear items are made of materials that become pliable when heated, they must be handled carefully during laundering to avoid the possibility of setting in wrinkles or creases that will be difficult to remove when the fabric has cooled. However, this same pliability makes

245

normal wrinkles and creases disappear from the fabric during laundering, since heat returns the fabric to its original "set."

Examples of brand names and trademarks include: Koratron, Penn Prest, Coneprest, Perma-Prest, Dan-Press.

To Launder Permanent-Press, Wash-and-Wear, and Synthetic Fabrics

Best laundering results will be achieved by using an automatic washer and dryer. As a matter of fact most manufacturers of permanent-press items recommend tumble-drying for best no-ironing results. Most washers and dryers provide special permanent-press cycles, which will allow you to wash in hot water, cool before spinning, and rinse in cold water. They also provide slower than average spin speeds which will also minimize wrinkling. If your washer does not have this cycle, you may be able to operate your washer manually by advancing the controls to cool down the wash water before spinning.

In general, wash from 5 to 10 minutes, using hot or warm water, depending upon the degree of soil. Rinse in cool or cold water.

Here are some tips that you may find helpful:

- Wash synthetics, wash-and-wear, and permanent-press fabrics frequently. Do not let them become too heavily soiled as soil will be harder to remove. This is apt to be a temptation because they look fresh longer during use.
- Wash small loads to cut down wrinkling.
- Wash whites separately. These fabrics may pick up color and soil from the water. Use a short washing time and a slow spin, if possible.
- Pretreat shirt collars and greasy spots with a detergent paste. Bleach may be used on white and color-fast permanent-press items, thus eliminating pretreatment, but check your hangtags or labels first. Some permanent-press finishes do not react well with chlorine and they may turn yellow.
- Use ample detergent, especially when using cooler water and/or gentle agitation. A cold-water detergent is essential for cold-water washing.

- Using a fabric softener in the rinse will minimize seam puckering and help to cut down on static electricity.
- Dry permanent-press in a dryer for best results. Remove immediately when dry. If it must be line dried, you may do some touch-up ironing.

    Tip: To reduce wrinkling on very special wash-and-wear dresses, dry over a plastic bag hung on a hanger. The bag will separate both sides of the dress, reduce clinging and wrinkling—and speed drying.

Stain- and Spot-Resistant Finish—This finish prevents spots, stains and general soil from penetrating the fabric and tends to resist water and oily stain. If you spill on such a fabric you can see the beads of liquid clinging to the surface, instead of being absorbed. If all detergent is not removed when you wash these fabrics, you may reduce or mask the effectiveness of these finishes. Thus it is especially important when laundering to rinse thoroughly.

If a stain-resistant finish has not been applied by the manufacturer of some item you feel may be subjected to lots of hard wear, you might consider sending it to a special fabric finisher. Or you might try finishing it yourself with stain-resistant aerosol spray, which can be purchased at notions counters or fabric departments. Scotchgard and Zepel are examples of soil-resistant finishes. During laundering or dry-cleaning the finish settles into the weave and dryer drying or pressing is necessary to restore its repellency.

Crease- and Wrinkle-Resistant Finish—This finish is applied to keep fabrics from wrinkling and creasing during wear or heavy use. Such treatment also makes them easier to iron.

Shrink-Resistant Finish—Many fabrics shrink in washing. A shrink-resistant treatment reduces possible shrinkage often to less than 1 percent.

One method used is the application of a *chemical* finish. Generally it is applied to wool, to control felting-shrinkage. The garment may still shrink slightly but not out of fit or shape. Dynalizing is one process.

This is not the same as *mechanical* preshrinkage given to fabrics before the garment is made. Sanforizing is one process. When

FABRICS AND THEIR CHARACTERISTICS

In addition to general characteristics of each fabric or textile family, each fiber has certain special characteristics that affect its performance and care. It helps in the care and use of these fabrics to understand these traits.

FABRIC	CHARACTERISTICS

Natural Fibers:

The natural fibers absorb moisture and withstand high temperatures. This means they are comfortable in warm weather, dry slowly, may shrink or stretch during laundering, unless specially treated.

WOOL

Sheds wrinkles, absorbs much moisture before it feels wet, fibers are covered with scales. If rubbed or soaked too long in hot water during laundering, the fibers swell and the scales lock. This causes permanent shrinking or felting.

COTTON

Durable, doesn't collect static electricity.

SILK

Absorbs much moisture before it feels wet, weakened by sunlight, can be damaged by strong soap, detergent, and high temperature.

LINEN

A crisp fiber, wrinkles easily unless finished to prevent this, yarns have uneven width giving fabrics a textured look.

Synthetic Fibers:

The synthetic fibers do not absorb moisture and soil. Soil adheres to the surface. They are also softened by high heat. This means they dry quickly, could be uncomfortable in warm weather as they hold heat and moisture. They shed wrinkles and require only touch-up ironing. Included in this group are the acrylics, nylons, polyesters, olefins, spandex, rayons, acetates, metallics, glass. In general they require warm temperature for laundering.

ACRYLIC

Lightweight soft fiber with the feel of wool, has a luxurious "hand," rubbing

GENERAL CARE	TRADE NAMES

Dry-clean, or machine washable if
treated, cold- or warm-water wash.
Cold- or warm-water rinses, gentle
agitation.

Color-fast cotton can be safely washed
and dried at high temperatures.

Dry-clean, unless given instructions for
laundering.

Generally can be safely washed and dried
at high temperatures. Iron at high
temperatures.

Remove oily stains before washing. Can be machine washed and dried at warm	Acrilan® Orlon®

FABRIC	CHARACTERISTICS
ACRYLIC (cont.)	causes tiny hairs on the fibers to bunch together into little balls or pills.
MODACRYLIC	Soft, resilient texture, dries easily, heavier than acrylic, fire-resistant.
NYLON	Strongest of all synthetic fibers, resists abrasion and scuffing, combines with many fibers to improve durability, snatches color even from color-fast items.
OLEFIN	Lightweight, strong, thermoplastic, heat-sensitive, nonabsorbent, excellent clean-ability.
POLYESTER	Resilient and returns to shape quickly, strong, resists wrinkling; springs quickly back to shape when crushed or twisted, may also appear dingy at warm temperatures from absorbed soil if not thoroughly rinsed.
SPANDEX	Has elasticity, has good holding power, and returns to shape quickly after stretching, is not weakened by perspiration or body oils.

GENERAL CARE	TRADE NAMES
temperatures. Wash items of fragile construction by hand. Iron at low temperatures. Brush pile surface with soft brush to prevent matting.	Zefran®
Machine or hand laundering may be used, depending upon strength of construction. Use warm water for laundering, iron at low temperature.	Dynel® Verel®
Remove oily stains before washing. Machine washable at warm temperatures, should be thoroughly rinsed to prevent graying from absorbed soil or soap left in garments, wash white separate from colored fabrics. White yellows with age. Use bleaches regularly to retain whiteness. Use a color remover to remove "yellow" that has occurred from age.	Caprolan® Antron® Cumuloft®
May be machine washed at warm temperatures, following specific instructions. Dry and iron at lower temperatures.	Herculon® Marvess® Merkalon® Polycrest® Vectra®
Pretreat oily stains before washing. Machine washable and dryable; pretreat collars and cuffs, some lint adherence can be reduced by using an anti-static agent in final rinse. Permanent-press items may be tumble-dried. Remove immediately.	Dacron® Fortrel® Kodel®
May be used with other fibers; these will determine care. 100% spandex may be washed and dried at low temperature settings.	Lycra® Vyrene®

FABRIC	CHARACTERISTICS
Non-fibrous Natural Fabrics: **GLASS**	Fibers of glass are brittle, not affected by sunlight, fire or mildew, repeated rubbing causes them to break.
METALLIC	Coated filaments won't tarnish, used for decorative purposes in draperies, table linen, braids, bathing suits; if suitable films and adhesive are used, they are not affected by salt water or chlorinated water.

Cellulosic Fibers:

The first man-made were produced from cellulose, the fibrous substance of many forms of plant life. Fibers share some characteristics of both synthetic and natural fibers. Each reacts individually to water absorption and high temperatures.

RAYON	A strong fiber, absorbs water, wrinkles, weak when wet and may shrink or stretch in laundering if not finished to prevent this.
HIGH MODULUS RAYON	Holds its strength when wet and is used mostly in blends to add strength and a soft silky hand.
ACETATE	Is beautiful but fragile, drapes well, heat-sensitive, usually is used where appearance is more important than durability.
TRIACETATE	Can be permanently heat-set into pleats, can be softened by heat, shaped or pleated, and then cooled to retain this shape, doesn't absorb moisture, dries quickly, and sheds wrinkles.

GENERAL CARE	TRADE NAMES
Generally needs to be hand washed to prevent breaking the fibers, although some more advanced processes may allow machine washing, ask about it when shopping or read labels.	Fiberglas® PPG® Beta®
Wash according to directions on hang-tags, labels.	Lurex®
Follow instructions for care. May be selectively washed or dry-cleaned, depending on specific fabric.	Bemberg® Cupioni® Fortisan®
	Zantrel® Avril® Regulon®
Most should be dry-cleaned. Fine delicate fabrics are best hand washed. Iron at low temperatures. Follow label directions.	Celanese® Avisco® Chromspun®
Observe any special instructions on labels and hangtags. Requires little special care because of fiber's resistance to high temperatures.	Arnel®

you see this label you will know that cotton or linen fabric will not shrink more than 1 percent in length or width when air (not tumble-) dried.

Check labels for the degree of shrinkage for washable woolens. Generally, woolens treated for shrink-resistance should not exceed 5 percent.

Flame-Retardant Finishes—These finishes retard burning and remain effective through many launderings. You can buy both clothing and home furnishings with flame-resistant finishes. It is a chemical treatment that prevents a fabric from supporting a flame.

Flame-resistant fabrics are especially desirable for children's wear. It should not be necessary to remind parents that children should be taught to be careful around fire, although dangers may arise from unexpected situations, such as with children when they want to help you cook. In the United States, effective July 29, 1972, law requires that all fabrics used in the manufacture of children's sleepwear up to size 6X must be flame-resistant.

Many flame-resistant finishes may be removed by successive laundry or dry-cleaning treatments, although there are never fibers looming on the horizon that will give permanent flame retardancy.

Water-Repellent Finish—This finish makes a fabric resistant to water, but not waterproof. Some of these finishes may be destroyed in laundering or dry-cleaning, while others are more permanent. You can now purchase spray finishes to restore water repellency or have it done by your dry cleaner. Some finishes are called "durable," others are "nondurable" to dry-cleaning. These latter may be labeled "renewable," meaning that they can be renewed by the dry cleaner.

Cravenette, Hydro-Pruf, Lovely On are examples of water-repellent finishes.

Waterproof Finish—Such finishes include application to a fabric of either rubber, lacquer, linseed oil compounds, or synthetic resins. They are completely waterproof, since these compounds totally close the fabrics' pores. Some may stiffen, however, during dry-cleaning. They should be "wet" cleaned. (See section headed Dry-Cleaning.) Reevair is one example.

Bactericidal and Bacteriostatic Finishes—Application of these agents helps to retard bacterial growth.

Anti-static Finishes—These chemicals are applied to fabrics used for carpets, automobile seat covers, etcetera, to discourage the development of static electricity in nonabsorbent textiles. Fabric softener is also used to control static electricity of washable synthetics. Use it in the final rinse or as directed, whether washing by machine or by hand. Many fabrics are permanently treated for "anti-static" qualities.

Mildew-Resistant Finish—This is a chemical finish applied to a fabric to prevent growth of mildew and mold. Used mainly on untreated rayon, cotton, and linen, this chemical helps to retard attack by mildew in moist, humid conditions or climates. Fresh-Tex is one example.

Moth-Resistant Finish—This, too, is a chemical applied to wool to make it resistant to attack by moths and carpet beetles. Examples include Berlou Mothspray, Dieldrin, Moth Snub, and Woolgard.

Perspiration-Resistant Finish—This is a chemical finish applied to a fabric to make it resistant to the damage caused by body perspiration. You'll find it used mainly on lining fabrics. Examples are Sanitized, Unifast, and Unidye.

BLENDS

Blends combine the desirable characteristics of two or more fibers. The number of different fibers and the amount of each will determine the performance of the blend. Follow care instructions for fiber which has the highest percentage.

Guidelines for judging blends:

- If more than three fibers are used in one fabric, the usefulness of each is limited.
- A fiber must comprise at least 25 percent of the fabric's total for its characteristics to be maintained.

There are these exceptions:

- As little as 15 percent nylon will strengthen a blend.
- As little as 2 percent spandex will add effective elasticity or control.

- Smaller amounts of a fiber may be used for decorative or textural effects, such as surface loops.

DOING THE WASH

SORTING

The first step in achieving good laundry results is proper sorting. Sort your laundry according to fabric, garment construction, color, and degree of soil; then separate it into loads that require the same water temperature, washing time, agitation and spin speeds, and laundry aids. One wrong garment in a load can ruin the load or the garment. For example, a red sock in a load of white or light-colored clothes can color the whole load pink. A pair of dark wool socks in a load of terry towels could become so covered with lint that you might have to throw the socks away.

What Makes a Good Laundry Load?

1. *White and light color-fast fabrics* should be washed in hot water (140°–160° F.) using an all-purpose soap or detergent.

    Heavily soiled examples include children's clothes, work clothes, T-shirts, socks, bath towels, sheets and pillowcases, tablecloths, dish towels, diapers (separate load).

    Medium or lightly soiled items might be washable dresses, shirts, blouses, handkerchiefs and underwear.
2. *Colored color-fast fabrics* should be washed in hot water (140°–160° F.) using an all-purpose soap or detergent.

    Heavily soiled examples include blue jeans, khakis, slacks.

    Medium or lightly soiled items might include bath towels, bath mats, colored sheets, pillowcases.
3. *Non-color-fast fabrics* should be washed in warm water (90°–110° F.) using an all-purpose soap or detergent.
4. *Synthetic and delicate fabrics should be grouped into white, light-colored, and dark-colored loads.* Wash them in warm water (90°–110° F.) using a light-duty or all-purpose soap or detergent, depending upon the item.

Note: It is important to sort the *lint givers* from the *lint receivers:*

Lint givers	Lint receivers
Chenille robe and spreads	Corduroy
Bath towels	Permanent-press fabrics
Throw rugs	Synthetic fabrics
	Socks

Your wash loads will probably fall into four or five of the following categories:

- White and light color-fast cottons and linens
- Bright or medium colors
- Dark colors
- Heavily soiled fabrics, such as men's work or children's play clothes
- All-white, sturdy permanent-press, wash-and-wear, synthetic fabrics, blends
- Colored permanent-press, wash-and-wear, synthetic fabrics, blends
- Delicate white lingerie, fabrics
- Delicate colored lingerie, fabrics
- Diapers
- Baby garments
- Special items, such as blankets, woolens, pillows, etcetera
    Caution: Follow the instruction book provided by the manufacturer of your laundry equipment. *The directions relate to situations that have been tested under specific conditions.* Also be sure to follow label directions for the laundry products you are using.

Preparing the Laundry

For best results, before you wash a load, close zippers, fasten hooks, tie apron strings, and close attached belts; mend any rips and tears; remove unwashable trimmings; empty pockets and brush out lint. Frogs and nails and puppy dog tails, in addition to crayons, tissues, and dollar bills, can cause trouble, notwithstanding jangled nerves and temper tantrums. Turn down cuffs and brush out lint. Turn woolens and knit garments inside out to prevent pilling.

Tips:

- To keep zippers in working condition, close the zipper before washing the article, and open it before drying.
- An easy way to remove lint and dirt from shirt pockets is to use a soft toothbrush.
- Turn all colored socks and blue jeans inside out when placing them in the washing machine. Any lint accumulation will be on the inside.
- Turn machine-washable wool or nylon socks inside out before putting them into the washing machine to keep them fluffy and lint-free.
- In each load of wash, include an *old* pillowcase. When the wash in the dryer or on the line is dry, put the clothes in the pillowcase for easy toting.

PRETREATING

Pretreat heavily soiled areas, such as collars, cuffs, pillowcases, feet of socks, with a soft brush and a paste of detergent and water or a liquid detergent. Generally, use the same detergent you are using for the wash load. Remove spots and stains before washing. Removing them immediately, when they occur, of course, is best, for they will "set" if allowed to remain in the fabric too long. Remember "time heals wounds, but sets stains." See stain-removal guide at the end of this chapter.

PRESOAKING

You may need to presoak heavily soiled items. Soaking fabrics that have protein-type stains such as milk, blood, etcetera, will help to loosen soil before washing cycle. You may use a regular laundry detergent or one of the enzyme presoakers. Follow package directions. Many washers have a soak cycle. If yours does not, use the regular wash cycle and stop after clothes have agitated for a minute. Soak fifteen to twenty minutes if using a regular detergent. If using an enzyme product, follow directions on the package. When you restart the washer, advance the timer dial until water begins to drain and complete cycle. Reset the controls, add detergent and start washer.

Washing loads by the pound is not really an accurate measure, because fabrics have varying weights and absorption qualities. For example, a full load of nylon or sheer curtains may weigh only two pounds.

It is best to load so that all articles will circulate freely in the washer. If you were to watch the load move about during agitation in a plastic display washer, you would notice that they turn over, disappear, and reappear again within frequent intervals. An even distribution of large and small pieces gets cleaner results. A load composed of just sheets will not wash as well as one that also includes smaller items such as pillowcases, men's shirts, and other small items. Wash large bulky items such as bedspreads or blankets one at a time.

Avoid overloading. Follow your instruction book and check the capacity of your washer. It is always best to underload. If you would like some idea as to the weight of your mixed load, here are some average dry weights to help you judge load size:

AVERAGE DRY WEIGHTS OF COMMONLY WASHED ITEMS

ITEM	NUMBER	APPROX. WEIGHT (IN POUNDS)
Double Bed Sheet	1	1½ to 2
Twin or ¾ Sheet	1	1 to 1½
Pillowcases	3	1
Bath Towels	2 or 3	1
Hand Towels	4	1
Linen Towels	6	1
Face Cloths	16	1
Luncheon Cloths	2	1
Luncheon Napkins	16	1
Diapers	6 to 8	1
Men's Shirts	2	1
Boys' Shirts	3 or 4	1
Socks	18	1
Women's Dresses	2 or 3	1
Girls' Dresses	3 or 4	1
T-shirts	3 or 4	1
Slips	3 or 4	1
Pajamas	3 pairs	1

Typical loads might include:

GENERAL	HEAVY FABRICS	PERMANENT-PRESS AND WASH-AND-WEAR
2 sheets	2 short coats	2 ladies' dresses or
2 pillowcases	2 pair overalls	4 men's shirts
2 bath towels	2 pair work pants	4 slips
2 shirts	2 work shirts	2 blouses or
3 hand or dish towels		sport shirts
4 washcloths		
4 undershirts		
4 pair shorts		
6 handkerchiefs		

HAND LAUNDERING

For hand washing, the water temperature should be comfortable to the hands. Always dissolve the soap or detergent completely before putting anything into the water. Carefully squeeze the suds through the fabric and rinse in two or more waters. Water may be squeezed out and additional water can be pressed out by rolling the items in a bath towel and patting gently.

If colors have a tendency to run, roll garments in an old terry towel to absorb excess moisture, then hang in front of a fan or breeze to speed drying. Always hang any garment or fabric which is to be drip dried without squeezing or wringing.

It is really impossible to give general instructions for hand washing as garments vary with fabric, construction, and finish. Save all loose hangtags, labels, and laundering instructions and follow them carefully.

Some Tips on Hand Laundering

- Have you ever had trouble emptying your bathroom sink of unnecessary suds after doing hand laundry? One young homemaker says that after she wasted loads of valuable time trying to get rid of them (she even lifted them out into the bathtub) she discovered that by washing her hands with a bar of soap, the lather helped to clear away the mound of suds.

- To launder fine old lace, baste it onto a firm piece of white muslin. Then wash it gently by squeezing in warm mild sudsy water—do not rub.
- When washing several pairs of stockings, make a loose knot near the top of the stockings to keep them in pairs.
- To wash white shoelaces easily, put them into a small jar with warm sudsy water. Close, shake several times, remove, rinse, and dry.
- Dip the hems of toddlers' and small children's dresses in light starch or use a spray starch. Skirts will look fresh and pert, and the top won't be stiff and uncomfortable.

CORRECTING LAUNDRY PROBLEMS

"Tattle-Tale Gray"—This is caused from sorting incorrectly; using insufficient detergent to remove soil from clothes and then hold it in suspension until rinsing and draining; too low a water temperature, using water that was not properly softened; or infrequent use of bleach.

To remove tattle-tale gray, use a soak bath in a concentrated solution of detergent* and hot water. Fill the washer about half full of hot water. If your washer has a water level selector set it at *low*. Add enough water conditioner to soften the water and 1 cup of oxygen bleach. Then add 3 or 4 cups of soap or detergent. Put clothes in the washer and soak for around 12 hours or overnight. As the water cools, the solution will form almost a gel.

After this long soak, turn the timer control to *drain*, just before the *spin* cycle. After the washer has completed the spin, advance the dial and let clothes run through a regular cycle, using hot water. Add enough water conditioner to soften the water. Dilute ½ cup of bleach in 1 quart of water and pour it into the washer after fill is completed. Do not add any soap or detergent.

After this soak bath, the next time you wash follow regular

* *Note:* For front-loading machines, use a low-sudsing detergent and follow specific instructions for your machine.

261

recommended instructions for both your machine and the detergent you use.

Yellowing—Yellowing in the center of sheets, pillowcases, and other items indicates a buildup of body oils. It is caused from using too low a water temperature; not enough detergent; or washing too short a time. To remove, wash in hot water, increasing the amount of detergent.

Yellowish Brown Lines—When brown lines appear on items that are ironed, you can be pretty certain that they are caused by a buildup of chemical salts from perspiration or detergent. It happens when you do not rinse properly, overload the washer, or use too low a water level.

Wash the items through a regular cycle without using water conditioner or detergent. This should remove the chemical salt buildup.

Yellowing Due to Chlorine Bleach—Yellowing may also be caused by using chlorine bleach on some resin-treated fabric finishes. To remove, rinse fabrics with water, then soak ½ hour (longer, if necessary) in a solution containing 1 teaspoon of sodium thiosulfate (available in drugstores or as "hypo" from photo supply stores) to 1 quart of hot water—which is safe for the fabric.

Lint—At end of wash cycle, if lint is clinging to clothes—men's socks, knits made of man-made fibers, permanent-press clothes—put them through another regular cycle, using a fabric softener in the last rinse.

Perspiration—The best method is prevention. Wash garments frequently.

To remove clinging perspiration odor from washable clothing, try adding four tablespoons of salt to each quart of water and let garments soak. Rinse, then put through a regular wash cycle.

WHEN YOU USE A CLOTHESLINE

Despite the increased popularity in the use of automatic dryers, many still prefer to use the clothesline, or if they don't prefer it, they are doing it out of necessity. While it is harder to lug the laundry to the clothesline, drying out of doors does give clothes a lovely fresh smell. An indoor line is also necessary for those bad-weather days. If you don't have an area where you can leave the line up at all times, consider one of the indoor retractable types. Hang it in a spare room or bathroom.

- *To hang sheets,* fold them double, hem to hem. Turn about three or four inches over the line and pin, or fold in half if that is easier for you (make sure the pins are snag-free and clean). Run your fingers down the selvage edges to make sure they are smooth. If you hang them this way, sheets will dry evenly and will be easier to iron. As a matter of fact, they may well be smooth enough so that ironing is unnecessary if you fold while faintly damp (only enough to feel coolish to the touch). If they are permanent-press sheets, then your ironing worries are over!
- *To hang men's shirts,* first fold double by bringing the two shirt fronts together, then hang by the tail, folding three or four inches over the line. Pin at the ends.

    We like to hang permanent-press shirts on hangers for drying. Secure the hangers to outdoor lines with clothespins.
- *To hang towels,* fold either one third or double over the line. Shake them vigorously, to restore softness and fluffiness. Never hang by one corner.
- *Hang clothes* into the prevailing wind so that pajama legs, sleeves, etcetera, will billow and smooth out as they dry.
- *Hang dresses,* trousers and pants, knitted garments, and any items you want to hold in their original shape on hangers and secure the hanger to line with clothespins.

Tips:
- To clean your outdoor clothesline, put it into a pillow-case or any similar casing. Tie the opening. Wash in your washing machine. After removing it from the washer, stretch and rehang.
- Wear a pair of lightweight cotton gloves inside rubber gloves when hanging wash on an outdoor clothesline in cold weather. This will help to protect your hands.

263

- Don't take time to sort socks before you hang them on an outdoor clothesline. Hang each sock as you pick it up, but leave a space for its mate.
- To clean clothespins, place them in a mesh bag and swish through warm sudsy water. Rinse, then hang over the line to dry.
- A small wire brush, such as those used for brushing suede shoes, is excellent for untangling the fringe on towels, place mats, guest towels, etcetera.

HOW TO LAUNDER JUST ABOUT EVERYTHING

We will attempt here to give you a basic idea of how to launder most items, both in automatic laundry equipment and by hand. (Check your washer and dryer instruction book first for any specific directions for your particular brand.) Observe hand laundering instructions carefully. Refer often to instruction books, hangtags, and labels.

Caution: Make sure all items are washable.

Baby Clothes—It is wise to select the easiest-to-care-for baby clothes you can find—those you can wash and dry with the least effort. Follow special hangtag and label instructions. Easy-care materials for baby clothes, especially those which thrive on dryer drying, include treated cottons, corduroy, flannel, plisse, seersucker, synthetics, and terry cloth. Wash and dry them according to fabric, degree of soil, and color. Use gentle agitation. Avoid overdrying.

Soak garments stained with milk, cod liver oil, orange juice in cold water immediately to prevent permanent stains. Formula stains are difficult to remove when old.

Place fragile lace or ribbon-trimmed dresses in a mesh bag with other delicate family articles and launder in warm water with a light-duty detergent, using gentle agitation.

Bedspreads—Buying the washable kind, preferably those made of permanent-press fabrics, can save you both time and money. Wash chenille and other lint-producing bedspreads separately.

Select the water temperature according to fabric and color. Use a short wash and a slow or gentle agitation to prevent tufts from pulling out. If gentle agitation is not possible, or bedspread is old and fragile, use the soak method as for woolen blankets. Then let machine run through regular rinse and spin cycles. Wash one double or two single spreads at once. Use a fabric softener in the last rinse to create a soft feel. To dry, use a dryer if possible, and remove while slightly damp. Shake several times, then brush lightly while on the bed. To line dry, hang over the line wrong side out. This will help to "fluff the tufts" as they rub against each other.

Dry-clean silk or rayon bedspreads unless label states "washable." If it does, follow the instructions.

To launder crocheted or knitted spreads, measure first, then launder with warm or cold water on the gentlest agitation speed possible, or preferably by using the soak method. (See Blankets, Wool—Soak Method, below.) When clean, stretch them to the correct size and dry on a flat surface. You may have to fold them to conserve drying space.

If your spreads are made of plastic, sponge them lightly while on the bed, using a damp sponge dipped in warm sudsy water. Rinse with a sponge wrung out of clear water and dry thoroughly.

Tip: It is a good idea to place new chenille spreads, draperies and throw rugs in the dryer for 5 to 10 minutes to rid them of excess lint.

Blankets, Wool (Machine Washable)—Treated wool blankets and other treated woolen items are machine washable. It is a good idea to look for a machine washable label when buying new blankets. Measure the blanket before washing. Follow the manufacturer's directions for laundering or use cold or lukewarm water for washing and rinsing, with gentle or slow agitation. Set washing time from between 2 and 5 minutes, unless machine instructions indicate otherwise. If blankets are badly soiled, pretreat bindings first, then agitate for one minute, stop the washer and soak for around 5 to 7 minutes. Restart the washer and let it finish through the gentlest cycle on your machine, preferably one designed for permanent-press. Fabric softener may be used

265

in the last rinse. If you do not have a gentle cycle on your machine, use the soak method that follows.

Blankets, Wool (Not Machine Washable—Soak Method)—Untreated wool may shrink in water. Agitation, handling when wet, and tumbling will also cause wool blankets and garments to shrink. If you have any doubts, have them dry-cleaned. If you decide to wash them, here are the general guidelines. Following them carefully will probably give you good results.

If bindings on blankets are soiled, pretreat by brushing gently with a detergent paste. Fill the washer with warm or cold water. Add liquid detergent or detergent granules (dissolved in a little warm water) and agitate to mix. *Stop the machine*, add blanket, pushing it under the water. Let it soak for about 10 or 15 minutes, depending on how soiled it is, turning the blanket once.

Use no agitation. Advance the control to drain, then fill with rinse water, using the same temperature as wash water. Stop the washer when fill is completed and let the blanket soak for about 5 to 8 minutes, turning blanket once again. Drain and repeat the soak-rinse process again if necessary; otherwise, complete the rinse-drain cycle. Spin washer to remove as much water as possible. You may wash one large or several small blankets at the same time.

Follow the same procedure for other woolen items, such as shirts or sweaters, or hand wash, using one of the cold-water or specialized detergents following specific instructions.

To dry woolen blankets try to avoid wrinkling and matting; most woolens should not be tumble-dried. Air drying is best. If the manufacturer says your blanket may be dried in an automatic dryer, follow specific instructions for the particular machine you own and the blanket label. In general stretch blanket to shape, then place in a preheated dryer with 5 or 6 clean dry bath towels to lessen the tumbling. Use recommended or regular heat for drying. Dry for 5 to 10 minutes, or *until just damp*. Remove blanket, stretch gently in both directions to shape. (If you have help for the shaping operation, you can do a better job.) Remove blanket from dryer while still damp, block to original size and drape to finish drying. When the blanket is dry, press the binding with a warm iron and pressing cloth. Be careful not to touch the iron to any part of the blanket fleece.

To line dry, hang blanket over two lines in the shade, preferably in a breeze. Pin binding edges together and straighten edges. (To prevent line marks on the blanket, string cardboard tubes from waxed paper over the line.) When the blanket is dry, brush it gently with a soft wire or nylon brush after it has dried to restore a soft nap.

To dry woolen garments and items washed by hand, squeeze gently and roll flat in a dry towel. Shape on another towel and spread flat to dry.

Blankets, Electric—Tip: To protect plug, stitch or pin the edge of the blanket over plug, or cover by sewing a sturdy piece of cloth over it, being careful to avoid the wires.

Wash as for wool blanket (soak method, above) if it is labeled machine washable. Do not dry in the dryer unless the blanket manufacturer says that this may be done. This may damage wiring coatings and the thermostats. Blanket may be dried by hanging over two lines, as for line drying woolen blankets above.

Caution: Do not stretch electric blankets because you may harm the wires.

Blankets: Cotton, Synthetics, Blends, Including Sheet Blankets —Use lukewarm or cold water, gentle agitation and light-duty soap or all-purpose detergent. If gentle agitation is not possible, or if blankets are old, use the soak method. Use a second rinse if desired with fabric softener in the last rinse. Dry according to dryer instructions or on the line as indicated above for wool blankets, not machine washable.

Curtains—Wash curtains when they begin to look soiled, especially, white and light-colored ones. Soil, fumes, dust, and sun can weaken them. Launder *nylon, polyester,* and *acrylic* curtains in an automatic washer on a warm-water setting and use a cool rinse if possible with gentle agitation for about 3 to 8 minutes depending upon soil. Permanent-press cycles are excellent. Shake out to remove excess water. Drip dry or machine dry, according to instructions for machine drying, use lowest temperature setting and dry only two or three panels at a time to avoid wrinkling. Rehang at windows while slightly damp. To hand wash, use lukewarm sudsy water, rinse thoroughly in cool water and hang on

267

line to drip dry. Use a mild oxygen bleach on white curtains to help retain whiteness. They will probably need no pressing, but if they do, use a warm iron.

For fiber glass curtains—see Glass Fiber.

For permanent-press curtains—see Permanent-Press, Wash-and-Wear.

For cotton and rayon curtains, wash in small loads, as overcrowding will wrinkle them.

Prewash or soak heavily soiled curtains to loosen soil. Sheer, old or sun-damaged curtains should be put into a mesh bag for protection. Some cotton fabrics may be resin-treated or finished; check labels, and if so, do not use a chlorine bleach which may discolor them. Use an oxygen bleach which is safe for all fabrics. Wash for about 5 to 7 minutes, using hot water for white and color-fast cotton and warm for rayon and non-color-fast curtains. Rinse with warm water.

Dry two or three panels at a time using correct dryer temperature for fabric. Avoid overdrying, which creates wrinkles. Remove from dryer while slightly damp. If you dry curtains by hand, hang over a clothesline, lining edges evenly.

To iron, see instructions in Ironing section.

Corduroy—Make sure the label says "washable" and follow instructions. Corduroy attracts lint from other fabrics. Turn inside out and wash with similar fabrics or materials. Test a small area to determine color-fastness. Bright colors may run. Handle according to garment construction and color. Wash for 6 to 9 minutes, using cold or warm water, depending upon color-fastness. Rinse with warm water. Dryer drying can eliminate need for pressing. Otherwise, press on wrong side, with a dry warm or steam iron.

Diapers—Many people now use a diaper service or disposable diapers, but if you have your own washer and dryer, there is no reason you can't do them yourself.

To make washing easier, rinse soiled diaper under cold running water immediately after changing baby. Then let soak in a solution of lukewarm water, a little detergent, and a laundry aid such as Borateem, Diaper Soft, or chlorine bleach until you are ready to put in the washing machine. Spin excess water from diapers before washing. When washing, follow directions for a white and light color-fast load.

Dry in the dryer or on a line in the sun. Fold according to baby's size. Never iron diapers; this retards absorbency.

Draperies and Slipcovers—Vacuum or shake to remove dust before laundering. Remove hooks and close zippers. Test for color-fastness, then use water temperature suitable for fabric and colors. If heavily soiled, use warm or cold water and detergent to soak or prewash. Then wash for 5 to 7 minutes, using hot water for color-fast cottons and warm for rayons and other synthetics. If material is fragile, old or weakened, use gentle agitation. Rinse in warm water. Dry slipcovers until slightly damp, then replace on furniture while still slightly damp or cool to the touch. They won't require ironing as they will dry to fit tightly. Do any touch-up ironing (pleats, ruffles, etcetera) before replacing on furniture. Be careful when laundering lined draperies as the materials may vary and the lining may shrink and pucker. If there is any doubt about washability, have them dry-cleaned.

Foam Rubber Bras—Wash in a mesh bag in the washer using warm water, light-duty detergent, and gentle agitation. Or wash gently by hand. Do not dry in any dryer with heat because foam rubber is combustible.

Girdles, Elastic Garments—Wash often. Body soil and perspiration may cause yellowing and deterioration of fibers. For spandex, wash in warm water and if necessary, use an oxygen bleach. Never bleach with chlorine. Some spandex may yellow from age. Spandex may be dried in the dryer, but follow specific instructions exactly. Do not dry rubber girdles or baby pants in the dryer.

Glass Fiber—Items made of glass fiber have the characteristics of glass and therefore should not be twisted, agitated, spun or tumbled, otherwise they may shred or break. However, some items may have machine washable directions. If so, follow them carefully. Otherwise, glass fiber should always be washed by hand. If

269

not machine washable, wash in the bathtub by swishing up and down in warm sudsy water. Rinse in clear water. Do not bleach glass fiber with chlorine bleach (unless otherwise directed) as the color may be only on the surface. Water does not penetrate glass fiber so it may be quickly dried by hanging. Never use a dry-cleaning solution on glass fiber, as this may remove the finish or color.

Gloves, Leather—If they have ever been dry-cleaned, do not wash by hand. Otherwise, if they are washable, wash them on the hands, using warm water and a light-duty or mild soap or detergent. Two exceptions are chamois and doeskin, which should be very gently handled. (Squeeze gently through warm sudsy water.) If cuffs and fingertips are heavily soiled, work in a little extra soap or detergent. Roll them off the fingers and hand, then turn right side out. Rinse all leather gloves thoroughly, then press out excess water in a clean towel. Reshape and fluff up fingers by blowing into them, or using special glove stretchers. Lay flat on a towel to dry. When almost dry, gently work with the hands to soften them.

Fabric: Wash white fabric gloves according to fiber in an automatic washer with a regular white load. Or hand wash them in warm or hot water (depending upon fabric and color-fastness) with a light-duty detergent. Always wash dark gloves by hand as they may fade and discolor other items. Press out excess moisture with an old towel; fluff and shape, then hang to dry, or flat dry on a towel, if you wish. To shape, put round-headed wooden clothespin into each finger before drying.

Wool: Draw a pattern of the gloves on brown paper. Hand wash in cool water with a cold-water special woolen or light-duty detergent and rinse well. Press out moisture with a towel and reshape to dry over pattern. Fluff or brush after drying.

Tip: Cut out cardboard patterns of children's woolen mittens when they are new. After each washing, slip the cardboard pattern into each mitten to avoid any possible shrinkage while drying.

Hose—Always wash a new pair before use. They will give you longer wear. Launder in warm water using a mild or light-duty soap or detergent. Squeeze suds through, rinse thoroughly, and roll in towel. Hang over a smooth rod, away from heat and sunlight.

Knits, Washable—Garments made of synthetic fibers such as polyester, nylon and acrylic will more likely keep their original size than knits made of cotton or rayon, even though they may stretch in wearing. Items made of a blend of synthetics and cotton and rayon will also hold their shape and size better than those of cotton or rayon alone.

Wash in the machine from 5 to 8 minutes, depending upon how soiled the items are. (If your washer has a special cycle for knits, follow specific directions.) Use gentle agitation, warm water for washing and warm or cold water for rinsing. Dry at medium or warm temperatures in the dryer according to fabric and remove while slightly damp. Reshape.

To dry by hand, roll gently in a towel and lay flat on another dry towel. Shape and air dry.

For woolen knits, follow label instructions. Tumble-drying is generally not recommended.

Tip: To remove "pills" that have formed on sweaters and other knitted items, first use fine sandpaper and "sand" gently. If this does not remove the pills, pull the cloth firmly over a curved surface (so the pills stand away from the material) then cut off *very carefully* with a small pair of scissors. To reduce pilling, turn the article inside out when laundering.

Mattress Pads—If badly stained, use warm prewash or soak. Then wash with hot water and bleach, if necessary. If washing one pad, add a couple of bath towels to balance the load. If pad is worn or not heavily soiled, use gentle agitation. Run through regular rinse and spin cycles, using warm water. To dry, use a dryer if you have one and remove when slightly damp. Stretch and straighten edges gently to reshape as quilted articles may pucker and shrink. To dry out of doors, spread over two lines. When partially dry, pull the edges straight and stretch gently. Shake gently several times while drying to fluff. Follow manufacturer's directions for polyester-filled pads.

271

Permanent-Press, Wash-and-Wear, and Synthetic Fabrics—See preceding section on Fabric Finishes.

Pillows (Feather, Down)—Make sure that ticking and seams are firm or sew the pillow into a pillowcase, to avoid the loss of feathers. Open the seams at corners, diagonally about one inch, then pin these openings. This will prevent the pillow from filling up with air and bursting.

Wash two pillows at a time or add a couple of bath towels if washing one, to balance the load. Use warm water, an all-purpose detergent, gentle agitation and a short wash. Pillows will float, so be sure to push them under the water. *Stop the machine* before doing so. Turn over during washing and rinsing. Let washer run through entire rinse and spin cycle, using warm water. Spin to remove as much water as possible. Shake pillows after washing.

Use a dryer if possible, on regular temperature setting, for maximum drying time to make sure that the feathers are completely dry, thus preventing mildew. For pillows with synthetic stuffing, wash as above for feather pillows, if the label is marked "washable." To line dry, hang by two corners in a breezy spot. Fluff and turn occasionally while drying.

Pillows, Foam Rubber—If machine washable, follow manufacturer's instructions. Foam rubber deteriorates with age, so pillows may split or crumble. *Do not dryer dry foam rubber.* In general, wipe foam rubber pillows on the outside with a dampened sponge. Dry with a clean soft cloth. For a more thorough laundering, squeeze carefully in lukewarm sudsy water. Rinse several times in cool clear water. Press between two terry cloth towels. Dry in a cool breezy spot.

Plastic Curtains and Other Plastic Items—Plastic will "balloon" and float in the water. Therefore, use special care when washing it. Wash and rinse in warm water using gentle agitation. Push the article under the water several times during the washing (stop the machine before doing so). Use an all-purpose detergent and bleach if necessary. Check for color-fastness before using bleach.

When spinning in the washer, check to make sure that the articles are not floating above the water as they may catch when spinning.

Plastic does not absorb water. Wipe off or hang to dry, or tumble plastic in the dryer with a few dry bath towels using an air-only setting. Plastic will soften when heated and could melt if allowed to overdry.

Tip: To keep plastic shower curtains from getting stiff after laundering, rub lightly with mineral oil, then wipe. This will keep the plastic soft and pliable, and will make it wear much longer.

Quilts, Comforters, and Afghans—Quilts and comforters filled with down, feathers, or wool should probably be dry-cleaned, as they are very hard to handle. Check labels to make sure fillings are washable before laundering, as cotton batting may slip and become lumpy. Washable quilts should have very close stitching. Use the warmer water temperatures depending upon color and fabric and gentle agitation. If gentle agitation is not possible, or if quilt is old, use the blanket soak method (see Blankets, Wool).

To dry, hang over two lines in the shade. Shake occasionally. To dryer dry, use regular heat setting following specific fabric instructions. Remove while slightly damp.

To clean woolen, crocheted, or knitted afghans, wash by hand using a cold-water detergent, following specific instructions. If you wish to launder them in a washer, follow instructions in use and care book.

Caution: Do not launder heirloom or antique quilts. Have them dry-cleaned.

Rugs (Washable Cotton and Synthetic Fibers)—Shake or vacuum before laundering. If rug has a tendency to shed lint, particularly when new, use a gentle agitation and wash for a short time. Choose setting for fiber and backing. In general use warm-water washes and rinses, unless labels indicate otherwise. Do not use hot water on rubber-backed rugs as heat will deteriorate rubber. It is better to wash two or three small rugs together for balance. If you wash only one small rug at a time, add bath towels to balance the load. A fabric softener in the last rinse will add

273

softness to the rug and will eliminate static electricity from synthetic fibers. Some synthetic fiber rugs should not be dried in the dryer with heat. Follow manufacturer's directions for drying.

Tip: Before washing a hooked rug, baste a strip of washable fabric along one edge. When you hang the rug on the clothesline to dry, attach the clothespins to the strip of material. The rug will retain its shape, without creases. After washing braided or crocheted rugs, lay them on clean paper (preferably on a porch or basement floor) and go over them with a rolling pin until perfectly flat. This will eliminate bulges and help the rugs to dry faster. Exercise extreme care in laundering these rugs. If you decide to wash them, use a soak method, as for Blankets, Wool (Not Machine Washable), or for Knits, Washable. Check first for color-fastness, then use warm-water temperatures, short wash cycles, and gentle agitation. *Do not* launder them if you have any doubts and especially if they are heirloom items. Have them dry-cleaned.

Sheets—Follow directions for white and color-fast loads or for permanent-press fabrics.

How to Fold Fitted Sheets

1. Hold sheet inside out the long way by putting a hand in each of the top corners.
2. Bring corners together with fingertips touching.
3. Turn left corner right side out and fit over right corner. Now you have one corner over the other, as a tailor folds a coat, shoulder to shoulder.
4. Smooth edges of sheet. Fit second set of corners together in same fashion.
5. Repeat, turning left doubled corner inside out and fitting over right doubled corner. All four corners are now nested neatly into one.
6. Smooth edges and place sheet on flat surface. Flatten pocket corner. Fold sheet into size best for your linen closet.

Shoes and Boots—Wash "washable" tennis shoes, canvas-type play shoes, rubber or plastic boots, rubbers, and overshoes with warm water and gentle agitation. Add some towels as a "buffer." If you use a dryer, use only air setting if possible. Do not dry rubber items or rubber-soled shoes in a dryer with heat. If you don't use a dryer, air dry in a breezy spot.

Stuffed Toys—Check any labels to make sure that stuffing and trim are washable. If eyes or other trim are glass, tie toy in a mesh bag or pillowcase or tie a nylon stocking over the head. Wash with warm water, using a gentle agitation and a cool rinse if possible. Add towels for balance in the washer, if necessary. If toy floats, press under water until wet. *Stop the machine* before doing so. Dry in dryer if stuffing permits. Do not dry items with foam rubber or kapok fillings with heat. To air dry, set or hang in a breezy place.

Sweaters, Synthetic (Nylon, Orlon) and/or Cotton—Button and turn inside out to prevent friction of fabric and pilling. Wash in the machine according to garment construction, fabric, and color. Wash white synthetics only with other whites as they pick up color readily. Do not wash with heavy fabrics as this may cause too much friction and pilling. It is a good idea to use a fabric softener in the last rinse. Dry flat on a towel or in the dryer, according to instructions. *To wash by hand,* swish in luke-warm sudsy water, using a light-duty detergent or a cold water detergent following specific instructions.

Tip: After washing a turtleneck sweater, roll the collar into place and put white crushed tissue paper under the collar. Speeds drying time and aids in reshaping the neckline.

Sweaters, Wool—Do not machine wash unless label says "machine washable."

Loosely woven and fine knit wool sweaters will require special attention. They could shrink if the garment is not made of treated "washable" wool. (See Blankets, Wool.) You may prefer to hand wash and hand block them, measuring before and after washing.

To wash by hand, use a cold-water detergent, following specific directions. In general, use 1 tablespoon of cold-water detergent designed specifically for wool to 1 gallon of cold water. Swish lightly to mix. Soak garment for 3 minutes, then rinse and squeeze gently to remove moisture. Roll lightly, avoiding wrinkles, in a terry towel. Block and dry flat on a turkish towel and pull gently back into shape.

If wool sweaters are labeled machine washable, follow manufacturer's directions, using a light-duty detergent and gentle agitation with a cold or lukewarm wash and a cool rinse. If your washer cannot provide these conditions, use the Blankets, Wool—Soak Method. Dry flat on a towel, or if the label so indicates, dry partly in the dryer at recommended heat setting using bath towels to "buffer" the load. Finish air drying on a towel.

Tip: To air dry woolen sweaters, gloves, or other items, pin them in shape on a turkish towel and hang the towel on the line. This helps them to dry faster and keep their original shape. Or, for indoor drying, extend a clean window screen reserved solely for that purpose over two chairs or the bathtub. Or buy a special screen designed solely for drying woolens indoors. Place a towel over the screen and spread the laundered article on it. The screen will allow the air to penetrate and insures quicker drying. To speed the drying time of a bulky-knit sweater after it is washed, insert a folded bath towel between the front and back of the article. The towel will absorb moisture and allow air to circulate more freely.

Tablecloths, Mats, Napkins—These may be made of many fibers. Use the washing conditions suitable for the fabric. Many of the stains which appear on table linen will come out if a cold- or warm-water soak or prewash is used, followed by regular washing. Bleach if necessary, according to fabric. To remove grease stains on permanent-press table items, apply full-strength liquid detergent to stains and let them set for a few hours or overnight. See guide to stain removal at the end of this chapter.

To iron a round tablecloth, fold it evenly and pin the edges together at intervals to help retain its shape. Iron it doubled.

Work Clothes—Shake or brush off any loose soil, mud, or sand. Empty pockets and cuffs. Use a cold or warm soak, or prewash clothes stained with plaster, flour, milk, blood, or food soils. Then wash in hot water with extra detergent. Two washes may be needed for some garments. Be sure to use enough detergent for heavily soiled clothes.

IRONING

Thanks to the development of wash-and-wear fabrics, permanent-press, new finishes, and the improvement of ironing equipment, ironing becomes less of a chore each year. Most ironing today is touch-up maintenance and pressing.

The Iron—Get the best one you can find. Today's dry, steam and spray-steam irons are designed to control the correct heat for the many different types of fabrics in your laundry. Many clothing manufacturers put ironing temperatures on their laundering tags, which is a great help.

As for your own iron, follow the manufacturer's directions for best results.

Tests have shown that steady, even heat, not pressure, is the key to successful ironing. Since today's irons are so lightweight, don't offset this advantage by pressing down too hard. Let the iron do the ironing.

The Ironing Board—A good ironing board is one that will not tip or collapse. It should have a sturdy metal top with adequate ventilation for steam to penetrate, and be lightweight and adjustable so you can select your most comfortable ironing height. You might consider adding a sleeve or touch-up board to your collection of ironing equipment. They are not expensive and they speed up small jobs. You also might like to consider one of the boards that can be lowered enough to allow you to sit while ironing. If you get one, use a chair or stool that will let you be comfortable without slumping over the table.

Where You Iron—The best arrangement is to set up your board where you can keep it up at all times. If this is impossible, most boards fold up easily and can be stored in any convenient location, preferably an ironing closet, where all other ironing supplies are tucked away.

The Light—The light for ironing should be just the same type that you'd have for reading. It should flood the ironing table

277

softly, preferably from over one shoulder so that you can see any wrinkles while keeping glare at a minimum.

Some General Rules:

- Begin by carefully sorting everything you are going to do. If you start the ironing by doing the articles requiring the lowest steam heat setting, you won't have to wait for cool-down to proceed to the articles that require higher settings. The new irons heat rapidly and they also are made to cool relatively slowly to make ironing a more economical job. When you've finished with the steam ironing, empty your iron and switch to the dry settings and higher temperatures.
- If you have any doubt about the temperature at which an item can safely be ironed, begin at a low temperature and gradually increase it if necessary.
- Straighten material on the ironing board. Use the palms of your hands and smooth from the center out. Fingers are apt to stretch the fabrics and pull them out of shape.
- Iron with straight strokes.
- Iron each section completely before you start on the next. Natural fibers should be ironed completely dry; man-made fibers left slightly damp.
- Collars, cuffs, sleeves, belts, and trimmings are ironed first, then the flat sections of the garment.
- White and light-colored cottons and linens are ironed on the right side, dark cottons and linens on the wrong side; silks and rayons on the wrong side; damask first on the right side, then on the wrong side.
- If folds in flatwork are always made in the same place, the wear on the fabric from creasing may cause the fibers to break. Sometimes fold in thirds and sometimes in fourths to avoid this strain.
- Make sure the ironing is dry before putting it away.

To Dampen or Not

Regular cotton and linen items still need to be dampened (unless your steam iron does a satisfactory job for you) and ironed carefully. Sprinkle or dampen with *warm* water. After dampening, roll in a towel and don't iron immediately. Wait an hour or so to enable the moisture to penetrate the fabric thoroughly and evenly. Use a high ironing heat. If you can't iron immediately, store in a plastic bag in a cool place—preferably in the refrigerator—to prevent mildew.

How to Iron What

Tablecloths. Fold these selvage to selvage, right side out. Iron both sides. Next, fold lengthwise. Iron again. Fold crosswise several times to fit linen closet or drawer. (Unless you put them over special poles designed for linen storage—see Chapter Eight.)

Pillowcases. These should be done at the temperature appropriate to the fabric. Iron closed end first, then both sides. Fold and iron in thirds lengthwise. Complete by folding in fourths crosswise to store.

Guest Towels. If they are monogrammed, embroidered, or appliquéd, iron on a thick bath towel so the designs will stand out. Then fold the towels in thirds lengthwise and once crosswise. If linen or cotton, dampen first.

Sheets. If you don't have permanent-press sheets which require no ironing, fold selvage to selvage and proceed as for tablecloths. To iron four thicknesses at once, fold hem to hem, then in half, bringing hem side to fold. Iron first on plain side then on hem side. If you do not want to iron regular muslin or percale sheets, remove them from the dryer or line and fold while very slightly damp.

Napkins. Iron wrong side up first, then right side. Fold small luncheon napkins in quarters, then in a triangle or oblong, as desired. Fold large dinner napkins hem to hem in thirds lengthwise, then in thirds crosswise. Remember that monograms and embroidery on all linens should be ironed on a heavy bath towel, dry, on the wrong side to prevent the pattern from pulling out of shape and being flattened.

Runners. Be careful with runners. If you do not iron them properly they may pucker and bulge. Iron lengthwise in one direction, then fold lightly to prevent creasing.

Dresses. Today's dresses seldom need more than touch-up, if they have been laundered properly. Turning the dress sleeves and all inside out, iron the sleeves first (on your sleeve board if you have one), beginning with the cuff, then the gathers, until all are smooth. Then slip the sleeve over the regular board as far as you can and do the shoulder and upper sleeve, as well as the front and back of the dress. Do the collar next from the points toward the center of the neck. Follow by doing the waist, back, sides, and front. Press skirt seams flat to give your ironing a nice finished look. Complete the job by turning the dress right side out and touching up special areas such as collar points, pockets, etcetera. Finish by putting on a hanger and fastening every other button.

Men's Shirts. "Now, who irons shirts these days?" was the comment from a young bride of six months. "Joe's are all permanent-press." But we found out there are those who do—and enjoy it. Others patronize the laundries. If you iron shirts, begin by ironing the collar on the wrong side, then on the right. Pull the collar tight and iron in from the points. Fold and iron the yoke first, moving outward to the cuffs and sleeves. Iron cuffs like the collar, then the body of the sleeves. Complete with the back first, then the fronts. Hang or fold and put away.

To Fold Shirts. Lay the shirt back on your ironing table, flat. Smooth from collar toward the tail and buttons, top, middle and bottom buttons. Turn with front facing down. Fold each side about halfway from collar to shoulder, laying sleeves lengthwise. Turn up tail about 5 inches, then fold to collar.

Slacks, Shorts, and Overalls. If they require ironing, turn inside out and iron pockets first. Then do waist and seams. Next iron the seat area. Press the legs inside out with seams flat. Do not crease. Finally, turn the garment right side out, touch up and crease where necessary.

Baby Clothes and Small Dresses. Iron as for regular dresses. They will look better if ironed on a sleeve or small board. That's the only way you're going to be able to do tiny sleeves without creasing and folding.

Some Common Ironing Problems

Scorching

Nonwashable fabrics, send to a dry cleaner.

Washable fabrics, launder according to fabric and finish.

Remember, scorching is caused when the iron gets too hot, when you leave the iron in one spot too long, or if you have not rinsed the garment properly and detergent remains in the fabric. If you are ironing starched items, it is a good idea to reduce the heat setting of the iron one unit.

To Remove Shine

Run a dampened sponge over the shiny area and press lightly over a pressing cloth.

Ironing Tips

- After washing and rinsing hair ribbons, dip in a cup of warm water to which a teaspoon of sugar has been added. Press out moisture in an old towel, then iron while damp. This will restore their natural body.
- Before ironing handkerchiefs, fold them in half and pull tight. Lay flat on the ironing board and iron up from the fold. This will prevent uneven edges. Continue ironing, and fold as desired.
- If starch sticks to the soleplate or bottom of the iron, let the iron cool and apply paste silver polish. Then wipe with a damp cloth and dry. Or you can remove rough and sticky spots from the iron by sprinkling a little salt on a piece of paper or cloth and running the hot iron over it. (Not for irons with Teflon soleplates)
- A clean ketchup or mustard dispenser also makes an ideal container for filling steam irons. Keep it near the ironing board to save steps.
- When ironing or pressing a pleated skirt, place the waistband on the wide end of the ironing board. Then hold the pleats in place as you iron from the top to the

281

bottom of the skirt. This will eliminate pinning or sewing the pleats in place.
- Store the ironing board on the inside of a closet door. Secure two clothes hooks to the bottom to form a resting place, then tack a wide elastic band or leather belt about 3 feet above the hooks. First slip the board into the band, then rest on the hooks.
- When ironing a blouse or dress with pearls or rhinestones, press very carefully face down on a turkish towel.
- To store your "things to be ironed" in an orderly fashion, tack a pillowcase (or other container) to the inside of a closet door. Drop the clothes in as you accumulate them, or keep a special basket or hamper for the purpose.
- When ironing long items, such as bedspreads, sheets, etcetera, place a chair or two in front of the ironing board and use it to prop the material as you iron.
- Keep an ice cube wrapped in a thin cloth handy when ironing. It's fine for dampening small areas.
- When you spray-starch a black cotton blouse or dress, spray the starch on the wrong side of the article, and press on the wrong side, too. This will prevent white marks and a shine.

PRESSING

Pressing is simply applying heat with or without steam to smooth or crease a fabric. Ironing is a complete operation of special smoothing after laundering which includes fabric surface, seam ironing, crease- and pleat-pressing or general touching up of wrinkled areas.

When pressing, in general:
- Use a steam iron or a dry iron with a pressing cloth.
- Always dampen pressing cloth (a treated cloth will allow you to use higher temperatures for pressing).
- Use a light up and down motion, rather than a sliding one as you do for ironing.
- Always brush clothes well. Don't forget pockets, cuffs, collars, etcetera.
- Never let the cloth get too dry.

- Lift cloth while pressing and brush up nap or surface of fabric.
- If you use a steam iron, wool items may be carefully pressed on the wrong side without a cloth. Use caution.

Special Pressing

Pressing While Sewing—Press all finished darts or seams on the wrong side, as they are finished. Iron with an up and down motion, pressing the seams flat and shape the darts with your iron as you go.

Blocking Hand Knits—Sweaters, knit dresses, knit vests, and socks should all be blocked. Stretch out the area to be pressed in the center of the ironing board, wrong side out. Pin securely to maintain the proper measurement. Avoid stretching out of shape or size. Hold your steam iron (on steam setting) above the area and let the steam penetrate the yarn fully.

To Press a Tie—While not altogether satisfactory, you may try by inserting a cardboard cut to fit the inside of the tie. Cover tie with a thick layer of cheesecloth and press very, very lightly with a steam iron.

Pressing Tips

- To remove an old hemline mark from a garment, make a solution of half vinegar and half water and then dip a pressing cloth into the mixture. Wring out the cloth, place over the hemline and press lightly.
- Wax paper used as a pressing cloth will remove creases from net hats and headpieces. It will help stiffen them as well.
- Paper toweling, when dampened, will make an excellent pressing cloth.

STAIN REMOVAL

Stain removal can be a paradox. It is at once a simple job and yet it does require more than just a simple understanding of the stain itself. We need to know a little something about the nature of the stain, as well as the *reactions* that take place when chemicals come in contact with common stains.

We are instructed at every turn to remove stains immediately, follow the directions carefully, and to be careful when using chemicals. This is important, but keep in mind that *if* you don't get to the stain immediately, you may still be able to remove it with some, if not a complete degree of success. Stains are a fact of life. Deal with them as you do any other phase of housekeeping. Know the facts.

It would appear that stain removal is a job for a chemist. But as we have said before, chemicals are not as foreboding as they seem when you understand their nature. For example, if directions call for an oxygen bleach to remove a stain, you are actually using either sodium perborate or potassium monopersulfate, both peroxygen bleaches. In the supermarket you can buy sodium perborate as Snowy Bleach. Or white vinegar is simply a low percentage (5 percent) acetic acid.

Stains may be either *greasy, non-greasy,* or a *mixture* of both.

Basic Understanding of Stains—Greasy stains, in general, may be easily removed by using an absorbent.

If materials are washable, greasy stains may or may not be removed by laundering. Before laundering, pretreat with a detergent paste or liquid detergent.

If a stain "pops up" after laundering, rub it with a little liquid detergent and rinse it with hot water. If that doesn't work, let the fabric dry, then use a cleaning fluid. If that doesn't work, try bleaching, following directions for bleaches.

Most non-greasy stains can be removed from washable materials by sponging them in cool water. If stain is heavy, soak several hours in cool water. Or use a bleach, as suggested in the following section.

Nonwashable Fabrics—For materials that are not washable, the cool-water sponge method is probably the best, but try it out first on an inconspicuous spot to determine results. Or try a little liquid detergent, rinse with cool water and pat lightly with a towel, then sponge lightly with alcohol, diluted with two parts water. *If there is any doubt about the fabric or using the recommended stain-removal method, consult a professional dry cleaner.*

For a mixture of non-greasy and greasy stains, treat the stain first for the non-greasy portion.

MATERIALS TO KEEP ON HAND
FOR STAIN REMOVAL

For Absorbing Greasy Stains:

Cornstarch	Sprinkle on stain and let
French Chalk	stand several hours or over-
Fuller's Earth	night. Brush lightly to re-
White Talcum Powder	move.

For General Stain Removal:
Spray Stain Removers. Follow container directions.

Bleaches (see general instructions):
Chlorine
Color Remover
Oxygen Bleaches
Hydrogen Peroxide (a peroxygen bleach, safe for all fabrics)

For Non-Greasy Stains (*solvents*):

Acetone (poisonous)	Used especially for nail polish, ballpoint ink.
Alcohol (poisonous)	Dilute with two parts water when used for acetates.
Banana Oil (poisonous)	Used especially for nail polish, ballpoint ink.
Turpentine (poisonous)	Used for paint and varnish stains.

General Chemicals:

Acetic Acid (10%)	Will neutralize stains caused by alkalis such as ammonia.
Ammonia (10% household ammonia)	Will neutralize stains caused by acids, safe for most fabrics, but dilute for silk and wool.
Vinegar, White (5% acetic acid)	Will neutralize stains caused by alkalis.

285

Cleaning Fluids (greasy stains):
   Follow container directions.
   Flammable
      Naphtha
   Nonflammable
      Perchloroethylene
      (poisonous)
      Trichloroethylene   Do not use on triacetates
      (poisonous)   such as Arnel or on polyes-
                                 ters such as Dacron or
                                 Kodel.

Most chemicals and cleaning materials may be purchased at drugstores, hardware stores and housewares departments. General bleaches, detergents, etcetera, may be purchased at grocery stores and supermarkets.

Caution: In general, highly flammable items used in the home include:

Acetone	Some Liquid	Turpentine
Denatured Alcohol	Household	Waxes
Gasoline	Cleaners	Wax Removers
Kerosene	Some Spot Re-	
	movers	

GENERAL DIRECTIONS FOR STAIN REMOVAL

* Treat stains as soon as possible. Many stains can be removed easily when they are fresh, but are difficult or impossible to remove later.
* Identify the stain, if possible. The treatment for one kind of stain may set another.
* Consider the fabric, finish and color before treating. The water temperature, type of stain remover or bleach, even the method, may vary depending upon the fabric or color.
* Before using any stain remover, be sure it will not harm the fabric, finish or color. The methods suggested below have been carefully tested, but there are exceptions, so

test a sample of material or a hidden part, hem, seam allowance, etc.
- Launder washable fabrics thoroughly after removing any type of stain.
- All cleaning fluids should be used in a well-ventilated room. Always dilute bleach before using; then rinse thoroughly from fabric.
- If in doubt about what caused the stain, try only cool water and cleaning fluid or powder. *Sponge with cool water* first and then let the fabric dry before applying the cleaning fluid.

STAIN-REMOVAL CHART

STAIN	AND LINENS WHITE COTTONS	OTHER WASHABLE FABRICS
Blood	Rinse or soak in cold water. Work detergent into any remaining stain. Rinse, if stain persists, put a few drops of ammonia on stain and repeat detergent treatment. Rinse. If necessary, bleach.	Same method, but if color-fastness is questioned, use hydrogen peroxide instead of ammonia.
Candle Wax	Scrape off excess with dull knife. Place stain between clean white blotters or several layers of facial tissue. Press with warm iron. Sponge with cleaning fluid. If spot remains, bleach.	Same method. Use oxygen-type bleach.
Chewing Gum	Rub with ice to harden. Scrape off excess with dull knife. Sponge with cleaning fluid.	Same method.

287

STAIN	WHITE COTTONS AND LINENS	OTHER WASHABLE FABRICS
Chocolate or Cocoa	Rinse or soak in cold water. Work detergent into stain. Rinse. If stain remains, bleach.	Same method. Use oxygen-type bleach.
Cod Liver Oil	Sponge with cleaning fluid. Launder in warm suds. Old stains are almost impossible to remove.	Same method.
Coffee or Tea— Black	Pour boiling water through the stain from a height of 1 to 3 feet. Bleach, if necessary.	Rinse or soak in cold water. Work detergent into stain. Rinse.
with Cream	Rinse or soak in cold water. Work detergent into stain. Rinse. Dry. If grease stain remains, sponge with cleaning fluid. Repeat, if necessary. If colored stain remains, bleach.	Bleach, if necessary. Use oxygen-type bleach.
Cream, Ice Cream, or Milk	Rinse or soak in cold water. Pretreat and launder. If ice cream is fruit or chocolate, treat stain as such.	Same method.
Cosmetics (Lipstick, Rouge, Powder)	Pretreat and launder or sponge with cleaning fluid. If color remains, bleach.	Same method. Use oxygen-type bleach.
Dye	Use a commercial color remover or method for other washable fabrics.	Rinse or soak in cold water. Work detergent into stain. Rinse, if necessary, bleach. They are not always possible to remove.

STAIN	WHITE COTTONS AND LINENS	OTHER WASHABLE FABRICS
Egg or Meat Juice	Rinse in cold water. If stain remains, sprinkle with meat tenderizer—let stand 15 to 20 minutes. If stain still remains, sponge with cleaning fluid or diluted bleach. Launder in hot water. The use of hot water at first may set stain.	Same method, but select water temperature suitable to fabric. Use oxygen-type bleach.
Fruit, Fruit Juices, Wine, or Ketchup	Same method as black coffee.	Same method as black coffee.
Grass	Work detergent into stain. Rinse. Sponge with denatured alcohol. Bleach, if necessary.	Same method, but if color-fastness is questioned, do not use alcohol. Dilute alcohol with 2 parts water for use on acetate.
Grease, Oil	Pretreat and launder in hot water. Dry, if stain remains, sponge with cleaning fluid. If necessary, bleach.	Sponge with cleaning fluid. Launder in warm water. If necessary, bleach. Use oxygen-type bleach.
Ink	Soak in cold water. Bleach. If a yellow stain remains after bleaching treat as rust stain. Certain inks require treatment with a color remover; some inks are impossible to remove.	Same method, but do not use color remover on colored fabrics.
Mildew	Wash in hot suds. Moisten with lemon juice and salt. Dry in sun. If stain persists, bleach. Old stains are hard to remove.	Same method but select water temperature, etcetera, suitable to fabric.

289

STAIN	WHITE COTTONS AND LINENS	OTHER WASHABLE FABRICS
Mustard	Soak in hot detergent water for several hours. If stain remains, bleach.	Same method, but select water temperature, etcetera, suitable to fabric.
Nail Polish	Sponge with nail polish remover or banana oil (test nail polish remover on seam first). Launder. If color remains, bleach.	Same method, but use only banana oil on acetate.
Paint	Sponge or soak in turpentine or banana oil. Launder. If paint has dried, soften first with lard or oil.	Same method.
Perfume	Rinse or soak in cold water. Work detergent into stain. Rinse. If stain remains, bleach.	Same method.
Perspiration	Pretreat. Launder in hot sudsy water. If fabric has been discolored, restore by applying ammonia to fresh stains or vinegar to old stains. Rinse. Bleach, if necessary.	Same method, but select water temperature, etcetera, suitable to fabric.
Rust and Iron	Apply commercial rust remover such as Whink, according to manufacturer's directions. Rinse. Or, if safe for fabric, boil stained article in solution of 4 teaspoons of cream of tartar to 1 pint water.	Same method but do not boil.
Scorch	Rinse or soak in cold water. Work detergent into stain. Rinse. Bleach, if necessary. Stain may be impossible to remove.	Same method. Try brushing woolens with emery board.

STAIN	WHITE COTTONS AND LINENS	OTHER WASHABLE FABRICS
Soft Drinks	Sponge with cold water. Some stains are invisible when they have dried but turn brown when heated and may be impossible to remove.	Same method.

DRY-CLEANING

Items that need dry-cleaning may be taken to a coin-operated dry-cleaning center or to a professional dry cleaner. In either case, it is advisable to clean anything before it becomes too heavily soiled and before stains have had time to set in permanently. Make sure you empty all pockets, fasten buttons and closures, do any necessary mending and remove trimming that cannot be dry-cleaned.

A professional dry cleaner has the expertise and equipment for spot-removal cleaning and pressing. They will do a better job on your dry-cleaning if you give them instructions for special care, point out location and cause of specific stains (pin a note to the stain), and don't rush your cleaning. The same-day or overnight service may be fine for an occasional emergency, but avoid making it the rule.

Professional dry cleaners may also offer services including dyeing, repairs, alterations, fur, leather and suede cleaning, pick-up, delivery, and storage.

Wet-Cleaning. When fabrics are so badly soiled that dry-cleaning will not remove the soil they may be further cleaned by a process known as wet-cleaning. Garments that may need bleaching or items that are so stained that they require the digestive action of enzymes are usually wet-cleaned.

While this process is not washing, it does remove the soil with water under carefully executed conditions. They are first dry-cleaned to remove solvent-soluble soil, then they are measured and, when necessary, restored to original size after wet-cleaning, then quick-dried.

291

CHAPTER FIVE

The Kitchen

Many estimates have been made as to how much time we actually spend in the kitchen. Of course this depends upon one's particular life-style, but it would seem that most of us spend close to 50 percent of our at-home working hours there.

It should be easy enough for you to make an exact estimate. Work it out just on the basis of the minimum time you would devote to meal preparation alone, not to mention all the other activities that emanate from or near the kitchen:

- ½ to 1 hour for breakfast
- ½ to 1 hour for lunch
- 1 to 2 hours for dinner

Considering four hours a day, seven days a week, this adds up to a minimum of 28 hours a week, 112 hours a month and 1344 hours a year. And then there are these other considerations:

- Time spent in using the kitchen as the *hub* for other daily activities such as cleaning.
- Time spent in food preparation for entertaining.
- Time spent in food preparation for special meals.

It soon becomes apparent that the kitchen *is* where most of the action is. It is also where the greatest concentration of utensils and tools is stored and used. Therefore, some degree of efficiency, organization, and careful thought can help to save hours of needless steps and wasted energies.

In her lifetime, the average American homemaker will wash and dry more than 1,500,000 pieces of silverware, dishes, pots, and pans.

The average American throws away from five to seven pounds of solid waste each day. That's over a ton a year—and the amount is increasing, according to the U.S. Department of Agriculture. This all adds up to work and these are just two examples.

Research has shown that simple reorganization of a kitchen can save 300 steps (from 500 to 200) in preparing and serving breakfast, 500 (from 700 to 200) in dinner preparation, and 450 (from 600 to 150) washing dinner dishes. In other words, with proper organization, cooking and cleanup can be cut by approximately one-third!

Using Our Kitchen—Ever since man first learned he could make fire he has had an insatiable desire to cook, not only to satisfy his basic need for nourishment, but also to entertain his friends.

Today the development of and interest in casual kitchen design allows us to choose from an enormous range of equipment and furniture, all geared to our own special needs.

How we interpret those needs depends upon how easy our kitchen will be to live and work in.

Plan your kitchen first with the idea of saving steps. Consider these alternatives. Would you prefer to take out the bottom of a double boiler from the cabinet next to the range and walk to the sink to fill it with water, then walk back again to the range, or would you rather remove it from the cabinet next to the sink first, fill it with water, *then* take it to the range? Taking vinegar from one cabinet, salt from another and oil from yet another to make a simple salad dressing can be avoided with good planning.

Planning for better organization just takes a little thought.

KITCHEN PLANNING

Whether you are remodeling a kitchen, designing a new home with a builder or architect, or just simply rearranging your present kitchen, you will find these basic rules a useful guide.

Forethoughts—If you are going to remodel or build, first decide what you want in a kitchen. What kind of storage? What, if any, kind of eating area? Any special hobbies for which you might wish to allocate space?

Shop around and get estimates. Don't base your decision on price alone but on quality of materials and workmanship. Now's the time to ask questions, change your mind. What is the room size, what kind of cook are you, how many people will there be in the kitchen at one time?

PLAN YOUR WORK CENTERS

A good kitchen is made up of appliance-based centers arranged for easy work flow. Working with a simple floor plan of your kitchen, decide how you'll arrange these basic centers:

- *The sink and cleanup center* is the most frequently used area—give it a choice location, depending upon the plumbing, of course. It centers around the sink and may include a dishwasher, waste disposer, trash compactor, with counter space on both sides of sink, storage.
- *The range or cooking and serving center* with ventilating fan and hood, forms the core of the cooking center. Put it close to the sink; more trips are made between these two areas than any other. Don't forget storage for both utensils and food, and a heatproof counter top.
- *The refrigerator* is the nucleus of your *mixing and food-preparation center*. Vital elements to include: wood chopping surface; specific appliances needed such as blender, mixer, can opener, etcetera; plenty of storage. Most time and motion experts would agree (we do, too) that this area should have a lowered counter top for more comfortable and energy-saving work. In general, a 32″ height rather than the standard 36″ is more comfortable for stirring or mixing. Make sure the refrigerator opens on the side toward the counter. It is possible to purchase them with either a right- or left-hand door opening.
- *An eating area* for casual family meals is becoming more and more popular. It may be a part of an adjoining family room or an actual part of the kitchen. Include serving and storing facilities.
- *Other centers* to include if you've the space or inclination —portable appliance center, a kitchen laundry, a hobby area (such as an indoor herb garden), or a desk.

Consider the Triangle

Whenever possible, the three major work centers should be arranged so as to form the points of a triangle.

The total working distance of the three sides should measure no more than 22 feet. The legs of the triangle should follow these measurements.

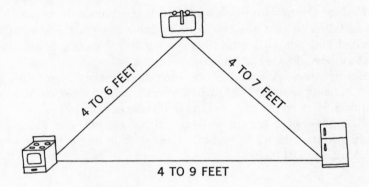

4 TO 6 FEET   4 TO 7 FEET

4 TO 9 FEET

- Between the sink and refrigerator—4 to 7 feet
- Between the sink and range—4 to 6 feet
- Between the range and refrigerator—4 to 9 feet

Be sure to keep the traffic flow away from the work area, if possible.

Maximum Measurements to Allow the Most Efficient Use of Space:
- Allow a total of 6 sq. ft. of shelf space for each person. Add an additional 12 sq. ft. of shelf space if you plan to entertain a great deal.
- Provide these minimums of counter space: 15″ to 18″ by refrigerator, 36″ to 42″ for mixing area, 36″ on right of sink, 30″ to 32″ to left of sink (unless you have a dishwasher, then 24″ should be ample), 24″ on both sides of range if possible.
- Depths: most base cabinets are 24″ from front to back (counters for base cabinets are 25″), most wall cabinets are 13″ deep, utility cabinets are 13″ and 24″ deep.

295

- Standard average heights include: 36″ counter height, 30″ to 32″ for mixing counters, 27″ to 29″ for sit down working. When planning counter heights, think about your own height. Most comfortable working heights are about 3″ below your elbow height. First shelf on wall cabinets 52″ from floor. Shelves to be used frequently should not be higher than 72″ from floor. Hang standard wall cabinets 15″ to 18″ above counter.

Built-in Ovens—Studies have found that separate ovens should be installed so that the top edge of the oven door when fully opened and pulled down is between 1 and 7 inches below the user's elbow, depending upon user's height.

Eating Areas—A seated person extends 20 inches from table, a person rising from table 32 inches, to walk behind a seated person requires 24 inches, to edge behind that same person, 16 inches.

Passages—For a person walking, 26 inches; between opposite work counter, 42 to 48 inches; where two or more people are working, 54 to 64 inches.

Basic Arrangements of Floor Plans

U-Shape Kitchen—Each work area is planned conveniently on one of three walls. In a large room, you can arrange cabinets with island or peninsula to separate work areas, cut traffic in work area down. Corner cabinets make use of "dead space."

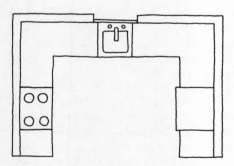

Two-Wall Kitchen—This "corridor" type is economical because there are no corners to turn.

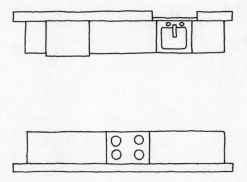

L-Shape Kitchen—This is practical and economical for two adjacent walls. It frees space along other two walls for dining, laundry, or other use. Can provide work counter space at corner.

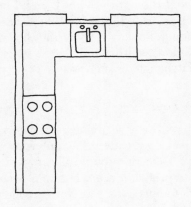

One-Wall Kitchen—Perfect for limited space in a narrow room, this plan is popular for small homes and apartments. Easy to install.

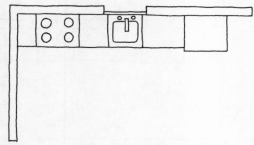

Islands and Peninsulas—If your kitchen area is large and spread out, an island or peninsula can draw areas closer together while dividing kitchen from laundry or eating area. At right angle from wall, peninsula adds counter, storage space. Sink and range units may be installed here, and wall cabinets suspended.

To Measure Your Kitchen

Start at any corner of your kitchen above the counter top height and *measure around* the entire room. Using ¼-inch graph paper, draw your kitchen to scale ¼ inch = 1 foot. (See ¼-inch rule on the scaled template, following.) Show the thickness of the walls, the door and window widths, and door swing. Don't forget to draw in existing kitchen items such as a sink that you want to keep.

To Lay Out Your Plan

Now that you have the measurements of your kitchen drawn on the graph paper, you are ready to lay out your plan. See accompanying template. Take this rough plan to your kitchen dealer so that you can interpret your needs to him more fully.

Use this scaled template to plan your kitchen. Trace the appliances and cabinets from the guide. Cut them out, then place or draw them over a piece of ¼-inch graph paper (buy it from a stationery supply store) to make your plan.

Note: Some products may vary slightly from these general measurements. Check the specific sizes with your dealer. Mark your plan lightly, as you may want to change it several times before making a final decision.

INVESTIGATE EQUIPMENT

After you have your plan in mind, determine the appliance sizes that will fit in your kitchen before shopping. Consult the section on appliances in this chapter. Shop around. Learn the major features offered—what they will or won't do for you—so you can decide if you want to spend extra money for them.

Built-in equipment helps make a kitchen appear neat, trim, and attractive, but if space is limited, remember that a built-in oven and cook top use more wall area than a free-standing range, and also that many free-standing ranges and refrigerators are designed with a built-in look—to save space and installation charges. A built-in oven can be placed outside the cooking center if it has a heat-resistant counter next to it. A built-in dishwasher is the most convenient. But if there's no space, the portable variety, easily stored in an out-of-the-way corner, is also available in convertible models that can be built in later.

Sinks are commonly either stainless steel or porcelain. Stainless steel is very durable, and though it will water spot in hard-water areas, it is fairly easy to care for. It comes in various gauges —the heavier gauge makes a better-quality sink. Porcelain-finished sinks are made of steel or cast iron and come in many attractive colors, which allows flexibility in decorating schemes.

SHOP FOR CABINETS

Cabinet exteriors (generally of wood, metal, or plastic laminate) should be practical to care for as well as attractive and stylish. The less trim, the easier they are to keep clean.

Cabinet interiors are important. Look at features and accessories—pull-out cutting board, breadbox, cutlery drawer, flour sifter, tray storage, slide-out garbage can, vegetable drawer, spice cabinets, slide-out shelves. Be sure you're getting quality construction in terms of drawers that glide easily, shelves that adjust, doors and hardware that work.

299

KITCHEN PLANNING TEMPLATE

DIRECTIONS

Use this scaled template to plan your kitchen. Trace the appliances and cabinets from the guide. Cut them out, then place or draw them over a piece of ¼" graph paper (buy it from a stationery supply store) to make your plan.

Note: Some products may vary slightly from these general measurements. Check the specific sizes with your dealer. Mark your plan lightly, as you may want to change it several times before making a final decision.

Base Cabinets

Corner—27" 9" 12" 15" 18" 21" 24" 27" 30" 36"

Wall Cabinets

Corner—27" 12" 15" 18" 21" 24" 27" 30" 36"

Appliances

Side-by-side Refrigerator—36"

Refrigerator —30"

Range—30"

Range—40"

Eye Level Double Oven Range—24"

Eye Level Double Oven Range—30"

Cook Top—32"

Cook Top—36"

Wall Ovens

Wall Ovens

Dishwasher

Freezer

Freezer

Single—30"

Double—36"

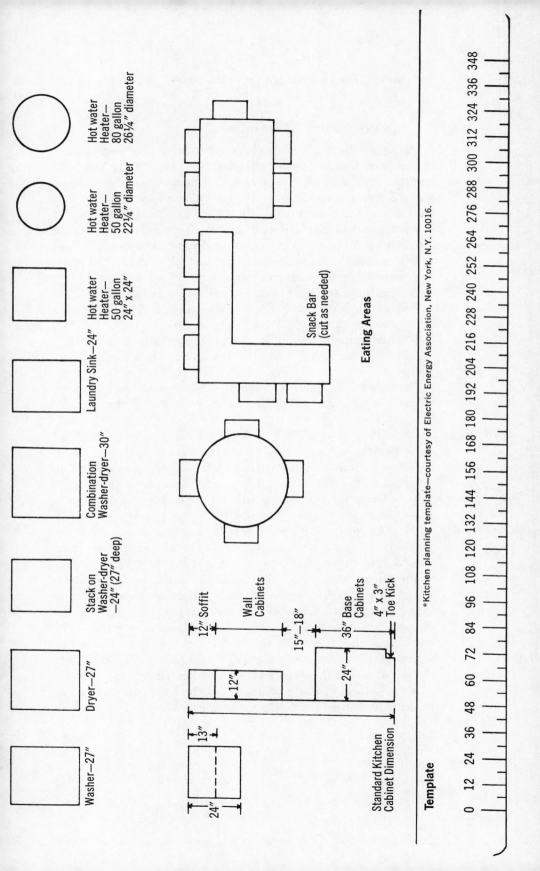

Washer—27"

Dryer—27"

Stack on Washer-dryer—24" (27" deep)

Combination Washer-dryer—30"

Laundry Sink—24"

Hot water Heater— 50 gallon 24" x 24"

Hot water Heater— 50 gallon 22¼" diameter

Hot water Heater— 80 gallon 26¼" diameter

24"

13"

12"

24"

12" Soffit

Wall Cabinets

15"—18"

36" Base Cabinets

4" x 3" Toe Kick

Standard Kitchen Cabinet Dimension

Snack Bar (cut as needed)

Eating Areas

*Kitchen planning template—courtesy of Electric Energy Association, New York, N.Y. 10016.

Template

0   12   24   36   48   60   72   84   96   108   120   132   144   156   168   180   192   204   216   228   240   252   264   276   288   300   312   324   336   348

LEARN ABOUT MATERIALS

Flooring—There is a wide choice of resilient floor coverings on the market. Look for newer ones that need no waxing. Vinyl, the best in terms of comfort, easy care, and durability, is highly resistant to grease and alkalis. Although quite expensive, there are now many grades of vinyl to fit a variety of pocketbooks. Tops in comfort are the cushioned varieties, which are extremely resilient. Linoleum is a popular, economical, and practical flooring, though it is less durable than the vinyls. Asphalt tile resists alkali stains and is suitable for use over cement. It is not too resilient or grease-resistant and hard to care for unless it is heavily waxed.

Rubber tile is extremely resilient and quiet, and while durable, it is not so resistant to grease, oil, and solvents.

Kitchen carpeting of nylon or polypropylene fibers is comfortable and amazingly easy to care for. You'll find a good assortment of styles and colors available.

Ceramic tile is lovely and durable, but it is difficult to clean, expensive, and not too comfortable. For care of flooring, see Chapter Three.

Brick, like ceramic tile, adds a certain charm, but it is difficult to clean and is not comfortable for long work periods.

Counter Tops—Different counter-top materials work better in different work areas, making it practical to use a variety of them in your kitchen. Laminated plastic is popular for general counter use—it is heat-resistant (but not heat-proof), and comes in a wide assortment of colors. Ceramic or glass mosaic tiles are popular in many areas for decorative general counter use; these should have epoxy plastic grout. A wood chopping-block surface is a useful addition, although it requires some special care. Stainless steel is durable, practical, and heat-proof, especially near range areas. Glass ceramic is a new counter material on the market. Available as inserts or as free-standing surfaces (like cutting boards), it is also excellent for the cooking area as it, too, is heat-proof. Ceramic tile is colorful and heat-proof, but it may crack. For care of these surfaces, see Chapter Three.

Wall Surfaces—Paint is undoubtedly the least costly and most practical wall treatment. It can be easily cleaned, if it is a top-quality gloss or semi-gloss enamel; it is also easy to touch up and redo.

A washable wall covering, especially those made of vinyl, can be a decorative plus. Be sure your wall covering is washable, or else treat it with a washable finish before putting it up.

Other popular wall treatments include brick or stone. The genuine thing is nice-looking but hard to care for; check the newer three-dimensional copies of these in cork, plastic, or glass fiber for ease of cleaning and resistance to fume damage. Ceramic tiles, vinyl sheeting, and laminated paneling are other easy-care possibilities.

WIRING, LIGHTING, VENTILATION

Don't skimp on wiring. (1) Provide separate 240-volt circuits for an electric range or built-in electric oven and cook top and electric dryer. (2) Separate 120-volt, 20-amp circuits for a re-frigerator-freezer combination, dishwasher and disposer (one circuit serves both), washer, and freezer. (3) One—preferably two—120-volt, 20-amp circuits for small appliances, a gas range, automatic ice maker, a compact refrigerator. (4) One 120-volt, 15-amp circuit for lights and exhaust fan. See that convenience outlets are placed no more than four feet apart along walls behind all counters and other work areas. Consult your utility or electrical contractor for an adequate wiring plan.

Plan for general illumination from ceiling panels, a luminous ceiling, or a large center ceiling fixture. Fluorescent fixtures with their low brightness and cool operating temperatures are recommended for general illumination. (Specify deluxe warm white.) A good rule to follow for a ceiling fixture is one that will provide 150 to 175 watts incandescent, or 60 to 80 watts fluorescent for each 50 sq. ft. of room. In addition, plan separate lights over sink and range (down lights are good), under wall cabinets over counters (fluorescent brackets work well), and decorative fixture for eating area. For more about lighting, see Chapter Two.

The cooking center needs ventilation. A hood-fan combination is the best if you can vent the fan to the outdoors. If venting is not possible, a nonducted fan will clean the air of fumes and grease, but does not exhaust hot air. Try to vent portable appliances if possible; be sure to vent a built-in barbecue.

PLUMBING AND HEATING

Try to work with existing plumbing, gas, and heating systems if they are adequate and work with your plan. If you are remodeling don't give up a good plan just because one of these systems is in the wrong place. Work with your contractor to find a reasonable solution.

GET PLANNING HELP

Kitchen dealers (generally cabinet dealers) specialize in drawing plans and installing kitchens. They are well trained and competent. There is generally no charge for the plans and estimates, but you are expected to buy their cabinets and let them do the installation.

Appliance dealers may have a trained staff to develop plans, or they may get help from distributors or manufacturers. Their main interest is in selling the appliances, but not in contracting complete kitchen installations.

Many electric and gas utilities offer free kitchen-planning help. Some utilities will plan lighting too.

Often good lumber dealers will provide plans free of charge and offer estimates. They will then furnish all materials and do the installation.

There are many architects who will draw plans and supervise installation for a fee. They are a good source of creative, unusual ideas that help to make the most of your kitchen.

If you're buying a development house, you can often catch your builder early enough in the construction to plan kitchen adjustments with him that will make your kitchen more practical for *you*.

FIGURE YOUR FINANCING

- Once you have received estimates and know how much you've got to spend (it may run from a minimum of $3000 for minor changes—possibly appliances, flooring, and rearrangement of shape using present cabinets—to over $10,000 for a complete overhaul), investigate your sources of financing.

- Before you look for financing, you should know, in addition to how much money you'll need, how large a monthly payment you can afford.
- Investigate the major types of home-improvement loans such as open-end mortgage, refinanced existing mortgage, second mortgage, an FHA-insured home-improvement loan (either long- or short-term), or a personal loan.

PERSONALIZE YOUR KITCHEN

Here are some bonus tips to help make your kitchen more functional, more personal:

- Plan drawer space at each work center.
- Shallow halfway cabinets or shelves installed between counter top and wall cabinets add to storage area for small items.
- Shallow shelves are often better for storage than deep ones.
- If you are low on drawer space, arrange wooden spoons and other kitchen tools bouquet-style in a handsome pitcher, canister, or wooden bucket next to the range.
- Use wall space by installing pegboard near your food-preparation area—hang gadgets, strainers, a portable cutting board on the pegs.
- Cut counter clutter with one of those four-in-one plastic turntable canisters.
- Reorganize the cabinet over built-in ovens, refrigerators, for storage of bulky kitchen items such as large platters, deep bowls, huge baskets (items not in use every day).
- Use equipment space-savers such as the combination portable appliances—a can opener-ice crusher; blender with juicer, ice crusher, mixer attachments; mixer with meat grinder, juicer attachments.
- A magnetic knife rack takes a minimum of space, stores knives safely and conveniently. There are magnetic hooks for other kitchen utensils, too, as well as wall-mounted dispensers and portable appliances.
- To create additional space in wooden kitchen cabinets,

install narrow shelves at the back and sides of the shelf to store glasses or small articles.

- Attach tiny baskets to inside of kitchen closet doors for envelope mixes, small cans of snacks.
- For more efficient storage of dishes, etcetera, organize cabinets with wire racks, lazy Susans, step-shelves, hooks.
- After lining a cabinet shelf, put a paper plate under each pot before storing it. This will keep the lining clean and the paper plate is easily replaced when necessary.
- If your kitchen is large enough, bring back the old-fashioned pantry. It's great as a supermarket for all your grocery needs.
- If you entertain a lot, why not build in a serving cart or bar under an open counter. Slide it out when you need it.
- If you've no room to build in a cutting board, or do not want to go to the expense of doing it, have one custom cut to fit over one section of the sink. Some of the new sinks come outfitted with cutting boards. Or simply buy a portable cutting board.
- A cork bulletin board, mounted on the side of a cabinet or on an available wall area, can be useful and decorative.
- How about a mirror on the inside of one cabinet door?
- If you are a recipe clipper, then forget where you "filed" them, install a rack on the inside of one cabinet door to hold them.
- It is not always necessary to enclose all the space under counters with base cabinets. Leave some open room for sit-down working. And then hasten to lower the counter for more comfortable working heights. We also feel that if you are "naturally neat," you may find that open shelves are more functional for storage of kitchen utensils used most often. This certainly saves stooping and bending to "hunt" for pots and pans. Most people, however, prefer cabinets that close to conceal the contents. It does cover "clutter" that can hardly be avoided at times.
- Drawer cabinets are more functional than base cabinets, because they provide "pull to you" storage.
- Consider installing two under-counter refrigerators in different areas, then plug in a freezer where you would normally install the refrigerator; raise the dishwasher to a higher level for a more comfortable working height.

- People are cooking and eating all over the house these days. Consider setting up a small decentralized "kitchen." It could be no more than an automatic coffeemaker in the bedroom to provide that first cup of morning coffee. Or a small, compact wood-grained refrigerator in the den or playroom.

  If you have provided special outdoor electric outlets on decks and terraces, these areas can literally become "outdoor kitchens" for casual living. Portable ovens, electric rotisseries, coffeemakers, frypans can serve as an outdoor "range." Outdoor gas braziers and grills provide built-in convenience for charcoal-type cooking.

PLANNED FOOD AND EQUIPMENT STORAGE

Staggering as it may seem, the average American family of four consumes about two and a half *tons* of food a year. Even though you do not buy it all at once—still, a bulk of it *has* to be stored. It has also been estimated that homemakers plan, buy, prepare, and serve almost a half billion individual meals a year.

Just storing food and the utensils needed to cook it requires a great deal of organization in time, energy and *space!*

What to Store Where

The best-planned kitchen simply will not work efficiently if things are stored inconveniently.

Take the time to plan storage for each work center. Remember to allow space for future purchases. Duplicate the small inexpensive utensils (such as measures, cutlery) that you'll need in more than one work area. Consider using storage aids such as perforated hardboard, wall hooks, open shelves, easily accessible floor-to-ceiling utility cabinets. Measure large utensils to be sure they'll fit.

Here we have listed everything (or so it seems) that you will find in a kitchen according to the place where you will need it the most and are most likely to use it first. This listing is divided into the three major work centers, described in the preceding.

You may not have enough room to arrange or place these things as suggested, or you may find other arrangements work better for

307

you. In any case, use this listing as a guide to good storage planning.

COOKING AND SERVING CENTER
(RANGE)

Utensils

Skillets and covers
Saucepans and covers
Dutch oven and cover
Casseroles
Griddles
Teakettle
Roasting pan
Cooking forks
  and spoons
Ladles, tongs
Spatulas, metal
Wooden spoons
Tongs
Meat thermometer
Deep-fat thermometer
Deep-fat fryer
Potholders

All small electric cooking appliances
  (to take advantage of range hood,
  unless you have a special small ap-
  pliance area with an appliance
  panel, separate convenience out-
  lets and a ducted or ductless hood
  above it for adequate ventilation)
Egg poacher
Pressure cooker
Large kettles, steamers
Double boiler, part not requiring
  water
Poultry shears
Wire cooling racks
Measuring cups and spoons
Hand mixer

Near serving and eating area

Serving platter
  and bowls
Table condiments
Toaster
Tablecloths and
  place mats

Everyday china, glassware,
  silverware (if not stored
  near dishwasher)
Napkins
Trays
Hot pads

Foods

Packaged cereals
Uncooked cereals
Pasta—noodles,
  spaghetti
Rice
Flour
Instant coffee,
  tea, chocolate

Condiments
Seasonings—salt, pepper,
  herbs, some spices
Sugar
Jellies, syrups
Canned goods

MIXING OR FOOD PREPARATION CENTER
(REFRIGERATOR/FREEZER)

Utensils

Baking utensils—
    cake, pie, loaf,
    muffin pans
Mixing bowls
Measuring cups
    and spoons
Can and bottle
    openers
Biscuit and cookie
    cutters
Cutlery
Wooden mixing spoons
Rubber spatulas
Rolling pins
Pastry cloths
Cutting bread and
    pastry boards
Corers
Scissors or shears
Grater

Custard cups
Cookbooks
Knife sharpener
Paper towels
Wax paper
Aluminum foil
Plastic wrap
Sandwich bags
Ice bucket
Canisters
Cookie jars
Cakebox
Breadbox
Skewers
Scoops
Casseroles
Food grinder
Flour sifter
Molds, ramekins

Foods

Baking powder
    and soda
Cornstarch
Shortening
Flour
Cake mixes
Spices and herbs
Flavorings
Jellies and jams
Spreads (nonrefrigerated)
Breads, cakes, cookies

Onions
Chocolate and cocoa
Salt and pepper
Raisins
Bread mixes
Pancake mixes
Sugar
Salad oil
Vinegar
Snacks
Canned foods

All *refrigerated* foods
(in the refrigerator and freezer)

309

CLEANUP CENTER
(SINK, DISHWASHER AND WASTE DISPOSAL FACILITIES
SUCH AS DISPOSER, TRASH COMPACTOR, GARBAGE CANS)

Utensils

Saucepans and covers
　(those requiring water
　most often)
Can opener
Slicers, peelers
Cutlery
Citrus squeezer
Strainers
Coffeepot
Bottom of double boiler
　(because you need water
　for it)
Funnel
Vegetable brushes
Pot scrapers

Colander
Measuring cups and spoons
Rubber spatula
Paper towels
Aprons
Dish cloths or sponges
Dish towels
Potholders
Garbage cans
Wastebaskets
Paper bags
Cleanser, soaps, detergents
Everyday china, glassware,
　and silverware (unless
　stored near eating area)

Foods

Dried peas and beans
Potatoes

Unrefrigerated fruit
Onions

MAJOR APPLIANCES—PURCHASE,* USE, CARE

Since the *range, refrigerator/freezer,* the *dishwasher,* and *garbage disposer* form the nucleus of your kitchen, it is important that they, and other kitchen-related appliances, be chosen to suit your needs—working habits, taste, and space requirements.

Always compare price in relation to convenience. Both vary according to the model. As features and conveniences increase, prices increase accordingly. Although an appliance may be an economy model, it should still perform the basic functions it was designed to do with quality and durability. Within a brand of appliance, the additional convenience features account for most of the added cost of each appliance in any line. It is important,

* *See also Chapter Fourteen.*

then, to decide just what your particular needs are, before making a final decision.

If you live in an apartment, there is usually no choice, for the appliances are pre-selected. On the other hand, if you are buying a house in a development or from a builder, there are usually certain choices within price limitations. If you are remodeling or building your own home, the entire choice is yours.

RANGES

When you purchase a range you will first have to decide whether you want gas or electric energy. In making the decision you will want to take into consideration your installation requirements, which fuel is available to you and its cost, and which you prefer using. Both have the same general features and cooking efficiency. Both offer cleanliness and efficient heat control, though some people like the fact that when they turn off a gas burner the heat immediately stops. On the other hand, the retained heat factor that electric units provide can be a plus. Both types have either infinite or fixed surface heat controls.

Before buying, consider these other features:

The Design—Styles include *free-standing ranges* which stand independently and come in a wide variety of sizes, colors, prices, and features. *Built-ins,* which are separate ovens and cooking tops, are installed independently, allowing for many different arrangements and heights. They do, however, take up more space than free-standing units. *Eye-level designs* are free-standing units with one oven on top and the other on the bottom or a cook top and oven mounted on a base cabinet. *Slide-ins* or *drop-ins* are free-standing styles that set between cabinets to resemble built-ins. Some come with finished side panels like complete free-standing units; others have unfinished sides. *Stack-on ranges* are set on a counter top or a special base cabinet. *Flat or "smooth-top" cooking surfaces* with the heat source located under smooth ceramic-glass material can be built in flush with counter tops or are available as complete electric ranges that have self-cleaning ovens. Gas models may also be available.

Cooking Capacity—There is a wide variety in the number and arrangements of surface units or burners in widths of 24″, 30″,

311

and 40″. Ovens may be single or double in varying sizes. Broiler units or burners are located either in the top of the oven or in separate compartments.

Note: If you do a great deal of entertaining, have a large family, cook several types of foods at once, consider a double oven.

Construction and Convenience—In *construction* look for outside finishes of porcelain or baked enamel, chrome or stainless steel; top and backsplash in one piece with rounded corners for easy cleaning; handles and switches of heat-resistant materials; convenient, easy-to-read and adjust controls; ovens with vents, lock-stop doors, several shelf supports to vary positions of racks; rust-resistant racks with lock stops to prevent tipping; broiler units or burners in top of oven or separate compartments; speed broilers which broil both sides of meat at once.

As for *convenience*, easy cleaning is of prime importance. Look for self-cleaning or continuous-cleaning ovens, removable doors and control knobs, oven liners. Other conveniences include automatic controls, time baking, meat probes, cook and hold temperature controls; ventilating fan and hood; electric ignitions for pilot lights; automatic lighting for top, oven and broiler burners on gas ranges; infra-red gas broilers; built-in storage; built-in rotisseries, appliance outlets (one automatic); thermostatically controlled surface units and burners ranging in temperature from 130° to 400° F.; warning lights on electric ranges to indicate when range surface units are on; warming areas.

How to Get the Best out of Your Range

To avoid heat waste, use cooking utensils having essentially the same diameter as the surface unit or burner. Adjust the flame on gas burners so it does not extend beyond the utensil edges. Check levelers occasionally to make sure the range is level. This is especially important if you bake many cakes, as they will rise unevenly. It is always wise to use the broiler pan that comes with your oven, as it is designed to control oven spattering.

To avoid blocking heat circulation in the oven when using aluminum foil, *do not* cover any openings in the oven bottom. In fact, it is best never to cover entire shelves or line an oven bottom with aluminum foil, as it may affect the browning of some foods. If you cover drip pans on range surfaces with aluminum foil, follow the contour of the pan and be sure to puncture the center hole and leave it free.

If your electric range does not operate, check the current to see if it is on or if a fuse has blown. The clock-timer may be set on automatic instead of manual or hand operation.

If your gas range does not operate, see if the pilot light is out, if the clock is set on "automatic" as above.

If your oven smokes, the temperature may be too high or it may need cleaning; stickers, tapes and packing materials may not have been completely removed from a new range; there may be a faulty catalyst in a continuous-clean oven; or there may be an oven cleaner residue.

If there is smoking during broiling perhaps drippings are not draining properly—check your broiler pan; or the door may be in the wrong position—it should be partially open for an electric range, closed for gas.

If there is oven steaming, this is normal when baking foods high in liquid, or the vent may be blocked.

If baked foods burn, perhaps the temperature setting is too high, pan is incorrect size, pan is placed incorrectly, or the oven is too crowded. *Always* lower the temperature 25° F. when using glass utensils. Dull aluminum utensils absorb more heat, shiny ones reflect the heat and produce lighter-brown baked products.

To Clean

Always follow manufacturer's specific instructions for your range. In general, wipe the surfaces, drip trays, reflector pans with a damp cloth or sponge wrung out in warm sudsy water, using a mild or light-duty detergent; wipe oven interior after each use before entirely cool; allow any porcelain enamel surface to cool before cleaning or use warm water for hot surfaces (see special instructions below); never scrape surfaces with sharp objects; never use oven cleaners, ammonia, or acids on range exteriors and metal surfaces or parts (especially aluminum); pull off control knobs, wash and dry gently (do not soak), then return to range. Surface and oven heating elements on electric ranges are self-cleaning. Soil burns away when units are heated. Oven vents, usually found under a surface unit, should be washed with hot sudsy water, dried, and replaced. If heavily soiled, clean with a detergent-filled steel wool pad.

Grates and burners on gas ranges lift out and should be washed in hot sudsy water, using a detergent-filled scouring pad for stubborn areas. Burners may be dried in an oven set on a low temperature. Make sure burners are replaced correctly and that air shutters are in same position as they were. Relight burners as soon as you replace them. If holes or parts become clogged, clean out with wire or pick.

Porcelain Enamel Surfaces—Porcelain enamel finish is essentially glass fused on steel at high temperature and is breakable if misused. It is acid-resistant, but if you do spill any acid food (such as lemon or other citrus fruit juices, or mixtures containing tomato or vinegar) you should wipe it up immediately. To wipe up spills when range is hot, use dry paper towels or a cloth dipped in warm water. Avoid the use of cleaning powders, harsh abrasives, or steel wool pads which may scratch the surface.

Stainless Steel Surfaces—Wash, rinse, then dry with soft cloth. To remove brown discolorations, use a powder cleaner such as Samae, which you can purchase in a hardware store or housewares department. Over a period of time stainless steel may darken.

Broiler Pans—Do not let soiled pan and rack stand in oven to cool. Drain fat, cool pan and rack slightly, then add detergent. Fill pan with warm water and spread cloth or paper towel over rack. Let it stand while finishing meal. Drippings should have loosened enough to wash with a sponge dipped in hot sudsy water. If not, use a detergent-filled scouring pad. Rinse and dry. If pan is not made of anodized aluminum it may be washed in dishwasher.

Note: If grid is lined with aluminum foil, be sure slits are made in foil to follow design of grid. If pan is lined with aluminum foil, cleaning is cut to a minimum.

Ovens—Preventive maintenance is the best method for keeping an oven clean. Food spatterings that are allowed to reheat and bake on will be difficult to remove. Clean regularly with detergent and water to remove greasy soil. An all-purpose household cleaning detergent, especially those containing ammonia, will remove much of the burned-on soil and grease. To loosen baked-on soil, place a saucer filled with a small amount of undiluted ammonia in the oven for several hours or overnight. If oven is heavily soiled, use a commercial oven cleaner, following container directions exactly. Be sure to use rubber gloves. Follow specific directions for Teflon liners or other coated surfaces.

Ventilating Hoods and Fans—If you have a ductless hood over your range or a range with a fan and filter system which is ducted to exhaust grease, heat, and cooking fumes to the outdoors, the charcoal grease filter may be cleaned and reactivated by oven heating. Follow your instruction manual. Replace these filters yearly. Wire-mesh filters may be washed in the dishwasher or soaked and brushed in hot sudsy water using a light-duty detergent. Rinse thoroughly and tap gently to remove excess water. Let dry thoroughly, then replace. To clean an exhaust fan wipe with a damp sponge wrung out in hot sudsy water.

For self-cleaning ovens (referred to as *Pyrolytic*), oven soil is reduced to a light ash during a separate high-heat cycle. The remaining ash can be removed with a damp cloth.

Clean door liner only outside the gasket, using a detergent-filled scouring pad, if necessary. Rinse well before cleaning. Avoid rubbing or getting any cleaning materials on gasket. Simply remove cooking utensils and set the controls to lock the door and clean the oven *according to the manufacturer's instructions*.

For continuous-clean models (originally referred to as *Catalytic*), oven soil is gradually reduced to a presentably clean condition on specially treated surfaces during normal baking or roasting operations. Wipe up any spills immediately. Clean all other surfaces as you would regular ovens.

Electronic Cooking

Another relatively new appliance is the electronic or microwave oven. It cooks with microwaves (high frequency), using primarily paper or glass utensils and offers the convenience of speedy cooking—a ten-pound roast in one hour or a baked potato in four minutes. It is available as a built-in, table, or counter-top

315

model, free-standing or eye-level type, or in a combination. Some models require 220/240-volt installation, others 110 or 115 volts. Those with browning elements offer the most convenience.

To Use and Clean Electronic Ranges—When microwaves have been used alone for cooking, the interior of the range can be wiped clean with a damp sudsy sponge, then rinsed and dried with a towel. When the conventional heat (browning), bake, or broil unit has also been used, the care is the same as that of a conventional electric range.

Use only utensils designed for cooking in microwave ovens. Do not use metal or aluminum foil, unless otherwise directed by the manufacturer. Always check the filter below the oven. Soiled or greasy ones can prevent air from cooling the magnetron tube, which may stop operation. Never operate the oven when the filter is not in place or when the door is open. If, by chance, the oven operates when the door *is* open, close it and *call a serviceman immediately*. To avoid any possible microwave loss or exposure, never place anything between oven frame and door such as a paper or cloth. Do not allow soil to build up on door seal, door surface, or oven frame. Follow specific cleaning instructions for your particular model.

How to Keep It Running Smoothly—If your electronic range does not operate well, perhaps the magnetron tube is overheated, the filter is dirty or greasy, the oven door is not properly closed, the timer is not set, or the "on" button is not pushed.

Induction Cooking

Looming on the horizon is another type of flat cooking surface which cooks food without conventional gas or electric heating elements. This cooking method induces heat directly into the pan. This new method is made possible by solid-state electronic circuits within the range. When cookware of magnetic material such as iron or steel is put over a coil, indicated by a pattern on the range top, the pan couples with the oscillating magnetic field created by the coil and heat is produced in the vessel itself; the range surface does not have to be heated to heat the vessel.

REFRIGERATORS

These days, newer refrigerators and freezers virtually beg us to save time by doing our marketing less often, and the wide variety of models available allows us to shop and store according to our personal needs.

Before you buy your next refrigerator, consider the size of your family, how fast it will grow in the next few years; your marketing habits (if you shop only once a week, you'll need more storage space than if you shop every few days); how many frozen foods you buy or freeze yourself (if you buy a lot, then you'll need a large freezer compartment or a separate freezer); available kitchen space; cost. If you entertain a great deal or drink lots of soft drinks, you may want a refrigerator with an icemaker.

The Design—Basically there are two types—the combination refrigerator-freezer and the conventional design.

The side-by-side combination combines a full-length refrigerator with a full-length freezer that maintains a minus 5° to plus 5° F. temperature range. The *bottom-freezer combination* also offers this temperature range. Freezer may be a roll-out drawer, or have a side-opening door with shelves and baskets that move out. The *top-freezer combination* also maintains this temperature range, though of the three combinations, it usually has the smallest capacity. It's good for a small family, one who needs a minimum of freezer storage.

The *conventional refrigerator* is the least expensive and offers the least convenience. The freezer compartment is not designed for long-term storage. It makes ice cubes and stores frozen foods for a limited time, but may not keep ice cream hard. Temperature range is from 0° to 20° F, averaging from 10° to 15° F.

The clean, sleek styling of free-standing units gives them a built-in look. Or you can buy the above models in true built-in units.

The compact refrigerator is great if you are short of space or if you want a second refrigerator in the kitchen, family room, or den.

Capacity is stated in cubic feet; shelf area in square feet. (See

317

section on certification seals.) New, thinner insulation allows larger capacities inside, with smaller dimensions outside. As for judging the capacity you need, fresh food compartments should provide approximately 8 cubic feet of storage for a family of 2 and 1 cubic foot for each additional person, plus 2 cubic feet for entertainment needs. The freezer space should provide approximately 2 cubic feet for each family member. It is always better to buy a little larger refrigerator than you need. It allows you to shop less often and provides extra space for entertaining and holiday foods.

Construction and Convenience—Look for outside finishes of porcelain or baked enamel; linings of porcelain enamel, corrosion-resistant aluminum, or sturdy plastic; shelves, baskets and drawers of rust-resistant metal or sturdy plastic that are easy to remove, replace, clean, and adjust; insulation of glass wool, glass fiber or foam, which is moisture-resistant and odorless; doors with sturdy hinges and a tight-sealing gasket; right- or left-hand door openings (you can purchase models that open on one side *or* the other depending upon placement); accessible controls with clear temperature indications. There are plastic or aluminum ice cube trays; lighted interiors; automatic ice cube and ice water dispensers; automatic ice cube makers, which require plumbing connections; seasonal controls; casters or rollers to allow you to easily clean floor and walls; doors that open from the inside to prevent children from being trapped; reversible hinge doors for interchangeable door openings; fast chill shelves or compartments; egg trays; compartments for special storage of dairy products, vegetables and meats.

Types of Defrosting

Defrosting very simply may be defined as the removal of accumulated frost. The means of removing this frost may be automatic or manual. You may manually defrost by turning the controls to *off* or by some other method such as hot water or heat. What this amounts to is that *you* may "wobble" across the floor, carrying a pan of defrost water to the sink, or the system itself disposes of it by automatic means.

There are, essentially, four types of defrosting you can buy.

A *manual-defrosting refrigerator* is a cabinet which has to be defrosted by hand. It is not automatic. Defrosting must be initiated and terminated by the individual.

A *semi-automatic defrosting refrigerator* is a cabinet in which you manually turn on the defrost system, but it is automatically stopped. The defrost water is automatically disposed of.

An *automatic-defrosting refrigerator* is a cabinet in which the defrost cycle is automatic. It is automatically turned on and off to remove the accumulation of frost on refrigerated plates or coils.

Caution: You may find a few models which are automatic defrost in the refrigerator section but must be defrosted by hand in the freezer section.

In a *frostless refrigerator-freezer,* both the refrigerator and freezer compartments never form frost. We feel that this feature, along with self-cleaning ovens, is one of the major breakthroughs in housekeeping convenience. Moisture that condenses on the inner wall of either compartment is quickly drawn off by the air circulated through the compartment by a hidden fan. The moisture freezes on the evaporator section of the refrigerating mechanism and is then melted off by small electric heaters that turn on periodically for very short periods. Buying this feature costs more and does increase your electricity bill, but you may find it is worth the time and energy you save.

How to Get the Best Out of Your Refrigerator

Keep your refrigerator set at the recommended temperature. The efficient operation of any refrigerator/freezer depends upon maintaining the proper temperature, air circulation, and humidity. The compartments in your refrigerator are there for a reason. The efficiency of your refrigerator is definitely increased if you use some organization in storage. To keep eggs unbroken and for ease of handling, use the egg storage compartments. They are often located in the door away from the coldest air, because eggs don't require as much cold as other foods. Neither does butter. Use your covered butter container because butter tends to absorb odors from other foods. Cover cheese tightly with a moisture-proof wrapping to keep it from drying out.

319

Meats, poultry and fish are more susceptible to spoilage than other foods. Keep these in the meat storage compartment, which should be the coldest part of the refrigerator, located immediately above or below the freezer. Theoretically, a meat keeper should maintain a temperature of 28° F. and have some air flow around the meats. But this, once again, is dependent upon the temperature of the main food compartment. A meat-holding drawer is not the same as a true meat keeper. Check your instruction book to see which type you have.

Fresh vegetables and fruits go in the crisper compartment, which is designed to maintain a high humidity and keep the produce fresh. Milk should be very cold. The milk-bar shelves are often located on the refrigerator door near the freezer area. This section will maintain the same temperature as the main food compartment as long as the door is not left open for long periods of time.

We'd like to be able to state unequivocally that your refrigerator should never go below 35° F. or above 41° F.; that eggs should be stored at x degrees and milk at y degrees. But, aside from the fact that refrigerator temperatures don't stay the same throughout the day, how cold your foods should be depends, for one thing, on how long you keep them. If you do not open the refrigerator door often, you can probably keep milk for a week because the temperature will remain around 34° F.

Tip: To determine if controls are correctly set, so the freezer section and the fresh-food refrigerated section will keep foods at their best, a good rule of thumb is to check the milk and ice cream. When milk stored inside the refrigerator is a good, cold drink, the refrigerator section will be around 36° F. to 38° F. When the freezer keeps ice cream very firm, the freezer will be approximately the proper 0° F.

For storage of all kinds of perishable foods, see section on Food Storage at the end of this chapter.

To determine the true temperature range of your refrigerator, keep a refrigerator thermometer in the fresh food compartment and a freezer thermometer in the freezer section.

Plan your arrangement of foods if at all possible. Avoid overcrowding, which hampers air circulation. Remove foods from cardboard cartons and heavy wrappings, which "eat up the cold."

Cover foods with lighter wrappings—plastic wrap, wax paper, or aluminum foil. Or use refrigerator containers. Cover foods tightly to prevent drying and to keep odors from spreading. Let foods cool before placing them in the refrigerator. Edit your leftovers regularly, and throw away stale foods.

How to Keep Your Refrigerator in Good Running Order

Place your refrigerator so that there is adequate space above, behind, and on the sides for free air circulation and to leave room for its own heat to escape properly.

If your refrigerator seems to be running more frequently than you think it should, there may be a leak through the door gasket letting warm air inside, the condensers may need cleaning, or there may be a frost buildup. Remember that frost-free models do require more running time and cost more to operate.

If moisture collects inside your refrigerator it may be a sign that you are opening the door too often. Hot, humid weather also may increase the rate of frost buildup and internal "sweating."

If your refrigerator has an unpleasant odor, make sure all foods such as onions, cabbage, etcetera, are covered. Clean your evaporator pan from time to time, and if the odor still persists, your refrigerator may just need a thorough cleaning.

If your cabinet vibrates, is noisy, or has a running water sound, the refrigerator may not be level or your floor may be weak or there may be something on top or behind the refrigerator.

If you find that foods are freezing in the refrigerator compartment, the temperature control dial may be set in too cold a position. Lower it.

To Clean

Wash the exterior of the cabinet and door gasket with warm sudsy water, rinse, and wipe dry. Do not use scouring powder or harsh abrasive cleaners. Polish cabinet occasionally with a creamy appliance wax.

To clean the inside, turn control dial to "off." Remove all food and shelves. Wash with a solution of 1 tablespoon baking soda in 1 quart warm water. Rinse with clear water then dry with a towel. Wash shelves, crispers, and ice cube trays in warm sudsy water, rinse, and dry.

Check your instruction book to determine the location of the condenser coils. They may be on the back or bottom of refrigerator. Make sure that nothing obstructs the space near the condenser, which can block air circulation. Dust the condenser every 2 or 3 months with the crevice tool attachment of your vacuum cleaner, or a long-handled brush. Failure to keep the condenser clean may cause excessive heat on the outside, vibration from pump, noise, and increased temperatures on the inside.

If you plan to be away for one or two weeks, allow the refrigerator to operate at the normal cold control setting. *For a longer absence,* disconnect the refrigerator cord from the wall outlet and remove all food. Defrost, clean the interior, and leave the doors ajar to allow room air to circulate within the cabinet.

Defrosting the Conventional Refrigerator

The refrigerator should be defrosted when frost in the freezer compartment is ¼-inch thick. When defrosting, be sure to follow specific directions in your instruction book; otherwise remove frozen foods, wrap them in heavy paper, newspaper, or place them in an insulated chest. Turn cold control to "off." Remove items from any trays located below the freezer. Fill one or two large pans with boiling water. Place in freezer compartment. Repeat until frost has melted. Wipe up defrost moisture. Empty tray or pan underneath. Clean the interior. Wipe dry. Turn cold control to original setting.

Caution: Never try to remove ice or frost with an ice pick or sharp object. You may puncture the lining and cause serious damage. You can purchase electric defrosting units which help to speed up the process. Make sure they are Underwriters Laboratories Approved (UL). Follow specific directions.

FREEZERS

A separate home freezer is a good buy if you:

- Have a large family
- Entertain a great deal

- Freeze home-grown or home-prepared foods
- Buy in quantity when prices are low
- Have the space

If you do decide to purchase a freezer, take advantage of it to store all the make-ahead meals and company food you can. A freezer can make your meal planning very simple if you use it properly. It can help you to market less frequently and be prepared for unexpected guests. One good trick is to cook double quantities and freeze the additional portions.

Design—The type of freezer you select will depend on the space you have and your personal preference.

The *upright freezer* requires approximately the same amount of space as your refrigerator. It has the advantage of easy to see and use shelf storage.

The *chest freezer,* the original freezer style, may take from 32 to 72 inches in width; 27 to 32 inches in depth. The height is around 36 inches or standard counter height (but remember, you have to account for and keep clear the space over it for opening and closing the lid). This type is generally kept in a pantry or some other room besides the kitchen. It requires more floor space, but the initial cost is less and it stores larger, bulkier packages.

The *compact freezer* is excellent if you are short of space. Compact freezers come in chest-style, top-opening models, and upright-style, front-opening models.

Capacity—In determining capacity, you need to consider the available floor space, family size, how often you shop, cooking and entertaining habits, and the freezer space in your present refrigerator. A common rule is 6 cubic feet per person.

Convenience—Look for a signal light to indicate that the current is off or that the temperature is too high; an automatic reset switch when the power returns; an adequate drain for easy water removal on nonfrost models; a removable basket or adjustable shelves for easier cleaning and loading; counterbalanced lid on chest freezers; certification seal indicating refrigerated volume and shelf space on upright models and refrigerated volume on chest models; a separate quick-freeze section; a well-lighted interior; easy-to-read and accessible controls; rollers or casters for mobility in cleaning.

How to Get the Best out of Your Freezer

Acquaint yourself with a few of the technical principles of freezing and using a freezer.

- Select good-quality foods—when properly packaged, freezing retains quality but does not improve it. The condition of the food when you put it in the freezer is the same condition in which it will be when you remove it.
- Buy foods when they are in season and prices are low, or when they are marked as specials.
- To manage a home freezer well, avoid overstocking on commercially packaged foods for they are always available and don't vary too much in price. Keep several weeks' supply but allow space mainly for baked goods, prepared dishes, and special foods for entertaining.
- Wrap foods in meal-size portions, or serving portions. There is less waste and foods thaw more quickly.
- Always use moisture-, vapor-proof materials, especially designed for freezing.
- Freeze a small quantity at a time. Put in no more unfrozen food than will freeze in 18 to 24 hours—more quickly, if possible. This amounts to about 2 or 3 pounds of food to each cubic foot of capacity. Quality essentially depends upon fast freezing. Fast freezing is usually done at near −10° F. or lower. Look for freezers with a fast-freeze section.
- Label packages accurately with name, portion, and date, and arrange foods so you can reach them conveniently.
- Keep a running inventory and use the foods that have been in the freezer for the longest period of time. Use foods within the recommended maximum storage period. See storage chart at the end of this chapter.

Packaging Materials—The Essential Key

Wrapping Papers—These should fold easily to form a tight seal. Use the "drugstore wrap" for best results: place food in center of sheet (large enough to enclose the food); bring longest edges together and fold over 1 inch; fold again over and over until edges are flat and tight against the food. Push out all air pockets. Fold and tuck under the ends; heat-seal or tape with freezer tape to make secure and tight. Another method is the "butcher" wrap, which is the cross-fold method butchers actually use.

- *Aluminum foil* is very flexible and can be easily self-sealed by folding over and crimping the edges. Heavy-duty aluminum foil is recommended for freezing.
- *Wax-coated laminated freezer papers* are especially recommended for meat, though they do not mold as closely to the foods. Seal with freezer tape and tie securely with strong cord.
- *Transparent plastic sheet wrap* is very flexible and air can be pushed out easily; some of the lighter-weight materials should be overwrapped for extra protection. Seal fold and ends with freezer tape.
- *Transparent plastic bags* have the same flexibility as plastic sheet wrap. Air can be pushed out easily and they can be fastened tightly with paper-covered wire twists.

Containers—Make sure containers have tight-fitting lids and are stackable. To fill, allow a headspace of ½ to 1 inch for expansion during freezing. Containers may be of foil which can go from freezer to oven; glass baking dishes (some can go direct from freezer to oven); waxed cartons; plastic containers; and glass jars.

Sealing Tape—Use special freezer tape. To heat-seal plastic sheet wrapping, use an iron set at "warm" or an electric heat sealer designed for freezer use; just barely touch the overlapped edges of the plastic sheeting to seal.

Labeling Equipment and Markers—A china marking pencil or grease pencil is useful for labeling and package identification.

Overwrap Materials—For long-term storage use stockinette (loosely knitted tubular cotton fabric), butcher paper, or cheesecloth and place over initial package.

Commercially Frozen Foods

Tip: When storing commercially frozen foods, be sure they have not thawed.

325

- Select foods that are solidly frozen. Do not purchase if they are soft to the touch.
- Buy frozen foods just before you go to the checkout counter.
- Carry them home in insulated bags.
- Store in the freezer immediately.

Can You Refreeze Thawed Foods?

Don't refreeze foods which have thawed completely. In an emergency, foods may be refrozen if food is still firm and ice crystals remain. However, these foods will have lower quality and less flavor. Use them as quickly as possible after they have been refrozen.

What and What Not to Freeze

The following are not recommended for freezing:

Bananas	Lettuce	Celery
Fresh tomatoes	Mayonnaise	Cooked egg white
Cream (unless whipped)	Custards	Cream pies
Gelatin salads		

Other than the above, most foods can be frozen. Onions, green peppers, and celery may be chopped and frozen for short periods, to be used in cooked dishes only.

MAXIMUM STORAGE TIME AT 0° F.

BAKED FOODS	MONTHS
Yeast bread	6 to 8
Rolls	6 to 8
Partially baked	4 to 6
Unbaked	less than 1
Cakes	
Baked	3 to 4
Baked, frosted	2 to 3
Unbaked	1 or less
Cupcakes	2 to 3
Baked cookies	8 to 12

BAKED FOODS	MONTHS
Pies	
Baked	1 to 2
Unbaked	3 to 4
Chiffon	1 or less
Quick breads, baked	2 to 3
Leftover cooked foods	1 or less
Sandwiches	1
Prepared foods	1 to 3
Stews and soups	2 to 3

DAIRY PRODUCTS	
Creamery butter	4 to 6
Heavy cream (40%)	2 to 3
Milk	2 to 3
Cottage cheese (uncreamed)	2 to 3
Cheese, Cheddar	4 to 6
Eggs: whites, yolks or whole	8 to 10
Ice cream	1

FISH	
Commercially frozen	1
Lean fish	6 to 9
Fatty fish	3 to 4
Salmon	2 to 3
Shellfish	2 to 3
Shrimp	
Fresh, unpeeled	up to 4
Cooked, unpeeled	3 to 4
Cooked, peeled	2 to 3
Crabs	1 to 2
Lobster	1 to 2
Oysters	1 to 2
Clams	1 to 2
Scallops	1 to 2

FOWL	
Duckling	3 to 4
Game birds	8 to 12
Geese	5 to 6

327

FOWL	MONTHS
Poultry	
Cut up, broilers	4 to 6
Whole	6 to 8
Creamed	2 to 3
Giblets	1 to 2
Turkeys, unstuffed	6 to 8
Creamed	2 to 3
Cooked chicken	2 to 3
or turkey	

FRUITS	
Apples, apricots*	16
Berries*	16
Blueberries	12
Cherries, sour	16
Cherries, sweet	12
Coconut	8 to 12
Cranberries	16
Currants	12
Dates, figs	8 to 12
Gooseberries, grapes	8 to 12
Juices	8 to 12
Melons	8 to 12
Mixed fruits	6 to 8
Oranges, grapefruit	8 to 12
Peaches*	16
Pears	6 to 8
Pineapple	16
Plums, prunes	8 to 12
Raspberries,* Rhubarb	16
Strawberries*	16

MEAT	
Beef	
Steaks, roasts	8 to 12
Frankfurters	2 to 3

* Storage times are for sugar or syrup packed fruit, with ascorbic acid added as needed. Dry packs do not store as long.

MEAT	MONTHS
Ground beef	2 to 3
Kidney, tongue	3 to 4
Lamb roasts	8 to 12
Most game	8 to 12
Pork	
Fresh pork	4 to 6
Pork, ground, unsalted	2 to 3
Variety meats	1
Veal	4 to 8

VEGETABLES	
Asparagus	6 to 8
Beans, green or wax	8 to 12
Beans, lima	12
Broccoli	12
Brussels sprouts	12
Carrots, cauliflower	12
Corn on cob, cream-style	8 to 12
Corn, whole kernel	16
Eggplant	8 to 12
Greens	12
Kohlrabi	8 to 12
Mixed vegetables	8 to 12
Mushrooms	6 to 8
Okra	12
Peas, black-eyed, green	12
Peppers	8 to 12
Potatoes	
French fried	2 to 3
Stuffed	2 to 3
Pumpkin, mashed	16
Squash, summer	8 to 12
Squash, winter	12
Sweet potatoes	12
Turnips	12

Defrosting and Cleaning the Freezer

Plan on defrosting and cleaning your freezer when your food supply is low.

To defrost:

Unless you have a frostless model you will need to defrost by hand. Follow specific instructions for your particular model. In general, defrost when the frost buildup is about ¼-inch thick. Use a rubber, wooden, or plastic spatula or paddle to scrape frost from the freezer walls.

Never use a knife or sharp instrument which could cause damage to freezer walls. On an upright freezer turn the cold control dial to "off"; on chest freezer, disconnect electrical cord from wall receptacle. Remove any food and wrap in heavy layers of paper. Place in refrigerator or store in an insulated chest or in a carton covered with heavy paper, newspaper, or a blanket.

Do not let water collect on the bottom of the freezer. Place empty pans on the very bottom to collect the defrost water. Or use towels to catch the frost. Scoop out additional frost with a clean dustpan. It will probably be necessary to place several towels across the bottom front of the freezer to keep any defrost water from dripping down the outside of the freezer.

To Clean:

Wash the interior with a solution of 1 tablespoon baking soda in 1 quart warm water; rinse and wipe dry. Connect the freezer, let it cool, then put the food away.

Wash the outside of the freezer cabinet with warm sudsy water, rinse, and wipe dry. Occasionally polish the exterior with a creamy appliance wax. Wipe gasket around door or lid frequently with a damp cloth.

Clean condenser every two or three months (follow instructions for your model), using the crevice tool or brush attachment of your vacuum cleaner or a long-handled brush.

In Case of Freezer or Power Failure

If your home freezer stops running and will be off for some time, you can take several steps to keep food from spoiling.

- Move the food to a locker plant if you have a lot of it.
- Add dry ice if you can get it. To prevent burns, wear gloves.
- Wrap food up in newspapers.
- Keep the freezer closed. Open it only to take out the food for moving to a locker plant, or to add dry ice.

Estimate how long the current will be off. Don't worry if you know you can have the freezer running again in a few hours.

When the freezer stops running, the power supply may be off or the freezer itself may be out of order.

- Try to find out how long the power will be off.
- Consult the instruction book to determine if there is something you can do to put the freezer back into operation. *Important:* Follow any specific instructions the manufacturer recommends in case the freezer stops.
- Try to find out how long it will take to get a serviceman to put the freezer back in running order.

Try to estimate about how long the food will stay frozen. With the freezer closed, food will usually stay frozen in a fully loaded cabinet from 36 to 48 hours; in a cabinet with less than half a load, not more than a day.

How long the food in your freezer will stay frozen depends on:

- The amount of food in the freezer. A full freezer will stay cold many hours longer than a freezer only a quarter full.
- The kind of food. A freezer full of meat will not warm up so fast as a freezer full of baked food.
- The temperature of the food. The colder the food, the longer it will stay frozen.
- The freezer itself. A well-insulated freezer will keep food frozen much longer than one with little insulation.
- Size of freezer.
- Some foods will not hold up as long as others. For example, remove and use all cream, cheese, and other dairy products as soon as possible.
- The larger the freezer, the longer the food will stay frozen.

If You Need a Freezer-Locker Plant

If you have one in your area, make arrangements well in advance with a local locker plant to take care of food in an emergency. Then, if an emergency occurs:

1. Call the locker plant to see if it is operating and, if so, whether it has room for your food. If space is available—
2. Wrap the food in plenty of newspapers and blankets, or use insulated boxes.
3. Rush the food to the locker plant.

If You Need Dry Ice

If locker space is not available and it looks as though the freezer will be off for longer than a day, use dry ice if you can get it. You may be able to buy dry ice from a local dairy or a cold-storage warehouse. The more dry ice you use, the longer the food will keep frozen:

- Twenty-five pounds of dry ice should hold the temperature of a half-full 10-cubic-foot cabinet below freezing for two or three days.
- Food in a fully loaded cabinet will stay frozen for three to four days if you put the dry ice in soon after the freezer goes off.
- Use 50 pounds of dry ice for a 20-cubic-foot freezer if it will be off for 36 hours.

Put heavy cardboard directly on the packages of frozen food and then put the dry ice on top of the cardboard.

As an extra precaution, you may cover the freezer with blankets, quilts, or some other covering. It will help to put crumpled newspaper or excelsior between the cabinet and the blankets.

Be sure to pin or fasten them so that they will not cover the air-vent openings. The power may go on unexpectedly and ventilation will be needed.

Information in this section was taken from the U.S.D.A. Bulletin #321, "What to Do When Your Home Freezer Stops."

DISHWASHERS

Dishes, of course, may be washed by hand or automatically in a dishwasher.

Hand dishwashing, if done properly, can be quite satisfactory, but it is time- and energy-consuming and does not sanitize as effectively as automatic dishwashing. As we said previously, the average American homemaker will wash and dry more than 1,500,000 pieces of silverware, dishes, pots, and pans in her lifetime, so it is wise to find the easiest and most sanitary method. (For washing dishes by hand, see later section in this chapter.)

Sanitizing the Dishes

Automatic dishwashers have proved to be the best method thus far of actually sanitizing dishes, glassware, silverware, and cooking utensils.

The Effect of Heat

Heat kills bacteria better than almost anything else, and in a dishwasher the heat is high throughout the entire dishwashing cycle. Normal water temperatures in models which have electric heaters to maintain or boost the incoming water temperature are 140° to 160° F. Drying temperatures are even higher.

With automatic dishwashing, you can wash dishes in water hotter than the hands can stand. The incidences of passing around colds and flu germs among family members have been known to be reduced with families using a dishwasher. Average temperatures of the water used in hand washing is about 100° F. With rubber gloves, of course, you can use hotter water.

Dishwasher detergents make water much more alkaline than hand washing detergents, which must be mild enough to be kind to the skin. This, of course, helps to destroy bacteria, which for the most part need a neutral atmosphere to survive. Dishwasher detergents also contain chlorine, which helps to disinfect as well as clean, as it does in laundering.

A dishwasher detergent complements the cleaning action of

the water. The action of the water by means of its overall distribution and circulation through the impellers and spray arms, coupled with the detergent's cleaning power, does the job you would otherwise do with your hands. Dishwasher detergents are essentially low-sudsing and they must also help to suppress the foam from protein food soils such as egg and milk. In addition they perform much the same functions as a laundry detergent—they "tie up" hardness-causing minerals, make the water wetter to loosen soils, emulsify oily or greasy soils, hold them in the wash water until they can be rinsed away, clean the surfaces of dishes, glassware, and flatware so that water will sheet off instead of forming drops of water which would leave spots during drying, and protect china patterns and metals from the corrosive effects of heat and water alone.

When Buying a Dishwasher Consider These Features

Design—There are free-standing, built-in, or portable models. If you are building or remodeling, no doubt you will want a built-in under-counter model. Otherwise you may choose a portable. If you think you may want to build it in at a later date, select a "convertible" front-opening portable. Tops may be either laminated plastic or wood. Portables should move about easily with easy-to-reach hose and electrical connections.

Capacity—While some manufacturers indicate capacity in terms of table settings, some do not. In either case, the important thing to note is that, with the exception of the under-sink dishwasher and economy portables, most all dishwashers hold all the pieces an average family is likely to wash at one time on any one day!

Construction and Convenience—Look for outside finishes of baked or porcelain enamel, stainless steel, or brushed chrome; rust- and scratch-resistant tub and door linings, spray arms, impellers and jets that assure good overall water distribution; racks that allow flexibility of random loading; automatic detergent dispensers and wetting agent or rinse dispensers which inject a liquid that helps water "sheet off" glassware and dishes to prevent spotting while drying; built-in grinders or filters to help eliminate hand rinsing and dispose of soft food waste.

Also look for controls to stop the machine for adding or removing dishes during washing; cycles for rinse and hold, pre-wash, regular wash, heavy wash for pots and pans, boosters for raising water temperatures that allow portable machines to use water from faucet while dishwasher is connected; good insulation to deaden sound special compartments for silverware.

Almost everything is dishwasher washable, with the exception of some wooden items, anodized aluminum, antiques, hand-painted, gold-encrusted or overglazed china, rubber utensils, some plastic ware which is not heat-resistant, items with cemented-on handles such as hollow-handled silver, pewter, cast iron, and dirilyte.

How to Use a Dishwasher

Make certain water temperature is between 140° and 160° F. Use dishwasher detergents only. Add the detergent immediately before operating the machine. If your water is hard, use a rinsing agent to prevent spotting. Use enough detergent to soften the water, suppress foam from food soils, and provide the necessary cleaning and suspension of soil. Follow package directions. When loading, place metal items away from detergent cups; do not place large objects next to detergent cups. This may block circulation of water which will prevent dispensing of detergent into the dishwasher. Place lightweight items securely on rack so that they are not moved by the force of the water.

To Clean

Generally the dishwasher tub is self-cleaning; however, if after long use in areas with hard water, a white film develops, wipe the tub with a damp cloth and a very mild household cleanser.

Check the bottom of the tub periodically to remove any small objects that may have become dislodged from the racks.

Wipe the outside of the dishwasher with a sponge dipped in warm sudsy water, rinse, and wipe dry. Clean occasionally with a creamy appliance wax. To clean laminated plastic tops, see section on laminated plastic in Chapter Three.

Wood top dishwashers are particularly vulnerable to heavy water usage. Should the top show warpage after unusual exposure

335

to moisture, wipe and keep top dry for forty-eight hours and the warpage should disappear.

To remove water stains, wipe with cloth saturated with non-toxic mineral oils or boiled linseed oil. (For more detailed care of all wood tops, see Chapter Three.) Should top become stained or dirty, sand with 000 or 0000 sandpaper and then wipe over sanded area with a cloth soaked in oil as above.

How to Keep Your Dishwasher Running Properly

Check the following points before calling for service:

- If the dishwasher leaks, perhaps you are using the wrong detergent. Use only *dishwasher* detergents. If leakage persists, call your serviceman.
- If you notice any unusual noise, check the items inside. The utensils may not be firmly placed, and water forces them to rattle. An especially small item may have moved from its original position.
- If there is detergent left in the detergent dispenser, water action may be obstructed. Be sure that a large plate, pan, or other item is not placed directly in front of the detergent dispenser.
- If there is spotting and filming on glasses and flatware, the rinse dispenser may be empty, or your water may not be hot enough. If you do not have a dispenser, use a solid rinse agent.
- If cycles do not seem to continue normally, check to see if push-button controls are on the proper setting.
- If you find brown stains in cups, tea or coffee may have been allowed to remain in cups too long. Rinse cups immediately if they are not to be washed within an hour. To remove stains by hand, use a little baking soda or a mild cleanser on a damp cloth.
- Dark spots on metal are often caused when detergent crystals are left standing on metal. This can be removed from silverware by vigorous rubbing with soft cloth and silver polish and from aluminum with a soap-filled scouring pad. Otherwise use a special cleaner designed for specific metals.

- If your dishes do not dry properly, the water temperature may be too low, or perhaps you may not be loading it properly. Dishes should not nest together. If problem persists, call a serviceman.

GARBAGE DISPOSERS

A garbage disposer promises to reduce food waste to small enough pieces to be flushed down the drain. It uses a round, spinning disk that whirls food against a shredding ring to pulverize it. Hammerlike impellers hold it there until it is fine enough to be flushed away. A shredding ring often includes cutting devices to shred fibrous foods. A good disposer will handle just about all of your wet garbage—corncobs and husks, fruit rinds, artichoke leaves, steak and rib bones, eggshells and coffee grounds. Follow your own instruction book, however, for specific directions as to what can and what cannot be put in *your* disposer.

Design—There are two types of garbage disposers. The *continuous-feed model* has a switch (usually on a wall) which turns on and off. A rubber backsplash fixed partially over the opening keeps the wastes and water from splashing out; more waste may be added while the disposer is in operation. In the *batch-feed model,* the waste is put into the disposer, the cover put on and locked to start the disposer, which then grinds a "batch" at a time; to add more waste the cover must be unlocked and lifted out.

Convenience Features—When you want to purchase a garbage disposer, look for heavy-duty motors, anti-jamming controls, circuit breaker or automatic reset switch to prevent overheating of motor; manual or automatic overload reset to protect against overloading; high-bulk cutters, grinding wheels and shredder hinge of tough, hard material; noncorrosive material such as stainless steel housings, epoxy, or other high-quality plastics; good sound control such as insulated sink mountings, insulated gaskets at connections, foam or fiber insulation or a sound-absorbing plastic body for the disposer itself.

Check Local Codes—Due to antiquated sewage systems in some communities, the use of garbage disposers is prohibited;

337

however, in other far-sighted communities they are required. Check local codes.

Installation—You can use a disposer with a septic tank if the septic tank is properly designed and of the right size for your family. It is properly sized if it meets the current FHA Minimum Property Standards for septic tanks. These provide for disposers, dishwashers, and automatic washers. Check with your local office.

How to Use and Care for a Garbage Disposer

The disposer is essentially self-cleaning. The motor is permanently lubricated and the shredder doesn't need sharpening. If unpleasant odors do develop, grind lemon, orange peels, or an ice cube. Flush the disposer occasionally by filling the sink with about 3″ of cold water, then drain. Allow disposer and cold water to run after grinding or after draining the sink of wash water. Some materials may be corrosive; flushing will pass them into the drain without injuring the disposer.

Caution: Avoid putting lye or other chemical cleaners into the disposer. Producers of some cleaners may warn you that their product is injurious to metals. Read the labels carefully. Warranties may be void when chemical damage is detected.

For the most satisfactory performance, grind all waste immediately; always use cold water and a fast water flow, making certain that the water is running before grinding the waste. Grind any fibrous matter slowly with other food wastes. Never put your hand in the disposer at any time—if necessary to probe, use a wooden spoon. Leave deflector in place during grinding to keep foreign objects from dropping into the disposer.

INCINERATORS

These appliances provide an easy, economical way of burning dry and wet garbage, paper, rags, milk cartons, sweepings and all kinds of assorted trash in the home, with the exception of tin cans, glass jars, and aluminum foil. Even if you own an in-sink garbage disposer, an incinerator will work hand-in-hand with it. Gas models require a ½-inch gas pipe connection. Venting and ducting are required to remove heat, smoke, and odor. Check special installation requirements or prohibitions with any local codes before installing one. There are indoor and outdoor models. While they are small cabinet-height appliances, kitchen installation is not recommended.

Convenience—Look for pollution-controlled devices which can assist in maintaining a clean environment. If you are shopping for an incinerator, check for special provisions of *smokeless* burning, durable liners for refuse or combustion chamber, ash drawers, pilot relight controls for gas models, insulation, grates, and safety seals.

For *proper use and care* make certain indoor units are vented properly. Avoid overloading the unit. Set the control according to the manufacturer's directions. Empty the ash drawer at least weekly, or as needed.

Trash Compactors

The newest major home appliance representing a significant step toward the solution of municipal waste disposal is the trash compactor. This appliance, which may be free-standing or installed under the counter, crushes metal cans, glass and plastic bottles, cartons, and most food waste or garbage. It proposes to eliminate the need for most kitchen trash, garbage, and waste containers, though it doesn't necessarily replace the garbage disposer. It will, however, handle a normal amount of wet garbage, which may be an important fact to those who live in areas where ordinances prohibit installation of disposers. The only items that should not be put in a trash compactor are those that are highly inflammable, combustible, or toxic, and smelly things such as fish and poultry trimmings.

About half the width of a dishwasher, a compactor is powered by a ⅓-horsepower electric motor requiring a 115-volt circuit. Waste is compressed into a water-resistant, polyethylene-lined Kraft bag which may be sealed and easily lifted out when ready for disposal once a week, when it is set out for pickup collection. It contains odor controls in the form of deodorizer sprays. A filled bag, ready for disposal, would weigh about 20 to 25 pounds.

To clean, remove the ram cover and wiper periodically and wash in warm sudsy water. To minimize the need for cleaning, wrap soft food waste in newspaper or cover it with several thicknesses of paper toweling before it is compacted.

How to Keep Your Trash Compactor Running Smoothly

If it does not operate, check to see if the drawer is firmly shut. Perhaps some trash has lodged behind or under the bin, the lock is not in "on" position, the "start" button is not pushed, latches not secure, or if in the case of some models, the unit is not at least ⅓ full.

PORTABLE OR SMALL APPLIANCES

The space-saving, multifunction concept has come into its own with small appliances as our needs increase and space grows more precious. Multi-appliance centers allow the use of a number of appliances to be operated from a single power unit. And increasingly, appliances have several attachments for performing additional functions. For this reason, it is well to consider the *functions* which you personally want your small appliance to do for you.

The variety and number of small appliances is growing so fast that we are barely able to keep up with them. There are well over 200 now on the market—and who knows how many more to come! Today's typical household owns on an average of 16 electric housewares.

Later in this section you will find a list of the most basic ones we need to run our kitchen efficiently—on up to a more sophisticated list for the gourmet-minded.

Here we will cover only the use and care of that basic list, with the addition of a blender, so popular these days for spreads and dips.

Food Preparation Appliances

Blenders—Blenders are versatile appliances. They cut, mince, puree, grate, chop, crumb, liquefy, and blend, often better than any other method.

340

In using a blender, make sure the container is firmly in place, and the lid is on securely before starting motor. Do not overload container. Always pour liquid (enough to cover the blades) or semi-liquids into the container first, when blending liquids and solids. Cut firm foods into small pieces. To grate or chop, add small pieces a few at a time to blender in which water has been added to the top of the blades. Process until the preferred texture is reached. Use a rubber spatula when needed to push food from sides of container, to mix ingredients, or to remove food. Avoid overblending. Remove container from motor base when motor has come to a complete stop. Cool cooked foods and liquids slightly before placing in blender. When motor is sluggish on a lower speed, switch to a higher one to complete processing. Clean the container by filling half full with warm water, add a few drops of a light-duty liquid detergent, cover, and blend briefly on low speed. Rinse and dry thoroughly. Or wash in dishwasher if directions permit. Clean motor base with a damp cloth, and dry.

Coffeemakers—Automatic coffeemakers assure easy and automatic coffeemaking. Thermostatic temperature controls "brew" coffee rather than boil it; hold coffee at serving temperature.

Always use a clean coffeemaker, freshly drawn cold water, and fresh coffee. It is a good idea to rinse the basket with cold water before adding coffee. This will keep the fine grounds from falling into the brew. Place your finger over the pump stem while filling basket to avoid clogging. Be sure stem is set securely in well. Fill container to maximum cup level, never over. Begin with a cold pot. Always disconnect coffeemaker after last cup is poured. Remove basket of grounds immediately after coffee has brewed, to prevent bitter oils from dripping down into coffee. Use a narrow brush or pipe cleaner to clean spout, stem, coffee level gauge. To clean aluminum interiors, add 1 to 1½ tablespoons cream of tartar to full pot of water and complete brewing cycle. To clean stainless steel or glass, see Chapter Three.

Frypans/Skillets—Electric frypans are excellent for frying, pan broiling, sautéeing, stewing, baking, roasting, even broiling in some cases.

Season nonstick finishes before using—wash, rinse, dry, then wipe surface with unsalted shortening or oil. After use, disconnect probe control, wipe clean with damp cloth; never immerse probe in water. Do not immerse a hot frypan in water—it may cause warping. Some immersible models may be washed in the dishwasher. Check use and care manual for specific instructions. Never immerse broiler units in water. Wash inside and underside of pan after each use with hot sudsy water to prevent buildup of greasy soil. Follow cleaning instructions for specific metal finish.

Food Mixers—Electric mixers are favorite standbys. They may be part of a motor-driven appliance center or a separate standard or portable unit.

Regardless of the type, place beaters in food before starting the motor; turn mixer off before raising beaters from bowl. Use rubber spatula to guide food into beaters. Adjust bowl position on standard mixers before mixing. Guide beaters of portable mixer evenly and constantly through batters. Disconnect mixer before cleaning. Beaters and bowls are dishwasher washable. Turn motor off before inserting or ejecting beaters.

Toasters—There are two basic types of toasters—the vertical pop-up for standard toasting and the horizontal oven-type for flat toasting or other uses.

To use one properly, set the control at "medium" to test personal preference, then adjust for brownness. Darker toast settings are suggested for whole wheat breads, frozen waffles, and other rich breads. Never use a fork, knife, or other metal tool to remove bread from toaster—it's an invitation to a shock and toaster damage. Clean crumb tray with a damp cloth, dry thoroughly before next use. To keep like-new exterior, wipe with damp sudsy cloth, rinse, and rub dry with soft dry cloth.

YOUR KITCHEN INVENTORY

After you have selected the appliances that will perform the major portion of your work in the kitchen, then consider the other tools and utensils you will need to complete your inventory of equipment.

Here is a list of basic kitchen tools, utensils, and small appliances to help guide you in selecting the items that make a kitchen work efficiently. This list includes both electric and nonelectric equipment. You will find duplications. Choose those items that best suit your needs.

To find out where to store all these items, see Work Center section earlier in this chapter.

TOOLS AND UTENSILS

A. *The basics:*

Saucepans with
  covers:
    1 or 1½ qt.
    2 or 2½ qt.
    3 or 4 qt.
Roast rack
French fry basket
Coffeepot
Griddle
Kitchen shears
Can opener
Vegetable peeler
Corer
Minute timer
Flour sifter
Rolling pin
Strainer
Saucepot: 5 qt.
Double boiler
Skillets:
  1 small
  1 large
  (with covers)
Teakettle
Dutch oven
Roasting pan

Casserole dishes:
  1 medium
  1 large
Custard cups:
  4 to 6
Pie plate:
  one 9-inch
Cake pans:
  two 8-inch or
  9-inch, 1 square
Cookie sheets: 2
Muffin pan
Loaf pan or dish
Bottle opener
Colander
Cutting board
Juice extractor
Mary-Ann measur-
  ing cups—metal
Liquid measuring
  cups—glass
Measuring spoons
French knife
Paring knife
Serrated slicing
  knife

Utility knife
Carving knife and
  fork
Thermometers:
  roast meat
  deep-fat fry
Potato masher
Rotary beater
Pastry blender
Metal spatula
Tongs
Ladle
Pancake turner
Grater
Long-handled
  slotted spoon
Long-handled
  basting spoon
Long-handled
  2-tine fork
Nest of mixing
  bowls
Pastry brush
Rubber scrapers
Wire cooling racks
Wooden spoons

B. *Add some of these for more completely equipped kitchens:*

Chicken fryer
Cook-and-serve
  utensils
Tube pan
Jelly-roll pan
Extra:
  saucepans
  skillets
  cake pans

muffin pans
cookie sheets
mixing bowls
casserole dishes
Egg poacher
Teapot
Roaster (covered)
Springform pan
Kitchen scale

Wire whisk
Grapefruit knife
Baster
Assorted cutters
  (for cookies,
  doughnuts,
  biscuits, etc.)
Pressure cooker

C. *Add some of these if you are a fancy cook:*

Tart pans
Molds and rame-
    kins
Omelet pan
Steamer kettle
Gem pan
Pizza pans
Tiered cake pan
    set

Corn stick pan
Other specialized
    utensils, such as
    casserole with
    warmer, bever-
    age server, fon-
    due cooker, etc.
Popover pan

Ice cream scoop
Mortar and pestle
Butter ball paddles
Garlic press
Melon ball cutter
Boning knife
Canisters for
    storing fancy
    ingredients

PORTABLE ELECTRIC APPLIANCES

A. *The basics:*

Skillet
Coffeemaker

Toaster

Hand mixer

B. *Add some of these for a more completely equipped kitchen:*

Blender
Can opener
Broiler/rotisserie
Dutch oven
Egg cooker
Griddle

Hot tray
Juice extractor
Meat grinder
Saucepan or sauce-
    pot

Toaster-oven
Standard mixer
Waffle iron/sand-
    wich grill

C. *Add some of these if you are fancy-minded:*

Casserole
Popcorn popper
Teakettle
Large coffeemaker
Deep-fat fryer
Roaster-oven
Coffee grinder

Kabob grill
Buffet cooker
Chafing dish
Plate warmer
Fondue cooker
Yogurt maker

Electric wok
Bun warmer
Pizza warming
    platter
Ice crusher
Ice cream freezer

POTS AND PANS

Underlying the festive appearance of today's colorful cookware, you'll find the same basic materials we've been using right
along—*aluminum, stainless steel, iron, glass,* and *glass ceramic.* A

new application of these materials through improved styling, finishes, and shapes has improved their performance by capitalizing on the best features of each material.

A good cooking utensil should spread heat evenly, create no hot spots, be strong, durable, and easy to clean.

- Look for flat bottoms, which will make the best contact with the source of heat.
- Lids should be close-fitting but not necessarily tight.
- Handles should be comfortable and easy to grip; long enough so that there's no danger of your hands touching the hot metal; made of a heat-resistant material so that they stay cool during cooking. If handles are detachable, make sure they grip the pan firmly when in use.
- Look for smooth, seamless surfaces, rounded corners, no crevices to harbor food or bacteria.
- Pan should be evenly balanced. To check balance, remove the lid and gently tap the handle. If the pan is balanced it will right itself promptly. Proper balance means more efficient cooking, easier carrying and pouring.
- Knobs on lids should be easy to grasp, of a heat-resistant material so they stay cool during cooking.

The Basic Materials

Aluminum—Spreads the heat quickly and evenly throughout the pan to completely surround the food that is being cooked.

Gauge, or thickness, is a good indication of quality and durability. The thicker the gauge, the costlier and more durable the pan. Consider, also, the use of the pan. The gauge, or thickness, of a frypan should be greater than the gauge of a cookie sheet, for example (8-gauge is thick, 20-gauge is thin).

Aluminum utensils are manufactured in a variety of ways. They may be cast (always a heavy gauge), stamped, or hydroformed (a process using water pressure to mold the metal). Although these methods affect the looks through shape and styling, they generally do not affect the cooking qualities.

Today there are numerous easy-clean finishes on aluminum utensils. You may find stainless steel bonded to the inside, or

345

nonstick Teflon, or newer, tougher versions of Teflon which are nonscratch as well as nonstick. Stains on Teflon from improper cleaning may impair the nonstick quality. (To clean Teflon, see Chapter Three.) Stains from high heat cannot be removed but generally do not impair the nonstick quality.

Colored porcelain enamel is a popular exterior finish for aluminum. Other exterior finishes include highly polished aluminum, anodized aluminum in colors (pretty but not dishwasher-proof), chrome plating. For care of aluminum, see Chapter Three.

Stainless Steel—Stainless steel is noted for its extreme hardness, sparkling appearance, and resistance to scratching.

Because stainless steel alone is a relatively poor conductor of heat, it is usually combined in some way with other metals to provide even heat distribution. You may find two layers of stainless steel sandwiching a core of copper, carbon steel, or aluminum through the whole pan; two layers sandwiching a core of iron with an aluminum-clad bottom; or stainless steel with an aluminum- or copper-clad bottom.

There are excellent stainless steel cleaners to help remove heat spots or streaking that may occur. For care of stainless steel, see Chapter Three.

Cast Iron—Cast iron heats evenly and retains the heat for a long period of time, making it excellent for long, slow cooking processes. Traditional cast-iron utensils are black, have no special finish, and are limited in variety to skillets, special baking pans, Dutch ovens, and griddles. (For information on how to season, see Chapter Three.)

Another variety of cast iron utensil has recently arrived in the stores. They are highly styled pots with pretty porcelain-enamel exteriors and Teflon or enameled interiors. Many designs have attractive wood handles. Because of the interior finish, they need no seasoning and are comparatively easy to clean. Because of their styling they are attractive for table service. For care of cast iron utensils, see Chapter Three.

Heat-resistant Glass—Glass utensils absorb and hold the heat well, but may develop hot spots. Some come with a wire grid to be placed between the heat and the utensil when cooking on an electric range. They clean easily but harsh abrasives should never be used as they may scratch the glass.

Glass Ceramic—Glass ceramic's heat distribution and cleaning qualities are similar to those of glass, but there the similarity ends. Glass ceramic is extremely tough and durable. It is resistant to temperature changes so it can go from freezer to oven or cook top with no danger of cracking, breaking, or warping.

Many glass ceramic utensils have detachable handles so they can be used as saucepan, skillet, or casserole. Without the handles, they make attractive serving dishes; some have cradles for buffet service.

Porcelain-clad Steel—Porcelain enamel is a glasslike substance fused to metal. Its cleaning properties are similar to those of glass. It absorbs and holds the heat well, but may develop hot spots with high heat.

Newer porcelain finishes are extremely durable and resistant to cracking and chipping. Some also have Teflon interiors. For care of porcelain-clad finishes, see Chapter Three.

Copper—Copper's beauty has always made it a popular cookware metal, even though it is a fast heat conductor and can create hot spots with high heat. Many gourmet cooks love the elegance of cooking in copper and are willing to watch the rate of heat absorption with the care that is required. Copper utensils are usually lined with tin; occasionally with stainless steel. Some have a core of other metals to aid in even heat distribution. There are excellent copper cleaners to help keep these utensils looking their best. For care of copper, see Chapter Three.

Teflon-lined Utensils—Many utensils are Teflon-lined, though exterior metals vary. For care of Teflon, see Chapter Three.

KITCHEN SHEARS

In far too many cases the household scissor wardrobe usually consists of a favorite pair which serves multiple duty for everything you can think of—paper, hair, wire, cord, etcetera.

In an ideal situation every well-equipped household should have one pair of each of those scissors that meets a *specific* need. High on our list of musts is a pair of kitchen shears. They are especially useful for snipping herbs, cutting cords from rolled roasts and trussed poultry. As a matter of fact, there are dozens of uses for kitchen shears that simply cannot be done well by any other method.

To care for them, keep them clean and dry and occasionally

lubricate screw with sewing-machine oil; wipe off the excess. Don't strain by using them to cut beyond their capacity. Don't cut objects for which scissors were never intended, such as wire, tin, or other thin metal.

KNIVES AND CUTLERY

It could be safe to say that a good cook's ability to work skillfully depends upon using the right knife. Here are the five special knives that we feel no good cook should be without.

Within each group there are several styles, and the one you select will depend upon your personal preference, which will determine the weight, length of blade, and size and fit of handle.

Here are the basic knives in the different styles, as well as a selection of specialty knives for other uses.

Paring Knives—These are the smaller knives of an assortment and also the most varied in size and shape. The blades are usually 2½ to 3" long, curved in or out, with pointed or rounded tips. Individual preference determines your choice. Since you use paring knives for so many small cutting jobs around the kitchen—paring onions and carrots, peeling potatoes, to name just a few—it is probably wise to have several on hand.

Utility Knives—These are the in-between knives that run a close race with the paring knife as a favorite "do-all." Blades are all shapes and forms with serrated, wavy, or straight edges. The usefulness of both the utility and the paring knives lies in their smaller size. The shape of the blade does not determine their use and is important only in how it works for you.

French Knives—Often called chef's or French cook's knife. These have a basic blade form that never varies, though the size and length of the knife and blade may. In use, the tip rests on the cutting board surface held by the palm of the left hand, while the rest of the blade is raised and lowered with the right hand to chop.

Carving Knives—These have long, curved blades to promote wide carving of generous slices of meat. Some are serrated. It is usually accompanied with a carving fork to anchor the meat.

Slicing Knives—These have serrated or wavy edges. A complete set of cutlery needs at least one serrated or wavy-edge knife for those certain foods that tear easily (such as bread and foam cakes).

Specialty Knives

In addition to the basic knives the following are exceedingly useful:

Butcher Knives—Heavy-duty knives that trim raw meats, cut lobster, etcetera. They are varied in size.

Grapefruit Knife—This knife has a thin, narrow blade that is curved and serrated. Ideal for coring and sectioning.

Steak and Poultry Slicer—A knife with a long, narrow blade that is curved. Excellent for delicate slicing jobs such as chicken, steak, and small roasts, especially smaller ones that have bones.

Household Cleaver—A specialty knife that's especially useful if you're a "from scratch" cook. Separates ribs and joints—tenderizes, too.

Swedish Cook's Knife—A favorite among many housewives who like the angled handle for better leverage when slicing firm breads, cheeses, etcetera.

Spatula—This has a long, narrow, blunt-edge blade with a round tip. A spatula's not meant for cutting, but for spreading frostings, folding omelets, and manipulating food in general.

Tomato Knife—This very narrow blade with serrated edge neatly slices fragile foods such as tomatoes.

These are just some of the many specialty knives you'll find at the cutlery counter.

Buying Tips for Cutlery

A good knife will last you a lifetime if you choose one of top quality and care for it carefully. A cheap-quality knife will always be dull and extremely irritating to use.

The blade should always contain a fairly high content of *carbon,* which helps to assure a constantly sharp edge. Low carbon content will also cause the blade to darken and stain. The addition of vanadium and chromium further improves a blade's quality—*vanadium* to strengthen the steel and help it to keep a sharp edge, *chromium* to help produce a stainless steel that resists rust.

The handle is attached to an extension of the blade called a tang. A full tang (which extends all the way to the end of the handle) and a half tang (which extends to the middle of the handle) are the most permanent attachments when fixed with two or more rivets. Any other method of attachment will, with use, loosen and become an annoyance and a hazard. The handles of good-quality cutlery are designed to fit your hand. Try the various brands until you find the one that is most comfortable for you. The material of the handle should be moisture- and stain-resistant. Most good knives have handles of hard wood or very high quality plastic.

Knife blades may have flat or hollow-ground edges. The least expensive is a flat edge which forms a "V" (or may be slightly rolled or "canalled" to resist damage by hard surfaces). This edge wears quickly and requires frequent sharpening. The hollow-ground edge has a curve on each side, gradually slimming the thickness of the knife to a sharp cutting edge. A good serrated or wavy-edge knife will also have a slight hollow grind. Different manufacturers have developed refinements of the hollow grind to improve the quality of their knives. Some are designed to help the blade edge retain its sharpness. These latter include a thin layer of tungsten carbide along the edge, or a special fine-toothed serration.

How to Care for Your Knives

- Store your knives properly in the rack or blade cover provided for them so the blades do not become nicked or scratched. Wall racks or boards which are magnetized provide excellent "protective" storage.
- Always use a wooden cutting board. Cut around, not into, a bone. Don't use a knife to loosen a lid or remove a bottle cap.
- Keep the blades away from high heat or hot flame.
- Keep the blades sharp. A dull knife is often more of a hazard than a sharp one used properly.

- Don't put your knives in the dishwasher unless the manufacturer's instructions specifically tell you that you may. Don't soak them either. This will damage the finish. Wash them in warm sudsy water, rinse well, and dry immediately.

OTHER KITCHEN IMPLEMENTS

All kitchen implements, the ones we have discussed on the preceding pages and these mainstays, should be able to take even the most rigorous use without too much damage.

Spatula, spoons, ladles, forks which you need for mixing, stirring, and cooking should be selected for their durability, safety, and ease in handling. Those made of stainless steel are usually the best, as porcelain-coated ones may chip and rust and chromium-plated ones will eventually wear and rust. New ones made of durable, heat-resistant plastic may also be a good choice, especially if used with Teflon-lined utensils. Handles should be well balanced and heat-resistant. Look at the way handles are joined. The shank should be driven well into or all the way through the length of the entire handle.

Measuring cups and spoons should adhere to the accuracy standards set by the American National Standards Institute. They are designed using specific standards for American recipes.

Mixing bowls may be made of tempered glass, ceramic, steel, aluminum, or heat-resistant plastic. The nested type of graduated sizes are among the best—as they offer a variety of sizes and take up the least amount of space.

Rotary beaters of the heavy-duty type, with sturdy blades and well-meshed gears that turn noiselessly and easily, are the best.

To care for kitchen tools and implements always rinse them as quickly as possible after use so food will not stick to them. As with knives, never soak these tools in water for long periods.

HOW TO CLEAN THE KITCHEN

The organized sequence of taking care of a kitchen can make quick work out of an otherwise disagreeable job.

351

Daily

Supplies:
- Cellulose sponge.
- Dishwashing mop or dish cloth.
- Dishpan and drainer.
- Scouring pads.
- Cleanser.
- Liquid detergent for dishes.
- Dishwasher detergent for dishwasher.
- Household cleaner.
- Paper towels.
- Broom and dustpan.

- Put food away.
- Wash the dishes after each meal or rinse and stack them in the dishwasher until the dishwasher is full enough for one load.
- Clean counters and wipe off soil from any appliances or items stored on the counter with a damp sponge wrung out in warm sudsy water, using a light-duty detergent. Rinse and wipe dry.
- Wipe off range and refrigerator with damp sponge, as above.
- Clean the sink with a damp sponge and cleanser after the last meal.
- Sweep and wipe up floor, if necessary.
- Carpet sweep or vacuum floor with kitchen carpeting, if necessary.
- Empty trash and garbage. Wipe out containers with detergent and warm water. Rinse, dry, and reline.
- Wipe off windowsills if dusty or sooty.
- Air out kitchen if necessary by opening the window or turning on the ventilating fan.

Weekly

In addition to supplies for daily cleaning:

- Mop and pail.
- Clean all parts of range that are heavily soiled—oven, drip pans, encrusted broiler pans. Soak heavily soiled

parts in a hot sudsy water. For special care, see special section on ranges.

- Vacuum curtains or brush off dust.
- Dust windowsills, shades, or blinds.
- Clean out refrigerator and throw away forgotten left-overs. Wipe out heavily soiled areas with damp sponge wrung out of warm sudsy water to which a little baking soda has been added. Rinse and wipe dry.
- Dust shelves and objects on them.
- Wipe off with a damp sponge wrung out of hot sudsy water the fronts, tops, and sides of all appliances, range, refrigerator, dishwasher, laundry equipment; also cabinets inside where crumbs have accumulated and outside; wipe off any other exposed surfaces such as plastic counters, metals, porcelain, wood counters.
- Clean crumb trays of toasters, toaster-ovens.
- Use drain cleaner, if necessary.
- Clean sink with damp sponge and cleanser.
- Clean garbage can and spray out with disinfectant.
- Hang up clean towels and replenish paper towels, if necessary.
- Sweep floor.
- Damp mop floor, if necessary.

Monthly

Try and space out these jobs so they don't pile up.

- Give range a thorough cleaning.
- Defrost refrigerator, if yours is not a frostless model. (Defrost when the frost is ¼″ thick.) Give it a thorough cleaning.
- Clean drawers and cabinets inside—reorganize, reline, and replenish supplies. Do one or two a week in rotation. Not necessary to do them all at once.
- Wash filters in ventilating fan and hood. This is important as accumulated grease can catch fire.
- Polish surfaces, cabinets, and appliances with an appliance wax.
- Polish pots and pans, silver, copper, brass, and pewter as needed.
- Wash windows inside.

Occasionally

- Clean lighting fixtures.
- Clean behind range and refrigerator.
- Remove and launder curtains, wash windows inside and outside.
- Clean windowsills, ceiling, woodwork.
- Clean all metal fixtures.
- Clean refrigerator condensers. See page 322.

KEEP YOUR KITCHEN CLEAN AS YOU GO—SOME TIPS

If you keep your kitchen clean as you work it will cut down on after-meal cleanup. If you are not the type, or it simply gets ahead of you, then you will have to set your own standards of working. At least you will know all the tricks, use them or not!

- Dirt and grime collect on the top of kitchen cabinets which are not flush with the ceiling. To simplify the cleaning job, cover the top with wax paper and use Scotch tape to hold it securely. Replace with new paper when necessary. Or, line wall cabinet tops with shelf liner and place seldom-used bowls, trays, and other kitchenware on top in a decorative arrangement. Or if you're more ambitious, enclose the space over cabinets for "dead" storage of items you seldom use.
- Save the plastic or paper trays that come with meat and vegetables—they make handy disposable trays for vegetable peelings, etcetera. Or spread out a newspaper to catch the waste, then fold up and throw away. Paper plates (the kind you buy in bulk on a bargain counter) are good, too.
- Wipe off salt and pepper shakers, spice containers, and shortening cans after each use.
- Keep paper towels and damp sponges handy for wiping up soil and spills.
- Work on rubber-backed throw rugs around range, refrigerator, and sink—helps to keep floor clean and makes it easy underfoot at the same time.
- Line the drawers with washable rubber or plastic lining,

or use several layers of lining paper. When the top one is soiled, throw away.

- Work with grease-shields around frying pans, or protect nearby surfaces with aluminum foil.

WASHING THE DISHES

Dishwashing, like other household tasks, needs to be organized.

If you would spend that very little bit of extra time while you are preparing the meal, to clean and wash up as you go, you'll be glad you did. This procedure may work for some—but *never* for others. Some are simply doomed to using every utensil in the kitchen and spreading them around on the counters everywhere until the meal is on the table. We'll wager to say, however, that those devoted to creating "kitchen-clutter-as-they-go" are in the minority, and with a little thought given to some semblance of preorganization, most people can develop the "clean-up-as-you-cook" and "scrape-rinse-and-stack-the-dishes-after-the-meal" routine very easily! See time management, Chapter One, for a tip or two!

If you are *really pressed for time* while cooking, at least fill the dishpan or sink with sudsy water and soak the soakables until you can wash them up later.

If you use a dishwasher, it is infinitely more useful to you to have it empty as you begin meal preparation. Then rinsing-and-loading-as-you-cook is a breeze. By the time you have the meal on the table, the kitchen is really quite presentable.

Washing Dishes by Hand

If you do not have a dishwasher, a fairly well-organized sink area and the right equipment can still let you get your dishes "squeaky clean."

You will need:

A container for scraps
A rubber pad or rack for sink to prevent breakage
A dishpan and drainer
A dishcloth or sponge
A dishpuff for glassware

Soap-filled steel wool pads
Plastic or rubber scraper
Hot water
Clean, soft lintless dish towels
Scouring powder
Light-duty liquid detergent

355

Tip: In addition to the dishwashing supplies under the sink, we like to keep a bar of soap in a container on the sink for quickie cleaning. Place it in a container containing a rack or teeth to elevate the soap and keep it dry. You might like to keep it on a sponge, which will absorb the drippings. Use the sponge then to swab off the counter or clean the sink.

- It is usually best to work from left to right. If you are left-handed, work in the opposite direction. Or if you prefer, a work pattern directed toward the dish-storage area is usually helpful. For example, if the dishes are stored to the right of the sink, have the work flow from left to right—stack dirty dishes on the left, drain and dry dishes on the right. If dishes are stored to the left, reverse the work flow.
- Scrape, rinse (preferably under hot running water), and stack dishes, placing first the larger pieces on the bottom and graduating them according to size. Use cold water for "eggy" and milk-soiled dishes. Look up *care of specific items* in the Index.
- Use a special light-duty dishwashing detergent.
- Wash glasses first, flatware next, eating dishes (cups and plates), then serving dishes. Use a dishcloth or cellulose sponge for dishes, and a glassware puff for cups and glasses. Keep a plastic scouring cloth or pad handy for scraping off encrusted food without scratching your china. Remove coffee stains from china cups with a little baking soda.
- Wash cooking utensils last—unless you washed them immediately after use. Look up care of specific utensils in the Index. Fill glass or ceramic casseroles with hot sudsy water to soak off burned-on food and make them easier to clean. Heat a little water in skillets and saucepans to release burned-on food. Keep special cleaners on hand for specific jobs.
- Set in drainer on drainboard and rinse with very hot water (150° F.) poured from a kettle, or sprayed from the tap. You may also rinse them under running water or dip them in a separate dishpan of hot water, then set in a strainer.
- It is best to let dishes air dry, then put them away. This

will help to avoid towel lint and spots. Glassware and flatware will sparkle more with towel drying, since it removes the last traces of water droplets which can spot when allowed to evaporate, especially in hard-water areas.

FOOD STORAGE

Fresh perishable foods should be used soon after they are harvested or purchased and stored at the right temperature and humidity.

Understanding Spoilage—When foods are kept too long or stored improperly, they spoil. Some kinds of spoilage make foods harmful to health; some do not, and it is not always possible to distinguish between the two kinds.

How Can You Tell If Food Is Safe?

Shall I eat this or throw it out? Is it safe? How can I be sure? These are all familiar questions we ask ourselves almost every time we look in the refrigerator or kitchen cupboard. This is one of the major problems in kitchen housekeeping.

Caution: Any time you are in real doubt, the safest course of action is to throw the item out.

A brief explanation, however, of what happens to food under certain conditions just might help to clarify the whole picture of food storage and its possible hazards.

Your first consideration in judging safety of food involves three things:

1. Whether or not the food is one that encourages the growth of illness-causing organisms.
2. Whether or not there are illness-causing organisms present in the food.
3. How long you have had the food and the temperature at which it has been stored.

357

Keep in mind that there is a difference between food *safety* and *quality*. Food may not taste good, and yet it might be safe.

For example, potato chips may taste rancid, indicating they are stale, but still safe. Safety concerns the presence of certain groups of bacteria such as *Salmonella, Staphylococcus, Clostridium botulinus,* etcetera, which can cause illness by producing poisonous toxins either within the food itself or within the intestinal tract after the food has been eaten. Then there are some microorganisms such as yeast and mold which grow in food but are not particularly dangerous.

Keep these essential facts in mind and chances are you will do a very good job of keeping the food that you handle safe and of high quality:

- *Bacteria* need food and moisture to survive. They thrive on some foods better than others.
- Protein encourages bacterial growth, *acids* slow it down. Foods such as meat, fish, poultry, eggs, and milk are moist and high in protein. Dishes made from these products with little or no acid are potentially dangerous; for example, puddings and meat pies.
- Foods low in protein, high in acid, or dry are more likely to be bacteriologically safe.
- *Dried* foods can be safely stored for fairly long periods at room temperature. If you add moisture, however, some bacteria may grow if the temperature is favorable.
- Foods high in acid, such as tomatoes and fruit juice, do not encourage growth of bacteria. Yeasts may develop and produce fermentation, but this affects flavor and quality, not safety.
- Harmful organisms must be in food in the first place in order for them to grow and cause illness. These harmful organisms enter the food through humans, insects, rodents, and soil. Contamination can be cut down by handling foodstuffs as little as possible and by maintaining careful cleanliness standards—washing your hands, keeping cutting boards and implements clean, etcetera. Scrub these items well, especially after use with raw meat and poultry.
- Bacteria grow quickly at warm temperatures and slowly, or not at all, at cold temperatures.

Low temperatures are required in the storage of many perishable foods. Low temperature retards quality losses in these foods and delays spoilage by slowing the action of the natural enzymes in foods and the growth of organisms always present in air, water, and soil.

How Cold Is Room Temperature?

The term "room temperature" usually means from 70° to 75° F. Use your judgment in determining how long any perishable food will keep at that temperature, remembering that most foods last longer at *lower* rather than higher room temperatures. Follow specific directions. One exception: When the term "room temperature" is applied to wine, a temperature of 60° to 68° F. is usually implied.

WHAT HAPPENS TO BACTERIA AT SPECIFIC TEMPERATURES*

TEMPERATURE	SAFETY ZONES
32° F. (safety zone)	At 32° F. or below most organisms survive but are not actively growing. Refrigerator frozen food compartments range from 0° to 20° F.; freezers, 0° F. and below. Foods stored too long at subfreezing temperatures may lose eating quality, but are safe, unless improperly handled before storage. Bacteria that survive freezing may grow again when food thaws.
32° to 45° F. (safe for short-term storage)	Some organisms survive but grow slowly if at all. Refrigerator storage prevents bacterial growth, at least for several days. Good management suggests using refrigerated foods promptly.

* Adapted from Home Economics Extension Leaflet No. 47. "When Is Food Safe?" Irene Downey and Marjorie Washbon, July 1969. Adapted with permission of the New York State College of Human Ecology, a statutory college of the State University, Cornell University, Ithaca, New York.

TEMPERATURE	SAFETY ZONES
45° to 140° F. (danger zone; safe only for essential preparation time)	Bacteria grow rapidly at temperatures just above refrigeration to warm serving temperatures. Growth is very rapid between 60° and 120° F. *Never* let the temperature of the food remain in this range for more than two hours, or more than four hours between 45° and 140° F. Some examples may be: 1. Keeping food warm for latecomers. 2. Holding foods several hours at room temperature, as done in very slow heating of potentially hazardous food—for example, roasting a stuffed turkey over 18 pounds. Stuffing may remain in the danger zone for almost entire roasting period and may never reach the safety zone of 165° F. (That's why overnight roasting at very low temperatures is not recommended.)
140° to 165° F. (very warm zone)	Many organisms survive, but do not actively grow. Moderately safe; very warm serving temperature; recommended for holding food, such as on steam tables, chafing dishes, etcetera.
165° to 212° F. (safety zone)	Most organisms are destroyed in a few minutes provided all food reaches 165° F. or above. One exception is *Staphylococcus*. No amount of heating will make food safe if this common organism has previously multiplied enough to produce large amounts of toxin.

What Can You Do to Prevent Spoilage?

- Cool foods quickly. If the quantity is large, cool before refrigerating by setting containers in cold water, or divide into smaller portions. If the quantity is small (for example, 4–6 servings), pre-cooling is a matter of personal choice. It is wisest to refrigerate the hot food almost immediately to avoid forgetting to do so. The refrigerator temperature may increase temporarily but this is of little significance if the quantity of food is small. Refrigerating in shallow containers will speed the removal of heat from the food.

- Boil non-acid home-canned vegetables before tasting. Unless recommended pressure-canning procedures are followed properly, there is always a chance that heat-resistant forms of *Clostridium botulinus* may survive and form a toxin during storage. This toxin is destroyed by boiling 15 minutes in the presence of air.
- While molds have been generally considered harmless, some strains are now known to produce toxins. Until further evidence is available it is best to throw out foods with mold since they have been stored too long anyway and have lost their flavor.
- Keep hot foods *very* hot and cold foods *very* cold.
- Refrigerate all perishable foods as quickly as possible.
- Don't trust odor alone. Food may look, taste, and smell good but not be safe.

STORAGE OF PERISHABLE FOODS *

FOOD	DIRECTIONS

Breads and Cereals

Breads   Store in original wrapper in breadbox or refrigerator. Bread keeps its freshness longer at room temperature than in the refrigerator. In hot, humid weather, however, bread is better protected against mold in the refrigerator than in the breadbox.

Breads will retain their good quality for 2 to 3 months if frozen in their original wrappers and stored in the home freezer.

Breads, rolls, and doughnuts—store in tightly wrapped moisture-proof wrapper under 75° for up to 5 days.

* Excerpted from U.S.D.A. Home and Garden Bulletin # 78, "Storing Perishable Foods."

FOOD	DIRECTIONS
Cakes	*Pound, layer, sponge cakes*—store in tightly wrapped moisture-proof wrappings up to 1 week. *Cream fillings, custard pie*—store in refrigerator no more than 2 days. Susceptible to bacterial growth. *Cookies*—will stay crisp in dry-tight container up to a month.
Cereals, flours, spices, and sugar	Store at room temperature in tightly closed containers that keep out dust, moisture and insects. Ready-to-eat cereals begin to deteriorate anywhere from 1 to 3 months. Store flour in dry airtight container at room temperature under 65°—*white* flour will keep up to a year, *whole grain* flour and *cereals-to-cook* from 2 to 4 months. During summer, buy flours and cereals in small quantities. Inspect often for weevils. They are vulnerable to high temperatures.
Dry mixes	Cake, pancake, cookie, muffin, and roll mixes may be held at room temperatures. Keep dry and tightly covered up to 1 year.

Eggs

Raw eggs	Store promptly in refrigerator. Eggs retain quality well in the refrigerator; they lose their mild flavor quickly at room temperature. To insure best quality and flavor, use eggs within a week. If eggs are held too long, the thick white may thin, the yolk membrane may weaken and break when the shell is opened. Refrigerate with small ends down. Never wash eggs as that removes natural coatings. Cover leftover yolks with cold water and store in the refrigerator in a covered container. Extra egg whites should also be refrigerated in a covered container. Use leftover yolks and whites within a day or two.
Dried egg	Keep in refrigerator. After a package has been opened, store unused portion in an airtight container with a tight-fitting lid. Dried egg will keep its good flavor for about a year if it is stored properly.

Fats and Oils

Most fats and oils need protection from air, heat and light. Fats and oils in partially filled containers keep longer if they are transferred to smaller containers in which there is little or no air space.

Butter, fat drippings, and margarine	Store, tightly wrapped or covered, in the refrigerator. These products are best used within 2 weeks. Keep only as much butter or margarine in the butter compartment of the refrigerator as needed for immediate use. Don't let butter or margarine stand for long periods at room temperature; exposure to heat and light hastens rancidity.
Cooking and salad oils	Keep small quantities at room temperatures and use before flavor changes. For long storage, keep oils in the refrigerator. Some of these oils may cloud and solidify in the refrigerator. This is not harmful. If warmed to room temperature, they will become clear and liquid.
Hydrogenated shortenings and lard	Most of the firm vegetable shortenings and lard have been stabilized by hydrogenation or anti-oxidants. These shortenings can be held at room temperature without damage to flavor. Lard that is not stabilized should be refrigerated. Keep these products covered.
Mayonnaise and other salad dressings	Keep all homemade salad dressings in the refrigerator. Purchased mayonnaise and other ready-made salad dressings should be refrigerated after jars have been opened.

Fruits

Plan to use fresh fruits promptly before they lose their best flavor. Because most fruits are fragile, they need special handling to prevent bruising. The softened tissues of crushed fruits permit the entrance of spoilage organisms that quickly break down quality.

Sort fruits before storing. Discard any bruised or decayed fruit to keep it from contaminating sound, firm fruit.

Apples	Store mellow apples uncovered in the refrigerator. Unripe or hard apples are best held at cool room temperature (60° to 70° F.) until ready to eat from 2 to 3 weeks. Use ripe apples within a week. Unripe apples will keep in the refrigerator from 1 to 2 months.
Apricots, avocados, grapes, nectarines, pears, peaches, plums, and rhubarb	When these fruits are ripe, store uncovered in the refrigerator. Use within 3 to 5 days. When unripe, allow to ripen in the open air at room temperature. Do not place in the sun.
Bananas	Store bananas at room temperature until ripe. After ripening, they can be stored in the refrigerator.
Berries and cherries	Keep whole and uncovered in the refrigerator or until ready to use. Washing and stemming these fruits before refrigerating results in loss of food value and increased spoilage. Use within 1 or 2 days.
Citrus fruits and melons	These fruits are best stored at a cool room temperature (60° to 70° F.). But short-time holding in the refrigerator is not harmful to their quality. If citrus fruits are held too long at too low a temperature, the skin becomes pitted and the flesh discolors. Use these fruits within a week. Citrus fruits stored at room temperature around 40° to 50° F. will keep from 3 to 6 weeks.
Pineapples	If fully ripe, these may be refrigerated for a day or two. Wrap them tightly to prevent other foods from taking up the odor of the pineapple. If pineapples are

Pineapples (cont.)	not ripe, hold them at room temperature until ripe, then refrigerate.
Canned fruits, canned fruit juices	After canned fruits and canned fruit juices have been opened, cover and store in the refrigerator. They can be safely stored in their original containers. Or transfer them to refrigerator jars or pitchers. (*See* Canned Food Storage, *page 370.*)
Dried fruits	Keep in tightly closed containers. Store at room temperature, except in warm, humid weather; then refrigerate.
Frozen fruit juices	Cover reconstituted fruit juice concentrates and keep in the refrigerator. For best flavor, keep in glass or plastic containers.
Jellies, jams and preserves	After these fruit products have been opened, store them, covered, in the refrigerator, unless directions state "store in refrigerator immediately after purchase."

Meat, Poultry, Fish

Cold cuts	Store in the refrigerator. Use within 3 to 5 days.
Cured and smoked meats	Store ham, frankfurters, bacon, bologna, and smoked sausage in the refrigerator in their original packaging. Uncooked cured pork may be stored longer than fresh pork, but the fat will become rancid if held too long. Bacon should be eaten within a week for best quality, a half ham in 3 to 5 days, a whole ham within a week. Ham slices should be wrapped tightly. Use within a few days.
Fresh fish, poultry, meat roasts, chops and steaks	Store all fresh meat, poultry and fish in the coldest part of the refrigerator, where the temperature is usually between 35° to 38° F. Loosen wrappings

Fresh fish, poultry, meat roasts, chops and steaks (cont.)	on fresh meat, poultry, and fish. They benefit from some circulation of air in the refrigerator. For poultry, short holding, 1 or 2 days, is recommended. Use fish immediately, otherwise freeze it. Roasts, chops and steaks may be held 3 to 5 days.
Ground and mechanically tenderized meats	Store loosely wrapped in coldest part of the refrigerator. Use within 1 or 2 days. Ground meats, such as hamburger and fresh bulk sausage, are more likely to spoil than roasts, chops, or steaks because more of the meat surface has been exposed to contamination from air, from handlers, and from mechanical equipment.
Leftover cooked meats and meat dishes	Cool quickly (container may be placed in cold water), cover or wrap loosely, refrigerate promptly. Use within one or two days.
Leftover stuffing	Remove leftover stuffing from chicken or turkey, cool immediately, and store separately from the rest of the bird. Use within 1 or 2 days.
Leftover gravy and broth	These are highly perishable. Cover, store in the refrigerator promptly. Use within 1 or 2 days.
Variety meats such as liver, kidneys, brains, and poultry giblets	Store, loosely-wrapped, in the coldest part of refrigerator. Use within 1 or 2 days. Remove poultry giblets from the separate bag in which they are often packed, rewrap loosely, and refrigerate.

Milk, Cream, Cheese

Fresh milk and cream	Store in refrigerator at about 40° F. Milk and cream are best stored only 3 to 5 days. Keep covered so they won't absorb odors and flavors of other foods. Rinse bottle or carton under cold running water, dry and refrigerate as soon as

Fresh milk and cream (cont.)	possible after delivery or purchase. If milk is delivered to your house, make arrangements to keep it from standing in a warm place or being exposed to sunlight. Exposure to sun impairs both flavor and riboflavin content of milk.
Dry milk	Keep dry milk—either nonfat or whole—in a tightly closed container. Nonfat dry milk will keep in good condition for several months on the cupboard shelf at temperatures of 75° F. or lower. Close the container immediately after using. Dry milk takes up moisture and becomes lumpy if long exposed to air. Lumps make reconstitution difficult. Dry whole milk is marketed only on a small scale, chiefly for infant feeding. Because of its fat content, it does not keep as well as nonfat dry milk; after the container has been opened, dry whole milk should be stored, tightly covered, in the refrigerator. Refrigerate reconstituted dry milk like fresh fluid milk.
Evaporated milk and condensed milk	Store at room temperature until opened, then cover tightly and refrigerate like fresh fluid milk.
Cheese spreads and cheese foods	After containers of these foods have been opened, store, covered, in the refrigerator.
Hard cheeses such as Cheddar, Parmesan and Swiss	Keep in the refrigerator. Wrap tightly to keep out air. The original packagings may be used. Stored this way, hard cheeses will keep for several months unless mold develops.
Soft cheeses such as cottage, cream, Camembert	Store, tightly covered, in the coldest part of the refrigerator. Use cottage cheese within 3 to 5 days, others within 2 weeks.

Vegetables

The fresher vegetables are when eaten, the better.

With only a few exceptions, vegetables keep best in the refrigerator.

The exceptions—potatoes, sweet potatoes, dry onions, hardrind squashes, eggplant, and rutabagas—keep well in cool rather than cold storage. (If you don't have a cool place, then by all means buy in small quantities and store them in the refrigerator for *short* periods in a plastic bag, especially to keep onions and potatoes from sprouting.)

Sort vegetables before storing them. Discard any that are bruised, soft, or that show evidence of decay or worm injury.

The vegetable crisper in your refrigerator performs better if it is at least two-thirds full. If crisper is less full than this, vegetables will keep better if they are put in plastic bags before going into the crisper.

Asparagus	Discard tough parts of stalks. Store in the refrigerator in crisper or in plastic bag. Use within 1 or 2 days.
Broccoli and Brussels sprouts	Store in refrigerator in crisper or in plastic bag. Use within 1 or 2 days.
Cabbage and cauliflower	Store in the refrigerator in crisper or in plastic bags. Use cabbage within 1 or 2 weeks, cauliflower within 3 to 5 days.
Carrots, beets, and radishes	Remove root tips and tops. Store covered in refrigerator. Use within 1 or 2 weeks.
Green peas and limas	Leave in pods and store in refrigerator. Use within a day or two.
Herbs	Store fresh herbs in a tightly covered jar in the refrigerator.
Lettuce and other salad greens	Store in crisper in the refrigerator or in plastic bags to hold down loss of moisture. Use within 1 or 2 days.
Onions	Store dry onions at room temperature, or slightly cooler, in loosely woven or open-mesh

Onions (cont.)	containers. Stored this way, they keep several months. They sprout and decay at high temperature and in high humidity. Keep green onions cold and moist in the refrigerator. Store in plastic bags. Use within 1 or 2 days.
Peppers and cucumbers	Wash and dry. Store in crisper or in plastic bags in the refrigerator. Use within 3 to 5 days.
Potatoes	Store in a dark, dry place with good ventilation and a temperature of 45° to 50° F. Light causes greening, which lowers eating quality. High temperatures hasten sprouting and shriveling. If necessary to store at room temperature, use within a week.
Spinach, kale, collards, chard, and beet, turnip, and mustard greens	Wash thoroughly in cold water. Lift these leafy green vegetables out of the water as grit settles to the bottom of the pan. Drain. Store in refrigerator in crisper or in plastic bags. Use within 1 or 2 days.
Sweet corn	Store, unhusked and uncovered, in the refrigerator. Use within 1 or 2 days.
Sweet potatoes, hard-rind squashes, eggplant, and rutabagas	Store at cool room temperature, around 60° F. Temperatures below 50° may cause chilling injury. These could keep several months at 60° F. but as little as a week at room temperature.
Tomatoes	Store ripe tomatoes uncovered in the refrigerator. Keep unripe tomatoes at room temperature away from direct sunlight until they ripen.

Miscellaneous Foods

Honey and syrups	Store at room temperature until opened. After their containers are opened, honey and syrups are better protected from mold in the refrigerator. If crystals form, dissolve them by placing container of honey or syrup in hot water.

369

Nuts	Store in air-tight containers in the refrigerator. Because of their high fat content, nuts require refrigeration to delay development of rancidity. Unshelled nuts keep better than salted because salt speeds rancidity. (If you are not certain when you will use them, store them in the freezer.)
Peanut butter	After a jar of peanut butter has been opened, it should be kept in the refrigerator. Remove it from the refrigerator a short time before using to allow it to soften.

For frozen food storage, see section on Freezers in this chapter.

CANNED FOOD STORAGE

Commercially canned food is safe unless the can is bulged or leaking. Always return bulged, leaking unopened cans to the store where they were purchased.

Cans Are Safe Storage Containers
Once They Are Open

A can that holds food has been thoroughly washed and inspected, and being commercially sterile, is more sanitary than most home containers used to store food. According to the U.S. Department of Agriculture, food may be left in tin cans after opening by putting a cover on the can and storing in the refrigerator.

Acid food, however, such as fruit and vegetable juices like tomato, may acquire a "tinny" taste and they should be poured into another type of container, such as glass or plastic.

Store canned foods in a dry place at moderately cool but not freezing temperatures. Avoid storage near steam pipes, radiators, furnaces, and kitchen ranges. Also avoid dampness, which might cause the container to rust.

Canned foods will keep safe and wholesome as long as nothing happens to the container to break the seal. A good rule, however, is to have a regular turnover once a year to keep foods in top quality.

CHAPTER SIX

Entertaining

Everyone loves a good party—and the hostess can enjoy it every bit as much as her guests if she knows the keys to successful entertaining: 1. People make a party—invite people who enjoy each other. 2. Plan ahead. Have all the preparations done so that when your guests arrive you can relax and enjoy them.

As you read through the tips and guidelines in this chapter, remember, too, that with today's informality, it is usually best to keep things simple, and that with the possible exception of strictly formal or state occasions, there are really no longer any hard-and-fast rules for entertaining.

Planning:
- First, decide what kind of party it's to be—a big holiday open house, a small dinner party, a cookout, a cocktail party? It's usually best to give the kinds of parties that you enjoy most.
- When you decide what kind of party and how many to invite, think about space, whether it's an outdoor or indoor party, and if it's a dinner party, how many you can seat and serve at your table. Don't invite more than you can entertain comfortably.
- Your guest list, particularly for a small party, should be considered carefully to make sure your guests will feel relaxed and enjoy each other. Don't hesitate to ask different types of people, because that makes an interesting party (your middle-aged banker neighbor might really enjoy meeting your young artist friend). But don't invite

371

people who will be at such odds with each other that it will cause real conflict.

- It's a good idea to invite some people who know each other but also to introduce a few new faces to the group.

Inviting:
- Whether you send invitations or call is up to you, but invitations are usually best for larger or more formal parties. If it is a simple little dinner party, a telephone or personal invitation is all that's necessary. Give enough notice, but not too much; ten days to two weeks is about right for a dinner party, and three to four weeks for any big party in the holiday season. Of course, spur-of-the-moment parties are the most fun of all. Follow the general customs in your community and your own life-style.
- Be specific about type of party and time when you invite. If it's for cocktails, say what time it's over, too: "Cocktails, 6 to 8." If it's for dinner or cocktail buffet, let the guests know—people want to know if they are invited for a meal or not.
- You need not specify dress, because the kind of party will indicate what's appropriate—and these days almost anything goes. The only exception would be a formal affair in which case you should write the words "black tie" on the invitation.
- Written invitations may be on your informals or you may use a party invitation. Just remember to add RSVP and your address or phone number if you want to know how many to expect. You may indicate "RSVP—Regrets Only," if you like.

GIVING PARTIES—SOME QUICKIE TIPS

The Food

1. Plan your menu or food several days ahead. Write it out and make out your shopping list from it. Don't forget any extra things you might need, such as candles, flowers, coasters, special napkins, etcetera.

2. If it is a dinner, serve as the main dish something you've made before successfully. It's great to develop a few specialties that friends can single out as specifically yours.

3. Plan other courses around your main course. Keep all the dishes fairly simple—make sure they complement each other: if your entree is rich, serve a light dessert. If meat is your main course, seafood is a good appetizer.

4. Prepare everything you possibly can ahead. This is most important. Make things a day ahead or more, things that will keep refrigerated or frozen and just need to be brought out and reheated. Don't ever try to do most of your meal preparation while your guests are having cocktails in the living room.

5. Especially if you have no help, keep things simple; one help is to serve the appetizers before dinner in the living room.

6. If you are planning a seated dinner, set your table ahead of time—don't clutter it, but always have candlelight and a centerpiece, no matter how simple.

7. If it is a cocktail party or cocktail buffet, or if you're serving cocktails before dinner, have the bar set up—liquor and glasses out, and have plenty of ice on hand.

8. Dinner time should be approximate, and food should "wait well" if possible. This helps you time your party right, to make allowances for a late guest and to feel the "mood" of the group and know when they're ready to eat. Don't rush them to the table, but don't let the cocktail hour stretch into hours and hours either.

The House—Before the Guests Arrive

1. Clean house a day ahead so that you do not have to wear yourself out the day of the party.

2. Allow a half hour or so, before you dress, just to do last-minute once-overs such as checking flowers, pillows, dust, etcetera.

3. Check to see if you have enough ash trays in the right places.

4. Give the bathroom(s) a once-over in case a child has used your guest towels, the toilet, or whatever.

373

5. Make provisions for coats, and especially if it is raining, umbrellas, raincoats, boots, etcetera.

UNEXPECTED GUESTS

1. If you've barely had a moment's notice that one or even six people are arriving unexpectedly either for cocktails or dinner, *keep your cool* at all costs.

2. Grab your cleaning basket or at the least a dust cloth, an empty container (we like an old shopping bag) and sail through each room dusting, straightening, and picking up clutter. Empty trash, ash trays in the container, then throw it all away. Fluff up pillows, check the bathroom, fill up the ice bucket, set out the quickest nibble or snack food in your pantry. Take a deep breath, look in the mirror, and answer the doorbell.

3. If they're coming for dinner have only the simple foods, for example, a casserole (whipped up from the larder), a green salad, some toasted bread or melba toast, spiced canned fruit compote for dessert, and pretend you've labored on it for hours! Or simply open up cans of crabmeat, tuna, meat spreads, etcetera, cut up a few fresh vegetable sticks and spread your cocktail snacks into dinner!

YOU

We can't say it too many times—give yourself time to relax *before* and *during* a party you have planned. Your good planning and determination to enjoy your own party are the two important keys to making it happen.

THE BIG COCKTAIL BUFFET

One of the most popular ways of entertaining today is the big bash. It can be either a plain cocktail party or a cocktail party combined with a simple buffet. Here is a useful guide:

- *Hire a Bartender:*
  Except for the smallest cocktail party things will run much more smoothly with one. If expense is no problem, hire a waiter or waitress too (see later discussion in this chapter).
- *Ice:*
  Have plenty. Make up lots of ice cubes in advance and store them in plastic bags in the freezer or buy a big bag or two a few hours before the party.
- *Glasses:*
  For a large cocktail party you may want to rent them from a caterer, but you can also buy simple, inexpensive glasses, plastic or glass, in the five-and-ten or supermarket. Have more glasses than the number of guests you've invited.
- *Liquor:*
  You needn't have a wide assortment of drinks and cocktails to offer—two or three choices are sufficient. What you serve depends on preferences in your group.

A BUYING AND SERVING GUIDE FOR DRINKS

Use this guide to determine how many drinks you will need for a specific occasion, and thus how many bottles of liquor you should buy. The number of bottles listed indicates the amount in volume, but you will want to increase the number of bottles since you no doubt will want to offer a choice of liquors. The most popular choices include Scotch, bourbon, rye or blended whiskey, and gin or vodka.

Note: We are indicating fifths, although to feel secure you may want to substitute quarts, except, of course, when you are offering a choice. Then fifths should be ample. The only other exception is a large cocktail party, during which time you will want to be doubly certain that you won't run low. It is always better to have more than you need. And no doubt you will use it over the long run. If, however, it is something you won't use or if you have a number of bottles you have not opened, your local friendly neighborhood liquor dealer may take some of it back.

When you know your guests well, then you can adapt this chart to "more or less." For example, chances are the average four people having pre-dinner cocktails won't consume 16 drinks, especially if you are having wine with dinner. Use the chart only as a guide, as we have indicated more than ample amounts just to be on the safe side.

NO. OF PEOPLE	NO. OF DRINKS PRE-DINNER COCKTAILS	LIQUOR (APPROX.)	NO. OF DRINKS COCKTAIL PARTY	LIQUOR (APPROX.)
4	8 to 16	1 fifth	12 to 16	1 fifth
6	12 to 24	2 fifths	18 to 26	2 fifths
8	16 to 24	2 fifths	20 to 34	2 fifths
12	24 to 48	3 fifths	25 to 45	3 fifths
20	40 to 75	4 fifths	45 to 75	5 fifths

In addition to spirits, include:

Dry sherry or an aperitif   Ginger ale
Dry vermouth   Tonic water
Soda water   Soft drinks for non-drinkers

For a cocktail party for 50, here more or less is what you'll need:

4 to 5 quarts of Scotch
4 to 5 quarts of vodka or gin
4 to 5 quarts of bourbon or rye
2 bottles of dry sherry or aperitif
Several large bottles of soda water, ginger ale, and tonic water
12 small bottles (or a few large ones) of cola or another soft drink

THE BAR

Set up the bar in an accessible place but not where the food is—that can cause traffic jams. The bartender will set it up, but if you're supplying the equipment, here's what you'll need:

- Tablecloth (with pad to protect table if it needs it)
- Cocktail shaker or martini pitcher
- Water pitcher

- Bottle opener
- Ice bucket with tongs
- Jigger measure
- Bar strainer
- Teaspoon
- Long spoon for mixing and stirring
- Corkscrew
- Muddlers
- Bar knife or paring knife
- Tray for passing
- Cocktail napkins
- Two linen towels
- Ingredients for special drinks—such as lemon twists or olives for martinis, onions for Gibsons, cherries and orange slices for whiskey sours

Hors d'Oeuvres

Have a few bowls of simple "nibble food" around—nuts, olives and celery and carrot sticks, chip and dip, cheese and crackers are a few suggestions. Then, some more substantial hors d'oeuvres. It depends on how elaborate you want to get, but it's usually best to have just a few popular, simple things. Here are some suggestions—two to four out of this group would be enough:

Shrimp with cocktail sauce
Small sandwiches
Stuffed eggs
Pâté with toast rounds or crackers
Crabmeat canapés
Chipped beef wrapped around squares of cream cheese and speared with toothpicks

Hot Hors d'Oeuvres

Serving hot appetizers is a little more difficult since someone has to check the oven or chafing dish, but it's nice to have at least one hot hors d'oeuvre. A few suggestions:

377

Meatballs with Cheddar cheese centers
Stuffed mushrooms
Broiled garlic-butter shrimp
Miniature pizzas
Rumaki (chicken livers wrapped with bacon and broiled)
Cheese fondue with French bread chunks

BUFFET FOOD

At a cocktail buffet the guests serve themselves at the buffet table, then they sit anywhere, or even stand, to eat. It's most important when having this type of buffet to serve food that requires just a fork, and bread and rolls that are already buttered.

Menu Suggestions

1.

Celery Fans and Carrot Curls
Crabmeat Salad Tartlets   Cheese Roll
Guacamole Dip
Sausageburgers   Chicken Livers
Rolled Smoked Salmon with Capers
Creamed Mushrooms on Waffle Squares
Pecan Tarts   Pound Cake
Coffee

2.

Assorted Relish Platter
Celery   Carrots   Olives   Cucumber
Meat Balls in Red Wine
Shrimp Louis
Lobster Newburg   Lamb Curry
Steamed Rice
Chutney   Almonds
Green Salad
Assorted Cheese   Crackers
Assorted Cookies   Assorted Chocolates
Coffee

Coffee

Though we've indicated it on the menus above, perhaps a special emphasis on the importance of coffee is in order. After a cocktail party of any duration your guests will welcome a cup, perhaps more, of piping hot coffee. It's *the* great stabilizer—made to order for any occasion. Have plenty of it available.

Prepare Ahead

Have all the food prepared ahead of time, covered in the refrigerator, ready to be heated if it needs it. Have the bar set up ahead—and clean your house the day before so you have only last-minute sprucing up to do.

SIT-DOWN DINNER PARTIES

THE SMALL INFORMAL DINNER

The small dinner party, for from about four to ten people, is probably the most popular way of entertaining today.

Setting the Table

Tablecloth or place mats? It's up to you—place mats are inexpensive, easy to wash and store, and they are correct for all except a formal dinner. If you use place mats, stick to the oval and rectangular shapes—the fancy shapes make a table look too busy. Tablecloths have one advantage: You can put more on the table without its looking crowded. Any colors go—as long as they blend with your china and the rest of the room.

Always have candles and if there's room on the table, a centerpiece—fresh flowers in a loose arrangement or a bowl of fresh fruit are always lovely. Candles should be tall and slim, centerpieces should be low; keep in mind that guests on opposite sides of the table want to see each other.

Serving

Appetizers are usually served in the living room with cocktails but may be served as a first course at the table. It just means a little more getting up and down from the table for the hostess. Serving may be done informally, passing the dishes around the table for everyone to serve themselves, family-style. Or, the hostess can serve. She has the plates in front of her, serves them and passes them around the table, serving the women first.

If you're serving meat that is to be carved at the table, the host can serve as he carves, or he may pass the plates on to the hostess who will serve the rest of the meal.

Condiments and bread or rolls are passed around the table. Desserts and coffee may be served at the table or later in the living room.

THE SEATED BUFFET

This is a dinner party where the guests serve themselves at a buffet table, then move to another table, which is already set, to sit down and eat. You can use a group of card tables with table-cloths for this, if you are using your dining table for the food or if it isn't large enough to seat everyone.

Menu Suggestions for Small Informal Dinners

1.

Boeuf Bourguignonne
Buttered Noodles
Green Salad   Hot Rolls and Butter
Strawberry Soufflé   Coffee

2.

Veal with Mushroom Sauce
Fresh Asparagus   Rice Pilaf
Orange and Chicory Salad   French Rolls
Apple Tarts   Coffee

3.

Chicken with Almonds and White Raisins
Cracked Wheat Pilaf
Buttered Brussels Sprouts
Endive and Pine Nut Salad
Sesame Sticks
Poached Pears
Coffee

a. *Salad Plate*
b. *Napkin (or place under forks or in napkin ring)*
c. *Salad Fork*
d. *Dinner Fork*
e. *Dinner Plate*
f. *Dinner Knife*
g. *Teaspoon*
h. *Bread and Butter Plate and Knife (optional)*
i. *Water Goblet*
j. *Wine Glass*

Here is another version of an informal table setting. The dessert spoon and/or fork are placed directly above the dinner plate. When you plan to serve soup as a first course, place the soup

381

spoon to the outside of the coffee spoon. Flatware is generally placed in order of use from outside in.

MORE FORMAL DINNER PARTIES—SEMI-FORMAL

This is a description of how to give a modern adaptation of a formal dinner party, more suited to our informal way of life and entertaining. Let's call it the semi-formal dinner.

- You will probably want to invite by invitation, though it need not be in the third person.
- Place cards, always in order at a formal dinner party, are suitable for this occasion. It will save any last-minute seating mix-up.
- They should read "Miss Bowen," "Mr. Johnson," etcetera. If there is a male guest of honor, he should be placed at the hostess's right, a female guest of honor at the host's right.
- Use a tablecloth: white, off-white, or a pale pastel. Fold each napkin into an oblong. Place on service plate. Or, if you are serving a first course, place to left of fork. This is the time to bring out your best china, crystal, and silver (although we hope you use it occasionally for your family meals, too).

The Need for Help

You'll probably want to have help for this meal—you'll have three or four courses, and you and the host could manage this dinner for about 12, but it would mean quite a bit of serving work for you; a maid to serve will make things smoother. If you do have a maid serve, be sure she knows how to do it properly: smooth service is very important at a formal-type dinner.

Instructions for the Maid

Just before dinner is served:
1. Fill goblets three-quarters full of water (it's easiest to pour if ice is already in glasses).
2. If bread and butter plates are being used, place individual butter pat or ball on each plate.
3. Set chair at each place, with front of seat flush with table edge.
4. Light candles.
5. If either fruit, fruit or seafood cocktails, oysters, or a paté are being served as the first course, place service on service plates before dinner is announced (although, with our less formal life-styles today, it is certainly permissible to dispense with service plates. In fact, they are not used much anymore except for the most *formal* of occasions). If the soup is the first course, place service on table just before or after guests are seated.
6. Serve the wine.

How to Serve

1. Serve hostess first, unless otherwise directed, then person to her right, and so on around the table.
2. Stand at left of each person to serve, remove, and offer dishes.
   Exceptions: Beverages and dessert silver should be placed from right to avoid reaching in front of a guest.
3. To exchange plates, remove used plate with left hand; place new one with right hand, standing at left side of each person.

383

4. Offer food by holding dish flat on palm of left hand. Offer side of platter or dish; see that handles of serving fork (at left) and spoon (at right) are pointed toward person being served.
5. For small dishes, use small tray. Service napkin should be used, like a tray, under dishes and trays, when offering food (not when exchanging plates).
6. Refill water goblets but do not lift them from table.
7. Before starting to serve, have everything ready for that course.
8. Serve hot food on heated plates; serve cold food on chilled dishes.
9. Handle lower part of goblets, never top; do not let thumb extend over rim of plates.
10. Do not start to remove a course until all persons have finished eating.
11. To remove dishes, remove all serving dishes and platters first; then used plates, glasses, silver, etcetera, then unused silver, salts and peppers, etcetera.

Serving the Main Course:
1. Bring heated dinner plates from kitchen, one at a time; exchange for first-course service (or serving plates). Or bring two dinner plates from kitchen at a time; leave one on serving table while exchanging other for first-course service. Take out two first-course services and service plates together.
2. Offer meat, then vegetables, gravy, bread, and relishes.
3. Take meat platter and vegetable serving dishes back to kitchen; rearrange for second servings.
4. If host carves, bring in carving set and place before him, then the meat. Stand at his left, and when he has arranged meat on dinner plate in front of him, pick it up with left hand and replace it with extra dinner plate in right hand. Take filled plate to hostess, removing her plate with right hand and placing filled plate with left hand. Repeat until everyone is served. Then pass other food.
5. If serving salad, it may be brought in individually and served before the main course, or if it is served with dinner, salad plate is to left of service plate at each place, and salad bowl is passed after the rest of the main course.

Or it may be served in the French manner with cheese just after the main course and before the dessert.

Serving Dessert and Coffee:
1. At each place, place dessert plate, with dessert fork (on left) or spoon (on right).
2. Or put dessert silver on small tray and place to right of each place. Then place dessert, which has been arranged on individual dessert plates.
3. Place cups and saucers to the right of each guest; pour coffee.

Adapting Maid Service to Hostess Service—No Maid

- Definitely plan to serve a first course in the living room.
- Plan to have the host serve the meat and the hostess serve the rest of the meal. In that case, place the carving set (if meat is to be carved), 1 serving fork and spoon to host's right. Set other serving pieces to hostess's right.
- Set the meat course and stack of hot plates in front of host.
- Set the rest of the meal in front of the hostess.
- Serve the salad with the meal.
- Remove all the dishes after the last person has finished eating and bring in the dessert.
- Serve coffee after the dessert either at the table or in the living room.

> *Tip:* Another method for serving is restaurant-style. Assemble the plate in the kitchen and serve to the guests. Seconds, of course, will be brought in from the kitchen in a serving dish.

> *Note:* Try to remove all the glasses from pre-dinner cocktails and snack or appetizer plates before the guests are seated for dinner. This takes some special maneuvering, but it can be done. You might serve the appetizer on a portable cart and have the guests return empty plates to the cart. At that time, place dirty glasses and empty snack dishes on the cart and roll into the kitchen.

385

Menu Suggestions for Semi-Formal Dinner Parties

Liver Pâté with Gherkin Pickles
Sirloin Tip Roast Beef   Yorkshire Pudding
Broccoli with Lemon Butter
Beet and Belgian Endive Salad
Oil and Wine Vinegar Dressing
Dry Red Wine
Lemon Ice with Red Raspberries
Sugar Wafers
Coffee

———————

Double Beef Consommé
Chicken Kiev
Orange Rice
Parslied White Asparagus
Spiced Peach Compote
Hot Rolls
White Wine
Mocha Torte
Coffee

———————

Mushrooms Vinaigrette on Lettuce
Roast Stuffed Pork Loin (whole or chops)
Brussels Sprouts with Water Chestnuts
Applesauce with Currants
Rolls
Dry White Wine
Steamed Fig Pudding
Coffee

———————

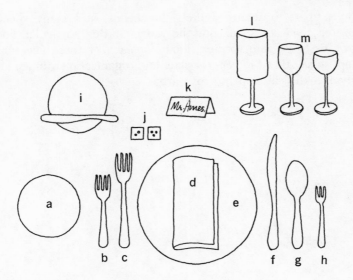

Semi-Formal Dinner Table Setting

a. Salad Plate
b. Salad Fork
c. Dinner Fork
d. Napkin
e. Dinner Plate
f. Dinner Knife
g. Soup Spoon
h. Cocktail or Oyster Fork
   (*place fish fork on the left side*)

i. Bread and Butter Plate and Knife (optional)
j. Individual Salt and Peppers (optional)
k. Place Card (optional)
l. Water Goblet
m. First Course Wine Glass (if one wine is served throughout meal, you need only one glass)

Bring in dessert spoon and/or fork and teaspoon or demitasse spoon with dessert and coffee or demitasse.

OTHER PARTIES

Besides the cocktail party, the cocktail buffet, and small dinner party, there are other very popular ways to entertain, particularly in today's casual life-styles. These include barbecues, picnics,

387

patio suppers, brunches, buffets, luncheons, and many special occasions. Neither space nor the range of this particular book allows us to go into specific detail for each of these occasions, except to say that the general planning, organizational hints, and party checklists all apply to any party.

CHAPTER SEVEN

On Stitching and Mending

You will surely save those familiar nine stitches when you do your mending on time. This is one instance where procrastination can literally become a disaster. We've heard the excuses, and to our chagrin, even indulged in them occasionally. "I've tried to sew and nothing holds," "I don't even know how to thread a needle," "I don't have time." But then there are excuses for everything one does not like to do. Mending is as inevitable as dusting, and almost as easy.

OUTFITTING A SEWING CORNER

Convenience is a matter of having everything you'll need at hand. There are two kinds of sewing centers: *the permanent sewing center* and *the portable one.*

The permanent sewing center is a small room or closet used exclusively for sewing, with a door you can close. You may create such a room by closing off the end of a hall with folding doors or possibly by making use of the space beneath a stairway. This is a true workroom where you don't have to hide the evidence between sessions. Glory be!

The portable sewing center can be in a corner of the kitchen, laundry room, dining room, or even the living room of a small apartment. The necessary equipment can be packed in anything

389

from a small basket to a cabinet set aside for this purpose. If you use a sewing machine it can be either portable or a cabinet model that blends with the rest of the furniture.

We like to keep mending kits in several places; this could be no more than a pincushion to hold threaded needles: one in the bedroom on the dresser, one in the bathroom, one near your ironing equipment and washing machine for unexpected repairs.

EQUIPMENT

Most of the supplies you'll need are simple and fairly inexpensive. If you've been sewing for a while, you'll probably need to fill in only a few items.

Scissors. You will need a pair 3 to 4 inches long for precision work and a pair 4 to 6 inches long for general use.

Shears are used for heavier work, have longer blades, and straight or contoured handles.

Needles come in several types and sizes. Hand-sewing needles range from #1 to #12—the smaller the number, the coarser the size.

Machine needles also come in various sizes. Your machine's instruction book will guide you.

Straight pins are a must. Brass dressmakers' or silk pins are best. If you use steel pins, don't leave them in fabric for any length of time.

Thread comes in sizes ranging from #8 (very coarse for heavy fabric) to #125 (very fine for lightweight fabric). Size 50 or 60 in mercerized cotton is used for most sewing, silk thread for silks, wools, and fabrics that mar easily, and nylon and Dacron thread for these fabrics. Keep a supply of black, white, brown, navy, and gray, and colors that match personal clothing and home furnishings.

A pincushion keeps your needles and pins ready for use. Get one filled with wool, ground cork, or hair.

A thimble that fits comfortably and is lightweight is a must for sewing.

MEASURING TOOLS

A tape measure with numbers on both sides gets used often. *A hem marker* will help with shifting hemlines. *A measuring gauge* is convenient for marking hem widths, measuring button-holes, and marking pockets.

SEWING MACHINE

If you do any real sewing and enjoy making your own clothes or accessories, a sewing machine is one of the best investments you can make. And if you can afford it even if you don't sew creatively, it can be a wonderful aid to making all necessary repairs.

OTHER SUPPLIES

A *work surface* 3 feet wide and 5 to 6 feet long is a great help. Ideally, have a large folding table. A *full-length mirror* is also a great asset. Double mirrors let you see both front and back of the garment. *Notions* such as thread, snap fasteners, hooks and eyes, buttons, seam bindings, tapes, trimmings, zippers, safety pins, iron-on tape, should all be kept handy.

MENDING AND REPAIR

Mending can be done by hand or machine, using basic repair and mending stitches. Most of it is done by hand. Everyone has to mend once in a while, such as repairing loose or ripped-off buttons, hems, hooks and eyes, snaps, thread loops, linings. And it seems that more and more it is not only the old garment that needs repairing, but the new one you bring home from the department store the very first time you put it on. To avoid this kind of disappointment check items carefully before purchasing. Select garments and furnishings that fit properly. Examine construction, inside and out, look for damaged areas and flaws. Make sure trimmings are sewed on firmly and that there are no dangling threads or loose seams or hems.

As to extensive repairing, that depends on the garment. If it is a good garment, you like it, and it still has a good deal of wear left, then it will be worth the effort. If not, and if you can buy a

391

new one fairly inexpensively, it may not be worth your time and effort to do a major repair job.

Whether or not you have or use a sewing machine, it is handy to know some of the basic hand stitches for quickie repairs. Select the stitch shown below that looks the most like the one originally used on the garment and adapt it to the particular item you want to repair.

BASIC STITCHES AND WHEN TO USE THEM

(See accompanying illustrations.)

Hemming Stitches—A *running* stitch is used if you want to space your stitches. In using this stitch, the thread remains under the fold. A *whip* or *slanted* stitch is excellent if you want close stitches. Here the thread is on top of the fold. A *slip* stitch is used mainly for protection against abrasive wear on skirts and the like. The thread runs inside the fold of the hem between the stitches. The hem is more durable if you can machine stitch the fold before using the slip stitch for hemming.

Note: Many times it is desirable to machine stitch the fold before hemming.

Overcasting Stitch—This makes an excellent seam finish to protect edges from fraying.

The Seed Stitch—This is another version of the back stitch. Tiny stitches show on the right side. This method is strong and practically invisible. Use it to mend zippers put in by hand or for repairing seams made from heavy fabrics. A long underneath stitch allows a space between tiny top stitches.

The Blanket Stitch—If you use this stitch to finish edges, make it large. If you use it to strengthen weak corners, make it very small.

The Catch Stitch—When you want to hold the cut edges of one fabric against the other, the catch stitch does just that. Many labels used in coats and suits are sewed in with this stitch.

The Lacing or Fishbone Stitch—This stitch is often used for delicate mending. The stitch is used when you want to pull two cut edges together either permanently or temporarily. Use these stitches spaced (a) to help reshape damaged areas before darning.

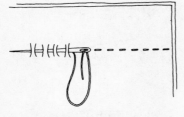

RUNNING STITCH

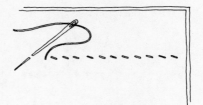

WHIP STITCH

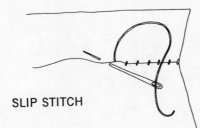

SLIP STITCH

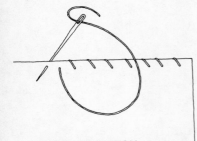

OVERCAST STITCH

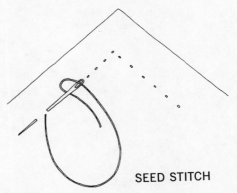

SEED STITCH

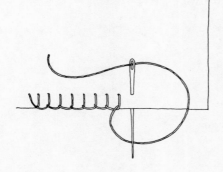

BLANKET STITCH

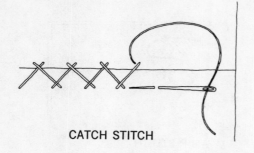

CATCH STITCH

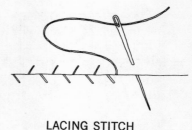

LACING STITCH

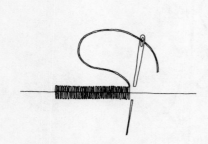

FISHBONE STITCH

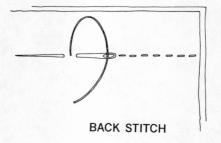

BACK STITCH

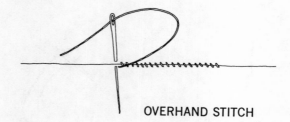

OVERHAND STITCH

BUTTONHOLE STITCH

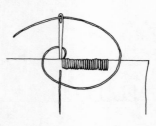

Back Stitch—This gives the appearance of machine stitching, but the underneath stitch is twice as long as the top stitch. Use it to mend seams that have been machine stitched, or for places hard to reach by machine, such as underarm seams, gussets, and plackets. The top stitching looks like machine stitching as each stitch meets the next.

The Overhand Stitch—This is to join two folded edges together. Take the stitches in the edges of the fold.

The Buttonhole Stitch—While this stitch is used primarily to **reinforce** machine-made buttonholes, it is excellent for sewing on hooks and eyes, and snaps. They will withstand harder wear and look better.

Hard-Wear Areas

Reinforce knees, seats of pants, elbows, especially in children's clothes, on old garments showing signs of wear, on new ones to prevent wear. The best method for most fabrics, other than knitted garments, is to use iron-on patches on the inside. For thinning elbows on wool sweaters, or for knees on loosely knitted pants, run a matching yarn invisibly through the knitting on the underside. On some men's sweaters it is possible to attach a leather elbow patch.

Iron-On Mending

This has become a very popular method of mending as it is very quick and easy, especially if you don't like to sew. The new iron-on fabrics are available in a multitude of colors and in both plain and jersey weaves. You can buy patches in corduroy, denim, and twill. Strips are available for repairing tears and rips in almost any fabric. Follow the instructions for application exactly.

That Stitch in Time

The real definition to "a stitch in time" is to catch those loose ones before they can do much damage to the garment or article.

Hems—Catch loose threads or rehem before they are completely undone.

395

Dangling Threads—Thread into a needle, bring to the wrong side if necessary, and fasten. If threads are too short, then resew.

Buttons, Hooks and Eyes, and Snaps—Resew, if they are loose, using tiny over and over stitches or the buttonhole stitch, being careful they do not show on outside of garment. If the thread has not come off completely, then sew over it. If buttons have a shank, then remove buttons and all loose threads, and resew.

SOME SEWING TIPS

Buttons

If the button gets much wear, then it should be applied with a shank. This will allow the buttonhole to fit nicely under it. To make a shank in buttons with holes (pierced buttons), make it with the thread you use to sew on the button.

The length of the shank will be determined by how thick the fabric is. A lightweight fabric needs a very small one, while a heavier fabric needs a long sturdy shank. As a matter of fact, even a shank button may require a thread shank for extra support. Using a single or double thread (if the fabric is thick); make a small knot. Take a small stitch on the right side of the garment where you want to sew the button. Stitch through entire thickness but do not go through facing; then take another stitch across the same spot. Next, sew through one hole in the button. Placing button over stitch, insert a toothpick or long straight pin between button and fabric, and take several stitches through each pair of holes. Remove toothpick or pin, pull button forward, then bring needle and thread between button and garment. Wind thread several times around thread to make a shank. Take several final stitches and secure thread by looping over needle to make a knot. Cut the thread.

To make a thread or button loop—Make a core of a few threads of proper length, then cover with a buttonhole or blanket stitch.

Zippers

Check to see that there are no loose or frayed edges on the fabric. If so, overcast to avoid catching in the zipper.

Pockets and Kick Pleats

At the top of the pocket or pleat reinforce with several over-hand stitches.

Seams

Reinforce sleeve, underarm and crotch seams with a back stitch by hand (see preceding list of basic stitches), or on the machine, over the first line of stitching.

Buttonholes

If they look frayed, go over them with a buttonhole stitch (see list of basic stitches), or use the zigzag machine stitch to make them firm.

PATCHING

To mend a tear or a fairly large hole, a patch is better than darning. Use a matching fabric. If the item has faded and shrunk and you are using a piece of new material, it may be faded and shrunk by washing it in detergent or soap and baking soda, then drying it in the sun. Take patch material for a ready-made garment from a facing, hem, pocket, or belt. Trim the damaged area all around, making a square or rectangle. Always follow the lines of the design or weave and work only on the straight of the grain. Cut the patch on precisely the same grain and match both lengthwise and crosswise threads. Match a design before cutting out a patch. Always use matched thread. (Also see section on iron-ons, preceding.)

Decorative Patches

Be creative. Think about using a decorative patch over damaged areas. For example, add a pocket over a tear (which you can mend with iron-on tape). Or:

- Use braid, rickrack, or ribbon to cover up wear or tear.
- Use appliqué in a special design in a contrasting fabric.

397

- Do some crewel embroidery in a splashy color.
- Patch a worn-out knee or elbow with a leather, denim, or contrasting fabric, then repeat it on the other one to make a matching design.

The Hemmed Patch

Cut the patch 1" larger than the damaged area, on all sides. Pin all around the hole, right side up. Clip into each corner of the hole diagonally about ¼". Turn under the raw edges around the hole and press evenly. Hem the edges to the patch with in-

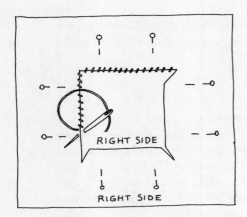

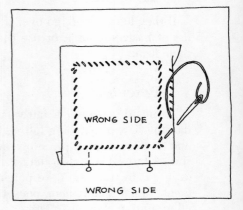

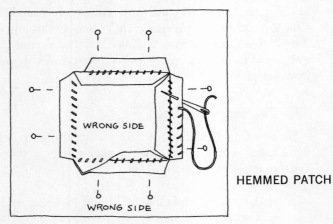

HEMMED PATCH

visible stitches (see list of basic stitches), being careful to take several of them at the corners. On nonwashable articles, trim patch edges to ¼″. Hem raw edge in place lightly. For washable ones, trim patch edges to ½″. To make a flat, invisible patch, trim patch to about ¼″, trimming off corners. Press seams open and overcast raw edges.

The Inset Patch

This kind of patch is almost invisible. Use it, however, on firmly woven materials where patch can be matched to design. It can be put in by hand or machine. Cut out damaged piece on grain of fabric in square or rectangle. Clip corners about ¼″ deep, diagonally. Turn edges under beyond the ends of the clips and press. Match the patch piece to hole and baste in place. Slip stitch (see list of basic stitches) folded edges of the hole to patch. Turn garment or item inside out and stitch patch in by handsewing an overhand stitch. Press seams open on lightweight fabrics and overcast edges. For heavier fabrics, press seam edges toward the garment then top stitch on right side.

INSET PATCH

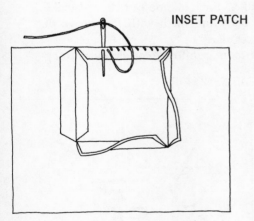
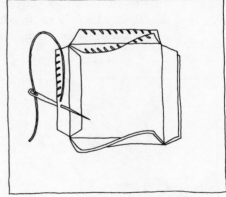

DARNING

Darning is done to give strength to weak spots or to mend tears, rips, snags, or small holes, though snags and small holes are done a little differently than tears or rips.

If appearance does not really matter, such as in sheets, work clothes, everyday slacks, etcetera, machine darning is stronger and faster than hand darning.

For hand darning, use matching thread or darning cotton. In homemade garments or items, draw the thread out of a leftover piece of fabric. For woolens, while we don't suggest that you "pull your hair out" over a mere darn, would you believe that long, single human hairs make a strong and almost invisible darn (on a similarly colored fabric, of course)? For knitted stretch and jersey fabrics, it is best to use thread which has some "give." Buy this special kind at the notions counters.

The keys to a good darn:

- Use a fine needle.
- Use short, single thread or yarn that matches fabric.
- Never knot the thread; let end extend on wrong side.
- Work on the right side.
- Never pull the thread up tight.

For tears and rips, draw the fabric together with a lacing or fishbone stitch (see list of basic stitches) before darning.

Next, bring the needle about ¼" to right side of tear and make rows of tiny running stitches back and forth with the weave of the fabric. Make the outside irregular.

For L-shaped and diagonal tears, reinforce corner by darning

DARNING TEARS AND RIPS

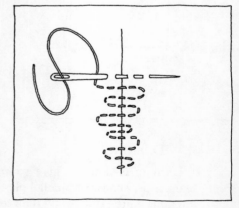

in both directions. (Or use iron-on tape if the tear can be mended fairly invisibly or if it is in an inconspicuous spot.)

For snags, small holes (moth-eaten areas or burns), trim ragged edges only, being careful not to change the shape of the hole. Sew lengthwise threads back and forth across the hole and as close together as the original weave or knit as possible. Work far enough into the fabric to strengthen the thin or worn area that may surround a hole. Then weave over and under threads crosswise, being sure to run the stitches past the hole to cover weak areas. (If there is no thin area and stitches can be made on the underside of a woven fabric, the darn will be less conspicuous.)

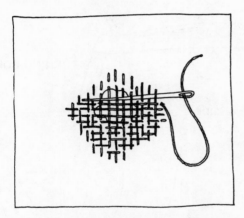

DARNING SNAGS

Tip: You can add strength to a darn by placing a piece of thin fabric on the wrong side and sew in with the stitches you take on the right side. Do not use this method on fabrics where the thickness might show. When placing the fabric on the wrong side, check to see that the grain matches the fabric grain. When you have finished the darn, trim the excess fabric.

How to Turn Collars and Cuffs

It is a well-known fact that collars and cuffs fray and wear out before the rest of the shirt or blouse. And it is still very much in vogue to be pennywise enough to turn them around to the unworn side.

401

Fold the collar or cuff in half and place pins close to the seam-line in the collar and neckband vertically in the center (or in the cuff and sleeve). For the collar, mark the position of the collar on the neckband with two pins on either side. Remove stitching carefully.

Reverse or turn the collar and reset into neckband, matching pins. Baste along original seamline, matching ends to pins. Machine stitch or use a good strong back stitch (see list of basic stitches) on inside of band over former stitching line.

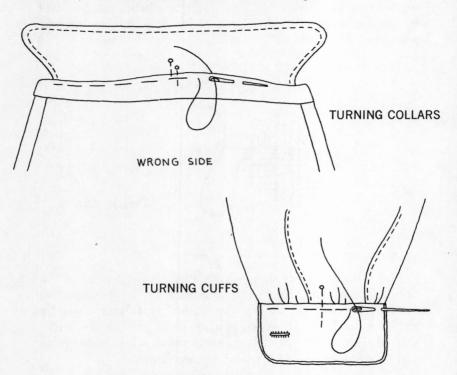

TURNING COLLARS

WRONG SIDE

TURNING CUFFS

For cuffs, turn and inset sleeve edge into cuff, matching pins. Baste and stitch as you do for collar above, on the outside of the sleeve.

How to Repair Hems and Seams

Hem. If the threads have loosened, remove loose threads and resew hem edge. If the seam binding has worn through, replace worn area. Remove it carefully, then stitch the new binding on the raw hem edge, preferably by machine, or by hand, using a back stitch (see list of basic stitches). Turn ends of seam binding under and rehem loosened area, selecting desired stitch from the list given in the preceding.

Seams. These should be sewed up immediately, preferably by machine, or by hand, using back stitch. For the underarm seams of raglan sleeves, which are often subjected to additional strain, reinforce them with seam tape, by placing tape over seam line, then stitching through it. *For gloves,* outside seams should be mended with the same stitch used by the manufacturer. They are usually whip stitches or running stitches. Use a very fine needle (or coarse if fabric demands it), starting without a knot. Secure stitching carefully and push thread ends inside the glove.

How to Repair Pockets

Need we emphasize the necessity of repairing a hole in the pocket? Sometimes the best method is to use the iron-on patch. But if the hole is in the corner, and they usually are, then sew a line diagonally across the pocket to conceal hole, either by machine or by hand, using a back stitch. If you need to replace the pocket, there are pocket kits available in the notions department.

Tip: Cover frayed or worn pocket edges on sports slacks and trousers with a narrow strip of contrasting fabric, suede, or leather.

When You Sew

- Put pins and needles in pincushions—never in your mouth, clothes, or furniture. Don't put any sharp objects in your lap.
- Store scissors and other sharp objects in secure places.
- Use sewing machine carefully and follow manufacturer's instructions on proper use. Turn off machine when not in use.

CHAPTER EIGHT

About Storage and Stashing

We've all said it at one time or another: "I don't have enough closet space." And yet we all know, the minute we find more storage space, we immediately discover we need more. Certainly we can all use more closet space. But what we are concerned with here, primarily, is using what space we do have to the best advantage, and in finding more storage space where none appears to exist.

Good storage that is both ample and convenient contributes to easier housekeeping, not to mention the amount of time and energy one can save in pulling things out and putting them back again. Rooms full of clutter create an impression of untidiness and chaos. It still seems to most of us who try to maintain some degree of orderliness that the key to efficient housekeeping lies within the familiar adage, "Have a place for everything and keep everything in its place." Unfortunately, that is easier said than done. To help you achieve the satisfaction of maintaining neat closets and drawers, we offer the following guides.

ANALYZE YOUR STORAGE SPACE

If you take a critical look at your present storage it can pay off in both appearance and convenience.

404

- Do you really need more space or is better organization the answer?
- Is everything that you have stored in the most logical place?
- Does the item take up more space than necessary? For example, do you have things stored in a box that is too large? Is a box necessary at all?
- Are items stashed away together that shouldn't be together?
- Do you have to move several items to get to something you use frequently?
- Are you storing things you'll never use again? Be ruthless in your editing of seldom-used items, then make a decision to throw, sell, or give them away.

HINTS TO PREVENT DISORGANIZED STORAGE

- Keep in mind that there are three kinds of storage: (1) things that are used regularly; (2) seasonal and occasionally used items; (3) seldom-used articles.
- Labels and lists will save time when you are hunting down something you need and haven't used for a while. Store all items you use most often at the place where they are used.
- Keep things covered as far as possible, to cut down on dust accumulation. Try not to stack or "stash" things away hoping to get back to them "later."
- Spruce up your storage areas with colorful accessories and shelf and drawer linings. It will encourage you to be tidy.

LOOK FOR STORAGE WHERE NONE EXISTS

A creative survey of every room in your home or apartment can lead to many good ideas for additional or more convenient storage space.

- If the space under your stairs is ample you might build in shelves. Or enclose the entire area, creating a closet for bulky items.

- Use basement joists for lumber storage, suitcases.
- For kids of all ages, create a mud room or area. All you need is a carefree floor and room for a low, slatted shelf and hooks. Boots and packages go on shelf, coats are hung on the hooks; make a place under the shelf for wet boots.
- Foldaway desks, ironing boards, and telephone caddies save space, speed work.
- Use drop-leaf table attached to wall or closet door for desk or table.
- Use small chests and cabinets as end tables and coffee tables; or, look for coffee tables that provide storage. More space-savers: storage hassocks, coffee tables that rise to full table height, and other convertible furniture pieces.
- If you have a fireplace, build some inexpensive bookshelves on either side by stacking unpainted bookcases or lining up those new steel and glass étagères, or even the wooden ones.
- It's still in vogue to have window seats with colorful cushions. Now you can cover them with gaily designed *vinyl* cushions that are washable. The window seat, hinged at the top, becomes a chest for all kinds of items —blankets, comforters, or whatever. (Or buy a chest and use it the same way.) Many stools with vinyl or leather tops are outfitted with narrow drawers beneath.
- Install or build bunk-type beds for children's rooms on top of unpainted chests of drawers.
- In extra spaces next to refrigerators or freezers, build narrow shelves on casters for kitchen items, such as paper goods, canned goods, etcetera.
- An old army or navy duffel bag can be put to good use. Hung in a pantry or closet corner, supported and held open by hanging the bag on two hooks through the grommet holes, it can be used to hold waste paper (emptied from smaller and more decorative baskets). Just empty when full. Also excellent for out-of-season sports equipment (helmets, cleats, pads, etcetera) in a boy's closet.
- A metal lunch box covered with a gaily patterned adhesive back paper is handy for storing monthly bills or canceled checks.

- Clothes hamper makes a good storage container for blankets and pillows. Sprinkle with moth crystals for out-of-season storage.
- A hanging basket attached to the inside of a closet door is handy to hold paper bags or other items. Or use one of the specially designed wire racks for paper bags.
- Pegboards with hooks provide handy storage in many rooms in your house.

STORAGE UNITS NOW ON THE MARKET

Aside from furniture units designed to store specific items such as silver or china, consider the following.

Shelves—Open shelf storage has come into its own. Things are easier to get at, convenient to reach, especially for frequently used items.

Wall Systems—Line or panel a wall with storage. Ready-mades can be installed to look like built-ins. Such storage units are excellent all over the house and in every room, for storing all kinds of things, both in closed cupboards and on open shelves. In the family or living rooms they can be used for decorative items, books, music equipment, radio, stereo and television, records, bar supplies, etcetera. In the dining room they are excellent for china and glassware, silver and linen. In the bathroom and kitchen, certain types, particularly those made of laminated plastic, are indispensable for towels, soaps, lotions, perfumes.

Room Dividers—Those which open on both sides contain much useful storage space.

Ready-made Racks—There are many many different kinds; they are useful for holding papers, cleaning supplies, clothes, shoes, china, kitchen tools, laundry and ironing, magazines, records, pots and pans, spices, tools, towels.

Stacked Cubed Storage—The newest, and most creative, way to have a whole storage system installed instantly.

Good storage is easier today than ever before. Furniture manufacturers produce pieces that bunch, line up horizontally, and stack vertically. Just take a walk through all the furniture stores,

407

notions departments, housewares and hardware stores if you want to feast your eyes on all the new and convenient units you can buy. Moreover, they allow you to exercise a good deal of creativity.

READY-MADES OR BUILT-INS

Unless you can do the job yourself, custom-made built-in storage is very expensive. If you own your own home or apartment, it may be worth it. However, there are so many ready-made bookcases, furniture, wall systems, shelves, chests, stackable units that can be installed to look built-in that it hardly seems worth it to spend the extra money. And the advantage is that you can take ready-mades with you, should you move.

CLOSETS

A toast to closets! Isn't it nice to be able to close the door on clutter. But unfortunately that's not what closets are for. They are for storage of all kinds. Keeping them in apple-pie order is ideal but almost impossible. Especially if there are not enough of them and if you are cramped for space. The most important thing about a closet is how it is planned and organized inside for easy access.

Ideally, there should be a closet in every bedroom and one for each person if possible. There should be one at the front entrance to the house and one at the back. There should be *at least* one linen closet (hopefully more), a "mud" room for wet and messy clothes, and another place to store heavily soiled clothes. However, there is not much you can do about this, except when you are buying or building a house.

LIGHTING AND VENTILATION

Don't forget to give some thought to ventilation and adequate lighting, especially for walk-in closets. If you do not have a vent in the closet, cut an opening at the base of the closet door. An on-off light switch that operates with the opening and closing of the door is convenient.

MAKING THE MOST OF YOUR CLOTHES CLOSETS

Keep these measurements in mind. Every closet should have enough space for the wardrobe of the person or persons occupying the room (3 to 5 linear feet for each person); a depth of 24 to 30 inches. A rod or rods should be placed so that garments clear the floor by 6 inches. Recommended heights are:

Robes and other long garments—72 inches
Dresses and coats—58 to 63 inches
Shirts, jackets, and skirts—45 inches

Distances recommended between shelves (made adjustable, if possible) are 7 inches for shoes and 8 to 10 inches for hats.

- Place two rods on one wall and use them for blouses, suits, and skirts.
- For evening clothes and long garments, to protect the hems, pin an old pillowcase or plastic bag over them.
- Stack or build tiers of shelves for small items at the ends of the closets—shoes, handbags, hats, etcetera. Place strips on shoe shelves to absorb moisture from damp soles. Sprinkle corners with cornstarch to help prevent odor.
- Hang tie and shoe racks on the backs of closet doors.
- Drawer units at bottom of the closet make efficient use of air space between clothes and floor.
- Install swing-out hangers for ties, skirts, and trousers at ends of closets.
- Stack see-through boxes on closet shelves; you'll save time locating stored items.
- If you are cramped for space, attach a towel rack to the inside of a closet door to hold several pairs of men's or women's slacks.
- Make a suitable hanger for small fur pieces by slipping a cardboard tube from a roll of wax paper over the bar of a wire coat hanger. Seal the cut end with tape and cover with a remnant of quilted fabric.

409

- Make a child's clothes closet from an old cedar chest. Attach casters to the corners of one end and turn it upright, then fit a pole across the inside.
- Tin boxes of the same size make excellent stack storage containers for children's woolen gloves, scarves, etcetera. Paint them in attractive colors, or cover with a gay adhesive-back paper.
- Give each child in the family a different-colored pillow case to hang on the inside of his closet door (or wherever). They are great laundry bags for dirty clothes— and kids'll love to help collect dirty clothes before laundering—maybe!
- To control dampness in a closet, fill an empty coffee can with charcoal briquets, punch holes in the cover, and place the container on the floor. A one-pound can filled with the charcoal is ample for a closet 3×5 ft.
- When you are storing clothing in garment bags for seasonal use, list each item and number the bag. Tape the list inside the closet door for quick identification.
- A small cloth bag hung on a hook on the back of a door of a child's closet is ideal for soiled socks. This makes it easy to check for pairs.
- If you do not have a dispenser for hanging mothballs in a closet, fill an old nylon stocking with mothballs and knot. Tack to back of closet or attach to hanger.
- To keep children's shoes together, clip them in pairs at the sides of the shoes with a pinch-type clothespin.
- To keep your "special" hat in perfect shape, use a plastic flower pot of the right size, turn it upside down and cover it with aluminum foil, adhesive-backed paper, or fabric.
- When cedar-lined chests and closets lose their aroma, sand the interior lightly. The sanding removes the dust and film from the wood, and restores the cedar odor.
- An inexpensive, yet attractive way to conceal packages and boxes stored on a top shelf of a clothes closet is to install a colorful and decorative window shade at the top of the space. Roll the shade down to the bottom of the shelf.
- A three-bar swinging towel rack attached to a closet door or wall makes a perfect holder for belts, for keep-

ing sizes, widths, and colors grouped together. It may also be used for holding necklaces and costume jewelry. Or cup hooks screwed into the inside of a closet door or on the inside wall are also handy for hanging belts. They take up very little space. Or twist a metal clothes hanger into a circle and attach shower curtain hooks to hold the belts.

- Screw two or three cup hooks into the closet door at different levels. Each hook will hold several blouses or children's dresses.
- To keep costume pins and flowers accessible, pin them onto a padded clothes hanger.
- To conserve closet space, hang a blouse on one hanger, and then hang the next hanger onto the first one, so that one overlaps the other.
- Don't discard spools after the thread has been used. These are excellent for fastening to a board or closet door, as pegs for hats, clothes, etcetera, for little tykes. Paint each spool a bright color as a decorative touch.
- Rubber bands wrapped around coat hanger ends will prevent clothes from slipping off and falling onto the floor of the closet.
- Discarded knitted ties make nice covers for wooden hangers. One tie will cover two or three hangers.
- To make a dark closet appear lighter, cover the floor with a piece of white linoleum, or use white vinyl tiles.
- Take advantage of wasted space at the top of a closet by adding an extra shelf or two to hold shoes and handbags. Or the rubberized racks used for stacking plates are excellent for elevating shelf space to hold handbags upright on the shelves.
- To create better space in a small clothes closet, divide the closet into sections; use one half for dresses and coats, and make two sections (one above the other), in the other half, for blouses, skirts, etcetera.
- If you have the space, file notches an inch apart on the top of a wooden clothes pole in your closet to keep your clothes from bunching up too close and wrinkling.
- As a space-saver for clothes, add shelves at the bottom of your small child's closet, thus utilizing the empty space. You can use the shelves for underclothes, shorts, slacks, even toys and games. Put hooks on the inside

of the closet door for hanging belts, pocketbooks, et-cetera.

- A towel bar placed on the back of the door of a boy's closet is ideal to hang trousers on at night.
- The cardboards packed with shirts from the laundry are just the right size and firm enough to use as "trees" for high leather or vinyl boots. Partly roll the cardboard, lengthwise, and put one inside each boot. This will help to keep the boot in shape.

FITTINGS YOU CAN BUY

In addition to the prefabricated closets, wardrobes, and chests you can buy, department stores feature a colorful array of closet fittings to help you organize your belongings. We must warn you, however, that if your closets are small they may take up precious space. Some of these items include:

- Garment bags.
- Transparent plastic boxes for hats, handbags, etcetera.
- Shoe racks.
- Bedding cases.
- Specialized hangers for all kinds of purposes—belts, skirts, pants.

YOUR DRESSER DRAWERS

There are a few partitioned dresser drawers with some divider space and slide-out jewelry racks; however, most of them are just empty spaces that invite confusion. If the contents of your drawers have a tendency to jumble and tumble, consider the following:

- Install partitions of your own, made of plywood, or use colorful boxes (without the lids, of course) for certain items.
- Invest in one of the rubberized silverware trays you can buy in the housewares department to hold all the as-

sorted trivia such as fingernail equipment or cosmetics not stored otherwise in a makeup chest or cabinet.
- Use special cases for lingerie and hose, shirts and socks.
- Line dresser drawers with colorful liners.
- To help keep odd-shaped bottles and cosmetic containers in place in drawers, securely tack a strip of elastic tape to the drawer and place bottles behind tape.
- To keep paper liners for drawers in place, cut a piece of cardboard to fit the bottom of the drawer; then cut the paper an inch larger all the way around the cardboard and fold the excess under the edge before placing it in the drawer.

LINEN STORAGE

We highly recommend *decentralization* of linen storage. Linen should be kept as close to the point of use as possible.

- Table linens in or near the dining room or eating area.
- Towels, washcloths, and bathroom linen in or near the bathroom.
- Dish towels in the kitchen.
- Bedding in or near the bedroom.

One homemaker with a family of ten had quite a job selecting sheets for the different-size beds. She solved her problem by using white sheets for double beds, striped ones for twin-size beds, solid colors for the youth bed, and floral sheets for the crib.

To save time and keep your linen closet neat, stack tablecloths with matching napkins between cardboards, then lift the cardboards and remove the set you want, without wrinkling the others.

When putting away linens, place the necessary number of matching pillowcases in the final fold of each sheet, making them easily available. This method can also be applied to other paired items, such as towels and face cloths.

Unfortunately most new homes have only one linen closet,

413

and that is usually too small. If you are in that predicament, here are some things you can do:

- Store the bedroom and bathroom linen in a closet near to them—or else on shelves or in a chest you might purchase for the purpose.
- Reserve one drawer in the kitchen specifically for towels.
- Or organize the linen closet you are using to the hilt. This may require some ingenuity, but it will pay dividends. (If you are building or remodeling, certainly give plenty of thought to the size, design of linen, clothes, cleaning, china, and glassware closets. For kitchens, see Chapter Five.)

ORGANIZATION OF THE LINEN CLOSET

1. It is a good idea to know the dimensions of linens when folded. Shelves for linen should be narrow, just deep enough to fit the size of folded items.
2. Consider a drop-leaf or pull-out shelf for straightening and sorting.
3. Rubber pull-out drawer fittings or trays are excellent for storing folded tablecloths, place mats, and small items such as guest and face towels.
4. Install deep shelves at the top for storing blankets, quilts, and infrequently used bedding. To store satin comforters, roll them tightly and put each one in a pillowcase. Cases serve as a dust cover and comforters won't slide off shelf.
5. If you can build your bottom shelf high enough you may have room to install a rod for hanging table linen on hangers for easy accessibility and less wrinkling. If you don't have space and wish to avoid wrinkles, fold them lengthwise over a drapery hanger (the kind that comes from the cleaners, with a paper tube over the wire), cover with a plastic bag, and hang in closet.
6. Label outer edge to indicate placement of linen, once good order is established. Things won't get mussed up so quickly this way.
7. Don't forget the specialized storage cabinets designed to match dining room and kitchen furnishings. They include

many shallow slide-out drawers for flat storage of cloths, napkins, and mats.

SAFE STORAGE OF CRYSTAL, SILVERWARE, AND ACCESSORIES

As for almost everything, there are furniture pieces specifically suited for storage of these items. Or put up ready-made or built-in shelves, cupboards, and drawers.

Tips:
- Store cups singly on their saucers or hang from rubber-coated hooks. Never stack, as it encourages chipping and damage.
- Make shelves for china high enough to accommodate the tallest pile. Keep piles fairly small, however, and plan spacing accordingly.
- Store glassware singly or at the most two deep.
- Lower or wider shelves might accommodate tall candlesticks, large serving dishes, pitchers, etcetera.

The most important thing to keep in mind is that all shelves should be shallow enough for easy accessibility.

Silver cupboards for hollowware should be lined with special fabric to prevent tarnishing. Never, *no never,* wrap any silver with transparent plastic wrap, regardless of how many of your friends tell you to do so. Tightly adhering plastic may cause your silverware to form pinhead-size black marks that are hard to remove. If you do use plastic wrap, and use your silver often, you may not have any trouble, but do it at your own risk.

Flatware may be stored in special silverware chests lined with felt to prevent scratching and tarnishing.

Or buy compartmentalized Pacific Cloth holders which then allow you to roll up silver by place setting or piece (i.e., all luncheon-size forks) and place in regular drawer. The cloth not only prevents scratching, but tarnishing as well.

415

BETTER STORAGE IN EACH ROOM IN YOUR HOUSE

BEDROOM

To free bedroom floor, use headboard storage units instead of nightstands.

A desk with a mirror hung behind it doubles as dressing table.

Make use of awkward spaces with built-in wall drawer and cupboard units. In the bedroom these can be especially designed for specific items—shirts, sweaters, lingerie, gloves, scarves.

Use open shelves in bedroom for convenient storage of jewelry, hats, sweaters, shirts—the things you use every day. However, this is good only if you are naturally tidy.

If you can afford it, replace bulky bedroom chests with a continuous row of built-in drawers or a series of small chests.

A vanity can be built with a tilt-top surface (with mirror under it) instead of a cosmetic counter.

If you're short on closet space, consider an old-fashioned armoire. You may want to remodel it yourself, to suit your storage needs.

Consider using the space under your bed for a sliding storage chest.

BATHROOM

Did you ever stop to take inventory of all the items that belong in or near the bathroom? Start a list and you'll wonder how the average bathroom ever handles them with a mere medicine cabinet and possibly some under-sink storage and maybe a small linen closet. Perhaps more than in any other room bathroom storage requires the most thought. Unless you have a new home, which you designed, along with the architect, no doubt you have a one- or two-bathroom house with minimal storage. In that case some creative thinking will help.

- Build in an overhead cupboard over bathtub. This would be especially adaptable if you have sliding glass shower doors. One ingenious young man did this, then installed a piece of plywood at an angle to make it resemble an overhead awning, which he then covered with adhesive-backed wallpaper.
- Tear out present small medicine cabinet and install a larger surface-mounted one.

- Use:
    Pole-mounted shelves.
    Standing towel racks.
    Open shelves installed on the wall.
    Toilet tank storage chests with sliding doors.
    Shelves mounted on back of door.
    Hooks everywhere.
    Built-in hampers under the sink.
    Utility cabinet installed against one wall.
    Unpainted chests, shelves, or bookcases arranged as a storage wall (if you like do-it-yourself projects and there is space for it).
- Stack several plastic vegetable bins in bathroom. They'll hold soap, sponges, etcetera.
- Install a series of towel bars on the bathroom door to increase storage. There'll be room for family, guest towels, and separating kinds of towels.
- Back-of-the-door shelves are good space organizers. A spice rack hung on the bathroom or linen closet door can hold shampoos and toiletries.
- An inexpensive remodeling job: drop ceiling above recessed shower or tub; tile underside and build storage space above.
- Under-sink cabinet in the bathroom can house pull-out built-in bins on casters for laundry, wastebasket, toilet tissue, cleaning supplies. You'll find it makes the floor easier to clean too.
- To preserve labels on medicine bottles, apply a thin coat of clear nail polish.
- To keep medicine bottles and other small articles from slipping off the glass shelves in the medicine cabinet, place half-inch adhesive tape along the front edge of each shelf.

417

- Kitchen spice racks attached to the inside of your linen closet door will hold the overflow from the medicine cabinet.
- You'll find a package of paper spoons a useful addition to your medicine chest. And disposable, too. Or keep a set of measuring spoons in your medicine cabinet so that, when one-half or one-quarter teaspoon of medicine is prescribed, you will be sure that correct amount is given. Wash them thoroughly after each use.
- Install a cabinet with a mirror in the bathroom for the children's use. Place it about three feet from the floor (or at desired height). The children can store their personal toilet articles in the cabinet, and the mirror will help them do a better job of brushing their teeth and combing their hair.

ATTIC AND BASEMENT

Attics and basements are more or less storage rooms in themselves and yet are often the most disorganized. We are more apt to let clutter accumulate when there is lots of room, than when we are limited in space.

It is important to:

- Protect certain stored items from heat in the attic (such as furniture which could dry out) by proper insulation.
- Protect all items from dampness in the basement, through insulation, waterproof sealers, or by installing a dehumidifier.
- Make some attempt at the most minimum of organization with shelves, cupboards, etcetera.

Hints for Attic Storage

- Shelves along all walls for storing flat items.
- Rods or clothes racks for storing garment bags.
- Triangular shelves or racks for under-eaves storage.
- Cardboard wardrobes such as movers use.
- Use nails and hooks everywhere.
- Label all boxes and keep a running inventory of what's in the attic.

For insect and moth protection, see section on pest control, Chapter Three.

Hints for Basement Storage

- Use free-standing steel shelves.
- Build or use free-standing shelves under the stairs.
- Nail wide boards to bottom of joists.
- Drop shelves from the ceiling.
- Use nails everywhere.
- Cover wall areas with pegboard, especially in the workshop. For more about workshop, see the following chapter.

Caution: Keep things up from the floor unless you have installed a protective coating and cover everything you can with plastic sheeting.

ENTRANCE HALLS AND PUBLIC AREAS

- Make a coat and hat rack by investing in a two-by-four at a local lumberyard; paint it and screw in some colorful hooks. Hang it near the entrance door for coats, hats, and scarves at the proper level so the small fry can reach it.
- Hinge the top of the bottom stair, if you have a staircase. This makes an excellent place to stow away such items as boots, baseball equipment, etcetera.
- Put a few clip clothespins on a wire hanger and hang on a nail in a convenient place, preferably near an outside door where the children come in from play. When they come in with wet caps and gloves, they can clip them conveniently onto the hanger.

GARAGE

If you do use your garage for storage, here are some ideas:

- Secure a strap to the garage wall, or wherever, to prop up bicycles.

419

- Suspend shelves from the ceiling over the cars.
- Line walls with perforated hardboard for hanging garden tools, bicycles, outdoor equipment of all kinds.
- Build out a shelf or cupboard over the car hood. Use all the overhead space you can to build racks for storing out-of-season items such as screens, awnings.
- Nail two-by-fours to the wall studs and suspend items from hooks.
- Assign sections of the garage (or wherever you can find the space) to various family members for their own storage areas. This helps to establish order, much the same way as large apartment buildings assign certain areas to tenants in the basement or storage room.

STORING MISCELLANEOUS ITEMS

BOOKS

No matter where or what kind of shelves you use to store your books, make sure you can reach them easily, that there is enough light to see the titles, and that if possible shelves are adaptable to take care of books of varying height.

If you are installing shelves, either built-in, custom-made, or free-standing ready-made or wall-hung systems, keep these sizes in mind: Books range from 6 to 9 inches wide and from 8 to 10 inches (preferably 12 for large picture books) tall. The average depth of a shelf is 10 inches. Make sure at least one shelf (or more if you are a collector) is 12 inches high to take care of large books.

CARD TABLES

If you are a card enthusiast, devote the easiest and most accessible place in your home to card table storage. Most people generally slide them into the side of a closet nearest to where they will be used. One family we know simply slides them (and the chairs) under the bed. Cover them with plastic sheeting if you don't want to dust them each time. An ideal place is a long, narrow closet (simple to build with plywood, for card tables, chairs, and ironing board).

Cards, Games, Etcetera

In the living room or family room (or where you entertain) have at least one or two pieces of furniture with drawer storage to house cards, bridge equipment, cocktail napkins, etcetera. If you play a lot of games, it might be worthwhile to create a special game cupboard.

CHROMIUM-TRIMMED ITEMS

These include things such as lawn furniture or baby carriages. Coat the chrome parts lightly with petroleum jelly to avoid rust and tarnish.

FOLDING BEDS, COTS

Where do you put these mammoth things? Even if you do have an attic or basement, it's not worth the effort to store them there for you have to cart them back and forth. Besides, they are too heavy. Stand the bed or cot in a spot where there is enough spare floor space and build a plywood cover to conceal it. Paint it the wall color or cover it with the same wallpaper used in the room to minimize its appearance. Top with some attractive indoor plants. Or you can buy fairly small furniture pieces that conceal fold-down beds or cots or almost anything else you have need for —bars, sewing machines, compact refrigerators.

GIFT WRAPPINGS

Assign one or two drawers in a base cabinet in the laundry room (if you have one) or in the most convenient space you can find to store all wrapping paper, ribbons, cards, scissors, tape, etcetera. It is also a good idea to have a counter or table close by for wrapping. If you can store gifts you collect or plan to wrap in the same area, that will be a convenience. Another good place to store gift wrapping is in the sewing area.

421

MAGAZINES, JOURNALS, CATALOGS

We recommend, if you do not want to become inundated with paper, that you cull the magazines that come into your house weekly and monthly.

- Keep a portable magazine rack near the chair in every room that is generally used for reading. When this is full go through it and throw away those magazines you don't want to keep. We use some handsome rattan baskets for this purpose.
- For those you do want to keep, such as professional journals or home-oriented idea books, find an accessible shelf and stack them neatly where you can use them regularly for reference. You can buy binders or cases for specific magazines from office-supply stores or directly from the publishers.

RECORDS AND SHEET MUSIC

We recommend, very simply, a record cabinet or rack. They are designed just *for* the purpose.

- Resealable plastic sandwich bags are perfect for keeping 45 r.p.m. records free of dust, scratches, etcetera.
- Get regular manila portfolios from an office-supply store and label each for sheet music.

SCREENS, SHUTTERS, FOLDING METAL CHAIRS

Suspend an overhead rack or shelf from garage ceiling, over the hood of the car, or invest in an outdoor metal storage bin for these large bulky items. To avoid damaging screens alternate their positions. Place one screen horizontally, the next vertically.

SKATES

To prevent from rusting, store in plastic bags or wrap in aluminum foil when not in use.

SNAPSHOTS

Classify them according to the year in which the pictures were taken, then put them in individual envelopes with the year written on the upper right-hand corner; file in a suitable container.

SPORTS EQUIPMENT

Whatever you do, don't store skis, fishing tackle, golf clubs, etcetera, in the back of a hall closet or in an otherwise similar situation. If you've ever done this, you'll know that they get tangled up with all the clothes and other paraphernalia. If you possibly can, devote one closet to sports equipment. If you can't afford that luxury, build a shallow cupboard out from the wall, wherever you can afford the space. Do you happen to have an unused door between two rooms? Then build in a closet on the side that has the most space to spare.

Another good way to store large sports equipment is on hanging racks and pegs in the garage.

TOY STORAGE

- Attach casters at each corner of a discarded dresser drawer or a similar container and use it to store small toys under a bed.
- Store crayons in a glass jar with a screw-on lid. When the children are coloring, they can see the particular color crayon they need without turning them all out on the table or floor.
- A clear plastic hanging shoebag makes an excellent storage container for small toys.
- A series of wicker or gaily colored wastebaskets make unusually practical and decorative storage units for children's toys. Store games in one, blocks and building toys in another, etcetera.
- Kids love old breadboxes. They use them for garages for small cars and trucks. They make an excellent garage for under-the-bed storage.

423

- To store trains and cars use an empty wine or liquor carton, complete with separations. Paint or paper the box with a gay color or design and leave it out as a decorative container in a child's room.
- The inexpensive cardboard jigsaw puzzles for children can be both educational and entertaining, but exasperating when they are scattered from one end of the room to the other. Staple a large manila envelope onto the back of each board that accompanies the puzzle, if there is a board to go with it. Otherwise, store each puzzle in a separate box or folder. Let the children be responsible for keeping track of the pieces.
- To keep children's modeling clay moist and pliable, wrap it in aluminum foil.
- Use colorful plastic napkin holders for excellent book racks for children's small hardcover storybooks.
- To solve the storage problem for bathtub toys, keep them in a nylon mesh bag and hang them wet over the shower or tub faucet. The toys will drip dry and are handy for the next bath session.

VACATION HOUSE OR SECOND HOME

The key thing to remember here is storage for proper protection of your home and furnishings, mainly from weather and household pests while the house is unoccupied. Here are some tips:

- Use as much metal as possible. Mice and other pests cannot attack it. Steel kitchen cabinets are preferable.
- If cabinets are wood, line all of them with aluminum foil or aluminum sheeting.
- Make sure all holes behind and under cabinets, around plumbing fittings, etcetera, are as small as possible.
- Plug up all cracks.
- Store bedding in metal chests.
- Cover chimneys with wire mesh or solid metal for protection from squirrels, birds.

THE HOME OFFICE AND RECORD-KEEPING

One of the most valuable aids to good housekeeping is having a place to plan and organize your work and store valuable papers. It can be as simple as a plain desk in the kitchen to the most elaborate "home office" in a den or study. It is no small wonder how much you can accomplish when you sit down to a well-organized desk.

There are a few very unusual people who can stuff everything in a drawer and be able to pull out just what they want when they want it. But most will agree that some degree of "office" organization is necessary in maintaining a smoothly run home. If your papers are scattered everywhere—in a shoebox, desk drawer, old scrapbook, lost—try to get them into order as quickly as possible.

Keep these items in your home file*:

1. Insurance policies (life, automobile, health and accident, property).
   The original policy is held by the company. Keep your copy of the policy at home where you can review it often. You could receive a duplicate if you know the company and policy number. Keep this information in a safe deposit box.
2. Tax returns (income, real estate, personal property, federal, state, local).
   Keep at least six years. The Federal Internal Revenue Service may question a return for any reason within the first three years after the due date of the return. If the taxpayer omits more than 25 percent of his gross income from the return, it may be checked at any time up to six years from the due date of the return.
3. Bank statements, deposit slips, check stubs, canceled checks.

* "Your Family Business Affairs," Iowa State University of Science and Technology, Cooperative Extensive Service; Ames, Iowa; April, 1966; HE-75.

Keep these at least three years and six years if used as evidence in tax deductions.

4. Receipts, receipted bills, sales slips, and annual statements of investment earnings.

Keep six years, especially if used as evidence for income tax deductions.

5. Social security stubs.

The card is carried with you. If it is lost, the stub will help you obtain a duplicate. Check every three years to make certain your earnings are recorded accurately.

6. Copy of will.

An unexecuted (unsigned) copy of the will should be placed in some accessible place such as a home file. It is a good idea for executors, trustees, or guardians nominated in the will to be informed of the contents of the will or to have an unexecuted file copy for their purposes.

7. Guarantees and warranties.

Write the date and place of purchase on the guarantee or warranty. Keep records of the type and date of repairs and persons repairing.

8. Records of expenditures and income (account books).

9. Household and other inventories.

An inventory is helpful in determining insurance claims in case of fire or theft. It is also helpful in deciding how much property insurance to carry and as a reference in checking age or price of an item. Another copy is kept in a safe deposit box.

10. Net worth statement.

Changes in net worth figures help you evaluate your financial progress.

11. Health records.

12. Employment records.

Records may be needed to obtain all the retirement and other job benefits. Proof of wife's earnings may be necessary for several purposes, including possible estate tax savings.

13. History of income, income tax, social security, and other payments.

14. Keys.

Other safe places may be found, but a file folder containing well-marked envelopes with a key sealed inside will eliminate the problem of lost keys.

15. Education records.
    Include teacher certificates, diplomas, report cards.
16. Reference materials.
    Information on appliances, home furnishings, insurance, etcetera, might be filed to use when you decide to purchase an item.
17. List of financial advisers.
18. List of items kept in safe deposit box and list of important papers in billfold.

Keep These Papers in a Safe Deposit Box:

1. Birth certificates, adoption papers, marriage certificate, divorce record, and death certificates. If you do not have these, contact the Vital Statistics Division, State Department of Health, or check with the county clerk or court.
2. Military service records.
    Discharge papers are needed to qualify for many veterans' benefits. Have papers recorded in county recorder's office. If lost and not recorded, it is a difficult and lengthy procedure to obtain a copy of the government's record.
3. Citizenship papers.
4. Passports.
5. Abstracts of title and deeds—including burial lot deed. Although burial lot deed and perhaps the will are in the safe deposit box, burial plans may need to be in a more accessible place.
6. Wills.
    Put the original executed copy in a safe deposit box, your attorney's file, or the office of the clerk of the district court. The safe deposit box is sealed upon death of the owner. A representative of the tax commission (often a bank employee), the attorney, and a representative from the estate will inventory the contents of the safe deposit box and remove the will within a few days after death.
7. Mortgages, security agreements, installment contracts, and other evidences of your debt (notes, contracts, liens).
    Also, keep evidence for at least ten years that debt has been paid, since legal actions on written contracts can be brought within ten years.

427

8. Evidences that others owe you (contracts).
9. Automobile title, truck title, etcetera.
   The title is needed when you sell a vehicle or borrow money using it as collateral. If the car is stolen, the title is evidence of ownership.
10. United States Savings Bonds.
    U.S. Savings Bonds can be replaced, but it may require several months.
11. Stock and bond certificates.
    The broker may hold these for you. To replace lost stocks or bonds can be expensive. It is advisable to attach purchase records to certificates.
12. Patents and copyrights.
13. History of income, income tax, social security, other payments.
14. Household and other inventories.
    In case of fire, an inventory kept at home might be burned, so this copy of the inventory would be needed. Include photographs of rare valuable items (antique guns, rings, paintings, etcetera) for identification purposes as well as insurance claims.
15. List of financial advisers.
16. List of important items in the home file.

THE DESK

Some of the supplies you might want at your desk:

Note pads	File folders
Pencils	Incoming and outgoing
Pencil sharpener	dividers
Paper clips	Ruler
Letter opener	Erasers
Scissors	Carbon paper
Writing paper	Blotter
Envelopes	Typewriter
Personal stationery	Radio
Post cards	Telephone
Stamps	Telephone book
Rubber bands	Address book
Scotch tape	

Finding a place to work and keeping things in some semblance of order is not too difficult. Here are some ideas you might want to consider:

- A small closet.
- Plan desk in the kitchen.
- Drop-leaf wall desk and file.
- Regular desk (in any convenient room).
- File "desk." Here is an idea you might find both colorful and practical. You can buy two two-drawer filing cabinets, lay a plank over both of them, paint them in bright colors, or cover with one of the new adhesive-backed papers, and *voila!* a desk. This is practical because you will find many things to store in a file drawer. Just as every good office owns a file for important papers, so should a home have one, too. Keeping records is important for obvious reasons.

How to Handle Current Business Papers

You might like to organize three boxes or containers to help keep your house "business papers" in order. Mark them "bills to pay," "paid bills," "miscellaneous." The miscellaneous box might be for letters to answer, school or club activities, etcetera.

Emergency Numbers

Keep a list hanging near the phone for emergency numbers—fire, police, ambulance.

Other additional numbers important to the running of a household are:

DOCTORS	HOUSEHOLD
General practice	Electric Co.
Pediatrician	Gas Co.
Obstetrician	Water Co.
Specialists	Telephone Co.
Dentists	Plumber
Veterinarian	Electrician
Drugstores	Air conditioning
Hospitals	Heating

Nurses (registered and practical)

PERSONAL

Husband's business
Next of kin
Nearest neighbor
Minister or rabbi

MONEY

Bank
Loan society

TRAVEL

Railroads
Airlines
Bus terminal

ATTORNEYS

DOMESTIC

Maid
Agency
Baby sitter
Caterer
Rental supplies
House cleaners
Dry cleaners
Window cleaner

MISCELLANEOUS

Garage
School
Newspaper
Locksmith

TELEPHONE SERVICE

Information
Long distance
Repair
Business office
Weather
Time

(Add your own personal numbers.)

CHAPTER NINE

Household Mechanics
and Minor Repairs

Anyone who has ever lived in a house knows the need for some mechanical knowledge. Even apartment dwellers soon realize that skillful management of all modern conveniences begins with a basic understanding of household utilities. These include electricity, gas, water.

ELECTRICITY

If:

- lights flicker and dim when an appliance is turned on
- heating appliances operate slowly (wasting electricity)
- fuses blow and circuit breakers trip
- radios fade or sound scratchy when an appliance is turned on
- television picture shrinks in size or winces
- there are too few outlets and switches where you need them
- there are "octopus" connections used to connect several appliances at once
- there are long cords strung all around rooms

then your home or apartment could be suffering from inadequate wiring.

ELECTRICITY AND HOME MANAGEMENT

Like water flows through pipes, electricity flows over the wires. Just as water is measured in terms of pressure and gallons, electricity is measured in terms of *amperes, volts,* and *watts. Amperes* measure how much electrical current flows over the wires, or the intensity and rate of the flow. *Volts* are a measure of the pressure behind the current. *Wattage,* the amount of power used, is determined by multiplying the number of amperes by the number of volts.

THE SERVICE ENTRANCE

The maximum amount of electricity which can come into the home at any one time is regulated by the capacity of the *electric service entrance* (the wires connecting the house to the power company's line). If you want more electric power, then the size of your service entrance must be increased.

When electricity enters the home, it passes through the service entrance *wires* to the *meter* and then to the main electric *panel.* In many areas of the country, everything except the meter is the responsibility and property of the homeowner.

Both the *size* and *number* of the wires in the service entrance determines the maximum amount of current which can enter the home at any one time. The larger the wire, the more electricity it can carry all at once. No matter how large the service entrance, the homeowner pays only for the current which actually registers on the meter.

SERVICE ENTRANCE LARGE ENOUGH?

Many people assume that their electrical service entrance is adequate if they have 220 or 240 volts. But actually, the wires have to be big enough to bring in enough amperage or sufficient power for all the equipment you're apt to want, or add, in this era of advanced technology.

Some very old homes, which have never been rewired, may still have obsolete 30-ampere, 120-volt service entrances, which supply, at most, only 3,600 watts. This is barely sufficient for lights and a few small appliances.

Homes built between about 1940 and the mid-1960s may have 60-ampere, 120/240-volt service entrance capacity, which supplies a total of 14,400 watts, and permits installation of one or two 240-volt appliances, such as an electric range and water heater.

Since the mid-60s, 100-ampere, 120/240-volt service has been mandatory for new homes in virtually all communities. This permits simultaneous use of lights and appliances requiring a total of 24,000 watts. If central air conditioning and/or electric heating are installed, 150–200 amperes (36,000–48,000 watts) may be required.

Electrical authorities today recommend 150–200-ampere service for new homes in order to allow a comfortable margin for the addition of future appliances with minimum expense for additional wiring.

You may see voltage requirements stated in the range from 110 to 120 volts (110, 115, or 120); from 220 to 240 (220, 230, or 240). These ranges generally are given to indicate that voltage will vary from 5 to 10 volts in any given situation. In some metropolitan areas, the voltage supplied is 208 volts. Appliances such as ranges, air conditioners, etcetera, should be converted or wired for this voltage before installation.

When installing a new appliance, have a qualified electrician verify that adequate electric service is available for the product, the addition of the appliance will not overload the circuit on which it is used, appliance circuits have been adequately grounded, three-hole receptacles and grounded outlets are properly polarized.

The main panel at the service entrance contains the main switches or main circuit breakers; usually, also, the individual branch circuit fuses or circuit breakers. In case of emergency or when repairs are being made, the main switch or main circuit breakers can be operated to cut off all electricity in the house.

Checking the size of the electric service entrance is often difficult and risky for the homeowner. The most reliable method is to call in an electrical contractor or a utility company representative.

30 AMPERES: OBSOLETE—usually 120 volt (found only in very old houses)

Typical 30 amp. fuse type main switch

Typical 30 amp. combination main breaker and branch circuit panel

Provides a basic electrical capacity of approx. 3,600 watts, adequate for lighting and a few small appliances.

60 AMPERES: OBSOLESCENT—120 and 240 volt (seldom found in new homes)

Typical 60 amp. fuse type combination main switch and branch circuit panel

Typical 60 amp. combination main breaker and branch circuit panel

Provides a basic electrical capacity of 14,500 watts, adequate for lighting, small appliances, electric range and water heater—no additional major equipment.

100–150–200 AMPERES: ADEQUATE—120 and 240 volt (100 amp. minimum required by most communities)

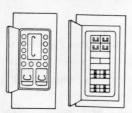

Combination main breaker and branch circuit panels

Panels of these capacities vary widely in appearance. Exact rating is shown on label

100 amp. provides an electrical capacity of 24,000 watts, adequate for lighting and small and major appliances, except electric heating and/or air conditioning.

150-200 amps, provides an electrical capacity of 36,000—48,000 watts adequate for lighting, small and major appliances, electric house heating and/or air conditioning, PLUS extra circuits for future expansion.

How Electricity Is Distributed Through Your Home

The branch circuit, which is "the electrical highway" from the service entrance to lights and outlets, is the key to the distribution of electricity throughout the home. There are three types of circuits generally in use today: *lighting and general purpose circuits, small appliance,* and *special purpose circuits.* Each one is protected by its own fuse or circuit breaker. Those serving convenience outlets located outside the house also should be equipped with a ground-fault interrupter. This is a safety device which provides protection against electrical shock due to small current leakages, or when electrical equipment is being used out of doors.

Convenience Outlets and Switches

Convenience Outlets—Many a new homeowner or apartment dweller finds that there are not enough convenience outlets. This is the lack which produces octopus plugs, multiple extension cords, fixed furniture arrangements, and inability to take advantage of new appliances because no convenience outlet exists for them. There is a remedy: to have an electrical contractor install additional outlets where they will do the most good—*provided, of course, that there is ample circuit capacity available.*

There are certain basic principles for the placement of convenience outlets which will allow you to get the most out of your electrical equipment:

- In living rooms, dining rooms, and bedrooms, and in family rooms or recreation areas, duplex outlets should be placed so that any point along the floor line of an unbroken wall is *within six feet of an outlet.* Additional outlets should be provided in any smaller but usable wall space, two feet or more in length.
- In a breakfast nook or a snack counter, outlets should be located at table or counter level.
- In kitchen work areas and in the workshop there should be outlets for each 4 feet of work space or fraction

435

DISTRIBUTION OF CIRCUITS IN AN AVERAGE-SIZED HOME

TYPES OF CIRCUITS	ARE LOCATED	TO PROVIDE POWER FOR	MINIMUM NUMBER AND SIZE OF CIRCUITS	EACH CIRCUIT PROVIDES CAPACITY OF
General Purpose Circuits	throughout the house	lighting outlets and convenience outlets except those in the kitchen, laundry, and dining areas.	one 15-amp circuit for each 375 square feet (if No. 14 wire is used)	1800 watts
			one 20-amp circuit for each 500 square feet (if No. 12 wire is used)	2400 watts
Small Appliance Circuits	in kitchen, laundry, dining areas	convenience outlets serving: 120-volt small appliances, such as a toaster, coffeemaker, iron, mixer, blender, can opener, casserole warmer, hot tray	two 2-wire 20-amp circuits or one 3-wire 20-amp circuit	2400 watts 4800 watts
Special Purpose Circuits	in kitchen, laundry, utility room	automatic washer one piece of major 120- or 240-volt equipment, such as an electric range, dishwasher-disposer, freezer, water heater, clothes dryer, room air conditioner*	one 2-wire 20-amp circuit, to laundry, plus one for each piece of equipment listed at left	2400 watts size and wattage depends on the ratings of the individual appliance

* 240-volt appliances, such as an electric range, water heater, and clothes dryer, must be each connected to a separate 240-volt circuit. These appliances cannot be installed in homes which are wired only for 120-volt service until the service entrance wires and equipment are changed to provide both 120- and 240-volt service.

436

measuring 1 ft. or more. The kitchen should also have an outlet to serve the refrigerator.

- In the laundry area, there should be at least one convenience outlet.
- Basement and utility rooms require an outlet near the furnace and at least one near the workbench location.
- Bathrooms should have an outlet adjacent to the mirror.
- Hallways require fewer outlets, one for every 10 to 15 feet.
- On porches and terraces, a weatherproof outlet should be placed every 15 feet, and one at front entrance.
- In the attic, one outlet is needed for general use.

Special Purpose Outlets—Not so long ago, special purpose outlets generally were found only in the kitchen, laundry and utility rooms. Today, however, they often are found in general living areas as well. For example:

- In living areas and bedrooms, special purpose outlets are needed for *room air conditioners* and for *electric heating equipment.*
- In bathrooms one or two special purpose outlets are needed for *built-in electric heating equipment* and a *built-in ventilating fan.*
- In the kitchen, the electric range or the built-in oven and cook top each require a special purpose outlet, as does built-in ventilating equipment, the dishwasher and food waste disposer, and the electric wall clock. See Kitchen Planning, Chapter Five.
- Laundry areas need special purpose outlets for the automatic washer, the clothes dryer, a ventilating fan, and the electric water heater, if it is located there. See Planning the Laundry, Chapter Four.
- Basement or utility rooms require special purpose outlets for electrical equipment used in connection with furnace operation, and of course for the water heater if it is not located elsewhere.
- Attics should have a special purpose outlet if a summer cooling fan is located there. Such fans should be switch-controlled from some other location in the house for ease of operation.

If you are planning to build or remodel a home, check with your local electric utility about your wiring requirements. Many companies will offer wiring plans to help you interpret your specific needs to your builder or architect.

FOR THE SAFE USE OF ELECTRICITY

- Avoid overloading the circuits.
- Always keep a bulb in lamp sockets. Failure to do so may result in a shock if a finger accidentally touches it.
- Never touch an electric appliance or cord with wet hands or when standing on a wet floor or when taking a bath or shower. Do not use radios or any electric appliance near the bathtub.
- Avoid the use of long cords which may be tripped over or damaged by vacuum cleaners, heavy furniture or by walking on them.
- Avoid the use of an extension cord unless absolutely necessary. If an extension cord must be used, be sure the wires are large enough to handle the load of the appliance. Most available cords have 18-gauge wire and are suitable only for light loads other than appliances (18-gauge is smaller than 16-gauge). An extension cord should never be used for permanent installation.
- Use caution in replacing fuses. Ordinary household circuits require 15-amp fuses. Using a larger fuse can be dangerous unless the circuit has been designed for larger fuses. If in doubt, consult a qualified electrician and rewire, if necessary.
- A three-prong (grounding) plug is provided on many major appliances for protection against shock hazards and should be plugged directly into a properly grounded three-hole receptacle or outlet. Never remove the third prong and plug it into a two-prong outlet.

Where a two-prong wall outlet is encountered, it should be replaced with a properly grounded three-hole receptacle by a qualified electrician. The third hole is connected to a wire in a separate grounding circuit which assures a safer grounding system. The grounding wire does not normally carry current to operate the appliance, but bypasses electrical current to ground in case of electrical fault.

GAS

Gas is available in two forms: natural or bottled gas, sometimes called LP (liquefied petroleum). Natural gas enters the home through a pipeline, much the same as water does. It is measured in cubic feet and registers on a meter much like electricity.

Bottled gas is used most often in outlying areas where natural gas is not available because there are no gas mains. It is supplied in tanks or cylinders, often two at a time—one for use and one for replacement (automatically by your bottled gas dealer and service agency). It may also come to you through a permanent tank connected to your house by a pipe. The tank may be filled on an automatically regular basis by truck delivery.

EFFICIENT AND SAFE USE OF GAS SERVICE AND APPLIANCES

Your appliances are functioning properly when the flame is pure blue. Yellow in the flame indicates that the air-gas ratio is incorrect. This may be caused by a dirty burner or clogged air supply. Make sure the mixture is in correct balance. Beyond simple cleaning, any adjustments should be made by an authorized serviceman.

FLUE CONNECTIONS

Gas water heaters must be provided with a connection to allow the flue gases to escape to the outside atmosphere. Space heaters are usually flue-connected. Flue connections must comply with the requirements of the municipal authorities having jurisdiction. Check with your local gas company.

GAS APPLIANCES

In general, input to a gas appliance is controlled through the use of a pressure regulator and proper size orifices. Therefore,

439

upon installation call in a qualified serviceman to assure the proper flow of gas.

Gas appliances require air for combustion and clearances shown on the appliance rating plate should be followed.

VENTING

Where the manufacturer's installation instructions call for connection to a vent or chimney, they should be followed carefully. The vent should be free from obstructions and inspected at least yearly by your gas company or an authorized serviceman.

Improperly adjusted gas appliances which are not vented correctly can produce carbon monoxide.

Gas appliances which use an external electrical supply should be grounded and wired as indicated for electric appliances.

RUBBER TUBING

Rubber tubing must *not* be used to connect appliances—it is unsafe and in most areas would violate local codes. Gas appliances must be connected with rigid metal pipe or approved flexible metal connections.

DRAFTS

Avoid drafts and breezes. Keep them away from open gas flames—especially where flames are low—the flame may be blown out. Keep curtains, loose sleeves, dust mops, and anything which will ignite easily away from your gas appliances.

THE FLAME

The gas flame, if properly adjusted, should not leave a black deposit on pots and pans. If you notice such faults, have the burner flame adjusted by an authorized serviceman. The flame should not curl up around cooking utensils. This can be avoided if the pan is the same size as the burner.

Lighting Oven Burners

For manual ignition, open oven door and broiler door. Light match and hold over lighting hole at bottom of oven or at burner through broiler door. Then, turn oven gas valve on full. If oven has heat control, set it above 300°. Make sure burner is fully lighted—then close oven and broiler doors. If burner does not light, turn off the valve, wait a few moments—then repeat the operation.

Note: When gas appliances are not in use, be sure the gas is turned completely off.

Gas Leaks

DO NOT LIGHT A MATCH if you smell gas or if you think there is a gas leak. *OPEN THE WINDOWS.* Then check to see if any burner valves are open or pilots unlighted. If you cannot locate the trouble, *call your gas utility or an authorized serviceman immediately.*

Ask for precautions to be taken until he arrives. All open flames and pilots should be extinguished. Do not hunt for a gas leak yourself.

When Changing from One Type of Gas to Another

In gas ranges and dryers, be sure burner orifices and pressure regulation are compatible. This should be done by a professional.

Gas Lines

Don't flex gas lines. Have loose gas fittings tightened, but not so much that it cracks the joint. If flexible tubing is used, it is intended to be flexed only when unit is moved. When you do, shut off the gas.

441

FUEL AND HEATING SYSTEMS

You will be confronted with many types of house heating systems. In most modern homes, these systems are automatic, though there may be some older homes which will require the burdensome task of "minding the furnace." Sizes of automatic heating plants may vary from the smallest counter-height kitchen units to those the size of a refrigerator to larger "plants," remotely installed in another section of the house.

Suffice it to say here, that whether your system is fueled by coal, oil, gas, or electricity, or whether it is forced air, radiant, hot water, or steam heating, each system requires a little different care.

Regardless of the fuel, here are some general rules to follow to help you achieve the best performance from the system you have.

- Follow specific instructions for your own heating system. If you don't have an operating manual, try to get one.
- Weatherstrip all doors, caulk cracks around windows and doors.
- Use storm windows and storm doors.
- Check your insulation to make sure there can be no heat loss.
- Be sure fireplace damper is closed when not in use.
- Don't block radiators or registers with furniture or draperies. Draperies and curtains should not touch baseboard heating vents or hinder free movement of air. There should be a clearance of 2 to 6 inches between draperies and vents.
- Try to keep daytime temperature consistent. This will help to conserve fuel.
- Be sure your thermostat is in the right location—on an inside wall, away from doors, windows.
- Check local utility.
- Don't leave windows or doors open unnecessarily during cold weather.
- Keep systems clean and in good repair. Have motors used for operating oil burners, pumps, blowers inspected

and serviced before each season's use, or at the end of the season. You may need replacement of new brushes or belts or removal of dust accumulation in older systems. Have heating system cleaned by a qualified serviceman. Check controls, flames, firepots, units, or burners. Change or clean all filters as recommended.

- If you want to cover a radiator decoratively, that in itself will cut down some heating efficiency. Design it to incorporate as much open space as possible.
- If you have your radiator painted, use as thin a coat as possible. Thick coats can insulate the heat.
- Open air valves on hot-water radiators occasionally to prevent "air lock." After hissing sound stops and water begins to drip slightly, close the valve.

FOR GAS HEATING SYSTEMS

It's generally best to leave the pilot light on through the summer to prevent excess moisture buildup. The gentle updraft in the chimney created by the pilot will also help keep basements dry and pleasant during humid summer weather. If pilot lights go out, automatic furnaces have an automatic 100 percent cut-off system. Follow relighting instructions exactly. When it is necessary on a manual system to relight the pilot, air out the gas chamber first, and open any nearby windows. This is to air out any gas accumulation in the chambers. If pilot keeps going out, call a serviceman.

The efficient operation of the furnace depends upon the proper balance of air and gas. If flame tips are yellow, then there is too little air; if flame jumps and dances above the burner, then there is too much air. Have an authorized serviceman make air adjustments.

FOR OIL HEATING SYSTEMS

To determine if your system is operating properly, check the flame. It is usually a yellow-orange and burns evenly. An uneven flame is usually caused from a clogged nozzle. If the flame is smoky, there is generally too little air. If flues pipes or heater leak this is what causes carbon deposits on walls and home fur-

443

nishings. If you need to have the burners adjusted, if you smell oil at all, if your unit stops, or if it does not seem to operate properly, call your serviceman. Do not attempt self-adjustment. Never stand near or in front of the furnace door when starting the burner.

FOR COAL FURNACE SYSTEMS

Remove the ashes daily. A buildup will affect the proper operation of the draft system, and cause possible damage to the grates. Always make sure there is a deep fire-bed. This means you will not have to add coal as often. Adjust the dampers to control how fast the coal will burn.

If the fire is too bright, you may be wasting coal. It is a good idea to keep a small fire in the center of the firepot, with ashes around the edges. Never lift ashes into the flames. That is what causes "clinkers." Always keep a small area of burning coal uncovered enough to burn off gases and ignite additional coal. Let the fire burn off gases when you add coal and before closing dampers at night. This will prevent any escape of dangerous carbon monoxide. Avoid overbanking fires at night. It will take longer to bring up heat in the morning. You will need to add more coal.

FOR ELECTRICAL HEATING

Follow the good general rules listed in the earlier section on electricty. If you have electric baseboard or ceiling cable heating, with individual room thermostats you can help keep energy costs down by lowering the temperature in unused rooms and keeping the temperature lower in areas such as bedrooms, etcetera. Check, also, the general rules listed above.

WATER SYSTEMS

A homemaker has two chief concerns with the water she uses every day. Is it *adequate* and is it *properly conditioned?* If there is not enough water at the times when we need it, managing the household will fall short on efficiency. It should be soft, pure and without minerals to play its role in housekeeping properly.

The Condition of Your Water

When you live in a large metropolitan area or a large community, there is not much you can do personally about the water before it is plumbed into the house except as a good citizen to speak up on all public issues that will improve the water supply. *Your control* begins with the water you bring indoors through your home plumbing system.

Soft or softened water makes housekeeping infinitely easier. (See Water, Chapter Four.) Your local water-softening appliance dealer can make an analysis of your water supply.

An unsightly ring around the tub after each bath, water spots on bathroom fixtures and wall tiles, spots and streaks on dishes and glassware. These could be signs that the water you are using is too hard.

To Soften Your Water

You can soften your water for each task performed, as we said earlier, when you use a *packaged water softener* except for showers and similar isolated household activities. And *detergents* are also formulated to help combat the hardness problem, as well. Or you can use a water-softening appliance.

Water-Softening Appliances

If you want to assure yourself of a continuous supply of soft water, you might consider installing an automatic mechanical water softener.

Home water-softening equipment contains ion exchange resins which have a definite capacity for removing hardness. When they reach their saturation point, these resins are recharged with salt obtainable from your water-softener dealer. The frequency with which this is done depends on the hardness of the water, hard-

445

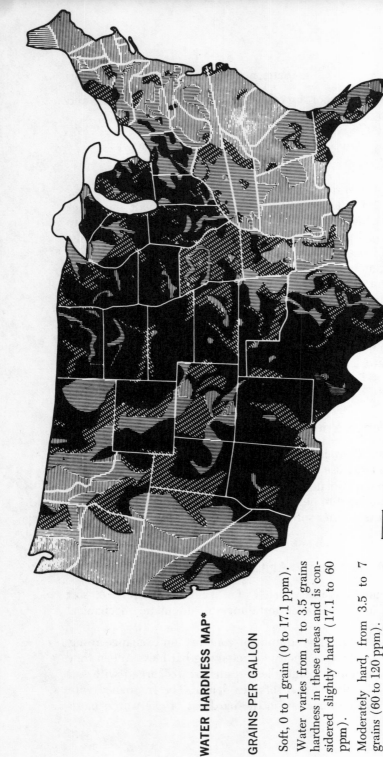

WATER HARDNESS MAP*

GRAINS PER GALLON

Soft, 0 to 1 grain (0 to 17.1 ppm).

Water varies from 1 to 3.5 grains hardness in these areas and is considered slightly hard (17.1 to 60 ppm).

Moderately hard, from 3.5 to 7 grains (60 to 120 ppm).

Hard water in these areas ranges from 7 to 10.5 grains hardness (120 to 180 ppm).

Very hard, over 10.5 grains (180 ppm). Such water causes serious housekeeping problems.

Slightly hard ½–3½

Moderately hard 3½–7

Hard 7–12

Very hard 12–20 plus

* This map is a general guide to hard-water areas. Water hardness is measured in grains per gallon or parts per million (milligrams per liter). Courtesy Culligan Water Institute.

ness-removing ability of the tank and the amount of water that is used. Recharging usually occurs automatically.

For best results, it is advisable to soften both hot and cold supplies. If hot water only is softened, the soft-water benefits are somewhat reduced since cold water is usually added to hot for most household tasks. Some find it economical to soften all water except that used in toilets. A water softener should also bypass the outdoor supply used for sprinkling and gardening. It should be installed near the water service entrance to the house.

There are three different ways you can have a water softener in your home:

- Buy one of your own.
- Rent one.
- Subscribe to a portable softening appliance service in which the dealer periodically will exchange an exhausted unit for a fresh one.

WATER HEATERS

Water that is *hot* enough and in large enough supply is essential to good housekeeping. Dishwashing and laundering results can be seriously affected by the lack of hot enough water. See dishwashing problems, Chapter Five. See laundering problems, Chapter Four.

You may buy either gas or electric models. Your choice may depend upon the cost of the fuel or the fuel you have available. It might be wise to check whether there is an "off peak" electric rate available. You will need 240 volts for an electric water heater. Check for certification of gas models.

There are two types of water heaters: The *quick-recovery* and the *standard storage type*. They are basically the same in construction and operation, except that the heating capacity of quick-recovery water heaters is greater. This means that, with extra heating facilities, water is heated more quickly. Often a smaller capacity quick-recovery heater can be selected to serve the same needs as the larger storage type.

Water heaters vary in capacity from 30 gallons to 100 gallons. There seems to be no simple way to determine the hot-water needs of a family, as size and habits vary. Your best rule of

447

thumb is to estimate needs generously, taking into account present requirements and future—larger family, structural additions to your home, etcetera.

In purchasing a new heater, check these buying considerations:

- What are your fuel requirements? gas? electric?
- Is the capacity large enough to give you a *constant* supply of hot water to meet all your needs? bathing? laundry? dishwashing?
- Would it be more efficient to buy a smaller capacity quick-recovery type or a larger standard storage type? Will it fit the allotted space?
- Have you estimated future needs for hot water as family grows and habits change?

For proper use and care:
- Locate the water heater as close to the hot-water outlets as possible.
- Locate the gas water heater as close as possible to a vertical vent for combustion products and good air circulation.
- Keep the thermostat set between 140° and 160° F.
- If you keep running out of hot water, check to see if your water heater capacity is too small.
- Check dripping faucets. A constant drip could cause a waste of 300 gallons a month!
- Make sure all water pipes are well insulated. Escaping heat makes your heater run more than necessary, increases fuel and water bills.

A drain valve is located at the lowest point in the tank so that you can drain accumulated mineral deposits when necessary, if you live in a hard-water area. They do not actually harm the tank or decrease the heating efficiency, but over a long period of time they may create a slight reduction in the capacity of the water heater.

WATER PURIFIERS

Water purification should be adequately maintained by your local water department, long before it reaches you, to provide a safe drinking supply. However, if you do want some control of taste, palatability, and odor of your own water supply, investigate the advisability and performance of home water purifiers. Though water conditioner people are just beginning to make a mere dent in the progress of home water purifiers, you will currently find several on the market. Their operation is based upon filtration. Some use charcoal and one type on the market works on a principle similar to human cells to reject contaminants. Instead of a cell wall, this uses a thin plastic membrane, like ordinary plastic wrap, as the barrier. The process is really reverse osmosis, if you remember your chemistry lessons well. Installation may be under a standard kitchen wall cabinet, wet bar, in the utility room or on any wall where a water line is available; requires no electrical connection; works on water pressure alone; processes 3 to 5 gallons of water a day and is excellent for use in steam irons, photo developing and printing, with household plants and for pets, tropical fish and humans! We only mention this here and *now* to indicate that progress is being made toward home water purification. No doubt changes are taking place this very minute.

SEPTIC TANKS AND WASTE DISPOSAL

A septic tank provides a storage chamber where sewage is digested by bacterial action. About 98 percent of the matter which goes into a tank is digested, 2 percent remaining in the form of sludge which settles to the bottom; and clear water is carried out into the filter bed or drain tile.

Most food wastes are:
- From 87 percent to 98 percent water.
- Easily digested.
- Fermented and spoil with a strong bacterial action.
- About 40 percent of the total sewage wastes in a private home.

Note: Excessive use of detergents, excessive grease, insufficient food and body wastes to maintain tank action, permitting excessive amounts of water, detergents, insoluble wastes, drain solvents, etcetera, to enter tank may all be detrimental to septic tank action.

449

A garbage disposer may be used in homes with septic tanks. See section on Garbage Disposers, Chapter Five, for source to determine recommended sizes of septic tanks.

INDOOR ENVIRONMENT

WHAT MAKES A COMFORTABLE HOME?

In addition to the familiar utilities of electricity, gas and water, we are becoming increasingly aware of the need to understand something of the physical nature of indoor environment—that is to say, the *comfort* of our personal surroundings.

Indoor environment is about the same as outdoor environment inasmuch as we are concerned with many of the same factors, such as:

- Heat ⎤
- Cold ⎦ Temperature
- Humidity
- Air movement
- Cleanliness of the atmosphere—dust, smog, fumes

And to varying degrees all these factors contribute to a person's well-being, comfort, and to the care and maintenance of the home itself.

HOW COMFORTABLE IS COMFORTABLE?

You are said to be *comfortable* when the heat loss and heat gain of the body are well balanced. If we are aware of the temperature—if we are too hot or too cold—we are not comfortable. If the air moves too fast or too slowly we feel a draft or we feel stuffy. If the air is too humid or too dry, we feel "clammy" or dry. Sound familiar? Some of the environmental factors mentioned above that directly affect our comfort are:

- Temperature   • Air Motion   • Humidity
- Cleanliness   • Odor   • Noise

TEMPERATURE

Let's look at some of the more familiar temperatures. We are all acquainted with a common thermometer which begins at 0° and goes up to 212°.

$$
\begin{array}{ll}
212° & \text{water boils} \\
\left.\begin{array}{l} 75° \\ 65° \end{array}\right\} & \text{comfort zone} \\
32° & \text{water freezes} \\
0° &
\end{array}
$$

On our common thermometer, the kind we're apt to find in any home, water freezes at 32° F. and boils at 212°. The comfort zone on an average thermometer is pretty narrowly defined at 75°. The indoor environment that we're controlling at 75° F. is against about 0° F. in the winter and 100° F. in the summer. So you see, temperature is a measure of the *presence of heat*, not a *measure of cold*. That's important to know, because we don't create cold, we only remove heat. Most people are comfortable in room temperatures at between 65°and 70° F. in the summer and 70° to 80° F. in the winter—provided the humidity is in proper balance. Heat, then, is added or subtracted from the home. The familiar measure of heat we all know is a BTU (British thermal unit). Most heating and cooling appliances are rated in BTU's per hour. One BTU is the amount of heat it takes to raise one pound of water one degree F. (about as much heat as that given off by one wooden kitchen match burning to ashes). Actually a furnace adds BTU's to the room atmosphere, while an air conditioner removes BTU's from the room.

One of the greatest indoor environmental controls ever developed is the air conditioner.

Room Air Conditioners

As we said, an air conditioner doesn't create cold, it just removes the heat that is in the room. The next time you go by an air conditioner on the outside put your hand on the louvers.

451

They'll be hot, and that heat you feel is actually the BTU's being removed from the room.

The four functions of a room air conditioner are to *cool, dehumidify, clean,* and *circulate* the air. When you turn the conditioner on, a fan or blower system draws in the warm, moist room air. The air goes through a filter which removes the dust, lint and other contaminants. It next passes over a cold surface which cools and dries it; then it is returned to the room. A thermostat maintains the inside temperature at the desired level. And grilles or air directors direct the flow of conditioned air so it will circulate without causing drafts.

Capacity—True comfort comes from proper capacity—neither too high nor too low. The capacity you choose is your most important decision. It is measured in British thermal units (BTU's). An air conditioner rated at 5000 BTU/hr. will remove 5000 British thermal units of heat from an area in one hour. Always check for the certification seal indicating the BTU/hr. rating for cooling capacity. This means the cooling capacity rating has been verified through a testing laboratory and is certified accurate.

The following are only very general estimates to give you an idea of what the various BTU capacities mean to you.

- A 4000 to 8000 BTU/hr. capacity will cool a small to medium, relatively inactive room.
- A 7000 to 15,000 BTU/hr. capacity will cool a large, active room or two closely related rooms.
- A 9000 to 24,000 BTU/hr. capacity will cool two, three, or even four rooms if they are situated so that the air can flow from one to another.
- A 25,000 to 34,000 BTU/hr. capacity may be able to cool a six-room house. But fans will be needed to help circulate the air through all the rooms, and the unit should be where one room does not get the brunt of the cooling.

Equally important in determining needed capacity are: the room exposure, insulation, type of wall, ceiling, roof, floor construction, number of occupants, exterior climate, and number of windows. Most dealers have charts that combine all this information to arrive at the proper model and capacity. If you would like a chart to help you figure it out yourself, write to Association of Home Appliance Manufacturers, 20 North Wacker Drive, Chicago, Illinois 60606, for their Cooling Load Estimate form. Fill it out and take it to the dealer.

Efficiency—After determining the size unit needed, consider efficiency. An efficient room air conditioner uses less electricity so costs less to operate. To determine efficiency, engineers have established a room air conditioner Energy Efficiency Ratio (EER). It is computed by dividing BTU/hr. by the watts of power used. EER is expressed in BTU/hr. per watt. Thus a unit with an EER of 8.8 is more efficient than one of 6.3, even though both have the same cooling capacity. The higher the EER of similar-sized models, the more efficient the electrical consumption and the lower the operating cost.

Styles—Most models are made for installation in a double-hung window; others for casement windows. Through-the-wall models are installed in an opening made through the wall. Some models have a reverse cycle setting and will *heat* as well as *cool*.

Wiring Requirements—Room air conditioners operate on 120-, 240- or 208-volt alternating current. You may be able to simply "plug in" your unit to a 120-volt, 15-ampere household circuit. This can be done, however, only if two requirements are met. They are: (1) the model must be designed to operate on 115 volts and 7½ or less amps; (2) the lamps and appliances already connected to that circuit, and likely to be in use at the same time as the air conditioner, must not exceed 860 watts in total rating.

Many local electrical codes require a separate, single-outlet circuit for 120-volt models using more than 7½ amps. In a few cities the code prohibits using a room air conditioner with any 120-volt circuit. To meet this requirement some models of relatively small capacity may be made for use with a 240-volt electrical supply. Check with your dealer.

For 240- or 208-volt room air conditioners, special wiring must be installed—unless, of course, the house or apartment already has a 240- or 208-volt circuit to serve the location where the air conditioner is to be installed.

Consult your electrician, public utility, or other qualified source to determine what additional wiring, if any, will be needed. Also what installation requirements are necessary.

For proper use and care:

- Correct location is very important—consider furniture arrangement and window placement.
- Wash filter periodically in warm sudsy water using a mild detergent. Rinse and wipe or shake dry. Or change it periodically according to instructions in your use and care manual.
- To avoid "freeze-up" at night when temperature drops, raise thermostat to middle setting and on medium or high fan speed.
- On hottest days, turn unit on a few hours earlier before temperature rises, or let it run continuously.
- Turn the unit off if fan motor fails to operate.
- Wait for at least two minutes before restarting after the unit or compressor has been shut off or the temperature control has been changed. Quick restarts may blow fuses.
- Do not attempt do-it-yourself installation unless the manufacturer specifically so instructs or provides a kit. Then carefully read the instructions.

Central Air Conditioning

An increasingly popular method for cooling newer houses is central air conditioning. This is particularly true where summers are severe or where year-round hot weather is a problem. In a central system, best installed when a house is being built, a centrally located unit cools and distributes cooled air to all rooms throughout the house, in much the same way as a heating system. If you have such a system or are contemplating one, be sure to follow specific use and care instructions for your particular brand.

HUMIDITY

Humidity is simply the amount of moisture present in the air. When you hear the term "relative humidity," that means that the air at any particular temperature has all the water it can hold. When the moisture level reaches its saturation point (or it is at 100 percent relative humidity), you may find that windows sweat, walls are moist, you feel "clammy" and perspire. When you have 100 percent relative humidity outdoors, you can be sure it is raining. If you have *too much moisture* indoors, you can reduce it as we said before with an air conditioner (which gives you a balanced control of air) or with a *dehumidifier.*

Dehumidifiers

This is a small portable appliance that weighs about 45 pounds. It is used primarily to protect your house and furnishings from warped wood, dampness, rust, and mildew.

Mildew is a real pest created from trapped or prolonged moisture. It affects leather, paper, wood, and natural fibers of cotton, linen, wool, and silk. It leaves stains and could cause complete decay of the material it attacks. For more about it, see Index.

The average portable dehumidifier can remove from 10 to 25 pints of water every 24 hours. (An air conditioner may remove from 100 to 200 pints every 24 hours.) Look for an automatic humidistat control so it will not run all the time.

In purchasing a dehumidifier, determine what areas of your home need dehumidification. Such non-air-conditioned or damp areas as basements, recreation rooms, storage areas, and vacation cottages usually require dehumidification. What water removal capacity is required? How large an area is to be dehumidified? What are the climatic conditions? Insulation and building construction? What method of water disposal do you prefer—automatic drain system? hose drain connection? collection pan?

Look for such features as an automatic overflow turn-off switch or signal light, casters for easy mobility, a humidistat, quiet operation, an easy-to-clean grille, condenser coil and pan, the certification seal which certifies water removal capacity at standard rating conditions.

For the best use and care locate the unit in an area closed to outdoor air and where air flow in and out of the unit is unimpeded and the dehumidified air can freely circulate within the room. Empty the manual drain pan regularly to avoid overflow. Do not place unit on damp floor areas or where water is likely to accumulate. Operate on a level surface for proper function of drainage system. Use as needed. Begin use around April up until the winter heating season begins, though some areas, depending upon geographical location, will require year-round use. You may need it whenever the heating system is not used.

To remove moisture without a dehumidifier, you may turn on the furnace in the summer, or use a space heater, preferably an electric one, which can be moved from room to room. If closets are too damp, keep a light bulb burning at all times. There may be certain chemicals available to control moisture. Ask your hardware dealer about them.

Humidifiers

If your indoor air is too dry, particularly in the winter months, you will realize that warm air has a greater capacity for holding moisture than cold air, which releases it. That's why, especially during the winter months, furniture may dry out and crack, sparks fly as you walk across the carpet, and your nose and throat feel dry. Or you may give someone a "shock" when you touch them. One antidote is to add moisture to the air with a *humidifier.*

When purchasing a humidifier, consider these questions:

What size do you need? What is the size of the area to be humidified? The desired relative humidity? The building's construction? The exterior climatic conditions? Which is more suitable—a self-contained console or table-top model?

Look for such features as an automatic control to prevent unit from operating when empty, a signal light to indicate low-water level, easily removed tank for cleaning, louvers directing air flow, the certification seal certifying capacity in terms of output of gallons per day at stated conditions.

For the best use and care manually fill reservoir every few days or as needed to proper level; clean water reservoirs frequently to guard against buildup of bacteria (it is wise to use a bacteriostatic agent which is sometimes available for purchase through a manufacturer); clean standing pad monthly—possibly replace it yearly; make certain humidistat is set for proper humidity level by watching for visible condensation. In hard-water areas, all parts that contact water should be of a noncorroding material. Connect to a 120-volt circuit. Remove water when not in use.

If you do not have a humidifier, it is possible to add moisture to the air by using a vaporizer, boiling water in an electric tea-kettle, or by setting a container of water on a heat source, such as a radiator.

CLEAN AIR

How Clean Is It in Your Indoors?

The cleanliness of air contributes greatly to the comfort of those who have to breathe it and to people who have to clean house. Many of us are bothered by the smog created from industrial facilities, traffic and automobiles, pollen, dust, and the atmosphere in general. And while much is being done to improve the outdoor pollution problem, there is not too much we can do about it individually, except to support the measures effected to correct it as soon as possible. But we certainly can do something about the control of indoor smog, soot, dust and other irritants. We can do something about controlling the soot and grease deposits on walls, discoloration of fabrics, and the air we breathe.

Air Filters

The secret to clean indoor air is filtering. All forced-air heating and cooling systems have filters which do a fairly good job on large particles, lint, and pollen. Air conditioners are particularly good in controlling pollen for allergy sufferers. A good filter should be able to remove the most minute particles from the air. Filters may consist of simple air strainers made of fibrous materials, or, as is becoming more and more common, consist of highly sophisticated electronic air cleaners which attract particles of dust through electronic means.

Electronic Air Cleaners—They come in portable units for one or two rooms or in a large size which can be connected to a furnace or central air-conditioning system. So far, they seem to be one of the best methods of consistently removing small particles from the air, through an electric charge that traps foreign particles. Regardless of the type you might use, it is, of course, important that you keep your windows closed. Obviously, then, you will need air conditioning during summer months.

457

Air Purifiers—These are portable units which contain one or more filters and a fan to draw room air through them, then out again into the room. They are not to be confused with the electronic type. See above. They can do a pretty good job of cleaning the air if the filters are good and if there is enough air capacity. As a matter of fact, in addition to a filter, top performance from any air cleaner (electronic or not), depends upon how well it handles the flow of air. Check to see how many cubic feet of air per minute it moves in relation to the size of room.

> *Caution: Air purifiers are not:*
> - Germ killers.
> - Do not cure depression and lift your mood.
> - Do not necessarily kill odors. In order to come close to any odor control an air purifier must contain an activated-carbon filter in addition to regular filters, despite any claims made to the contrary.

Ventilating Hoods and Fans

A ventilating hood and fan installed over the kitchen range to exhaust cooking fumes to the outdoors is a must if you want to control the cleanliness of kitchen air. It should be deep enough to cover all or most of your cooking surface and go no more than 26 inches above the surface. Thirty inches is maximum. It should contain a good grease filter and a good fan. The filter should be at least a half-inch thick, and removable for easy cleaning. A good ventilating hood and fan installed properly should blow out up to 85 percent of all cooking fumes with an air removal capacity of at least 300 c.f.m.

If you cannot install a hood, then consider an exhaust fan installed in the wall behind the range, installed from one to two feet above the cooking surface, or in the ceiling above. The fan should have an air removal capacity of at least 300 cubic feet per minute (c.f.m.), for an average-sized kitchen.

If you cannot duct or exhaust fumes to the outside, or if your range is too far from an exterior wall, then consider a *ductless hood and fan*. While this is not as satisfactory as those which exhaust to the outdoors, it is an effective substitute, and better than none at all. They contain both regular and charcoal filters which clean the air before it is discharged and recirculated back into the room. This type of unit removes smoke, grease, and odor, but not moisture and heat.

Bathroom fans can do an excellent job of removing excess moisture and providing necessary ventilation. They should have an airflow capacity of at least 100 c.f.m.

How to Control Household Odor

It is an amazing thing, but sometimes the cleanest houses inadvertently have the most unpleasant odors. And it is the people who live there who notice it the least. That familiar television commercial referred to it as "housitosis"—and it was just about on target. You probably could recognize the most familiar unpleasant ones: the lingering headiness of stale smoke; tell-tale reminders of last night's supper—cabbage, garlic, fish, burned roast; closet "smog"; unaired hampers.

As a pleasant contrast, think of the homes you've walked into that smell like fresh wax, clean sheets, perking coffee, and home-made bread. Those homes have the very breath of springtime or the exhilaration you feel after the smell of new-mown hay.

Though we have said these things before in different sections throughout this book, here, because they bear repeating, are a few tips to make your house smell fresh and clean:

- Air out your rooms as often as possible.
- Air out clothes, closets, bedding frequently.
- Follow all the good cleaning techniques and don't forget to clean the cleaning equipment, dust cloths, *sponges*, mops.
- Be sure hampers, garbage cans and waste containers are given special attention; clean and spray occasionally with a disinfectant or sanitizer.
- Install a ventilating fan and hood in the kitchen to vent or absorb cooking odors. Be careful not to burn foods.
- Cull potato, onion, and apple storage bins for rotten culprits.
- Wipe ovens clean after each use.
- Use sanitizers, especially on floors and in hidden corners.

459

- Keep spray deodorizers in strategic areas—bathrooms, kitchens, baby's room.
- Cut down on household humidity and moisture which will control mildew, a chief cause of odor.
- Use scented sachets in closets and drawers.
- Hang deodorizers in garbage cans and in bathrooms. Use special tank deodorizers in toilet bowls.
- Investigate the uses of air cleaners or air purifiers that contain activated carbon filters.
- Burn candles and incense to absorb unpleasant cooking odors.
- Place a bowl of ammonia and water (2 tablespoons ammonia to 1 cup water) in a room filled with smoke.
- Keep a bowl of dried rose petals and other garden flowers on a hall table.
- Hang fresh herbs such as sage, rosemary, thyme in the kitchen to dry.
- Keep a vase of dried eucalyptus in the living room.
- Burn candles during cocktail parties to clear out smoke-filled rooms. (Be sure they are well secured in candle holders and cannot tip over or drip.)

How to Control Noise

If you simply want to cut down on everyday noise, keep in mind that there are two primary sources of noise—the *airborne* sounds and those that result from *impact.* When someone talks loudly, the sound is airborne; if they walk heavily or throw something on the floor, that is an impact sound.

- Install carpeting with padding or resilient flooring underneath to avoid impact sounds.
- Apply acoustical materials to ceilings, walls, and floors to help reduce airborne sounds. All these factors can help reduce the noise level by 50 percent.

And don't forget:
- Tighten all loose nuts, bolts and screws that might rattle and squeak.

If you are building, begin with preventive medicine:

- Build sound conditioning into the house in the first place.
- Site the house so the bedrooms lie farthest from the street.
- Stagger inside doors so that sound won't flow in a direct line.
- Put closets, storage walls, and fireplaces between rooms to act as sound absorbers.
- Use insulation around pipes and ducts.
- Make sure heavy-duty appliances are cushioned and are provided with sound-deadening features.
- Isolate utility rooms and areas where noise may be concentrated.
- Use acoustical materials whenever you can—on ceilings, walls.

Great strides are being made by manufacturers of home appliances to make them quiet in all areas of their operation.

As we indicated at the beginning of the chapter, and as you no doubt have begun to realize as you leafed through the chapter, the skillful management of any household indeed depends upon some understanding of the utilities that make it run.

Almost as important is acquiring some experience, limited as it may be, in making simple household repairs.

THE HOME WORKSHOP

One young man, telling us how unhandy he is around the house, said, "Let something go wrong, and I am all thumbs." Moreover, his wife can't fix anything either. Between them they're in a tight spot if the sink is suddenly clogged or if a fuse blows. What they need are a few simple directions on how to repair the minor mishaps that occur around the house with some regularity.

And occur they will! The very fact that most everything around us in a home is either mechanical, breakable, or damageable means that eventually we are going to have to cope with breakdowns, cracks, leaks, drips, tears, scratches, stains, and almost anything else you can think of, know-how or not. When there

461

are emergencies we usually have to cope immediately—or call in an expert. Usually you can't reach them right away and when you do it can be a fairly expensive job. So, unless it's something you can't or shouldn't do without some professional expertise, it can be a source of pride and an economic security to learn a few do-it-yourself repairs and simple workshop techniques.

TOOLS

A few good and simple tools are necessary and they can be contained very nicely in one good family-sized tool box.

- A *hammer*—make sure it is well balanced. The claw type is your best choice as it is used for general purposes. It drives and pulls out nails with the least damage.
- *Pliers*—buy the slip-joint type which have an adjustable two-position pivot for gripping various size objects.
- *Screwdrivers*—a standard (about 7 inches) type to fit most screws has a blade wider than the shaft. A Phillips type to fit cross hole screws instead of the slot type. You can buy them in sets of four sizes.
- *Steel tape ruler*—for measuring.
- *Awl*—a hand tool for making holes (resembles a short ice pick).
- *Wrench*—for loosening or tightening bolts.

Experienced handymen tell us that if you have the tools above as well as an assortment of nails, screws, nuts and bolts, faucet and hose washers, sandpaper, glue, machine oil, wire, friction tape, rubber tape, fuses, turpentine, putty for sealing, spackle to repair plaster cracks, plastic wood to repair holes and cracks in woodwork, etcetera, that you should be pretty well outfitted for more than just minor repairs and household tinkering.

If you want to do a more complete stocking job, add the following:

- *Hand drill*—for making small holes in wood, metal, and plastic.
- *Bit brace*—buy the one with a conventional auger bit. This is excellent for making larger holes in wood and average-sized ones in metal.

- *Crosscut saw*—for sawing wood cross-grain. If you are planning to build shelves of any kind, this is a necessity.
- *Level*—to make sure planes are level and even.
- *Power tools*—if you plan on becoming an accomplished handyman, go to your nearest hardware store or carpenter shop and have a good session on the tricks of using power tools. Most likely they will recommend that you begin your collection with a simple power drill which not only drills holes, but will handle sanding jobs as well.

APPLIANCE REPAIRS

If you have any problems with household appliances, both large and small, check first with your instruction book to detect possible causes. *Do not attempt to repair other than the most minor of ailments, such as changing a fuse or repairing a cord.* It is important that they be properly serviced for your own safety and to protect your guarantee if the product is still in warranty. However, before you call your serviceman, check the following points:

- Check the plug. Is the appliance plugged in? Is it turned on?
- Has a fuse blown out?
- Are the prongs of the plug loose? Stretch to tighten.
- Check the outlet. Is it operative?

For some specific appliance problems, check individual appliances. See Index.

DOORS

Swelling—This usually happens in humid, damp weather; it is also an indication that room is too humid. (See preceding sections on dehumidifiers and air-conditioning systems.) Locate area and rub it with wax or soap. This may not work if swelling is excessive. If not, sandpaper area, or shave off some wood with a planing device. Be careful not to sand or plane too much since swelling decreases as humidity decreases. You may end up with a very loose door.

Note: Sticking or binding are also common problems caused by expansion of wood in damp weather or softening of paint on hot days or with the sagging of the door as a new house settles.

Dragging or Binding at Bottom—Sometimes with installation of wall-to-wall carpeting or floor tiles, the door will not open or close easily. Smooth bottom surface by swinging it back and forth over a strip of coarse sandpaper.

Rattling or Sagging—May be due to loose hinges. If the space between latch and framework is wider at one end than the other the hinge probably needs to be tightened. Try removing the screws one by one and repair either with plastic wood or wood filler in each hole before returning screws. Or replace present screws with longer ones.

Squeaky Doors—Apply a few drops of all-purpose oil on top of the hinge and move the door back and forth, until the squeak disappears.

Loose Doorknobs—Check to be sure all screws are tightened. If this doesn't do the trick, chances are you need new screws, probably slightly longer than the present ones with a blunt end. If this doesn't help, the shaft should be changed.

ELECTRICAL REPAIRS

HOW TO CHANGE A FUSE

Every homeowner needs to know how to change a fuse or reset a circuit breaker. Either one is a simple and completely safe job if you know how.

- First disconnect lamps and appliances in use when circuit went out.
- Open main switch or pull out section of panel labeled "main" in the service entrance, to cut off current while working at the branch circuit box.

- Identify the blown fuse—when a fuse blows, the transparent section becomes cloudy or blackened.
- Replace the blown fuse with a new one of proper size. The small sizes screw in and out just like light bulbs. Make sure your hands are dry; stand on a dry board or rubber pad, if possible. If the blown fuse is a cartridge type, located in the pull-out section, it can be removed and replaced by hand pressure.
- Close the main switch, or replace pull-out section, to restore service. Throw away the blown fuse.

Important note: The fuse contains a metal link which melts and cuts off electricity from the branch circuit before the circuit wires become overheated from an overload or a short circuit. Electricity will remain "off" in that circuit until the cause of the difficulty has been removed, and the fuse replaced.

The new fuse must be the correct size. A larger size eliminates the protection provided by the correct size. Fuses *should* blow, when an overload causes them to do so. That is the signal that something is wrong. When an *oversized* fuse is used, permanent damage to the circuit wires within the walls, ceilings, and floors may result. *This could cause a fire.* Never put a penny behind a fuse. This only eliminates your protection devices. There is nothing to "blow"!

Kinds of Fuses

- Screw-in fuses come in sizes from 15 to 30 amperes. Most home circuits which use No. 14 wire should be protected by the 15-ampere size. If wires are heavier than usual, 20-ampere fuses will be safe.
- Nontamperable fuses are screw-in fuses, but the threads differ in size to prevent replacement by the wrong size fuse.
- Cartridge fuses are used for main lines and for special heavy-duty circuits.
- Time-delay fuses will not blow during the temporary overload placed on circuits by motor-starting, yet they will guard against a sustained overload.
- Circuit breakers look like small switches.

HOW TO RESET A CIRCUIT BREAKER

- Disconnect lamps and appliances in use when circuit went out.
- Return handle to "on" position.

Important note: The circuit breaker performs exactly the same function as the fuse, but in a slightly different way. When an overload or a short circuit occurs in the branch circuit, the circuit breaker automatically trips open. No electricity will flow over that circuit until you have reset the circuit breaker, *after removing the cause of the difficulty.*

WHAT CAUSES SHORT CIRCUITS AND HOW YOU CAN PREVENT THEM

A defective appliance or cord can create a short circuit which also might cause fuses to blow or circuit breakers to trip open. It is wise to:

- Check all portable lamps and other electrical equipment for possible defects in the equipment itself and for frayed or broken cords.
- See section on appliance safety.
  For more on the home wiring system, see *Electricity* in Index

HOW TO REPLACE A BROKEN PLUG

- Disconnect the lamp or appliance and separate the plug from the wires by removing the screws that hold them in place with a screwdriver.
- Locate the worn area and cut the cord off at that point with a pair of heavy scissors.
- If the cord has a molded rubber covering, make a small cut in the end of the cord, between the two wires, then pull them apart about 2 inches.

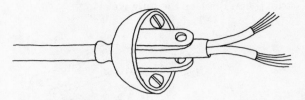

- Remove the insulation from each of the two exposed sets of wires for about ¾″ from the end. Make sure the wires are not cut or broken so that all of the original strands are exposed for the new connection.

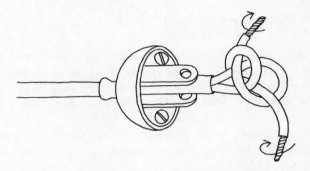

- Twist the strands of wire together, keeping the two wires separate.
- Push the cord up through the plug and tie the two wires with an Underwriter's knot.

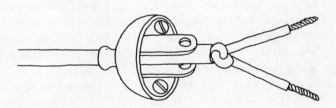

- Pass each wire around its prong to reach the screw.
- Wind the exposed bare section of the wire around the screw in the same direction as the screw itself is turned

467

to tighten it. Make sure no bare wires are visible. If so, trim them. Replace the plug covering.

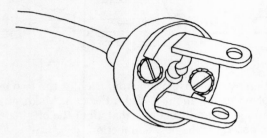

How to Repair a Lamp Cord with a Self-Wiring Plug

For light-duty cords, utilize "rip cord" wire covered with rubber or plastic insulation. To repair quickly, use the self-wiring plug. Such plugs open to receive the rip cord, then snap shut to puncture the insulation, automatically making contact with the conductors.

Tip: Use plug-in outlet protectors when you have inquisitive children who enjoy investigating convenience outlets with all sorts of metal toys and objects.

HANGING A PICTURE

If you have no wire or hanger on the back of the picture, screw or secure one small screw eye into each side of the picture frame on the back, about one third of the way down from the top. Loop a piece of picture wire (or any thin wire) or strong cord from one "eye" to the other. Allow enough give or slack so that it feels taut when pushed half the distance to the top.

Pull the string or wire taut and place *picture hook* under the center of it, as it will hang on the wall. Measure from the hook's nail down to the bottom of the frame. To hang, mark on the wall with a pencil point where you want the bottom of the frame to be. Then measure up from that mark the distance to the top where you plan to drive the nail. (The measurement you took above.)

HOW TO HANG A PICTURE

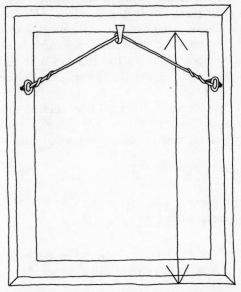

Cover spot where you plan to drive the nail with a little piece of masking tape to protect the plaster and keep it from cracking. Then drive in hook and nail. If you hang it higher or lower than you anticipated, correct it by shortening or lengthening wire. If the picture keeps tilting and moving from side to side, secure it to the wall by sticking a little floral or modeling clay to back of frame. It may stain the wall—use a light color.

HANGING SHELVES

First locate two studs inside the wall, at the height where you plan to hang the shelf. To find the stud, tap the wall lightly with the handle of a screwdriver or a small hammer. As you tap you will hear a "hollow" sound. When you come to a stud the sound is "solid." Next, mount standard shelf brackets in the size to match the shelf width. Hold brackets up where you plan to hang them (measured up from the floor) and over the studs. Make a pencil

469

mark through screw holes. Set the bracket aside. Drill through the wall into the stud at the pencil mark with an awl, or drill. Use 1½″ screws to fit the holes in the brackets. (Use a Molly bolt or toggle bolt if shelves are heavy, if walls are thin or when hanging shelves without studs. Ask your hardware man about this.)

Place the wooden shelf on the bracket and slide it into the right position and drive shorter screws into it through bracket holes.

Or: Mount standards in the wall first, then insert brackets into the standards and place shelves into position. Ask for specific hanging instructions when purchasing ready-mades.

HANGING CURTAIN RODS
AND DRAPERY HARDWARE

It is best to ask for specific hanging or mounting instructions for the type of hardware you are using, as window trims and out-fittings vary.

To repair a dangling cord on a traverse rod—When the cord is looped through a spring pulling on the wall, close the curtains, pull out the knot in one end of the center carrier until the cord is taut. Reknot.

If the curtain does not close at the center of the window—on a traverse rod, open the curtains all the way. Loosen cord looped around the hook found on the back of one of the center carriers. Push the carrier as far as it will go to the side of the window, then tighten the cord by pulling on one end. Reloop around the hook.

HOW TO SECURE FASTENINGS

Fastenings such as nails, screws, bolts, etcetera, require some technique in application in order to make them as secure as possible. Here are a few tips you will find handy:

- To drive a nail hold the nail, point on the wood, with the thumb and index finger of your left hand. Hold the hammer close to the end of the handle, not up near the head, with your right hand (vice versa if you're left-handed). Give the nail head several light hammer taps. Be careful. What you are aiming to do here is to drive the nail far enough into the surface of the wood or whatever, so that it will stand alone. Then hit the nail a little harder with the hammer to drive it in as far as you wish. If it starts to lean one way or the other, tap it lightly to straighten it.
- To remove a nail you must first work it up enough to slip the hammer claws underneath it. If it is raised slightly the job will be easy. To raise a standard nail (the common type with a flat head), tap the nailed joint apart slightly, then tap it back together without hitting the nail. If this doesn't do it, slip a very thin, but blunt instrument underneath the head to force it up slightly.
- To start small screws, make a shallow hole in the wood with an awl or toothpick-like instrument, then put the point of the screw into the hole and turn it with a screwdriver.

PLUMBING REPAIRS

Plumbing breakdowns—singing toilets, stopped-up drains, leaky faucets—are virtually inevitable sometime, somewhere.

LEAKY FAUCETS

When a closed faucet begins to drip, it is a pretty good indication that it needs a new *washer*. Close the stop-valve shutting off the water to the faucet. Grasp the handle firmly with one hand, using a wrench in the other to unscrew the nut around the faucet. Cover the nut with a soft cloth to protect the faucet finish. When you have released the faucet handle, thus freeing the washer, loosen and remove the screw in the center of the washer with a screwdriver. If it is hard to loosen try adding a little oil and tap it gently with the wrench or screwdriver. Insert a new washer,

471

dull side down. Replace the screw on the shaft of the handle and tighten the nut.

If yours is a ball-type faucet with a lever handle, it will be necessary to change the ball assembly. First, turn off the water and unscrew the entire faucet, then loosen the nut or screw which secures the ball. If the axle which holds the ball assembly is worn out, the entire part must be replaced. Ask your hardware dealer to give you explicit instructions for the faucet you buy.

Improved and new faucet designs are constantly being introduced. Some make mixing easier, eliminate dripping. If you have any that you do not understand, ask your hardware dealer about instructions for repair, *before* you need them. If a *shower head drips,* possibly the supply valve has not been fully closed, or the valve itself needs repair.

FAUCET ASSEMBLY

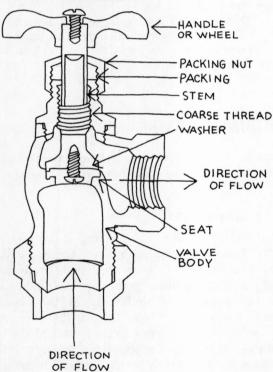

CLOGGED DRAINS

If water is slow in draining, check for any lint, hair, or other matter which may have collected in the strainer or drain. Use a piece of heavy wire to pull it out, or if it has twisted around the stopper pipe, use paper toweling to pull it off. Use one of the commercial drain cleaners recommended for opening clogged drains, following directions exactly. If this doesn't work, try using a plunger, often called a "plumber's friend or helper." Pour hot water down the drain and plunge the cup up and down until it loosens the material clogging the drain. If this has not helped, try a drain cleaner once again. Then work with the trap below. Place a bucket under the trap and unscrew the plug with a pair of pliers or monkey wrench. Use a long-handled metal brush or a long coil-spring wire, sometimes called a "plumber's snake" or drain and trap auger, to clean out the inside and twist an opening into the grease or whatever is clogging the drain. When you have done this, replace the plug and flush the sink with scalding water. If this doesn't work or if you have any doubt about your ability to do this, you'd better call a plumber.

If water from faucet comes in slowly or if one faucet slows down when another is turned on the pipes may be too small or clogged. Low pressure may also be the result of a slowdown in street main pressure. Check with your water company or check pressure regulator on home water supply.

NOISY PIPES

Water hammer sometimes occurs when a faucet is suddenly closed or if the water pressure is too high. If pipes are too small, too much pressure may cause hammering sounds. Check pressure regulator at water supply. *Whistling* sounds may be due to improper installation of pipe edges, valves, and faucets. A hammering noise in a faucet when it has just been turned on or off usually means a loose cap nut, a worn spindle, or a worn-out washer. If the thread on a spindle is worn out, you will have to install a new faucet.

473

FROZEN PIPES

Shut off the water immediately upon discovering the freeze. If they are not thawed rapidly, pipes may burst. Open the faucet and begin thawing at this end, working toward the thawed area. If it is a waste pipe, work from the lower end. If you can reach the pipe easily, wrap cloths around the pipe and pour boiling water over them. An electric pad or an iron used on the outside of the pipe is a slower but effective method. Stand on a rubber mat while working with these appliances. If the pipe is not accessible, call in a plumber.

LEAKING PIPES

Turn off the water until you can get a two-part leak clamp to cover the leak. (Most easily fixed in a straight line pipe.) If this doesn't work, call the plumber.

LEAKING OR NOISY RADIATORS

May be clogged radiator valves. First, tighten the valve. If that doesn't work, it probably needs cleaning. Turn off the radiator and let it cool. Then remove valve at stem. If the valve is not too dirty, it may become unclogged easily by hitting it against a soft object to loosen the soil. If this doesn't solve the problem, soak valve in hot sudsy water, white vinegar or kerosene. Swish back and forth to loosen soil. Rinse and dry thoroughly. If this fails, you probably need a new valve. Check with a qualified serviceman.

TOILETS

Running or Leaky Toilets—A simple but temporary remedy is to jiggle the flush handle, to assure proper positioning of the ball valve in the tank. This, of course, doesn't solve the problem permanently. The lift rod may be bent; make sure the guides connected to the overflow pipe are lined up properly. If this is not the case, the rubber ball valve needs to be replaced. Shut off the water supply and flush the toilet to empty tank. Unscrew the rubber ball valve and replace with a new one of the same size. If the rod is badly bent or corroded, it must also be replaced with one of the same size. Turn on the water supply once they have been replaced.

Overflowing Toilet Bowls (or water level too high)—This means that the trap or waste pipe is clogged. Use a plunger at the outlet and work it up and down quickly to loosen clogging. Or use a wire closet auger (buy it at the hardware store) to clear obstruction.

Low Water Level in Bowl—Refill is not working properly in toilet tank. Unscrew refill valve and clean or replace it.

Low Pressure Flushing—Water level in tank is low or it does not fill properly. Try bending float rod upward.

Overflow Pipe Fills with Water—Bend the float rod down to lower the ball valve. If it still overflows, unscrew the ball to see if it contains water. If so, replace with a new one.

WINDOWS

Windows That Stick—Rub the groove in which the sashes run with wax. Wait until weather and wood are dry to rub with wax as this will protect the wood from future dampness.

Window Will Not Open—It may be "painted" shut. If so, run the steel blade of an old knife up and down in the crack between sash and stop. Be careful!

Window Shade Won't Roll Up—Spring is probably unwound, won't catch, too stiff or broken. If it is unwound or won't catch, fix the shade in place and roll the shade by hand. Replace shade in brackets. It should roll properly. If not, repeat process.

Window Shades Snap Upward—Raise shade all the way up and remove from brackets and try again. If it is still tight, repeat process.

475

SOME TIPS ON PAINTING

Don't believe what they say. Unless you're a miracle worker it is not possible to paint a room in the morning and have guests at night. But it is possible these days to paint a room very quickly—one or two days—and get it back into working order with comparative ease. Newer paints, better equipment, and a great deal of enthusiasm will help to accomplish the job with dispatch.

Here are a few good tips to help the job along:

1. Repair any cracks or holes in the plaster. For the more simple ones you can do the job yourself. To fix a hairline crack or small hole, buy a pack of patching plaster at any paint or hardware store or an especially prepared commercial product designed expressly for the job. Follow the directions—usually applying it with your thumb or a putty knife.

2. After all the cracks and holes have been filled, dust the walls, ceilings, and windowsills. If your walls and surfaces are heavily soiled with grease and grime, they should be washed thoroughly.

3. If you plan to use a brush, buy only one of a good quality—either pure bristle or synthetics such as nylon. They will last longer and do a better job. Besides, the bristles will stay in. One of the worst problems you will face in the middle of a paint job is to pick out tiny hairs from freshly painted walls!

4. You will need several brushes—a 4″ flat paintbrush which you can also use for enamel; a paint and varnish brush for all areas (3″ wide for a woman, 4″ for a man); a flat trim brush, 3″ wide; and an all-purpose 1″ brush for finer detail work.

5. We mentioned above that quality brushes have sturdy bristles and that is true. However, even the best new brushes have a few loose bristles. You can remove them by revolving the handle quickly between your palms or by tapping the bristles sharply against your hand.

6. Soak a new brush in linseed oil for a couple of days, then squeeze out the oil and comb bristles straight.

7. To use the brush, dip it into the paint to a depth of about 2″. Avoid overloading it. Tap out excess paint against inside of the can. Apply paint with bristles flat against the surface. Don't push ends into corners. Hold the brush firmly, but lightly and don't force the ends into corners. Never allow a brush to stand on its bristle ends.

8. If you plan to use a brush for several days, suspend it overnight in linseed oil to keep bristle ends from touching the bottom. As for cleaning your brushes, it is a good idea to ask your paint dealer what to do as the procedure may vary with the type of paint. Many new brushes can be rinsed off with water. There are special brush cleaners you can purchase at the paint store. Follow the directions. When brushes are dry, comb or straighten out the bristles and wrap them in aluminum foil or plastic wrap to keep out air and moisture and to help them keep their shape.

9. For painting with a roller, follow specific directions for both paint and roller for best results. Directions vary with different types of rollers.

10. Roller painting is really very easy. It allows you to work quickly and continuously and produces professional results. Always keep the paint flowing so that the edges won't have a chance to dry and leave overlap marks. After you have spread your paint with crisscross strokes, finish with long, vertical ones. This will help compensate for any unevenness in your paint coat. When you finish painting, clean both the brush and roller immediately according to directions. If you allow them to dry you cannot use them again.

Note: Remember to cover all your furniture with plastic drop cloths, as well as the floor areas around the walls.

CHAPTER TEN

About Health, Fatigue, and Safety

Housekeeping is certainly not a sedentary job, to say the least. And with housekeeping, as in any other active work, good health is important. Suffice it to say that we will do all we can to keep ourselves up to par for our health's sake alone. That is just good common sense.

But there are things we can do to help maintain a safe and healthy environment in which to live—and to make housekeeping easier.

CHRONIC FATIGUE

Time and motion experts will generally agree that in most cases when we complain of housework making us tired, it is usually from boredom, lack of interest, or using the wrong methods, *not from overwork*. Although we can't overlook the fact that doing too much for too long will make us "dog tired"!

On one of those days when you are especially tired (if you have any energy left at all) think back over your activities and study these *7 Ways To Reduce Fatigue*. Perhaps therein lies a clue to your own fatigue.

    1. Don't overdo; leave some of the work you planned for today until tomorrow.

2. Make sure what you are doing is necessary; perhaps the job needn't be done at all.
3. Use your head to save your heels; save steps.
4. Delegate some of the work.
5. Don't *make* work; take some shortcuts.
6. Keep your tools in good working order.
7. Take some time out—regardless.

Energy and Fatigue

Budgeting energy is just as important as budgeting time.

Lifting a load above your shoulders can add as much as 25 percent of your weight to the weight of the object you are lifting. Lifting a load from the floor to the table adds 40 percent of your body weight to the weight of the object.

Energy is the resource we need to work. It is measured by calories. A calorie is the amount of heat that is necessary to raise the temperature of one gram of water one degree centigrade. If one 8-ounce glass of whole milk has 165 calories, that means this much milk will supply the body with that much energy to use. The amount of energy we need and consume will depend upon the type of work we are doing—light, moderately heavy, or heavy. One can accomplish just so much light work in a given amount of time. If it is moderately or very heavy work, you will accomplish less, depending upon the degree. Energy is best calculated or budgeted in connection with time. That's what *time and motion* is all about.

Light work may be classified as paring potatoes, ironing napkins, beating batter, or using a vacuum cleaner on a rug; *moderately heavy work* as dusting, using a carpet sweeper, using certain vacuum cleaners, polishing floors, emptying clothes from a washing machine, putting up and removing a clothesline; *heavy work* as sweeping a floor, washing clothes by hand, hanging clothes from a basket on a floor; *extremely heavy work* as sweeping a rug with a broom.

We all have a certain amount of energy to use—and when we have used it, we get tired. This is *fatigue*. We need to rest and nourish our bodies with good food to replenish the energy we use up. Therefore:

- Take time to rest.
- Eat balanced meals (watch overeating—it is the excess calories we don't use that we store into *fat*, which slows down our energy!).

ENERGY AND CALORIES

To give you an idea of how you use calories, here is a chart showing you the average number of calories used for normal activities:

ACTIVITY	APPROX. CALORIES USED FOR EACH 5 MINUTES
Sitting Eating Sewing by hand Talking on phone Knitting Typing Lying down	5 to 10
Dressing Peeling potatoes Playing piano Driving Polishing furniture	10 to 15
Making beds Ironing Mopping, wet	15 to 25
Carrying loads upstairs Gardening Walking fast	25 to 30

Now, how can we interpret all these energy statistics into meaningful terms? The chart* on page 481 shows the amount of energy you will use under varying conditions:

* H. C. Sherman and C. S. Lanford, *Essentials of Nutrition,* Macmillan Co., New York, 1940, p. 77.

FORM OF ACTIVITY	CALORIES PER HOUR FOR EACH POUND OF BODY WEIGHT	PERCENT OF INCREASE OVER LYING STILL
Awake, lying still	0.50	
Sitting at rest	0.65	30
Standing relaxed	0.69	38
Walking 2.6 miles per hour	1.30	160
Walking 3.75 miles per hour	1.95	290
Walking downstairs	2.36	372
Walking upstairs	7.18	1336

When it is suggested that you "sit" to do as much of your housework as you can, referring to the chart above, this means the more strain you work under, the faster you work, or the longer you stand, the more energy you use. As you can see, sitting burns less calories per hour than standing, thus you use less energy. Walking slowly uses less calories, thus less energy than walking fast. Transpose this into working slowly versus working fast and you can see why the more energy you use the more fatigued you will become.

What this really amounts to is budgeting your energy as you budget your time. Learn to work more slowly. Sit when you can. Avoid unnecessary climbing of stairs. You'll get more done in the long run.

Some tips on how to stand, sit, lift, work and walk properly, when working around the house. This makes a big difference as to how you feel at the end of the day.

- Your posture is important.
- Stand up tall—head erect, shoulders straight, stomach flat. Many years ago in gym class we learned by the "initial system" how to remember this rule: *"TTI"*—"Tuck Tummy In." Apply the same idea to your buttocks. Tuck them under, too! Obviously you cannot always work in this erect position. You will need to bend, stoop, lift, carry and reach, but try, even in these positions, to maintain good physical form.

481

- Walk easily, moving from the hips, toes ahead, and on the outside of your foot.
- Work with precision, using both hands when possible.
- To push or pull, stand up straight. Keep back straight and let your legs do the work. Push at middle of object. Put as many small things in or on carts as you can.
- To reach, use a stool and stand close to object.
- To lift things from floor, bend knees and squat down; keeping back straight, use legs to push up.
- To lift things from table, pull object close to body and lift.
- To carry heavy loads, distribute weight in shopping bags.
- Work at convenient heights. Change your position often.
- To iron, adjust the board to proper standing or sitting height.

What are the most convenient and comfortable working heights? First determine your own height, then consider that in performing certain hand-arm motions connected with food preparation and cleaning, people 5 feet 2 inches to 5 feet 5 inches tall spend the least energy working at counter heights of 32 to 36 inches from the floor. Ironing boards are more comfortable to work at when adjusted to a height of around 36 inches. When loading and unloading a clothes dryer, these people again spend the least energy when the center of the opening of the dryer is 38 inches from the floor and the clothes are transferred to or from a basket on a table 29 inches from the floor.

Built-in oven heights are determined according to the energy one expends when using them.

When working while sitting, the counter or work surface and chair should be arranged so that one can work with the elbows about waist level. In the kitchen some counter or work surface area should be planned with free space underneath for sit-down working and at a height providing sufficient clearance for the knees.

Sinks with shallow bowls, around 3½ inches deep, allow you to sit comfortably for working. For jobs performed while sitting on a standard chair (about 17 inches from the floor) the height of the work surface should be from 24 to 30 inches. For sit-down working at a counter 36 inches high, an adjustable stool is handy.

Using the proper tools and equipment can also help to conserve energy. The design of all household equipment and furnishings is based on average human dimensions. Location of controls, levers, handles are considered in relationship to average comfortable working heights. Always look for controls that are placed conveniently between elbow and shoulder heights.

Storage design is also important in conserving energy. Are you aware that it takes about 19 times as much energy to get something 3 inches from the floor as to get it at elbow level? See Kitchen Planning, Chapter Five, for cabinet and counter dimensions.

You can determine how convenient work and storage facilities are if you can stand about a foot away from the wall and move your arm freely from the shoulder so that the hand makes a large circle. Let someone record the high and low points of your own circle. A small circle made by moving the arm from the elbow can help you determine the most comfortable arrangement of things used most often. A good rule of thumb to remember is to store all things near the place where they are used most frequently and at comfortable heights for your reach based upon your usual positions for working in a particular situation, whether sitting or standing.

It has been suggested that the following situations are often associated with creating fatigue and that most of them occur in homemaking tasks.*

1. A long period of mental or light physical work in a restricted or uncomfortable position.
2. A long period of work in a standing position.
3. A long period of making continuous postural adjustments, such as when riding in a car.
4. A period, possibly short, of heavy physical exertion.
5. Working at a disliked task.
6. Working at an unaccustomed task.
7. Working at a task that requires close attention or extreme alertness (like writing this book, for instance).
8. Working under pressure, for instance when meeting a deadline.

* *Work in Home,* by Rose E. Steidl and Esther Crew Bratton, John Wiley and Sons, Inc., 1968.

9. Working without sufficient knowledge or information.
10. Emotional stress, whether working or not.

KEEPING A SAFE HOME

It is true that most accidents that occur in the home are the result of carelessness. It is also true that by taking precautions and following certain basic safety rules you can avoid most, if not all, accidents. Throughout this book you will find reference to safety—the safe use of appliances and products, safe working methods, proper handling of chemicals, etcetera. Heed them, for often they can mean the difference between serious or minor injury, and indeed, life or death.

Other important safety precautions should be taken in cases of fire, illness, and the use of medicines.

IN CASE OF FIRE

If you suddenly find yourself involved in a small fire—keep your cool. If it is minor, such as a grease fire in the oven, simply turn off the oven and throw some salt or baking soda into the fire to smother it. *Never water!* If it is on top of the range, again turn off the heat and do the same thing—or use a portable fire extinguisher you should keep at hand for such purposes.

If you have any doubt at all about your ability to control even the smallest fire—call the fire department immediately. The following are important tips to keep in mind regarding any fire that may occur in the home:

- In case of a bad fire, get everyone out first, then call fire department. Don't go back in for valuables.
- If you awake at night and smell smoke, don't fling open bedroom door. Touch handle; if it is hot, do not open door; if you do not need to alert other family members make your escape through window or stay in room and wait for rescue—stuff rugs and blankets under the door to keep out smoke as long as possible. If doorknob is cool,

484

open door cautiously. Use knotted sheets for window escape.
- Close any door which will confine the fire.
- Never try to fight a fire in a room filled with smoke—the fumes and lack of air are dangerous.
- A woolen blanket or other heavy covering will help to smother a small fire.
- Keep a box of baking soda near the range. As we said before, it is excellent to throw on grease fires to smother them. You can also use a pan cover handled by a long fork.
- Baking soda is also good for fires in ash trays, wastebaskets, upholstered furniture.
- Place fire extinguishers throughout the house for emergencies. Ask your local fire department to recommend the proper type.

To Avoid Fire Hazards

- Keep storage areas free of flammable fluids, paper, oily rags.
- Store flammable fluids, such as kerosene and gasoline, outside in clearly labeled and fire-safe containers.
- Discard oily rags or furniture polish cloths in covered metal containers. Storing any old rags, newspapers, etcetera, in warm areas may cause spontaneous combustion.
- Never leave rubbish, kindling, paints, turpentine, etcetera, near furnace or stove.
- Never throw dust into a fire, empty vacuum cleaner bags, or throw powdery materials such as sawdust, cereal, or flour into incinerators or fires. To do so may cause an explosion and consequently a fire!
- Be very careful when using paints; use quick-drying paints containing volatile solvent only in well-ventilated areas; burn paint rags or place in covered metal container immediately; never place a can of paint on a range to heat—put it in a pan of hot water.
- Don't smoke in bed.
- Store kitchen matches in a tightly closed metal container; make sure packs of matches are out of children's reach.
- Put out lighted matches and cigarettes in ash tray or

485

nonflammable receptacle—never in wastebasket. When you empty ash trays, make sure all cigarette butts are completely out.

- Never strike a match in an area where you smell gas.
- Locate towel racks away from range so towels cannot fall onto heating units or burners.
- Clean oven and broiler pan regularly to prevent accumulation of grease.

FIRST AID

Your best friend in case of emergency is a copy of a good first aid manual, such as the one published by the American Red Cross. You should be able to obtain a copy at your local chapter for a nominal charge, or buy one in a good bookstore. Or invest in a good home medical guide. Ask your doctor for a recommendation.

The three serious emergencies—breath stoppage, heavy bleeding, and poisoning—should be handled *immediately*. A basic knowledge of what to do may mean the difference between life or death, as there is often not even enough time to call a doctor. Keep the facts handy, as well as those for minor injuries and illnesses.

A First Aid Kit

Keep a portable first aid kit where it can be quickly reached at all times. The druggist will help you in organizing a basic one. Or you can buy them already prepackaged. In addition to your first aid kit, these materials and medicines should be important supplies kept in or near the medicine cabinet:

Bandage, gauze type	Band-Aids
Absorbent cotton	Adhesive tape
Mercurochrome, iodine or	Antacids
Merthiolate	Bicarbonate of soda
Boric acid powder or liquid	Smelling salts
solution	Ace bandage
Rubbing alcohol	First aid scissors

ILLNESS

There may be times when you will find yourself caring for a bedridden patient. Here are a few good tips that you may find handy, both for your convenience and for the patient's comfort:

- Set up a tray or tray-table near the bed. Outfit it with paper cups, water, medicine and tissues. Place a disposable container next to the bed, particularly in the case of a patient with a cold or flu.
- Make provisions for feeding patient comfortably.
- Make any special notes as to doctor's recommendations.
- Ask the patient what you can do to make him comfortable. Keeping the room as neat as possible and remaking the bed as often as necessary are important factors in his comfort.
- The sick room is no place for hordes of friends and visitors. Don't be afraid to ask smokers not to smoke. If hospitals can have rules, you can too.

MEDICINES

It is a good idea to take inventory every now and then and throw out the leftovers of old prescriptions, pills, and medicines. Prescriptions if held too long will deteriorate and must be discarded. In fact, they are no longer potent as a medication and might even cause problems if used.

Safety Rules in Medicine Handling:
- Keep medicines out of the reach of children.
- Keep harmful and habit-forming drugs in a safe and special place.
- Keep all poisons in the medicine cabinet and out of the reach of children.
- Separate family members' prescriptions by assigning a small box for individual use. Keep these weeded out also.

487

Reprinted courtesy of American Druggist Magazine, 1972.

MEDICAL EQUIPMENT FOR HOME USE

These are helpful to have for times of illness:

A thermometer (ask your doctor for the type he recommends)

Medicine dropper

Paper cup dispenser or small nonbreakable glass for medicine

Measuring spoons

Eye cup

Ice bag

Heating pad

Hot water bottle.

CHAPTER ELEVEN

Household Help
and Services

Although few of us today can have full-time help, there are times when we must rely on outside services for a specific job or time period. In addition, as the number of working women increase, so will the demand for good household help. Since 1950 the number of married women in the labor force has risen notably by approximately 250 percent, and today 60 percent of all working women are married and over 5½ million heads of households are female.

Whether you employ help full-time or only for a specific task, organizing the work to be done in your own mind will allow you to get the best service possible. This does not necessarily mean spending an entire evening "getting ready for the cleaning lady," but knowing what should be done, and in what order, does pay great dividends. Professionally trained help will generally want to use their own methods, but you still can set your own priorities as to what does get done first. If you are dealing with untrained help, your own knowledge will be invaluable in pointing out the best way in which to do a cleaning job.

ROLE-PLAYING AND HOUSEWORK

As for the changes taking place with regard to family role-playing, one survey we encountered indicated that the time contributed by husbands for household work is less than is often assumed and that it does not increase with the hours of wives' paid employment. A wife still does most of the in-the-home work (whether she works away from home or not), although husbands seem to be spending an increasing amount of time with their children.

WHAT KIND OF HELP DO YOU NEED?

There are many household services that can come to the rescue when you need them. Here is an overview of who you might need and how they can help:

The Cleaning Lady—A good cleaning lady can be the greatest find you will ever make. You might want to hire her one day a week or for a few hours every day. To find such help you can contact a cleaning agency, advertise, or check the ads in your local newspaper or, best of all, act on the recommendation of a friend. Often, within a particular neighborhood, several families will share the services of one cleaning woman.

Housekeeper—A housekeeper will be your best consideration if you have a full-time job and if you have older children, especially of school age. Your greatest consideration is the need for the running of an orderly household without too much interruption of daily or normal routine. She can be responsible for running the household, doing general cleaning, overseeing an occasional cleaning lady, doing the cooking, and looking after school-age children. Her duties will depend upon your needs, of course, and her expertise.

We must caution you that having a full-time housekeeper or a maid (even a part-time one) requires a good deal of organization on the part of the homemaker, the family, and the housekeeper. A family cannot expect a housekeeper to do all the work, since she has been hired only for specific duties. Other tasks must be shared by family members, if possible.

The Cook or Housekeeper-Cook—If there is a special job you want your housekeeper to handle you must train her. This is especially true of cooking. If she has never cooked before you will have to teach her the basics. It is a good idea to check her reading ability if you expect her to follow recipes—particularly if you want her to learn your special ones for family and for entertaining. If you want her to do any table or "hostess" serving, you must show her exactly how it is to be done. Don't assume that she will know how to set the table the way you like it to be set. Draw a diagram and keep it handy for these occasions.

Aside from the housekeeper-cook, there are full- or part-time cooks, and this is usually their only job. Some come in just for dinner preparation and cleanup; others will come in for company dinners.

Baby Sitters and Nursemaids—Check to see if there is a good day-care or child-development center in your community for youngsters of pre-school age. For older children there are many clubs and activity groups after school where they can have fun and be well taken care of until you get home from work.

If you have very small infants, you may wish to consider hiring a trained baby nurse. They are very expensive but may fill the bill for a limited time.

> *If you need a baby sitter or nursemaid:*
> - Put an ad in the local newspaper, stating exactly what you want—including hours, age and number of children, whether you require housekeeping, a driver's license, and how much you will pay, or at least some indication of fee.
> - Check "situations wanted" in the newspaper—someone may be looking for just the kind of job you offer.
> - Contact a child care (or household help) agency. This is a little more expensive, but you can give the agency your requirements and they will do the screening for you.
> - Consider an *au pair* girl. You can make contact through an agency, though you must be prepared to face the problems of hiring sight unseen and the frequently changing working-visa regulations.

Some additional procedures to follow are:

- Check references carefully—it's a good idea to ask for two, at least one whose children the applicant has cared for. Calls to the references will tell you what you need to know and this is essential for your peace of mind. In addition, careful questioning over the phone often elicits more honest information than is provided in a written recommendation.

- Narrow applicants down (from your telephone conversations) to two or three and ask them to come for interviews when your children will be there so you can see how they hit it off with them.
- Outline thoroughly what you expect her to do before she takes the job.
- Plan to pay more if you want housekeeping done, too (but if you ask her to do housekeeping, make sure she has the time). However, most regular baby sitters won't mind doing a few light chores and errands, as well as taking care of children's meals and children's laundry.

If you are a working mother with small children, your primary interest is in securing responsible loving care for them during the hours you are away. Here are some tips that may be of help:

- Be sure to leave a list of important phone numbers. These should include: fire department, police, children's doctor, and those which probably will be used most frequently—two or three close friends who are usually at home and who will be willing to help if there is a minor problem. Of course be sure and leave your own working number.
- Tell your sitter in case of a very serious medical emergency, such as a fall producing unconsciousness, severe bleeding, or choking, to telephone the police rather than try to get through to the doctor. They can come with the necessary medical aids. These may seem to be unpleasant ideas to consider, but you will be happier away from home if you feel assured that all such emergencies will be properly handled if they ever do occur.
- Remember that people who are especially good with children may not be as efficient at keeping the house neat as you would like. If this is not carried to an extreme, overlook the problem. The years when your children are little pass very quickly. You can take care of the clutter the days you are home.
- If your sitter doesn't cook dinner, prepare double portions when you cook and freeze the leftovers. She prob-

493

ably will be willing to start heating a defrosted casserole which will minimize your last-minute preparations.

- If you have just started back to work, consider leaving the sitter little notes to read to your children at lunch or when they come home from school.
- If you have a new sitter ask a friend to casually drop by the first week on the pretext of dropping something off.
- If you have young children make sure your sitter knows the priorities of her job: say that you would prefer she played with the toddler than fuss over the housework if she is responsible for that as well.
- Tell the sitter clearly the rules you have established for raising the children.
- If you ever disagree with your sitter's position on a disciplinary matter, discuss it with her later, not in front of your children.

RULES OF THE GAME IN HIRING HELP

Agencies—Look through the yellow pages for reliable recommendations. Generally a day worker is paid by the agency. The agency bills you. You might also secure help through the state employment agency, or the local community groups. Be especially cautious about hiring someone from abroad—someone you have never met. It has often not worked out for many and varying reasons. On the other hand, you may be lucky to realize a very pleasant relationship.

THE INTERVIEW

Determine what your needs are before you ever say "hello." During the interview, establish:

- Why she left her last job. Previous experience.
- Her requirements, your requirements.
- How many days she is to work.
- Arrival time, quitting time. Be specific. What does "after dinner" mean?
- If she lives in, exactly what time does she start? Quit? Hours and days off? Where and what are her facilities?

- Wages. What is her basic pay? How much overtime does she get? Method of payment.

Salary is usually based on the going rates within the community. Wages today range anywhere from $1.35 (low) to $2.25 an hour, depending upon where you live and what the job entails. The *cost* of having full-time help is expensive. But cost is relative when you begin to balance it against the dollar value of time, health and energy, particularly when both parents are carrying heavy burdens of full-time jobs, family rearing and home maintenance. Of course wages are only one part of the cost of having help. There might be agency fees (usually a percentage of the monthly wages), carfare, lunch, etcetera.

- *Holidays.* Exactly how much time does she get off and when? Will she observe a *national* holiday if she works at home? If the *banks are closed,* does that mean she doesn't work either?
- *Schedule and Duties.* Which rooms are to be cleaned? How? How much laundry is she to do? Ironing? Does cleaning include windows, floors? How about shampooing of rugs and upholstery? (This is generally *not* considered part of a cleaning lady's job.) If you have appliances, be sure to instruct her how to use them—give a demonstration. Do you expect her to do any marketing? If you expect her to cook, take time to explain, early on, just what kinds of foods you or your family like. Teach her some of your recipes.
- *Flexibility.* Can she go away with you in the summer or whenever? What will her duties be?
- Answer her questions as well as asking your own!

YOUR WORKING RELATIONSHIP

A good working relationship for both employer and employee might be one based upon the code of standards suggested by The National Committee on Household Employment. Some of the factors considered include:
- Any employee who receives $50 or more per quarter from any employer should be covered by Social Security. For more information on employer tax payments, write or call your local District Director of the Internal Rev-

495

enue Service. Ask them to send you Circular H which will describe the procedure you should follow. The Internal Revenue Service will assign you an "employer number" and send you a form every three months. This form will come to you automatically until you notify them that you no longer have an employee in your home. You will need the Social Security number of your employee as well as a record to keep track of her wages. It is also advisable to carry some homeowner's liability insurance to cover accidents.

- Agree in advance upon how your employee should be paid and how much time and overtime will be involved.
- If you have a day worker and for some reason will not require her services, notify your employee at least a week in advance, or pay for her services.
- Outline clearly just what your employee's schedule should be and what specific duties it includes (see section on The Interview, preceding).
- As for sick leave, legal holidays, and vacations:
Employees who work one day a week should receive one day of paid sick leave a year. If an employee works full time, she should receive a minimum of six days of paid sick leave a year. Full-time employees should receive two weeks of paid vacation after one year. If an employee works only one day weekly, she deserves one day of paid vacation for every six months she works. If she has been in your employ for a longer period, naturally there should be some increase in vacation with pay. If you have a live-in employee, she is entitled to a minimum of eight legal holidays annually, with pay. A full-time employee who does not live in should receive the equivalent of six legal holidays annually, with pay. If an employee works one day a week, she should be entitled to one paid legal holiday a year, if that holiday falls on one of her regular working days.

For more information on the suggested code of standards, write to The National Committee on Household Employment, 1346 Connecticut Avenue, N.W., Washington, D.C. 20036. They will provide materials on developing standards, existing training programs and sample contracts and will answer any specific questions you may have regarding the current status of hiring domestic employees. They will also supply you with names of organizations in your area affiliated with The National Committee.

TRAINING

Progress has been made in the last few years to assure the domestic worker a better status than ever before. Standards of work have been set in some communities as to wages, hours, vacation time, duties, and health requirements. The growing concern for elevating both the work standards of the domestic worker and her own attitude toward her job has led to the establishment of the Household Management Training Programs, financed by a grant from the United States Department of Labor. These training programs are now operative in several cities across the country. Study of latest developments in household equipment, care of fabrics, food preparation, laundering, cleaning methods are stressed. To find out more about this, order the pamphlet entitled "If Only I Could Get Some Household Help," published by the Woman's Bureau of the U.S. Department of Labor, Government Printing Office, Washington, D.C., (free).

Your best bet on training help, however, is to train them yourself. To do this effectively, you must know how to do the job first. Try to work out some method of communication which is clear and concise if you are to be away from home for long periods—notes, bulletin board or blackboard, and typewritten schedules to which she can refer for orders and sequence of cleaning. If she begins to get in the habit of doing something contrary to your methods or technique, nip it in the bud before the habit becomes a lasting one. Don't assume she "knows" what you are thinking.

OTHER SERVICES

Caterers—There are individual caterers who will come in for special occasion dinner parties only. They usually suggest menus and will give you a choice of menus for varying fees. They may or may not bring their own ingredients (if they don't they give you a market order to have ready upon their arrival). They pre-

497

pare the food, serve it, and clean up the kitchen. They often have access to a bartender's service in case you need one.

There are large-scale catering services who will plan and give a party from soup to chairs! They supply the food and any necessary equipment you need. There are also main dish "take-out" services who offer you a choice of main dishes, salads, breads, desserts, etcetera. You must give them an order ahead of time and they will have it delivered at a specified time.

Look for all these services in the classified directory on the yellow pages under *Caterers*. Fees will vary.

Waitresses, Bartenders—If you need help in serving a buffet, dinner, or cocktail party, check local agencies for specific services for waitresses and bartenders. They usually come in and serve food you have prepared yourself, then do all the after-party cleanup. Fees are hourly, usually with a four-hour minimum. Check with local agencies or friends for going rates.

Professional Cleaning and Repair Services—For special occasions, heavy spring and fall housecleaning, when illness slows you down, when there is a working mother in the home and there is no help, when families are helping aged parents who live alone, it is often important to pay for the convenience and competence of a professional cleaning service. Many of these services are available through the classified directory and the yellow pages. They are expensive services but (using first-class equipment and heavy-duty tools) they do their job fast and well.

Complete Housecleaning Services—This is a complete service performed by several men (and sometimes women) who come in and give your house a thorough cleaning. Such operations offer two types of service:

- *Special one-time services* provided generally on a week's notice. This might cover anything from moving furniture, dusting moldings, washing walls, or cleaning windows, to giving a house a top-to-bottom cleaning which may take several days.
- *Scheduled cleaning services* are those provided to regular customers either on a weekly, biweekly, or monthly basis.

SPECIALIZED SERVICES

While overall cleaning services are able to do any kind of housecleaning job and do it well, you may be likely to get somewhat better results on specialized jobs from firms that deal in special operations.

Window Cleaning—While we take these services for granted, this is an extremely dangerous job and requires good training—more so than you might suspect. The most important thing to make sure of in hiring a window cleaner is that he is fully insured against accidents to himself and his men.

Rug and Carpet Cleaning (Also Upholstery)—Rugs and carpets cleaned by professionals can often come out "looking like new," as these men are trained to handle special problem spots which you might not be able to remove yourself. Many of these firms also clean upholstered furniture.

Floor Cleaning—If your wood floors look dull and lifeless, a professional floor refinisher can revive them. He will scrape, stain, and refinish. A professional floor waxer can help revive smooth-surface flooring. Even though you have an electric floor polisher/scrubber, it may pay occasionally to have a professional work on your floors.

Venetian Blind Cleaning and Repair—When venetian blinds get to that hopeless stage of dinginess, you may find that a venetian blind cleaning service (often a venetian blind retail store) will perform miracles. Tapes and cords can be replaced or changed to match another color scheme. They may also be cut to fit other windows. They will be able to tell you whether or not it is economically worth doing a refit job or to buy new ones.

Shade Repairing—They can be made smaller. Rollers and pulls can be replaced. If your particular shade is not washable, have a professional do it.

Furniture Refinishing—If your furniture has chips, nicks, or has warped, you can make minor repairs at home. Or there are special furniture repairmen who will come to your home and service it there, making any necessary repairs to chips, nicks, and cracks.

499

Marble Polishing—As marble gets older it may begin to lose some of its luster. When moisture rings and stains overtake home remedies, a marble expert will remove a sheet of the surface with an abrasive grit. The surface is restored to its original luster by persistent buffing.

Silver Repairing—Professional silversmiths should do all repairs and can restore silver pieces to their original condition and color. If sterling silver is badly stained and has deep scratches they can be burnished out. Dents are removed. In silverplate, after removing dents, stains, and scratches, the piece will have to be replated.

For Miscellaneous Problems—To clean badly stained stone, brick, and other masonry surfaces which do not respond to home treatments, see Index for page references. You may want to hire a building cleaning contractor with sandblasting and steam-cleaning equipment. The fees are high and the mess is almost unbearable.

CHAPTER TWELVE

Living with Pets

Your home is your pet's home, too. And just as with other members of the family, they contribute their share to housekeeping. The only difference is that they can't help with the chores—unless there is a new course in obedience training about which we are not aware. They have toys that require storage, they leave a trail of dirty dishes, their paws bring in "footprints," and they have to be housebroken or toilet trained, or else!

In homes where there are children old enough to care for pets, the care and feeding of animals contribute immeasurably to teaching youngsters how to handle responsibility at an early age. Regardless of where the responsibility lies, here are some tips to make the job easier and more pleasant.

THEIR EATING HABITS

- Sloppy eaters increase work and many pets are sloppy eaters. Use paper place mats, plastic sheeting, several sheets of paper toweling, or vinyl under the dish. To keep the dish from moving, cement a rubber jar ring to the bottom.
- To keep the ears of long-eared dogs out of their food, invest in a new dish, one that is narrow and has sloping sides. One friend suggests cutting the sleeve from an old sweater and slipping it over your dog's head at mealtime.

501

- Animals require a balanced diet, especially dogs and cats. And just as humans require special diet instructions from their physicians for specific reasons, so should a veterinarian be consulted for overweight or underweight dogs or cats or for any other specific problems. The dog foods you buy on the market which furnish a well-balanced meal are usually identified as a complete food, which gives the animal its regular nutritional requirements.

- While other foods contain just one ingredient, e.g., meat, fish, or poultry, they may be supplemented with the complete foods, either mixed together or fed to the pet separately. Fresh foods such as cooked eggs, meat, fish, and milk may also be mixed with regular pet foods as nutritional supplements. As to feeding them bits of food from table leftovers, this is permissible if they are mixed with their food at the regular, established eating time. This, of course, is to make sure that they eat their own food and don't develop the habit of waiting for the scraps.

- Be careful of feeding dogs and cats meat or fish with bones, and particularly chicken bones, which splinter into small pieces. Dogs especially like to chew on bones, and while it is not necessary from a nutritional standpoint, be certain they are large and hard enough not to splinter. Or give them a dog biscuit or a toy bone.

- Water dishes for dogs who are kept outdoors often get overturned. To keep this from happening, the Pet Food Institute suggests driving a stake into the ground and placing the tube of an angel food cake pan over it. Nothing short of a tornado could tip it over.

WHAT TO DO ABOUT CARPET STAINS

- If a kitten or puppy is not housebroken it is best to keep him off the carpeting. Urine will quickly discolor carpeting if it is not removed immediately. Even after removal, some traces of odor may linger. Actually the danger of lingering odor, while possibly not detectable by humans, is that a pet's sensitivity to smell is so keen that it may trigger the instinct again.

- To remove animal urine stain, first blot up as much of it as possible before it has had time to absorb. Next, sponge the spot with lukewarm water and blot again. Then mix one teaspoon of white vinegar with three teaspoons of lukewarm water. Apply this to the stain with a medicine dropper and gently rub the area with a rotary motion, working in from the outer edge. Allow the solution to remain for fifteen minutes and blot. Mix one teaspoonful of a light-duty nonalkaline detergent (the kind you use for fine fabrics) with a cup of water. Apply this mixture on the spot with a sponge. Complete with another application of clear water and blot again to remove the moisture.

- Don't be shocked if your well-trained, housebroken cat suddenly begins to have accidents. Sexually mature, unaltered cats, particularly males, will deliberately spray to attract the opposite sex. A cat kept indoors will indulge in this habit around the house. If your cat does have this problem, the best solution is to have him spayed or neutered.

- To keep a kitten's sand or toilet box hidden, invest in one of those decorative screens or enclosed boxes you can buy from a pet shop.

- And for the "sand" box, there is a commercial cat litter made of a special gravel-like clay. While more expensive than plain sand or shredded newspaper, it does a good job of preventing unpleasant odors.

THE PROBLEM OF SHEDDING HAIR

- To avoid constant hair shedding on upholstery, clothing, and carpets, brush your pet's coat regularly:
- Set your pet up on a table or bench, on a rubber mat so he will have a firm footing.
- To keep your own clothes hair-free, wear an apron that covers front, back, and arms.
- If your cat or dog is not frightened by the sound of the vacuum cleaner, the brush attachment makes an excellent tool for removing loose hair.

503

BATHING A DOG

- When bathing your dog, a rubber mat in the bottom of the tub will help him feel secure.
- To keep the drain from becoming clogged with dog hair, stuff it with a nylon scouring net.
- Be careful when bathing a dog in the winter that he doesn't become chilled. Rub him down with a towel first, then use hand-type hair dryer to hasten the drying. Be careful of his ears and eyes while using the dryer.

PETS AND FURNITURE

- If you are the permissive type who does not mind your cat and dog lounging on the furniture, just as any other family member, you'll find that a sticky tape lint remover or a dry cellulose sponge picks up hairs quickly, between vacuuming.
- If you have just acquired a kitten, you'll soon find out that it begins scratching and your furniture is the victim. To prevent damage to your furniture, get a catnip-treated scratching post. Or make one of your own out of carpet. To train him, scold him firmly, then move him away from the furniture to the scratching post or pad.

STORAGE FOR PET SUPPLIES

- Somewhere near the back or front entrance find a special cupboard or area to keep all your pet's accouterments—dog collar, coat, etcetera.
- The familiar shoebag we have mentioned so many times as a handy storage container is especially good for holding pets' toys, balls, bones, catnip, mice, flea powders, and grooming tools.

- A hook is excellent for collars, leashes and towels for cleaning wet paws.
- Convert old bath towel into paw wipers by cutting a strip of toweling about 10 inches wide. Fold over and stitch the ends to form pockets large enough to fit your hands. Bind the raw edges with bias tape.
- A chamois is excellent for drying your pet's coat if he has been out in the rain or snow, especially for a long-coated dog.

KENNELS

If you have need for using a kennel, check the following points:

- Look in the yellow pages for a listing of the ones in your area.
- Check outdoor facilities for exercising if you plan to be away for any length of time.
- Make sure they keep a well-groomed kennel—clean cages, floors, free of odor.
- There should be a veterinarian on duty or one on call at all times.
- Make sure the cage is big enough for your pet to stand in and move around. He should have his own.
- Ask about food and drinking water. Will they supply the normal diet your pet is used to eating?
- Investigate heating and air-conditioning facilities.
- What are the kennel's requirements as to acceptance of pets?
    1. Inoculations.
    2. Signing contracts or waivers of immunity, to treat a dog without owner's permission in case of illness.
- Fee.

CHAPTER THIRTEEN

Moving

There probably isn't anyone who looks forward to the chore of moving, but everyone has to go through it occasionally—some people even frequently, in our mobile society of today. Let's face it, moving is work, but with the right kind of planning and packing ahead, and the careful selection of a moving company, moving day can be fairly smooth and efficient.

CHOOSING A MOVER

The best way to select a moving company is by personal recommendation or reputation of the mover. The large, well-known national and international companies are safe bets for reliability and efficiency. When choosing among these companies, their prices are competitive and will be approximately the same for most moves. However, if you want to save some money, some of the smaller local companies may charge less per hour. Be sure you check them out, however, if you do not know anyone who has recently used them—sometimes trying to save money by hiring an unknown company can end up costing you more in the long run (if they take longer for the move than estimated or if they are careless and damage some of your furniture). A reliable company will be insured in case of accidentally damaging your property.

GET ESTIMATES

Movers will come to your home and give you a fairly close estimate of what your move will cost. Get two or three estimates and you'll have a good idea of what price is about right. Be as exact as possible when the estimator visits as to what is to be moved—if there are any large pieces in the attic or somewhere that you've forgotten to show the estimator, the cost of the move will be more than you anticipate.

Checklist: What to Do Before Moving Day:
- Have major appliances such as refrigerators and washing machines serviced for protection during shipping.
- Curtain rods, towel racks, and wall brackets should be removed and packed prior to loading date.
- Items not to be moved should be tagged individually and left with any special instructions.
- Plan to carry articles of extraordinary value with you or send them by insured registered mail or by Railway Express.
- Discontinue utilities—notify all utilities to discontinue service and make final readings.
- Notify post office, magazines and newspapers, insurance companies, friends, etcetera, of your change of address.
- Obtain transcripts and records from schools, banks, doctors, etcetera, if you are moving a distance.
- Examine and make sure that the inventory record of your household goods is accurate as to number of items and condition of furniture.
- Be sure all agreements between you and the carrier are in writing on the order.
- Notify the mover's representative and driver where you can be reached during the move and on arrival at your new residence.

IF YOU DO YOUR OWN PACKING

If you decide to do your own packing it will save you a fair amount of money. To be sure your goods will arrive at your new home in good condition, pack with care. Remember these tips:

- Get large cartons from the mover—they will deliver these cartons to you as soon as you want them after contracting for the move. The nominal fee you pay for large cardboard cartons (and you get part of it back when you return them after unpacking) is well worth it, because they make your packing quicker and easier. Some smaller boxes are useful for books and small items—you can get strong ones from liquor stores.
- Mark boxes that are packed with breakables "Fragile" or "Glass." Pack with plenty of paper around each breakable item and on sides, bottom and top of box. (Use old newspapers—and use them generously.)
- Label your cartons, put similar types of items in same box, and pack by room. For instance, your labels might read: "Kitchen—pots," "Kitchen—glasses," "Living room —knickknacks," "Bathroom—fragile." This way you can look at the cartons quickly and tell the movers where to put them in your new home.
- Start to pack early—a few weeks before moving day. You can begin by packing a few cartons with decorative objects and other items that you have no daily use for. Each day you can pack a few cartons until, the last day before the move, you can pack up the necessities.
- So that you can pack all your kitchen utensils, plates, etcetera, plan to eat from paper plates and utensils on moving day and the evening before—or eat out.
- Use pillows, blankets, towels, and other soft articles for packing around glassware and other fragile and heavy objects. This will protect the breakables and alleviate the weight of heavy cartons.
- Carry with you your most important personal papers and valuables. Also certain fragile items that are particularly hard to pack such as pictures and mirrors if your move is a local one. Movers will crate these items if you can't take them with you, but every extra service like this costs something. If you carry valuables such as pictures or mirrors in the back of a station wagon, for instance, lay them carefully on blankets and pillows to protect them.
- Try not to have too many small boxes—movers can work faster with large cartons and, remember, you usually pay by the hour.

- If you have any special problem furniture pieces, such as a grand piano or an extra-long sofa that won't fit on the elevator in your new apartment building, let the movers know about it ahead of time so that they can make any necessary special arrangements. A friend had an eight-foot sofa which would not fit in the elevator at her new building, and it sat in the lobby for a while, much to the displeasure of fellow tenants. No matter what anyone tried, it would not fit on the elevator, and her apartment was on the 28th floor. Finally two young men agreed to walk it up the stairs for her—for a generous fee!

GETTING THE NEW HOUSE OR APARTMENT READY

- Make sure as far as possible that the house or apartment is ready for the movers. If painting is to be done, floors cleaned and waxed, do this before the move.
- Check to see that utilities are in working order—electricity, water, gas, and telephone.
- Place light bulbs in all overhead or ceiling fixtures. Have extras ready for lamps.
- Mark special areas in rooms for placement of large furniture and leave spaces in rooms for placing specific boxes marked for these areas.
- Clean kitchens, bathrooms. Have cabinets and closet shelves cleaned and lined, ready for storage items.
- Have carpeting laid and draperies hung before the move, if possible.
- Leave floors free so padding and area rugs can be laid before furniture is placed.
- Clean windows if possible.

AFTER YOU HAVE MOVED IN

Try to work fast to make your new house look like a home. You'll be amazed how cozy, cheerful, and lived-in a new house can look with a few quick decorating tricks.

- Before you do anything else, hang the curtains. If your draperies are suddenly too short or too narrow for your new windows, line with a print or contrasting color and let lining turn into a cuff all around. Make tiebacks to match.
- Hang some pictures as soon as you know the definite position of your furniture.
- Put your books in the bookcases. Never mind what order they're in, for now. Books are a bright, decorative, personally yours note.
- Light the lights. Do you have enough lamps, indoors or out, to do justice to the new house? Do you have enough outlets? Even the prettiest, most settled home looks dreary and dismal with inadequate lighting.
- If you didn't bring house plants with you, buy some. Living plants do wonders to create a "living" feeling. Larger ones are good for filling in problem corners—not to mention solving the too-little-furniture problem.
- Buy some fresh flowers.
- Unpack your accessories—ash trays, knickknacks, art objects. Just having them around will make you look settled.
- Set a pretty table. Camping out for a while is fine, but how much more time does it take to put out your prettiest mats and light the candles?
- Light a fire in the fireplace (if you have one) the very first night if you can. (If it isn't the season, substitute a group of flickering candles or armfuls of fresh, glossy leaves. Don't sit there staring at an empty, gaping hole.)
- Don't forget the "little touches." This is the time to do things backwards. Ordinarily, you wouldn't fuss with fancy finishing touches until everything else was in apple pie order. Now, we suggest you ignore those unpacked crates and disorganized closets and set a pretty silver bowl piled with shiny apples on a living room table.
- Compose a "still life" of vegetables in the kitchen. You'll be surprised how many big things will go unnoticed.

SOME QUICK DECORATING TIPS
FOR PEOPLE "ON THE MOVE"

Though these are good decorating tips that can apply to any situation, they are especially good for people who move often—and in particular if you *rent*.

Don't choose large, overscaled upholstered pieces, such as an eight-foot sofa, which may not fit in your new living room or will limit your furniture arranging.

Select adaptable, go-anywhere furniture—tables and chairs, chests, etcetera, which will be equally at home in a living room, dining room, or bedroom. Avoid matching suites. There's no rule that says dining room chairs have to match the table or a bedroom lamp has to look "bedroomy."

Choose a dining room table that can be expanded with leaves rather than a massive banquet table.

As we suggest in the chapter on decorating, buy a few good pieces, the very best you can afford. They not only weather moving better but will give you a sense of unity and pride of ownership whichever roof they are under. It's better to fill in with second-hand bargains that you can brighten up to taste and leave behind without tears than to settle for mediocre furniture that you won't like any better one place or the other.

Until you feel fairly "settled," keep your overall scheme neutral in color so that you can have the fun of changing wall colors, pillow accents and accessories.

Since built-ins are out, take advantage of wall units that combine shelves, chests of drawers or doors, glass-front cabinets, desks—all of which can be combined in many different ways. They can be placed against the wall or used as free-standing room dividers, and they are movable.

Wall-to-wall carpeting can be removed and recut, of course, but area rugs are much more practical.

Shop for a folding screen (couldn't be more packable) that could be a room divider in one house, a decorative accent in another.

Investigate the "paper" or heavy cardboard furniture available —especially for children's rooms.

Fabric-draped tables are a favorite decorating trick. They can solve many a problem and are especially tailored for people on the move since any round table will do (even a circle of plywood on a stand) and the cloths can be changed at will.

Consider the advantages of slipcovers instead of reupholstering. Since the cost is about half, you can afford to give sofa and chairs a new look more frequently.

CHAPTER FOURTEEN

On Purchasing Wisely

ON BECOMING AN INFORMED CONSUMER

This is, indeed, an age when we are learning to be smart shoppers and good consumers in spite of ourselves. There has never been a time when people were more conscious of the marketplace with its goods and services and what it means in terms of buying value and satisfaction. We are reminded at every turn just what responsibilities each of us has to himself—the manufacturer, the retailer, the government, and the consumer. This is an age of probing, question-asking, and seeking for quality, durability, integrity, and values in the products we buy for ourselves and our homes.

The way we spend our money and what we spend it for is influenced to a large degree by our sense of values and the goals we have defined for ourselves and our families. Our sense of values are the standards by which we live. Out of these standards, of course, come our goals and plans for the future. This, naturally, will determine how we spend our money.

How to Become Informed

To be a skillful and informed shopper it is important to get as many facts about the products and services you want as possible. Keep a clip file on all sorts of household goods you may be in the market for now and in the future. Then set about collecting all the information you can about these topics which will help you to become a better shopper and thus get more for the money you spend. You can collect these ideas from everywhere—newspaper and magazine articles, manufacturers and their associations, colleges and universities, extension services and bulletins, advertising (factual ads that act as buyers' guides), manufacturers' consumer service booklets, fact tags, hangtags and labels, seals of certification, safety seals, standards, business-sponsored publications such as those offered by insurance companies, banks, finance companies, etcetera, consumer education booklets published by the government agencies at local, state, and federal levels, and material produced by trade associations and manufacturers.

The art of becoming well informed is getting more complex because we need to know more about more things, yet it is becoming easier because there is more information around. Everyone is consumer-conscious—the government, the manufacturer, the retailer, and most of all, the consumer.

SMART SHOPPERS PLAN FIRST, COMPARE VALUES

It is a smart shopper who will take time to plan a major purchase in advance. It is important to decide how much you can and will pay for products and services before you begin to shop for them. Good planning imposes a control on your budget and, consequently, will curtail overspending. You may be able to save money by spending a little time and energy pre-shopping before you make decisions. Here are some guidelines:

- Compare prices of similar merchandise in different stores until you find what you want.
- Collect point-of-sale information, brochures. Study advertisements thoroughly.
- Look for sales and special prices. Study a bargain. A bargain is not a bargain unless it meets a need.
- If possible, avoid crowds of people and "rush hour" stampedes.
- You'll get better attention from sales personnel during "off" hours.
- If you are shopping during "peak" hours, save time by making a list and knowing exactly what you want and where to look for it.

- Take advantage of telephone shopping and delivery in large department stores if time is a factor.
- Consider just how a product will be used, how long you want it to last and what features are most important to you.

PURCHASING ON CREDIT

It is a wise and noble thing to buy only as much as you can pay for. However, it may be that some of us will never "catch up" long enough to acquire a few of the things, at least, that we want or really need. All of which means that some time or other we will be buying on credit. The key to buying on credit is to understand all the facts before you buy, and to try to work within a budget, even if you are "paying money to buy time," for that is just what you do when you buy on credit. When you buy on time or "on the installment plan" you are paying out more than when you buy for cash. Moreover, when you get an installment loan, you are paying back more than you receive!

When you hear such claims as "easy terms," "easy payment," "no down payment," beware. Nothing is a bargain when you pay more in the long run than the price tag indicates.

Let us say in the beginning: If you can pay cash or by check, do so. Subscribe to the use of charge accounts or credit cards only when you know you have the money to support it. If not, take time to plan your purchases, for when you buy for the first time on credit, you immediately set out to make a name for yourself, good or bad. There are various groups and agencies that maintain complete records and files of all your credit transactions. A good credit rating is the best reference you can have. On the other hand, a bad credit rating can be your worst enemy. Do everything you can to maintain good credit:

- Plan your purchases; budget ahead. See page 18.
- Don't buy more than you need.
- Pay your bills on time.

Remember, it's easy to fall into a credit habit. It's easy to say "Charge It." But it's hard when for some sudden reason your income takes a turn for the worse, to meet the payments, if you're in the swim over your head!

515

How credit works. The Truth in Lending Law, which became effective in July 1969, covers all credit for personal, family, household or farm use up to $25,000 and all real estate transactions. It is a federal law which, although it does not fix a maximum charge for credit, requires that your creditor must disclose to you the true and total cost of credit and that he must state finance charges in both dollar amounts and in *annual percentage rates.* These charges should include all costs involved. NO HIDDEN CHARGES. When you see the cost in dollars, you will know immediately how much money you are paying for the time you are buying. The annual percentage rate is a good guide when comparing charges from one place to another.

Suppose you want to buy a television on time. If you are told that the interest will be only 1% a month on the unpaid balance, that means, as low as it may seem to you, that you are paying 12% a year, or:

MONTHLY	ANNUAL PERCENTAGE RATE
1½%	18%
2	24
2½	30

Get All the Facts Before You Buy:
- Know the total amount you will pay.
- Read and understand a contract before you sign it.
- Keep a copy of anything you sign in a safe place.
- When you make any kind of payment, get a detailed receipt. A canceled check is always a good receipt.
- Be sure to keep up payments.

QUALITY

Quality is what makes up the character and fineness of a product determined by its materials, design, and workmanship. It is usually available in three types:

1. High quality means you will pay a higher price for the best material and workmanship. It usually means that the product will last longer.

2. Medium quality usually promises excellence in materials and offers a durable and practical product. Expect a medium-price range.

3. Lower quality means that material and workmanship are quite acceptable, but the product promises a limited or short-term life span. Price will be relative.

Follow These Guidelines When Actually Purchasing a Product:

- Plan ahead and pre-shop before making actual decisions.
- Buy from a reliable and reputable dealer. Take this to mean a dealer who has a good reputation and has proved to be a leader in his community, one who lives up to his promises, offers good service, and cares whether or not he has satisfied his customers.
- Buy a good brand name from a well-known manufacturer or retailer.
- Study labels. Read them thoroughly, and keep seals, hangtags, and instruction books.
- Ask questions and don't settle for anything until you have satisfied your curiosity.
- Read guarantees and warranties.
- Study contracts and read them fully before signing anything.
- Find out what the products are made of, how they work, how to use and take care of them, how long they should last.
- Ask about price.
- Don't shop for price alone. Buy only what you need.
- Insist on seeing advertised merchandise. Keep the ad until the merchandise is delivered and you are satisfied.
- If you know *what* you want, then you cannot be "baited" and "switched" to another product. If you know what you want, you can avoid a "spiff," when the salesman tries to switch you to another product because he will make more money on it.
- Beware of hidden charges, such as delivery, installation, or other service charges.
- Ask if you can return the merchandise if you are not satisfied.

SHOPPING THE SALES—
TO HELP YOU SAVE MONEY

January—Sales: After-Christmas, furniture, winter clothes, January white sales of sheets, pillowcases, and towels, small appliances, sports equipment.

February—Sales: Furniture, rugs, mattresses, china, glassware, housewares, curtains, notions, women's coats.

March—Sales: Clothing and home furnishings are expensive before Easter.

April—Sales: After-Easter clothes clearances.

May—Sales: White sales, TV sets, soaps, cleaning aids, women's underwear, housecoats, pocketbooks.

June—Sales: TV sets, refrigerators, storm windows, dresses, piece goods.

July—Sales: Used cars, washing machines, refrigerators, summer clothes, shoes.

August—Sales: Tires, white sales, furniture, mattresses, rugs, curtains.

September—Sales: Cars, tools, hardware, piece goods, housewares, china, glassware.

October—Sales: Cars (lowest of year), Columbus Day coat sales, women's underwear, and housecoats.

November—Sales: Veterans' Day sales of coats and dresses, blankets, piece goods.

December—Sales: Toys and gifts may be reduced in mid-December, women's and girls' coats, men's and boys' suits.

Watch for special sales in your local areas. There are sales all year long and, nowadays, they don't seem to follow a monthly pattern.

Some Tips on Sale Shopping
• Ask if items are returnable.
• The best shopping days are the first and last. On the first day you will get a better selection, and on the last day they may have cut the prices even more.

- Check the original price to see how much you will save.
- Inspect merchandise carefully to make sure it is a bargain.
- Think about shopping expenses in relation to how much you are actually saving. If you have had to pay a high cost for your personal time, transportation, baby sitter, lunch, etcetera, you may not be saving much after all.
- Consider repair costs. If you have to pay to put an article into working condition, it may not be worth the purchase.
- Ask if guarantees are still in effect. They should be, regardless of a sale.

CHECK SEALS OF CERTIFICATION AND SAFETY

Look for the safety or certification seals of the following organizations for safety, performance, and durability.

1. *The UL Seal of the Underwriters Laboratories, Inc.*, found on the body of an appliance (not the cord) means that UL tests and evaluates the product design to see that it meets the recognized safety requirements.

2. *The American Gas Association Blue Star Seal* on a gas appliance is placed there by the manufacturer and is his certification that a prototype has been tested at the AGA laboratories and has been found to comply with the American National Standard for safety, durability, and performance.

519

3. *The Association of Home Appliance Manufacturers* (AHAM) *Certification Seal* means that a key performance or capacity characteristic of the product has been established through tests designed by AHAM and performed by an independent laboratory. AHAM certifies the BTU/hr cooling capacity, amperes and watts rating on air conditioners; BTU/hr heating and cooling capacity, amperes, and watts of combination heating and cooling room air conditioners; water removal capacity of dehumidifiers and output of gallons of water per day for humidifiers; and the net refrigerated volume and net shelf area of refrigerators and freezers.

4. *The International Fabricare Institute* (IFI) *Certified Washable and Dry Cleanable Seals* mean that products undergo tests covering each element of manufacture which could contribute to satisfactory wear and laundering. These tests cover: shrinkage, color-fastness, light-fastness, gas-fading, perspiration reaction, tensile strength, bleeding, crocking, general appearance after laundering and dry-cleaning, and any other characteristic which may affect the product's satisfactory service. The International Fabricare Institute is the national trade association for the laundry and dry-cleaning industry and is the successor to the American Institute of Laundering and National Institute of Drycleaning.

5. *The American National Standards Institute* (ANSI) is the national clearinghouse and coordinating agency for voluntary standardization in the United States. It approves a standard when it receives evidence that all national groups concerned with the development of a particular standard have been given an opportunity to cooperate in the standard's development and have reached substantial agreement on its provisions. Standardization may be in definitions, dimensions, specifications, test methods, safety, labeling. ANSI also represents the interest of the United States in international standardization work.

6. Some magazines test products and indicate their approval or recommendations based upon their specific standards before products are accepted for advertising.

7. *Testing Services.* Such services may be conducted by business, government, or private organizations. Results may appear on seals or labels found on products or printed in publications, such as Consumer Bulletin, published by Consumer's Research Inc., or Consumer Reports, published by Consumers Union.

PURCHASING MAJOR APPLIANCES

Before You Buy a Major Appliance, Check:
- The appliance specifications against the space you have available.
- Any installation requirements necessary—electric, water, and gas connections—against the facilities in your home.
- The durability in construction, finishes, controls, sound insulation, doors, and handles. Open and close doors, pull out drawers, ask about quality of materials. If it looks and feels strong, then chances are it is.
- The capacity needed.
- The various models and styles available—free-standing, built-in, or portable.
- The guarantee or warranty. Read it carefully and understand all the terms.
- The availability of authorized service, service contracts.

- Hidden costs of delivery, installation, and operation.
- The advisability of budgeting for appliance repairs.
- Look for seals of safety and certification that indicate products have been tested and checked for safety and/or performance and durability. They include the UL Seal of the Underwriters Laboratories, Inc., the Blue Star Seal of the American Gas Association Laboratories, the AHAM Certification Seals of the Association of Home Appliance Manufacturers, and The International Fabricare Institute Certified Washable and Dry Cleanable Seals. See the preceding section for what these seals look like and what they mean.

After You Buy the Appliance:
- Study your instruction manual for use and care.
- When something goes wrong, before calling for service, check plugs, fuses, pilots, and controls—review instruction manual. More than one-fourth of all service calls are unnecessary when this is done.
- When you do require service, call your dealer, the service agency he recommends, or an authorized organization "franchised" by the manufacturer to repair your brand.

If a problem develops which you cannot resolve locally with your dealer or servicing agency, write or call the manufacturer giving all the details. If you are not satisfied with the action taken by the manufacturer, write to:

1. *For gas appliances,* Gas Appliance Manufacturers' Association, 1901 N. Ft. Meyer Drive, Arlington, Virginia 22209.
2. *For all other appliances,* Association of Home Appliance Manufacturers, 20 N. Wacker Drive, Chicago, Illinois 60606.
   These two organizations, along with the National Retail Merchant's Association, have established an independent consumer complaint panel called MACAP (Major Appliance Consumer Action Panel) who can take action on any complaints you may have.

UNDERSTANDING GUARANTEES AND WARRANTIES

These two terms are used interchangeably.

Remember that when you buy a major appliance (or any major durable product) you are also buying a warranty. It costs the manufacturer to fulfill the warranty terms and that cost is part of the price you will pay for the appliance. Make certain that each product you purchase has a warranty that provides you with protection that is meaningful. Become familiar with warranty contents and terminology. Treat the warranty just like a convenience feature on the appliance.

Before you purchase any appliance, answer the following questions, as recommended by the MACAP:

- Does the warranty cover the entire product? Only certain parts? Is labor included?
- Who is responsible for repairing the product? the dealer? a service agency? the manufacturers?
- Who pays for repairs? parts? labor? shipping charges?
- How long does the warranty last on the entire product? on individual parts or assemblies?
- If the product is out of use because of a service problem, or if it has to be removed from the home for repair, will a substitute product or service be provided? By whom?

Note: Keep your warranty contract and the sales check for future reference. Record the date of purchase and model number.

SERVICE AND MAINTENANCE

Because appliances and many other products such as television sets, etcetera, are mechanical, they can occasionally break down. Some may also require care and cleaning periodically. Obtaining necessary service can, at times, become an extremely trying experience. One of the purposes of a warranty is to provide fast, virtually cost-free service to the customer during the period of time when any basic defects in the appliance's workmanship and ma-

523

terials should show up. When a product is out of warranty, service costs will depend upon parts, labor, and sometimes a transportation "mileage" charge for getting to the job, especially if it involves some distance.

To obtain satisfactory service, make certain that your service is provided from an authorized or franchised representative of the manufacturer. (It is a good idea to arrange for service at the time of purchase.) Keep telephone numbers of service agencies handy for ready reference.

Consider purchasing a service contract if your product is out of warranty. Make certain it contains a regular maintenance agreement. *One caution:* Do not sign any contract unless you know and understand the exact terms and cost.

SHOPPING FOR SERVICES

Buying services is often an elusive thing. When you purchase a product it is a tangible thing you can see and feel. It is possible to examine it for specific characteristics. But when you are selecting or buying a service or an intangible, it is important to be particularly careful in the questions you ask and the values you will receive for your particular needs. Ask every question you can think of, regardless of whether you think it trite or not!

PROFESSIONAL—DOCTORS, DENTISTS, LAWYERS

Today's market is so complex that it requires some skillful probing and question-asking before you consult *any* professional service.

Check references through professional directories and associations; note whether or not they are graduates of accredited schools and are licensed to practice in your state; check fees before services begin; ask about allowances from medical insurance and plans; check for office hours, home calls in the case of doctors and, in particular, the hospitals with which they are associated. It is not unusual for you to ask a doctor or a lawyer what their fee is before you make a decision.

FINANCIAL—INSURANCE, BANKS, CREDIT FIRMS, INVESTMENTS

Check their reliability and whether or not they are licensed to do business in the state; ask about costs and methods of payments; what kind of benefits will you receive, percentage in bank services, coverage of insurance, how much credit and the cost of payments, value and growth of investments, etcetera; check terms of all financial contracts before signing anything.

PRIVATE SERVICES—LAUNDRIES, DRY CLEANERS

Check location, hours, speed, pickup and delivery; advantages of cash and carry—how much will you save; find out who handles complaints and what kind of adjustments can be made.

GUIDES FOR DOING THE WEEKLY MARKETING

HEALTH AIDS AND DRUGS

Drugstores today are selling a lot more than drugs as we know them. And keep in mind that other stores—discount houses and supermarkets—also sell drugstore supplies. It is possible to save money by shopping for medicines, toiletries, and cosmetics at discount houses, some department stores, discount drugstores, and "ten cent" stores. And private label brands, often the stores' own brands, may cost much less than well-known nationally advertised brands. Check with your doctor about the reliability of all kinds of drugs and medicines under private labels. You may be able to save a great deal that way. However, in some cases a lower price can mean poor quality.

Particularly talk to your doctor before buying diet pills, vitamins, and other "cures." They might be injurious to your health, unless your doctor prescribes them for you. Watch out for vague claims of cures for arthritis, baldness, and other "miracles." Not so.

525

Simple remedies such as disinfectants, headache pills, and similar products are safe to buy without consulting a doctor. But for severe pain or fever, check with your doctor. Don't put the druggist on the spot. As for prescriptions, ask your doctor if it is refillable without another one, or if it is possible, ask him to give "refill" instructions on the original prescription.

FOOD MARKETING

Marketing is not an easy job these days. An average family of four consumes approximately 2½ tons of food a year. There are well over 8,000 products in today's supermarkets. This array of food and its consumption is at once a staggering and exciting thought. But, like the growing number of laundry and cleaning aids, it can be a confusing issue. Since housewives the country over prepare well over half a billion meals a year, it is becoming increasingly more important to know how to shop wisely and economically, what with the wide choice of products, the increase in food prices and the fact that food spending accounts for a sizable share of your income.

A shopping list is your best guide to smart shopping. It will help you save time, money, and energy.

- Keep a market order pad handy to list the things you need. Organize it according to the departments in the supermarkets and arrange it in order as you come to the items in the aisles of the markets.
- Check the menus and recipes for special ingredients. Check all your storage areas for any missing staples or ingredients—refrigerator, cupboards, and pantry. Note styles, brands, flavor, and other preference of ingredients.

Some Useful Tips:
1. *Study the newspaper ads* before you make up your shopping list. Check for the specials and decide on the quantity you need.
2. *Be an early shopper* if you want the best choice in meats and produce.

3. *Know your supermarket.* Become familiar with its regular prices, so you will be able to recognize bargains. Keep up to date on current prices.

4. *Compare prices.* Learn to recognize the best buys . . . compare sizes—sometimes the largest or jumbo size may not be the most economical. Buy in quantity only *if* you can store and use that amount; *if* large sizes cost less per ounce of food than smaller packages; *if* lower prices are offered on quantity purchases. In figuring the cost of food, figure it based on the cost per portion. If a roast costs $1.39 a pound, and it will serve six, that means it costs around 23¢ a serving.

   Unit pricing, the cost per ounce or pound of food items, is a comparatively new method of price indication. Grocers are adopting unit pricing by indicating the price per unit on the package or by displaying unit pricing posters with the various cost breakdowns or by inserting a tag with the price on the shelves where the item is located.

   Tip: There are shopping computers you can carry in your purse to help you compare prices and find the best buys. Look for them in housewares departments and hardware stores.

5. *Learn to read labels.* By law, every can and every packaged food product must state on the label the net contents (weight or liquid measure), list ingredients, indicate whether any artificial flavors or colors have been added, describe dietary characteristics (sugar- or salt-free). Labels of canned products identify the variety or style of the product, for example, whole green beans or cut green beans; or if it's fruit, whether or not it is packed in heavy or light syrup, in water or perhaps in its own juice. The best canners will indicate the number of servings.

   Look also for nutritional labeling which gives you the nutritive values of the package's content.

   For a chart of commonly used can sizes, see the following section. Today we identify can sizes by weight or fluid measure, but in older recipes you may find the manufacturers' terms used instead, thus their explanation on the chart, also.

   Labels on packaged mixes and dehydrated foods not

527

only contain a list of ingredients and additives, but instructions and recipe variations as well.

6. *Open dating* refers to the date on a packaged food which indicates the last day of sale. This, of course, is the customer's assurance that he is buying a product at the peak of freshness and before it is "pulled" from the store shelves.

7. *Food companies and supermarket chains offer specials* at certain times of the year, sometimes just before the new crop of fruits and vegetables goes for canning. These specials vary from area to area. Try to get the "feel" of your area, the rhythm of your store; watch for the "loss leader," the item on which the store loses money, but does it to lead you to the store.

8. *Make the meat department manager your friend.* If you want a special cut of meat that isn't in the meat case, ask him to have it cut for you. He'll translate unfamiliar names such as "California Roast," which in the East is just the middle of the chuck, or "Newport Roast," which is the first rib cut.

9. *An occasional "impulse buy"* is part of the fun of marketing. But if you don't have a market order and depend only on the shelves and displays to dictate shopping, you won't get the most for your dollar.

10. *Remember that day-old baked goods* are usually sold at considerable savings. They're just as fresh as if you had bought them yesterday and left them on your own shelf.

11. *On Saturdays, an hour or two before closing*, there are often real buys in the produce and baked goods departments.

12. *At the checkout counter,* help the checker and yourself:
    • Group your order by categories—meat, dairy, produce and fruit, canned and packaged goods.
    • Group your two for something or three for something items, so you aren't charged for individual cans or packages.
    • Watch the register tally to be sure the "special" price is rung up rather than the regular price, which may happen inadvertently. It is good business to watch the register tally, anyway. Might save a few pennies here and there.

COMMON CONTAINER SIZES

Labels on cans or jars of identical size may show a net weight for one product that differs slightly from the net weight of another due to the differences in the density of the foods. An example would be baked beans (1 lb.) and blueberries (14 oz.) in the same size can. (Chart courtesy Nat'l. Canners Ass'n.)

	CONSUMER DESCRIPTION		
INDUSTRY TERM	APPROX. NET WEIGHT OR FLUID MEASURE (CHECK LABEL)	APPROX. CUPS	PRINCIPAL PRODUCTS
8 oz.	8 oz.	1	Fruits, vegetables, specialties* for small families. 2 servings.
Picnic	10½ to 12 oz.	1¼	Mainly condensed soups. Some fruits, vegetables, meat, fish, specialties.* 3 servings.
12 oz. (vacuum)	12 oz.	1½	Principally for vacuum-pack corn. 3 to 4 servings.
No. 300	14 to 16 oz.	1¾	Pork and beans, baked beans, meat products, cranberry sauce, blueberries, specialties.* 3 to 4 servings.
No. 303	16 to 17 oz.	2	Principal size for fruits and vegetables. Some meat products, ready-to-serve soups, specialties.* 4 servings.

Specialties—Food combinations prepared by special manufacturers' recipes.

No. 2	1 lb. 4 oz. or 1 pt. 2 fl. oz.	2½	Juices, ready-to-serve soups, some special-ties,* pineapple, apple slices. No longer in popular use for most fruits and vegetables. 5 servings.
No. 2½	1 lb. 13 oz.	3½	Fruits, some vege-tables (pumpkin, sauerkraut, spinach and other greens, to-matoes). 7 servings.
No. 3 cyl. or 46 fl. oz.	3 lb. 3 oz. or 1 qt. 14 fl. oz.	5¾	"Economy family size" fruit and vege-table juices, pork and beans. Institu-tional size for con-densed soups, some vegetables. 10 to 12 servings.
No. 10	6½ lb. to 7 lb. 5 oz.	12–13	Institutional size for fruits, vegetables, and some other foods. 25 servings.

Meats, fish, and seafood are almost entirely advertised and sold under weight terminology.

Infant and junior foods come in small cans and jars suitable for the smaller servings used. Content is given on label.

HOUSING

CHECKLIST FOR APARTMENT HUNTERS

- Be sure it suits your needs, for space, convenience, at-tractiveness.
- Check closet and storage space—older apartments and even houses are sometimes short on this. If there isn't

enough storage space in the apartment for trunks, bicycles, and such, ask if there is a storage room for this purpose in the building, and if so what are the security protections (things have a way of disappearing from these storage areas unless they are locked up carefully).

- Is there enough cross-ventilation in the apartment, and is it light and sunny where you like it to be?
- The windows in the apartment should be of good size and placed well; they should be supplied with screens and storms, blinds or shades.
- Ideally, the building should be soundproof. Listen for talking, plumbing, and footsteps from other apartments and hallways.
- Heating (and air conditioning, if the apartment has it) should be clean and effective, with individual room controls.
- Kitchen appliances should be in good condition.
- Check doors, casings, cabinets and any built-ins to see if they are well fitted.
- If you are signing a new lease, the apartment should be clean and newly decorated or painted.
- What extras if any does the apartment offer—such as air conditioning, carpeting, dishwasher, garbage disposer, fireplace, balcony?

Building Services:
- Does the building have indoor or outdoor parking space; if so, at what extra charge?
- If the building is not a new, fireproof building, are there adequate fire escapes?
- There should be convenient trash collection and disposal facilities—an incinerator room on each floor is convenient.
- What are the laundry facilities in the apartment building, if any? Most new, large buildings do have coin-operated washers and dryers for the tenants.
- What other services does the building offer? If it is a large high-rise building there may be 24-hour doorman service, which is an added safety factor, and there may be a package room to accept packages for you when you are not home. If these kinds of services are important to you, a new, large building is a good bet. Some of them even have maid and valet services, and health clubs with swimming pools.

531

- If you have to walk up more than two or three floors, does the building have an elevator? Buildings with more than four floors should have elevators.

- *How much rent can you afford to pay?* There's an old guideline that still holds true: your rent should not exceed your weekly take-home income. With today's high rentals, particularly in major cities, many people find they have to pay more than this percentage in rent, but this can become a strain. Remember to figure in electricity, telephone, gas and commutation costs as regular monthly expenses beyond your rent. You can afford to pay more in rent in a building where utilities are included in the rental price.

- *Read that lease.* When you are about to rent an apartment or a house, read the lease carefully before you sign it. Not many one-year leases are offered these days, so chances are it will be a two- or a three-year lease. If you are quite sure of staying three years at least, the longer lease is an advantage because the rent cannot be raised during that time. In other words, you should ask for the longer lease. When a lease is up, rent usually goes up as well.

- If there's a chance you might have to move again before the lease is up, be sure you have a sublet clause or some other means of getting out of the lease which doesn't cost you too much.

- Always check a lease, too, for whether or not pets are allowed, and what you are responsible for in the apartment; in other words, if you accidentally damage a wall or floor, or a counter top, will you have to pay for the damage? If you apply anything to the wall—wallpaper, cabinets—will you be responsible for removing it when you move? Be especially careful about this when you are renting a furnished apartment or home.

CHECKLIST FOR HOME BUYERS

Buying a house is the biggest financial transaction ever faced by the average family. It's vitally important to look carefully and to buy wisely.

- Choose the community and neighborhood first. When you decide *where* you want to live, then you can start to look for a specific house.
- Check the local newspapers. It's a good idea to first follow up on ads that are placed by owners—if you can buy direct you'll save the broker's fee. (These ads will often say "Principals Only.") Next, follow up any other ads placed by brokers that sound interesting.
- Register with a few brokers. Remember, the more you register with the more calls you'll be getting to go to see houses, etcetera, so if your house hunting is an almost full-time, concentrated effort, register with several; if you want to take your time and look leisurely, register with only one or two.
- Investigate all the local builders and developers and compare values.
- Does the community and neighborhood offer schools, churches, recreational facilities, physical attractiveness, zoning and spaciousness suitable to your needs and desires (you want to protect yourself from an area becoming overcrowded).
- In figuring what price you can pay for a house, have you considered interest and amortization of the mortgage, taxes, insurance, fuel, gas, water, electricity, telephone, minimum repairs, commutation or upkeep of car if used for daily transportation?
- Is the house well constructed? (It is wise to get expert advice on this, for much construction detail is hidden. Get an architect, for a nominal fee, to look over the house you are considering; he will give you a reliable opinion on its soundness.)
- Look for an architectural style which is attractive to you, which looks well on its site and mingles well with the houses near it.
- Does the house suit your tastes and needs—for now and in the future, especially if you plan to stay permanently and your family is still growing.
- Do the house and property suit your family's life-style? For instance, if you love to cook out and spend a lot of time outdoors, is there a patio or nice attractive lawn area for this? If you like privacy, is the house secluded

533

enough? If your family is sports minded, is there space for a basketball "court" or baseball diamond?

- Are the living room, family room and playroom large enough for family and guests?
- Does the house have that family room with fireplace you've dreamed of, or that paneled den or library with built-in bookshelves you've always wanted?
- Is the kitchen well planned (see Chapter Five), with good-quality appliances that suit your needs?
- Are heating, plumbing, and electricity adequate and in good condition? These are the nitty-gritty facts about a house that we most often overlook. Sometimes no one bothers to check—but do check heating and plumbing or have someone do it; these are important factors in a house and if they are not in good shape they can run you into a great deal of trouble and money.
- Can all areas of the house be reached from a hall without passing through one room to get to another?
- Are the entrances and hallways big enough to prevent traffic congestion?
- Are the windows, doors, and closets of rooms arranged to provide ample wall space for furniture arrangements? Are there properly fitted and easy-to-operate screens and storm windows?
- Does the house lend itself to future expansion?
- If the house has multiple levels, are the rooms arranged so you can do daily housework without climbing innumerable short flights of stairs?
- Is there easy access from the kitchen to the outdoor service area or back yard?
- Is there space enough in the kitchen for informal dining? Or an informal dining area adjacent to the kitchen?
- Are the bedrooms and bathrooms well separated from the living and working areas of the house?
- Are there sufficient bathrooms and fixtures to handle the morning rush?
- Are there enough bedrooms to provide separate rooms for the children when they grow older?
- Do windows in bedrooms provide good natural ventilation and light?
- Is there any area that can be used as a workshop and for storing paint and necessary tools?

- Is there adequate storage in the bedrooms?
- Is there sufficient space provided for storing linens, cleaning materials, food, and bulky items such as outdoor furniture, sporting equipment and bicycles?
- Are storage areas (both indoor and outdoor) easily accessible?
- Are attic and/or basement (if any) in good shape, and dry, with good storage space or expansion possibilities?
- Is garage large enough and is it in good condition? Is there access to it from house? What about driveway and walks?
- Are the floors level wood with smooth finish and no gaps; and are the walls smooth, without hollows or cracks?
- Is the roof leakproof and in good shape; and is the insulation adequate for warmth and soundproofing?
- Is the carpentry work in the house well done, with properly fitted joints and moldings?
- Outside, is there an enclosed yard if you have small children?
- Is the property well landscaped and cared for? Are there plantings that will bloom again, and are the lawn and trees healthy?
- Does the land slope away from the house? Is the soil dry and firm? Is there good drainage of rain and moisture? There should also be noncorrosive gutters and downspouts on the roof, connected to storm sewer or splash block to carry water away from the house.
- Is copper or aluminum flashing used over doors, windows and joints on the roof?
- Is siding material on house in good condition, solid brick and masonry free of cracks, and foundation walls solid?
- Make sure that all steps and stoops are sturdy and in good condition and that windows and doors are adequately weatherstripped.
- What extras does the house offer: fireplace, air conditioning, porches, new kitchens and baths, built-ins, appliances, garbage disposal, attractive decorations, carpeting, draperies?

Bibliography

GENERAL

Association of Home Appliance Manufacturers, Chicago, Illinois. *Home Appliance Education*. (A bibliography of selected industry, government, college and university educational aids related to all phases of homemaking.) 1972

United States Department of Agriculture. *Consumers All, The Yearbook of Agriculture*. 1965

United States Government. *Consumer Product Information*. Public Documents Distribution Center, Pueblo, Colorado. (An index which lists approximately 200 selected Federal publications on how to buy, use and take care of consumer products. Some are listed below under specific chapters.) Winter, 1973

ONE: MANAGING TIME, MOTION AND MONEY

Eisen, Carol. *Nobody Said You Had to Eat Off the Floor; A Psychiatrist's Wife's Guide to Housekeeping*. David McKay Company, New York. 1971

Gilbreth, Lillian M.; Thomas, Orpha Mae, and Clymer, Eleanor. *Management in the Home*. Dodd, Mead and Company, New York. 1954, 1959

Ketchum, Lucille. "Management in Families/Organizing for Family Living." (Extension Bulletin #551) Cooperative Extension Service, Michigan State University, East Lansing, Michigan. 1969

———. "What to Do About Housework." (Extension Bulletin #E–606) Cooperative Extension Service, Michigan State University, East Lansing, Michigan. (Adapted from Faith Prior, University of Vermont.) 1972

Oppenheim, Irene. *Management of the Modern Home.* The Macmillan Company, New York. 1972. See Chapter 6: "Using Time and Energy."

MONEY

Cohen, Jerome B., and Hanson, Arthur W. *Personal Finance.* 3rd ed. Richard D. Irwin, Homewood, Illinois. 1964

Fetterman, Elsie. "Family Spending Plan Book." Cooperative Extension Service, College of Agriculture, The University of Connecticut. Storrs, Connecticut. 1968

Institute of Life Insurance. "Money in Your Life." New York. 1970

Margolius, Sidney. *How to Make the Most of Your Money.* 2nd rev. ed. Hawthorn Books, New York. 1966, 1969, 1972

Money Management Institute. "Children's Spending." Household Finance Corporation, Chicago, Illinois. 1973

———. "It's Your Credit—Manage It Wisely." Household Finance Corporation, Chicago, Illinois. 1973

———. "Reaching Your Financial Goals." Household Finance Corporation, Chicago, Illinois. 1973

———. "Your Savings and Investment Dollar." Household Finance Corporation, Chicago, Illinois. 1973

United States Government. Consumer Product Information. "Budgeting for the Family." (Bulletin #0100–1826) Public Documents Distribution Center, Pueblo, Colorado, 1972

TWO: DECORATING FOR EASIER CARE

Bowers, Mabel Goode. *Decorate Your Way.* Charles Scribner's Sons, New York. 1968

Formenton, Fabio (Pauline L. Phillips, trans.). *Oriental Rugs and Carpets.* McGraw-Hill, New York. 1972

Hubul, Rheinhard. *The Book of Carpets.* Praeger Publishers, New York. 1970

Katz, Marjorie. *Instant Effect Decorating.* M. Evans and Company, New York. 1972

Liebetrau, Preben. *Oriental Rugs in Color.* The Macmillan Company, New York. 1963

Money Management Institute. "Your Home Furnishings Dollar." Household Finance Corporation, Chicago, Illinois, 1973

THREE: CLEANING THE HOUSE

GENERAL

MacNab, Marian, and Purchase, Mary. "Housecleaning Handbook for Young Homemakers." (Extension Bulletin #1136) Cornell University, Ithaca, New York. 1968

Moore, Alma Chesnut. *How to Clean Everything*. Simon and Schuster, New York. 1952, 1960, 1968

The Porcelain Enamel Institute. "Cleaning Tips for Kitchen, Laundry, Bathroom." Washington, D.C. 1969

The Soap and Detergent Association. "Housekeeping: A Simplified Guide." New York. 1965

United States Government. Consumer Product Information. "Vacuum Cleaners; Their Selection, Use and Care." (Bulletin #2200–0081) Public Documents Distribution Center, Pueblo, Colorado

FURNITURE

Alexander, Alice Mae. "Care of Valuable Possessions: Furniture, Tapestries, Rugs, Textiles, Paintings, etc." (Bulletin #GH 2066) Extension Division, University of Missouri, Columbia, Missouri. 1971

————. "Cleaning May Restore Furniture." (Bulletin #GH 2414) Extension Division, University of Missouri, Columbia, Missouri. 1971

Grotz, George. *The Furniture Doctor*. Doubleday and Company, New York. 1962

FLOORS

"Finishes for Wood Floors in Your Home." (Bulletin #GH 5305) Extension Division, University of Missouri, Columbia, Missouri. 1954

Wiegand, Elizabeth. "Facts About Floor Care." (Extension Bulletin #1157) Cornell University, Ithaca, New York. 1966

RUGS AND CARPETS

(See also, Chapter Two: Decorating for Easier Care)

Association of Home Appliance Manufacturers. "How to Identify Appliance Finishes." Chicago, Illinois. 1972

Association of Interior Decor Specialists, Inc. Aids to Interior Decor. "Fabric Care—Carpets, Rugs, Draperies, Upholstery." Arlington, Virginia

HOUSEHOLD MATERIALS

Caselman, Marilyn W. "Materials and Finishes for Household Equipment." (Bulletin #GH 4316) University of Missouri, Columbia, Missouri. 1970

Ehrenkranz, Florence, and Inman, Lydia. *Equipment in the House.* 2nd ed. Harper and Row, New York. 1966

Humphries, Glenda M. "Materials and Finishes Used for Household Equipment." (Extension Home Economics Bulletin #147) Florida Cooperative Extension Service, University of Florida, Gainesville, Florida. 1971

What's New in Home Economics. "Facts About Finishes." Dun-Donnelley Publishing Corporation, New York. March, 1971

PEST CONTROL

"Common Household Pests." Bulletin #P 52) Illustrated. Extension Division, University of Missouri, Columbia, Missouri.

United States Government. Consumer Product Information. "Controlling Household Pests." (Bulletin #1273) Public Documents Distribution Center, Pueblo, Colorado. 1971

FOUR: OF DIRTY CLOTHES
AND THE LAUNDRY BASKET

Changing Times. "Soaps, Detergents and Why Nobody Can Say What's Best." The Kiplinger Magazine, Washington, D.C. June, 1972

Hardy, Mamie; Basset, Elsie Cronthamel, and Hawkins, Mary, *eds. Textile Handbook.* American Home Economics Association, Washington, D.C. 1960, 1963, 1966, 1970

National Safety Council. "Strange Killer, Carbon Tetrachloride." Chicago, Illinois

Pattison, Arlean. "Plan a Workroom for Laundry and Other Activities." (Bulletin #562) Extension Division, Washington State University, Pullman, Washington. 1966

Purchase, Mary E. "The Big Detergent Question." *Journal of Home Economics,* American Home Economics Association, Washington, D.C. April, 1972

The Soap and Detergent Association. "Judging How Much Laundry Detergent to Use." New York. 1972

————. "Soaps, Detergents and the Environment." New York. 1972

United States Government. Consumer Product Information. "Clothing and Fabric Care Labeling." (Bulletin #7700–108) Public Documents Distribution Center, Pueblo, Colorado. 1972

———. Consumer Product Information. "Washers and Dryers." (Bulletin #2200–0079) Public Documents Distribution Center, Pueblo, Colorado. 1972

FIVE: THE KITCHEN

American Gas Association. "Your Gas Kitchen and Laundry." Washington, D.C. 1973

Birge, Emagene; Schneider, Rita Marie, and Habeeb, Virginia Thabet, eds. *Handbook of Household Equipment Terminology.* American Home Economics Association, Washington, D.C. 1959, 1965, 1970.

Caselman, Marilyn. "Freezers, Use and Care." (Bulletin #GH 4457) Extension Division, University of Missouri, Columbia, Missouri. 1972

———. "Trash Mashers or Compactors." (Bulletin #GH 4421) Extension Division, University of Missouri, Columbia, Missouri. 1972

Edison Electric Institute. *The Portable Appliance Buyers Guide.* New York, 1972

Farmer, La Verne. "Selecting a Dishwasher." (Publication #624) Agricultural Extension Service, University of Tennessee, Knoxville, Tennessee. 1972

———. "Selecting a Refrigerator." (Publication #629) Agricultural Extension Service, University of Tennessee, Knoxville, Tennessee. 1972

Habeeb, Virginia T. *MACAP Handbook for the Informed Consumer: An Educational Guide to the Purchase, Use and Care of Major Appliances.* Major Appliance Consumer Action Panel, Chicago, Illinois. 1973

Metal Cookware Manufacturers Association. "Consumer Information Guide." Fontana, Wisconsin. 1971

———. "A Guide to Metal Cookware and Bakeware." Fontana, Wisconsin. 1971

Oson, Wanda and Robert. "Selecting and Using a Portable Microwave Oven." (Family Living Fact Sheet #29) Agricultural Extension Service, University of Minnesota, St. Paul, Minnesota. 1972

United States Government. Consumer Product Information. *Keeping Food Safe to Eat.* (Bulletin #0100–1571) Public Documents Distribution Center, Pueblo, Colorado. 1972

541

SIX: ENTERTAINING

Corinth, Katherine, and Sargent, Mary. *All About Entertaining: Everything You Need to Know to Have a Fabulous Social Life.* David McKay, New York. 1966

Habeeb, Virginia T., 1966; Crawford, Frances M., 1972. *The American Home All-Purpose Cookbook.* M. Evans and Company, New York.

Staley, Lucy. *New Trends in Table Settings.* Hearthside Press, New York, 1968

Truax, Carol. *The Weekend Chef.* Doubleday and Company, New York. 1961

SEVEN: SEWING AND MENDING

Farmer, La Verne. "Buying a Sewing Machine." (Publication #620) Agricultural Extension Service, University of Tennessee, Knoxville, Tennessee. 1972

Ley, Sandra. *America's Sewing Book.* Charles Scribner's Sons, New York. 1972

Mager, Sylvia. *A Complete Guide to Home Sewing.* Gramercy Publishing Co., Division of Crown Publishing, with Simon and Schuster, New York. 1971

United States Government. Consumer Product Information. "Clothing Repairs." (Bulletin #0100–0778) Public Documents Distribution Center, Puebla, Colorado. 1970

EIGHT: ABOUT STORAGE AND STASHING

Fetterman, Elsie. "Record of Important Family Papers." (Bulletin #68–36) Cooperative Extension Service, College of Agriculture, The University of Connecticut, Storrs, Connecticut. 1968

Schuler, Stanley. *The Complete Book of Closets and Storage.* M. Evans and Company, New York. 1969

Schwenk, Frankie, and VerPloeg, Marcena. "Your Family Business Affairs." (Bulletin #HE–75) Cooperative Extension Service, Iowa State University of Science and Technology, Ames, Iowa. 1966

NINE: HOUSEHOLD MECHANICS AND MINOR REPAIRS

Appliance Manufacturer. "Controlling Appliance Noise." Vol. 20, No. 7 (July, 1972) pp. 48–51

542

Behrens C. "Think Quiet." *Appliance Manufacturer,* Vol. 20, No. 7 (July, 1972) pp. 44–47

Caselman, Marilyn. "Air Pollution in the Home" (Paper, Fifth Annual Air Pollution Conference) College of Engineering and Extension Division, University of Missouri, Columbia, Missouri. 1972

Daniels, George. *The Unhandy Handyman's Book.* Signet Books. The New American Library, New York. 1966

DeBusk, Kenneth E., and Farmer, La Verne. *The Care and Simple Repair of Household Equipment.* (Extension Publication #273) Agricultural Extension Service, University of Tennessee, Knoxville, Tennessee. 1971

———. *Electricity in the Home.* (Extension Publication #608) Agricultural Extension Service, University of Tennessee, Knoxville, Tennessee. 1971

Family Handyman Magazine. The Family Handyman Magazine's Home Emergencies and Repairs. (JSE 72–971) 1971

Peet, Louise Jenison, et al. *Household Equipment.* 6th ed. John Wiley and Sons, Inc. 1970

Schuler, Stanley. *How to Fix Almost Everything.* Pocket Books, New York. 1970

United States Government. Consumer Product Information. "Noise in the House." (Bulletin #5500–0074) Public Documents Distribution Center, Pueblo, Colorado. 1972

———. "Paint and Painting: Selection, Preparation and Application." (Bulletin #2200–0066) Public Documents Distribution Center, Pueblo, Colorado. 1971

———. "Room Air Conditioners." (Bulletin #2200–0074) Public Documents Distribution Center, Pueblo, Colorado. 1972

———. "Simple Plumbing Repairs." (Bulletin #0100–1033) Public Documents Distribution Center, Pueblo, Colorado. 1970

TEN: ABOUT HEALTH, FATIGUE, AND SAFETY

Greene, J. I. "Heart Rate and Daily Activities of Housewives with Young Children." *Ergonomics,* Vol. 15, No. 2 (March, 1972) pp. 139–146

National Safety Council. "The Anatomy of a Fire." Chicago, Illinois

———. "Family Emergency Almanac." Chicago, Illinois

———. "Home Accident Facts." Chicago, Illinois

———. "Take 10: A Fire Safety Checklist." Chicago, Illinois

Sherman, H. C., and Lawford, C. S. *Essentials of Nutrition.* The Macmillan Company, New York. 1940

Steidl, Rose E., and Bratton, Esther Crew. *Work in the Home.* John Wiley and Sons, New York, 1968

United States Department of Agriculture. *Consumers All, The Yearbook of Agriculture.* P. 121, "To Save Energy." 1965

ELEVEN: HOUSEHOLD HELP AND SERVICES

Christensen, Ethlyn, and Schlick, Mary D. "Household Employment: New Careers in an Old Business." *Word* Magazine. February, 1969

Edmiston, Susan. "While We're at It, What About Maids' Lib?" *New York* Magazine. Vol. 4, No. 26 (June 28, 1971)

Koontz, Elizabeth Duncan. "New Horizons: Household Employment and the Home Related Arts." (Paper, Conference on Consumer and Homemaking Education) California State Department of Education and the California State Board of Education with the California Community Colleges. Anaheim, California. November, 1970

National Committee on Household Employment. *Code of Standards For Employee—Employer Relationship,* Washington, D.C.

National Safety Council. "You're in Charge." (A leaflet for baby sitters) Chicago, Illinois

United States Department of Labor. *Labor Laws Affecting Private Household Workers.* Employment Standards

TWELVE: LIVING WITH PETS

Aistrop, Jack. *Enjoying Pets.* Vanguard Press, New York. 1955

Baird, Jack. *The Standard Book of Household Pets.* Halcyon House, Garden City, New York. 1948

Lewis, Howard J. *The Complete Book of Pet Care.* Random House, New York. 1956

Whitney, Leon Fradley. *The Complete Book of Home Pet Care.* Doubleday and Company, New York. 1950

THIRTEEN: MOVING

Dodson, Gardner. *Making the Most of Every Move.* Putnam, New York. 1958

Randall, Margaret. *The Home Encyclopedia of Moving Your Family.* Berkley Publishing Corp., New York. 1959

United States Federal Supply Service. *Federal Handbook for Prepara-*

tion of Household Goods for Shipment and Storage. Washington, D.C. 1958

FOURTEEN: ON PURCHASING WISELY

American Gas Association. "A Consumer Guide to Gas Range Selection," Washington, D.C. 1973

The Better Business Bureau. *Consumers Buying Guide: How to Get Your Money's Worth.* Rutledge Books, and The Benjamin Company, New York, 1969

Everybody's Money. "Know Your Seals and Tags" Vol. 12, No. 2 (Summer, 1972) pp. 8–10

Money Management Institute. "Your Equipment Dollar." Household Finance Corporation, Chicago, Illinois. 1973

————. "Your Housing Dollar." Household Finance Corporation, Chicago, Illinois. 1973

————. "Your Shopping Dollar." Household Finance Corporation, Chicago, Illinois. 1973

Appendix
Reader's Own Notes

Research continues to bring changes in the formulation of household products, the design of equipment, home furnishings and the nature of fabric content. With these changes come new methods of home care and consequently the products that help to improve techniques. We have brought you the latest information right up to press time, but no doubt changes have emerged even in this short span of time.

As these changes occur, you may wish to do your own updating. Make notes of any new directions, information, product changes that you gather from magazines, advertising, bulletins, newsletters, and from radio and television. These pages have been provided for your convenience.

SUBJECT	PAGE NUMBER

SUBJECT

PAGE NUMBER

SUBJECT

APPENDIX

SUBJECT   PAGE NUMBER

APPENDIX

SUBJECT   PAGE NUMBER

SUBJECT

PAGE NUMBER

Index